# Oxford
## Pocket
# School
# Spelling
# Dictionary

Robert Allen

Education Consultant Michele Chapman

OXFORD
UNIVERSITY PRESS

# OXFORD
UNIVERSITY PRESS

Great Clarendon Street, Oxford OX2 6DP

Oxford University Press is a department of the University of Oxford.
It furthers the University's objective of excellence in research, scholarship,
and education by publishing worldwide in

Oxford New York

Auckland Bangkok Buenos Aires Cape Town Chennai
Dar es Salaam Delhi Hong Kong Istanbul Karachi Kolkata
Kuala Lumpur Madrid Melbourne Mexico City Mumbai
Nairobi São Paulo Taipei Tokyo Toronto

Oxford is a trade mark of Oxford University Press
in the UK and in certain other countries

© Oxford University Press 2001

Database right Oxford University Press (maker)

First published 2001
Second edition 2003
Pocket edition 2004

British Library cataloguing in Publication Data available

ISBN 0-19-911195-2

10 9 8 7 6 5 4 3 2 1

Typeset in Arial

Printed in Italy by Canale

Do you have a query about words, their origin, meaning, use, spelling,
pronunciation, or any other aspect of the English language? Visit our
website at www.askoxford.com where you will be able to find answers
to your language queries.

# Introduction

The *Oxford Pocket School Spelling Dictionary* is a special dictionary designed to help students with their spelling. Generally speaking there are three main areas of spelling difficulty for users of English whatever their age.

- Some words are difficult because they have unusual or unpredictable features. **Eighth**, **guard**, and **niece** are often spelt wrongly because they have awkward letter sequences. **Disappear** and **embarrass** are confusing because some letters are doubled while others are not. Words such as **desperate** and **separate** seeminconsistent because one has an e in the middle where the other has an a for no apparent reason.

- Then there are words that are easily confused. **Vain**, **vein**, and **vane** sound the same but have very different meanings. Some words change their spelling according to how they are used. For example, **dependant** as a *noun* is spelt with an a, but as an *adjective*, it is spelt with an e.

- The third type of difficulty arises when suffixes and endings are added to words. It is not easy to remember to keep an e in **changeable**, to replace y with i in **happily**, and not to double the p in **galloping**.

With increased interest in spelling, reading, and writing in schools today we hope that the *Oxford Pocket School Spelling Dictionary* will provide a valuable tool offering useful strategies for dealing with spelling difficulties. We also hope that it will support teachers and parents whose task is to enable young writers to become confident, accurate spellers and to express themselves with a voice of their own.

# How to use this book

## Entries

Words are listed alphabetically in **blue** and the part of speech or word class (e.g. *noun*, *verb*, *adjective*) follows in italic. If the word has endings (called inflections), these are also listed in black below the headword.

Decide on the first sound of the word you are looking for. Some first sounds can be confusing. If you cannot find the word you are looking for, use the **Try also** tips which will guide you to other possible spellings.

## Footnotes

Some words have footnotes attached to them. These identify words that you need to check that you have the right meaning. For example, at **bite** you will find a footnote to tell you that there is another word that sounds like it but is spelt a different way, **!byte**. Words that sound the same but are spelt differently are called homophones. Some footnotes also give extra information on usage and grammar.

## Panels

There are about 250 panels which highlight particular problems. For example, you may want to know which words are spelt **-able** like **bendable**, and which ones are spelt **-ible** like **accessible**. Or you may want to know how you form plurals of nouns ending in **-f** such as **calf** or **roof**. Use these information panels to build your knowledge of spelling rules and practices.

It may be useful to keep a spelling jotter for new words. When using a new word, say it aloud several times before you write it down. When you go on to use it in your writing, try not to copy it but to write the word from memory.

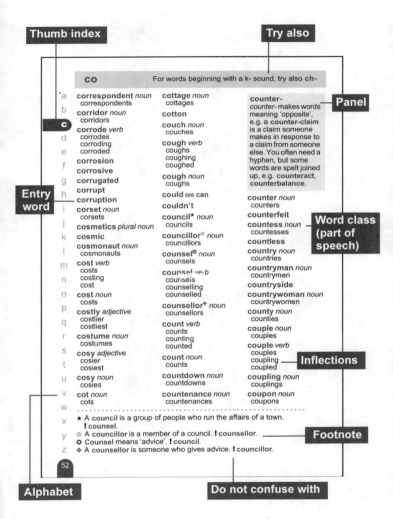

**Thumb index**

**Try also**

**co**     For words beginning with a k- sound, try also ch-

a
b
**c**
d
e
f
g
h
i
j
k
l
m
n
o
p
q
r
s
t
u
v
w
x
y
z

**Entry word**

**Panel**

**Word class (part of speech)**

**Inflections**

**Footnote**

**Alphabet**

**Do not confuse with**

**correspondent** *noun*
correspondents

**corridor** *noun*
corridors

**corrode** *verb*
corrodes
corroding
corroded

**corrosion**

**corrosive**

**corrugated**

**corrupt**

**corruption**

**corset** *noun*
corsets

**cosmetics** *plural noun*

**cosmic**

**cosmonaut** *noun*
cosmonauts

**cost** *verb*
costs
costing
cost

**cost** *noun*
costs

**costly** *adjective*
costlier
costliest

**costume** *noun*
costumes

**cosy** *adjective*
cosier
cosiest

**cosy** *noun*
cosies

**cot** *noun*
cots

**cottage** *noun*
cottages

**cotton**

**couch** *noun*
couches

**cough** *verb*
coughs
coughing
coughed

**cough** *noun*
coughs

**could** see can

**couldn't**

**council★** *noun*
councils

**councillor☆** *noun*
councillors

**counsel○** *noun*
counsels

**counsel** *verb*
counsels
counselling
counselled

**counsellor✚** *noun*
counsellors

**count** *verb*
counts
counting
counted

**count** *noun*
counts

**countdown** *noun*
countdowns

**countenance** *noun*
countenances

**counter-**
*counter-* makes words meaning 'opposite', e.g. a **counter-claim** is a claim someone makes in response to a claim from someone else. You often need a hyphen, but some words are spelt joined up, e.g. **counteract**, **counterbalance**.

**counter** *noun*
counters

**counterfeit**

**countess** *noun*
countesses

**countless**

**country** *noun*
countries

**countryman** *noun*
countrymen

**countryside**

**countrywoman** *noun*
countrywomen

**county** *noun*
counties

**couple** *noun*
couples

**couple** *verb*
couples
coupling
coupled

**coupling** *noun*
couplings

**coupon** *noun*
coupons

................................................................

★ A council is a group of people who run the affairs of a town. ! counsel.

☆ A councillor is a member of a council. ! counsellor.

○ Counsel means 'advice'. ! council.

✚ A counsellor is someone who gives advice. ! councillor.

# Aa

**-a**
Most nouns ending in -*a*, e.g. **amoeba**, **gala**, have plurals ending in -*as*, e.g. **amoebas**, **galas**. A few technical words have plurals ending in -*ae*, e.g. **antennae**.

**aback**

**abacus** *noun*
abacuses

**abandon** *verb*
abandons
abandoning
abandoned

**abbey** *noun*
abbeys

**abbot** *noun*
abbots

**abbreviate** *verb*
abbreviates
abbreviating
abbreviated

**abbreviation** *noun*
abbreviations

**abdomen** *noun*
abdomens

**abdominal**

**abduct** *verb*
abducts
abducting
abducted

**abide** *verb*
abides
abiding
abided

**ability** *noun*
abilities

**ablaze**

**able** *adjective*
abler
ablest

**-able and -ible**
You add -*able* to a verb to make an adjective that means 'able to be done', e.g. **bendable** means 'able to be bent'. Some adjectives that have this meaning end in -*ible*, e.g. **accessible**, **convertible**, and **incredible**. You cannot use -*ible* to make new words as you can with -*able*.

**ably**

**abnormal**
abnormally

**abnormality** *noun*
abnormalities

**aboard**

**abode** *noun*
abodes

**abolish** *verb*
abolishes
abolishing
abolished

**abolition**

**abominable**

**aboriginal**

**Aborigines**

**abort** *verb*
aborts
aborting
aborted

**abortion** *noun*
abortions

**abound** *verb*
abounds
abounding
abounded

**about**

**above**

**abrasive**

**abreast**

**abroad**

**abrupt**

**abscess** *noun*
abscesses

**abseil** *verb*
abseils
abseiling
abseiled

**absence** *noun*
absences

**absent**

**absentee** *noun*
absentees

**absent-minded**
absent-mindedly

**absolute**
absolutely

**absorb** *verb*
absorbs
absorbing
absorbed

**absorbent**

**absorption**

**abstract** *adjective* and *noun*
abstracts

**abstract** *verb*
abstracts
abstracting
abstracted

**absurd**
absurdly

**absurdity** *noun*
absurdities

**abundance**

**abundant**

**a**

b

c

d

e

f

g

h

i

j

k

l

m

n

o

p

q

r

s

t

u

v

w

x

y

z

**abuse** *verb*
abuses
abusing
abused

**abuse** *noun*
abuses

**abusive**
abusively

**abysmal**

**abyss** *noun*
abysses

**academic**

**academy** *noun*
academies

**accelerate** *verb*
accelerates
accelerating
accelerated

**acceleration**

**accelerator** *noun*
accelerators

**accent** *noun*
accents

**accent** *verb*
accents
accenting
accented

**accept★** *verb*
accepts
accepting
accepted

**acceptable**

**acceptance**

**access** *noun*
accesses

**access** *verb*
accesses
accessing
accessed

**accessibility**

**accessible**

**accession** *noun*
accessions

**accessory** *noun*
accessories

**accident** *noun*
accidents

**accidental**
accidentally

**acclaim** *verb*
acclaims
acclaiming
acclaimed

**accommodate** *verb*
accommodates
accommodating
accommodated

**accommodation**

**accompaniment**
*noun*
accompaniments

**accompanist** *noun*
accompanists

**accompany** *verb*
accompanies
accompanying
accompanied

**accomplish** *verb*
accomplishes
accomplishing
accomplished

**accomplished**

**accomplishment**
*noun*
accomplishments

**accord** *noun*
accords

**according**
accordingly

**accordion** *noun*
accordions

**account** *noun*
accounts

**account** *verb*
accounts
accounting
accounted

**accountancy**

**accountant** *noun*
accountants

**accumulate** *verb*
accumulates
accumulating
accumulated

**accumulation**

**accuracy**

**accurate**
accurately

**accusation** *noun*
accusations

**accuse** *verb*
accuses
accusing
accused

**accustomed**

**ace** *noun*
aces

**ache** *noun*
aches

**ache** *verb*
aches
aching
ached

**achieve** *verb*
achieves
achieving
achieved

**achievement**
achievements

**acid** *noun*
acids

**acidic**

**acidity** *noun*

. . . . . . . . . . . . . . . . . . . . . . . . . . . . . . . . . . . . . . . . . . . . . . . . . . .

★ To accept something is to take it. **!** except.

**acknowledge** *verb*
acknowledges
acknowledging
acknowledged

**acknowledgement** *noun*
acknowledgements

**acne**

**acorn** *noun*
acorns

**acoustic**

**acoustics**

**acquaint** *verb*
acquaints
acquainting
acquainted

**acquaintance** *noun*
acquaintances

**acquire** *verb*
acquires
acquiring
acquired

**acquisition** *noun*
acquisitions

**acquit** *verb*
acquits
acquitting
acquitted

**acquittal** *noun*
acquittals

**acre** *noun*
acres

**acrobat** *noun*
acrobats

**acrobatic** *adjective*
acrobatically

**acrobatics**

**acronym** *noun*
acronyms

**across** *adverb* and
*preposition*

**act** *noun*
acts

**act** *verb*
acts
acting
acted

**action** *noun*
actions

**activate** *verb*
activates
activating
activated

**active**

**activity** *noun*
activities

**actor** *noun*
actors

**actress** *noun*
actresses

**actual**
actually

**acupuncture**

**acute**

**Adam's apple** *noun*
Adam's apples

**adapt** *verb*
adapts
adapting
adapted

**adaptable**

**adaptation**

**adaptor** *noun*
adaptors

**add** *verb*
adds
adding
added

**adder** *noun*
adders

**addict** *noun*
addicts

**addicted**

**addiction** *noun*
addictions

**addictive**

**addition** *noun*
additions

**additional**

**additive** *noun*
additives

**address** *noun*
addresses

**address** *verb*
addresses
addressing
addressed

**adenoids**

**adequate**

**adhere** *verb*
adheres
adhering
adhered

**adhesive** *noun*
adhesives

**adhesion**

**adhesive**

**Adi Granth**

**adjacent**

**adjective** *noun*
adjectives

**adjourn** *verb*
adjourns
adjourning
adjourned

**adjournment**

**adjudicate** *verb*
adjudicates
adjudicating
adjudicated

**adjudication**

**adjudicator**

**adjust** *verb*
adjusts
adjusting
adjusted

**adjustment** *noun*
adjustments

**a**

administer *verb*
administers
administering
administered

administration *noun*
administrations

administrative

administrator

admirable
admirably

admiral *noun*
admirals

admiration

admire *verb*
admires
admiring
admired

admirer *noun*
admirers

admission *noun*
admissions

admit *verb*
admits
admitting
admitted

admittance

admittedly

ado

adolescence

adolescent *noun*
adolescents

adopt *verb*
adopts
adopting
adopted

adoption

adoptive

adorable
adorably

adoration

adore *verb*
adores
adoring
adored

adorn *verb*
adorns
adorning
adorned

adornment

adrenalin

adrift

adult *noun*
adults

adulterer

adultery

advance *noun*
advances

advance *verb*
advances
advancing
advanced

advanced

advantage *noun*
advantages

advantageous

Advent★

adventure *noun*
adventures

adventurous
*adjective*
adventurously

adverb *noun*
adverbs

adversary *noun*
adversaries

adverse

adversity *noun*
adversities

advertise *verb*
advertises
advertising
advertised

advertisement *noun*
advertisements

advice

advisable

advise *verb*
advises
advising
advised

adviser *noun*
advisers

advisory

advocate *noun*
advocates

advocate *verb*
advocates
advocating
advocated

aerial *adjective* and
*noun*
aerials

**aero-**
You use *aero-* to
make words to
do with the air
or aircraft, e.g.
**aerobatics**.
If the word is a long
one you spell it with
a hyphen, e.g.
**aero-engineering**.

aerobatic

aerobatics

aerobics

aeronautical

aeronautics

aeroplane *noun*
aeroplanes

aerosol *noun*
aerosols

aesthetic
aesthetically

★ Use a capital A when you mean the period before Christmas.

4

**affair** noun
affairs
**affect★** verb
affects
affecting
affected
**affection** noun
affections
**affectionate**
affectionately
**afflict** verb
afflicts
afflicting
afflicted
**affliction** noun
afflictions
**affluence**
**affluent**
**afford** verb
affords
affording
afforded
**afforestation**
**afloat** adjective and
adverb
**afraid**
**afresh**
**African** adjective and
noun
Africans
**aft**
**after**
**afternoon** noun
afternoons
**afterwards**
**again**
**against**
**age** noun
ages

**age** verb
ages
ageing
aged
**aged**
**agency** noun
agencies
**agenda** noun
agendas
**agent** noun
agents
**aggravate** verb
aggravates
aggravating
aggravated
**aggravation**
**aggression**
**aggressive**
aggressively
**aggressor**
aggressors
**agile**
**agility**
**agitate** verb
agitates
agitating
agitated
**agitation**
**agitator** noun
agitators
**agnostic** noun
agnostics
**ago**
**agonizing**
**agony** noun
agonies
**agree** verb
agrees
agreeing
agreed

**agreeable**
**agreement** noun
agreements
**agriculture**
**agricultural**
**aground**
**ahead**
**ahoy**
**aid** noun
aids
**aid** verb
aids
aiding
aided
**Aids**☆
**ailing**
**ailment** noun
ailments
**aim** verb
aims
aiming
aimed
**aim** noun
aims
**aimless**
aimlessly
**air⊙** noun
airs
**air** verb
airs
airing
aired
**airborne**
**air-conditioned**
**air-conditioning**
**aircraft** noun
aircraft
**Airedale** noun
Airedales

a
b
c
d
e
f
g
h
i
j
k
l
m
n
o
p
q
r
s
t
u
v
w
x
y
z

★ **Affect** means 'to make something change'. **!effect**.
☆ Use a capital A when you mean the disease.
⊙ You can use a plural in the phrase *to put on airs*.

5

**a**

airfield *noun*
airfields

air force *noun*
air forces

airgun *noun*
airguns

airline *noun*
airlines

airlock *noun*
airlocks

airmail

airman *noun*
airmen

airport *noun*
airports

airship *noun*
airships

airstream *noun*
airstreams

airtight

airy *adjective*
airier
airiest
airily

aisle★ *noun*
aisles

ajar

akela☆ *noun*
akelas

alarm *verb*
alarms
alarming
alarmed

alarm *noun*
alarms

alas

albatross *noun*
albatrosses

album *noun*
albums

alcohol

alcoholic *adjective*
and *noun*
alcoholics

alcoholism

alcove *noun*
alcoves

ale✪ *noun*
ales

alert *verb*
alerts
alerting
alerted

alert *adjective* and
*noun*
alerts

algebra

algebraic

alias *noun*
aliases

alibi *noun*
alibis

alien *adjective* and
*noun*
aliens

alienate *verb*
alienates
alienating
alienated

alienation

alight

alike

alive

alkali *noun*
alkalis

alkaline

alkalinity

Allah

allegation *noun*
allegations

allege *verb*
alleges
alleging
alleged

allegedly

allegiance *noun*
allegiances

allegorical

allegory *noun*
allegories

allergic

allergy *noun*
allergies

alley *noun*
alleys

alliance *noun*
alliances

allied

alligator *noun*
alligators

allot *verb*
allots
allotting
allotted

allotment *noun*
allotments

allow *verb*
allows
allowing
allowed

allowance *noun*
allowances

alloy *noun*
alloys

all right

all-round

all-rounder

ally *noun*
allies

................................................................

★ An aisle is a passage in a church or cinema. **!** isle.
☆ Akela is a Scout leader.
✪ You can use a plural when you mean 'different types of ale'.

**ally** *verb*
 allies
 allying
 allied

**almighty**

**almond** *noun*
 almonds

**almost**

**aloft**

**alone**

**along**

**alongside**

**aloud★**

**alphabet** *noun*
 alphabets

**alphabetical**
 alphabetically

**alpine**

**already**

**Alsatian** *noun*
 Alsatians

**also**

**altar☆** *noun*
 altars

**alter❂** *verb*
 alters
 altering
 altered

**alteration**

**alternate**

**alternate** *verb*
 alternates
 alternating
 alternated

**alternately**

**alternation**

**alternating current**

**alternative** *noun*
 alternatives

**alternative**

**alternator** *noun*
 alternators

**although** *conjunction*

**altitude** *noun*
 altitudes

**altogether**

**aluminium**

**always**

**amalgamate** *verb*
 amalgamates
 amalgamating
 amalgamated

**amalgamation**

**amateur** *adjective* and *noun*
 amateurs

**amateurish**

**amaze** *verb*
 amazes
 amazing
 amazed

**amazement**

**ambassador** *noun*
 ambassadors

**amber**

**ambiguity**
 ambiguities

**ambiguous**
 ambiguously

**ambition** *noun*
 ambitions

**ambitious**
 ambitiously

**amble** *verb*
 ambles
 ambling
 ambled

**ambulance** *noun*
 ambulances

**ambush** *noun*
 ambushes

**ambush** *verb*
 ambushes
 ambushing
 ambushed

**amen**

**amend** *verb*
 amends
 amending
 amended

**amendment**

**amenity** *noun*
 amenities

**American** *adjective* and *noun*
 Americans

**amiable**
 amiably

**amicable**
 amicably

**amid✢**

**amidships**

**ammonia**

**ammunition**

**amnesty** *noun*
 amnesties

**amoeba** *noun*
 amoebas

**among✱**

**amount** *noun*
 amounts

a
b
c
d
e
f
g
h
i
j
k
l
m
n
o
p
q
r
s
t
u
v
w
x
y
z

. . . . . . . . . . . . . . . . . . . . . . . . . . . . . . . . . . . . . . . . . . . . . . . . . . . . . . . . . . . .

★ **Aloud** means 'in a voice that can be heard'. ❢**allowed**.
☆ An **altar** is a raised surface in religious ceremonies. ❢**alter**.
❂ **Alter** means to change something. ❢**altar**.
✢ You can also spell this word *amidst*.
✱ You can also spell this word *amongst*.

7

**a**

amount *verb*
amounts
amounting
amounted

amphibian *adjective and noun*
amphibians

amphibious

ample *adjective*
ampler
amplest
amply

amplification

amplfiier *noun*
amplifiers

amplify *verb*
amplifies
amplifying
amplified

amputate *verb*
amputates
amputating
amputated

amputation

amuse *verb*
amuses
amusing
amused

amusement *noun*
amusements

amusing

an★

anaemia

anaemic

anaesthetic *noun*
anaesthetics

anaesthetist

anaesthetize *verb*
anaesthetizes
anaesthetizing
anaesthetized

anagram *noun*
anagrams

analogous

analogue☆

analogy *noun*
analogies

analyse *verb*
analyses
analysing
analysed

analysis *noun*
analyses

analytical

anarchism

anarchist *noun*
anarchists

anarchy

anatomical

anatomy

> **-ance** and **-ence**
> Most nouns ending in
> *-ance* come from
> verbs, e.g.
> **disturbance**,
> **endurance**. Some
> nouns end in *-ence*,
> e.g. **dependence**,
> **obedience**, and you
> need to be careful not
> to misspell these.

ancestor *noun*
ancestors

ancestral

ancestry *noun*
ancestries

anchor *noun*
anchors

anchorage *noun*
anchorages

ancient

anemone *noun*
anemones

angel *noun*
angels

angelic

anger

angle *noun*
angles

angle *verb*
angles
angling
angled

angler *noun*
anglers

Anglican *adjective and noun*
Anglicans

Anglo-Saxon *adjective and noun*
Anglo-Saxons

angry *adjective*
angrier
angriest
angrily

anguish

angular

animal *noun*
animals

animated

animation

★ You use an instead of a before a word beginning with a vowel, e.g. *an apple*, or before an abbreviation that sounds as though it begins with a vowel, e.g. *an MP*.

☆ You will sometimes see the spelling *analog*, especially when it is about computers.

**animosity** *noun*
animosities

**aniseed**

**ankle** *noun*
ankles

**annex** *verb*
annexes
annexing
annexed

**annexation**

**annexe** *noun*
annexes

**annihilate** *verb*
annihilates
annihilating
annihilated

**annihilation**

**anniversary** *noun*
anniversaries

**announce** *verb*
announces
announcing
announced

**announcer**

**announcement** *noun*
announcements

**annoy** *verb*
annoys
annoying
annoyed

**annoyance** *noun*
annoyances

**annual** *adjective*
annually

**annual** *noun*
annuals

**anonymity**★

**anonymous**
anonymously

**anorak** *noun*
anoraks

**anorexia**

**anorexic**

**another**

**answer** *noun*
answers

**answer** *verb*
answers
answering
answered

**-ant and -ent**
Many adjectives end
in -*ant*, e.g.
**abundant**,
**important**. Some
adjectives end in -*ent*,
e.g. **dependent**
(**dependant** is a
noun), **permanent**,
and you need to be
careful not to misspell
these.

**antagonism**

**antagonistic**

**antagonize** *verb*
antagonizes
antagonizing
antagonized

**Antarctic** *adjective*
and *noun*

**anteater** *noun*
anteaters

**antelope**☆ *noun*
antelope *or* antelopes

**antenna** *noun*
antennae *or* antennas

**anthem** *noun*
anthems

**anthill** *noun*
anthills

**anthology** *noun*
anthologies

**anthracite**

**anthropologist**

**anthropology**

**anti-**
*anti-* at the beginning
of a word makes a
word meaning
'against something' or
'stopping something',
e.g. **antifreeze** means
'a liquid that stops
water from freezing'. If
the word you are
adding *anti-* to begins
with a vowel, you use
a hyphen, e.g.
**anti-aircraft**.

**antibiotic** *noun*
antibiotics

**anticipate** *verb*
anticipates
anticipating
anticipated

**anticipation**

**anticlimax** *noun*
anticlimaxes

**anticlockwise** *adverb*
and *adjective*

**anticyclone** *noun*
anticyclones

**antidote** *noun*
antidotes

**antifreeze**

a b c d e f g h i j k l m n o p q r s t u v w x y z

★ The noun from **anonymous**.
☆ You use **antelope** when you mean a lot of animals and **antelopes**
when you mean several you are thinking about separately.

9

a
b
c
d
e
f
g
h
i
j
k
l
m
n
o
p
q
r
s
t
u
v
w
x
y
z

**antipodes★**
**antiquated**
**antique** *adjective* and
*noun*
  antiques
**antiseptic** *noun*
  antiseptics
**antler** *noun*
  antlers
**anus** *noun*
  anuses
**anvil** *noun*
  anvils
**anxiety** *noun*
  anxieties
**anxious**
  anxiously
**anybody**
**anyhow**
**anyone**
**anything**
**anyway**
**anywhere**
**apart**
**apartment** *noun*
  apartments
**apathetic**
**apathy**
**ape** *noun*
  apes
**aphid** *noun*
  aphids
**apiece**
**apologetic**
  apologetically
**apologize** *verb*
  apologizes
  apologizing
  apologized

**apology** *noun*
  apologies
**apostle** *noun*
  apostles
**apostrophe** *noun*
  apostrophes
**appal** *verb*
  appals
  appalling
  appalled
**appalling**
**apparatus** *noun*
  apparatuses
**apparent**
  apparently
**appeal** *verb*
  appeals
  appealing
  appealed
**appeal** *noun*
  appeals
**appear** *verb*
  appears
  appearing
  appeared
**appearance** *noun*
  appearances
**appease** *verb*
  appeases
  appeasing
  appeased
**appeasement**
**appendicitis**
**appendix**☆
  appendixes *or*
  appendices
**appetite** *noun*
  appetites
**appetizing**

**applaud** *verb*
  applauds
  applauding
  applauded
**applause**
**apple** *noun*
  apples
**appliance** *noun*
  appliances
**applicable**
**applicant** *noun*
  applicants
**application** *noun*
  applications
**applied**
**apply** *verb*
  applies
  applying
  applied
**appoint** *verb*
  appoints
  appointing
  appointed
**appointment** *noun*
  appointments
**appraisal**
  appraisals
**appraise** *verb*
  appraises
  appraising
  appraised
**appreciate** *verb*
  appreciates
  appreciating
  appreciated
**appreciation**
**appreciative**
**apprehension** *noun*
**apprehensive**

. . . . . . . . . . . . . . . . . . . . . . . . . . . . . . . . . . . . . . . . . . . . . . . . . .

★ A word Europeans use for Australia and New Zealand.
☆ You use **appendixes** when you mean organs of the body and
  **appendices** when you mean parts of a book.

10

**apprentice** *noun*
apprentices
**apprenticeship**
**approach** *verb*
approaches
approaching
approached
**approach** *noun*
approaches
**approachable**
**appropriate**
**approval**
**approve** *verb*
approves
approving
approved
**approximate**
approximately
**apricot** *noun*
apricots
**April**
**apron** *noun*
aprons
**aptitude** *noun*
aptitudes
**aquarium** *noun*
aquariums
**aquatic**
**aqueduct** *noun*
aqueducts
**Arab**★ *noun*
Arabs
**Arabian**★ *adjective*
**Arabic**☆
**arabic**☆
**arable**
**arbitrary**

**arbitrate** *verb*
arbitrates
arbitrating
arbitrated
**arbitration**
**arbitrator**
**arc**○ *noun*
arcs
**arcade** *noun*
arcades
**arch** *noun*
arches
**arch** *verb*
arches
arching
arched
**archaeology**
**archaeological**
**archaeologist**
**archbishop** *noun*
archbishops
**archer** *noun*
archers
**archery**
**architect** *noun*
architects
**architecture**

**-archy**
-archy at the end of a word means 'rule or government', e.g. **anarchy** (= a lack of rule) and **monarchy** (= rule by a king or queen). The plural form is -archies, e.g. **monarchies**.

**Arctic**
**are**
**area** *noun*
areas
**arena** *noun*
arenas
**aren't** *abbreviation*
**argue** *verb*
argues
arguing
argued
**argument** *noun*
arguments
**arid**
**aridity**
**arise** *verb*
arises
arising
arose
arisen
**aristocracy** *noun*
aristocracies
**aristocrat** *noun*
aristocrats
**aristocratic**
**arithmetic**
**arithmetical**
**ark**✛ *noun*
arks
**arm** *noun*
arms
**arm** *verb*
arms
arming
armed
**armada** *noun*
armadas

★ You use **Arab** when you mean a person or the people, and **Arabian** when you mean the place, e.g. *the Arabian desert*.
☆ You use **Arabic** when you mean the language, and **arabic** when you mean numbers, e.g. *arabic numerals*.
○ **Arc** means a curve. **!ark**.
✛ **Ark** means a boat. **!arc**.

a
b
c
d
e
f
g
h
i
j
k
l
m
n
o
p
q
r
s
t
u
v
w
x
y
z

11

## ar - as

**a**

**armadillo** *noun*
armadillos

**armaments**

**armchair** *noun*
armchairs

**armful** *noun*
armfuls

**armistice** *noun*
armistices

**armour**

**armoured**

**armpit** *noun*
armpits

**army** *noun*
armies

**aroma** *noun*
aromas

**aromatic**

**arose** see **arise**

**around**

**arouse** *verb*
arouses
arousing
aroused

**arrange** *verb*
arranges
arranging
arranged

**arrangement**

**array** *noun*
arrays

**arrears**

**arrest** *verb*
arrests
arresting
arrested

**arrest** *noun*
arrests

**arrival**

**arrive** *verb*
arrives
arriving
arrived

**arrogance**

**arrogant**

**arrow** *noun*
arrows

**arsenal** *noun*
arsenals

**arsenic**

**arson**

**artefact** *noun*
artefacts

**artery** *noun*
arteries

**artful**
artfully

**arthritic**

**arthritis**

**article** *noun*
articles

**articulate** *adjective*

**articulate** *verb*
articulates
articulating
articulated

**artificial**
artificially

**artillery** *noun*
artilleries

**artist** *noun*
artists

**artiste** *noun*
artistes

**artistic**

**artistry**

**asbestos**

**ascend** *verb*
ascends
ascending
ascended

**ascent** *noun*
ascents

**ash**★ *noun*
ashes

**ashamed**

**ashen**

**ashore**

**ashtray** *noun*
ashtrays

**Asian** *adjective* and *noun*
Asians

**aside**

**ask** *verb*
asks
asking
asked

**asleep**

**aspect** *noun*
aspects

**asphalt**☆

**aspirin** *noun*
aspirins

**ass** *noun*
asses

**assassin** *noun*
assassins

**assassinate** *verb*
assassinates
assassinating
assassinated

**assassination** *noun*
assassinations

**assault** *verb*
assaults
assaulting
assaulted

. . . . . . . . . . . . . . . . . . . . . . . . . . . . . . . . . . . . . . . . . . . . . . . . . .

★ The tree and the burnt powder.
☆ Note that this word is not spelt *ash-*.

b
c
d
e
f
g
h
i
j
k
l
m
n
o
p
q
r
s
t
u
v
w
x
y
z

12

assault *noun*
assaults

assemble *verb*
assembles
assembling
assembled

assembly *noun*
assemblies

assent

assert *verb*
asserts
asserting
asserted

assertion

assertive

assess *verb*
assesses
assessing
assessed

assessment

assessor

asset *noun*
assets

assign *verb*
assigns
assigning
assigned

assignment *noun*
assignments

assist *verb*
assists
assisting
assisted

assistance

assistant *noun*
assistants

associate *verb*
associates
associating
associated

associate *noun*
associates

association *noun*
associations

assorted

assortment

assume *verb*
assumes
assuming
assumed

assumption *noun*
assumptions

assurance *noun*
assurances

assure *verb*
assures
assuring
assured

asterisk *noun*
asterisks

asteroid *noun*
asteroids

asthma

asthmatic *adjective*
and *noun*
asthmatics

astonish *verb*
astonishes
astonishing
astonished

astonishment

astound *verb*
astounds
astounding
astounded

astride

astrologer

astrological

astrology

astronaut *noun*
astronauts

astronomer

astronomical

astronomy

**-asy**
Not many words end in -asy. The most important are **ecstasy**, **fantasy**, **idiosyncrasy**. There are a lot of words ending in -acy, however, e.g. **accuracy**.

ate★ see **eat**

atheist *noun*
atheists

atheism

athlete *noun*
athletes

athletic

athletics

atlas *noun*
atlases

atmosphere *noun*
atmospheres

atmospheric

atoll *noun*
atolls

atom *noun*
atoms

atomic

atrocious
atrociously

atrocity *noun*
atrocities

attach *verb*
attaches
attaching
attached

attached

attachment *noun*
attachments

★ **Ate** is the past tense of eat e.g. *I ate an apple.* **!eight.**

a
b
c
d
e
f
g
h
i
j
k
l
m
n
o
p
q
r
s
t
u
v
w
x
y
z

**a**

**attack** *verb*
attacks
attacking
attacked
**attack** *noun*
attacks
**attain** *verb*
attains
attaining
attained
**attainment**
**attempt** *verb*
attempts
attempting
attempted
**attempt** *noun*
attempts
**attend** *verb*
attends
attending
attended
**attendance** *noun*
attendances
**attendant** *noun*
attendants
**attention**
**attentive**
**attic** *noun*
attics
**attitude** *noun*
attitudes
**attract** *verb*
attracts
attracting
attracted
**attraction** *noun*
attractions
**attractive**
**auburn**
**auction** *noun*
auctions

**auctioneer**
**audibility**
**audible**
**audience** *noun*
audiences

**audio-**
*audio-* makes words with 'sound' or 'hearing' in their meaning. Some of them have hyphens, e.g. **audio-visual** (= to do with hearing and seeing).

**audio-visual**
**audition** *noun*
auditions
**auditorium** *noun*
auditoriums
**August**
**aunt** *noun*
aunts
**auntie**★ *noun*
aunties
**au pair**☆ *noun*
au pairs
**aural**✪
**austere**
**austerity**
**Australian** *adjective* and *noun*
Australians
**authentic**
authentically
**authenticity**
**author** *noun*
authors

**authority** *noun*
authorities
**authorize** *verb*
authorizes
authorizing
authorized
**autistic**

**auto-**
*auto-* at the beginning of a word means 'self', e.g. **autobiography** (= a biography of yourself), **automatic** (= done by itself). But some words beginning with *auto-* are to do with cars, e.g. **autocross** (= car racing across country).

**autobiography** *noun*
autobiographies
**autograph** *noun*
autographs
**automate** *verb*
automates
automating
automated
**automatic**
automatically
**automation**
**automobile** *noun*
automobiles
**autumn** *noun*
autumns
**autumnal**
**auxiliary** *adjective* and *noun*
auxiliaries

........................................................

★ You can also spell this word *aunty*.
☆ **Au pair** means a young person from another country who works in your house.
✪ **Aural** means 'to do with hearing'. **!** oral.

14

availability
available
avalanche *noun*
avalanches
avenue *noun*
avenues
average *adjective* and *noun*
averages
average *verb*
averages
averaging
averaged
avert *verb*
averts
averting
averted
aviary *noun*
aviaries
aviation
avid
avoid *verb*
avoids
avoiding
avoided
avoidance
await *verb*
awaits
awaiting
awaited
awake *adjective*
awake *verb*
awakes
awaking
awoke
awoken
awaken *verb*
awakens
awakening
awakened
award *noun*
awards

award *verb*
awards
awarding
awarded
aware
awareness
awash
away
awe
awed
awful
awfully
awhile★
awkward
awoke see awake
awoken see awake
axe *noun*
axes
axe *verb*
axes
axing
axed
axis *noun*
axes
axle *noun*
axles
Aztec *noun*
Aztecs
azure *adjective*

# Bb

babble *verb*
babbles
babbling
babbled
baboon *noun*
baboons

baby *noun*
babies
babyish
babysit *verb*
babysits
babysitting
babysat
babysitter *noun*
babysitters
bachelor *noun*
bachelors
back *noun*
backs
back *verb*
backs
backing
backed
backache *noun*
backaches
backbone *noun*
backbones
background *noun*
backgrounds
backing
backlash *noun*
backlashes
backlog *noun*
backlogs
backside *noun*
backsides
backstroke
backward *adjective* and *adverb*
backwards *adverb*
backwater *noun*
backwaters
backyard *noun*
backyards
bacon
bacteria
bacterial

a
b
c
d
e
f
g
h
i
j
k
l
m
n
o
p
q
r
s
t
u
v
w
x
y
z

★ Awhile means 'for a short time', e.g. *Wait here awhile*. You spell it as two words in e.g. *a short while*.

15

## ba

a  b  c  d  e  f  g  h  i  j  k  l  m  n  o  p  q  r  s  t  u  v  w  x  y  z

**bad** *adjective*
worse
worst
badly

**baddy** *noun*
baddies

**badge** *noun*
badges

**badger** *noun*
badgers

**badger** *verb*
badgers
badgering
badgered

**badminton**

**baffle** *verb*
baffles
baffling
baffled

**bag** *noun*
bags

**bag** *verb*
bags
bagging
bagged

**bagel** *noun*
bagels

**baggage**

**baggy** *adjective*
baggier
baggiest

**bagpipes**

**bail★** *noun*
bails

**bail☆** *verb*
bails
bailing
bailed

**Bairam** *noun*
Bairams

**Baisakhi**

**bait** *noun*

**bait** *verb*
baits
baiting
baited

**bake** *verb*
bakes
baking
baked

**baker** *noun*
bakers

**bakery** *noun*
bakeries

**baking powder**

**balance** *noun*
balances

**balance** *verb*
balances
balancing
balanced

**balcony** *noun*
balconies

**bald** *adjective*
balder
baldest

**bale○** *noun*
bales

**bale✛** *verb*
bales
baling
baled

**ballad** *noun*
ballads

**ballerina** *noun*
ballerinas

**ballet** *noun*
ballets

**ballistic** *adjective*

**balloon** *noun*
balloons

**ballot** *noun*
ballots

**ballpoint** *noun*
ballpoints

**ballroom** *noun*
ballrooms

**balsa**

**bamboo** *noun*
bamboos

**ban** *verb*
bans
banning
banned

**banana** *noun*
bananas

**band** *noun*
bands

**band** *verb*
bands
banding
banded

**bandage** *noun*
bandages

**bandit** *noun*
bandits

**bandstand** *noun*
bandstands

**bandwagon** *noun*
bandwagons

**bandy** *adjective*
bandier
bandiest

. . . . . . . . . . . . . . . . . . . . . . . . . . . . . . . . . . . . . . . . . . . . . . . . . . . . . . . . . . . . . . . . . . . . . . . . . .

★ **Bail** means 'money paid to let a prisoner out of prison' and 'a piece of wood put on the stumps in cricket'. **! bale**.

☆ **Bail** means 'to pay money to let a prisoner out of prison' and 'to scoop water out of a boat'. **! bale**.

○ **Bale** means 'a large bundle'. **! bail**.

✛ **Bale** means 'to jump out of an aircraft'. **! bail**.

**bang** *noun*
bangs

**bang** *verb*
bangs
banging
banged

**banger** *noun*
bangers

**banish** *verb*
banishes
banishing
banished

**banishment**

**banisters**

**banjo** *noun*
banjos

**bank** *noun*
banks

**bank** *verb*
banks
banking
banked

**banknote** *noun*
banknotes

**bankrupt**

**bankruptcy**

**banner** *noun*
banners

**banquet** *noun*
banquets

**baptism** *noun*
baptisms

**Baptist\*** *noun*
Baptists

**baptize** *verb*
baptizes
baptizing
baptized

**bar** *noun*
bars

**bar** *verb*
bars
barring
barred

**barb** *noun*
barbs

**barbarian** *noun*
barbarians

**barbaric**

**barbarism**

**barbarity** *noun*
barbarities

**barbarous** *adjective*

**barbecue** *noun*
barbecues

**barber** *noun*
barbers

**bar code** *noun*
bar codes

**bard** *noun*
bards

**bare**☆ *adjective*
barer
barest

**bareback**

**barely**

**bargain** *noun*
bargains

**bargain** *verb*
bargains
bargaining
bargained

**barge** *noun*
barges

**barge** *verb*
barges
barging
barged

**baritone** *noun*
baritones

**bark** *noun*
barks

**bark** *verb*
barks
barking
barked

**barley**

**barman** *noun*
barmen

**bar mitzvah** *noun*
bar mitzvahs

**barnacle** *noun*
barnacles

**barnyard** *noun*
barnyards

**barometer** *noun*
barometers

**barometric**

**baron** *noun*
barons

**baroness** *noun*
baronesses

**baronial**

**barrack** *verb*
barracks
barracking
barracked

**barracks**○ *plural noun*

**barrage** *noun*
barrages

**barrel** *noun*
barrels

. . . . . . . . . . . . . . . . . . . . . . . . . . . . . . . . . . . . . . . . . . . . . . . . . . .

★ You use a capital B when you mean a member of the Christian Church.

☆ **Bare** means 'naked' or 'not covered'. **!bear**.

○ **Barracks** is plural but sometimes has a singular verb, e.g. *The barracks is over there*.

**barren**

**barricade** *noun*
barricades

**barricade** *verb*
barricades
barricading
barricaded

**barrier** *noun*
barriers

**barrister** *noun*
barristers

**barrow** *noun*
barrows

**barter** *verb*
barters
bartering
bartered

**base** ★ *noun*
bases

**base** *verb*
bases
basing
based

**baseball** *noun*
baseballs

**basement** *noun*
basements

**bash** *verb*
bashes
bashing
bashed

**bash** *noun*
bashes

**bashful**
bashfully

**basic**
basically

**basin** *noun*
basins

**basis** *noun*
bases

**bask** *verb*
basks
basking
basked

**basket** *noun*
baskets

**basketball** *noun*
basketballs

**basketful** *noun*
basketfuls

**bass** ☆ *noun*
basses

**bassoon** *noun*
bassoons

**bastard** *noun*
bastards

**bat** *noun*
bats

**bat** *verb*
bats
batting
batted

**batch** *noun*
batches

**bath** *noun*
baths

**bath** *verb*
baths

**bathing**
bathed

**bathe** *verb*
bathes
bathing
bathed

**bathroom** *noun*
bathrooms

**baton** ○ *noun*
batons

**batsman** *noun*
batsmen

**battalion** *noun*
battalions

**batten** ✛ *noun*
battens

**batter** *verb*
batters
battering
battered

**batter** *noun*

**battery** *noun*
batteries

**battle** *noun*
battles

**battlefield** *noun*
battlefields

**battlements**

**battleship** *noun*
battleships

**bawl** *verb*
bawls
bawling
bawled

**bay** *noun*
bays

**bayonet** *noun*
bayonets

**bazaar** *noun*
bazaars

**beach** ✱ *noun*
beaches

**beacon** *noun*
beacons

**bead** *noun*
beads

........................................................................

★ **Base** means 'a place where things are controlled'. ! **bass**.
☆ **Bass** means 'a singer with a low voice'. ! **base**.
○ A **baton** is a stick used by a conductor in an orchestra. ! **batten**.
✛ A **batten** is a flat strip of wood. ! **baton**.
✱ **Beach** means 'sandy part of the seashore'. ! **beech**.

**beady** *adjective*
beadier
beadiest

**beagle** *noun*
beagles

**beak** *noun*
beaks

**beaker** *noun*
beakers

**beam** *noun*
beams

**beam** *verb*
beams
beaming
beamed

**bean**★ *noun*
beans

**bear**☆ *verb*
bears
bearing
bore
borne

**bear**☆ *noun*
bears

**bearable**

**beard** *noun*
beards

**bearded**

**bearing** *noun*
bearings

**beast** *noun*
beasts

**beastly**

**beat** *verb*
beats
beating
beat
beaten

**beat** *noun*
beats

**beautiful**
beautifully

**beautify** *verb*
beautifies
beautifying
beautified

**beauty** *noun*
beauties

**beaver** *noun*
beavers

**becalmed**

**became** see **become**

**because**

**beckon** *verb*
beckons
beckoning
beckoned

**become** *verb*
becomes
becoming
became
become

**bedclothes**

**bedding**

**bedlam**

**bedraggled**

**bedridden**

**bedroom** *noun*
bedrooms

**bedside**

**bedspread** *noun*
bedspreads

**bedstead** *noun*
bedsteads

**bedtime**

**bee** *noun*
bees

**beech**○ *noun*
beeches

**beef**

**beefburger** *noun*
beefburgers

**beefeater** *noun*
beefeaters

**beefy** *adjective*
beefier
beefiest

**beehive** *noun*
beehives

**beeline**

**been**✣ see **be**

**beer** *noun*
beers

**beet** *noun*
beet *or* beets

**beetle** *noun*
beetles

**beetroot** *noun*
beetroot

**before**

**beforehand**

**beg** *verb*
begs
begging
begged

**began** see **begin**

**beggar** *noun*
beggars

**begin** *verb*
begins
beginning
began
begun

**beginner** *noun*
beginners

**beginning** *noun*
beginnings

. . . . . . . . . . . . . . . . . . . . . . . . . . . . . . . . . . . . . . . . . . . . . . . . . . . . . . .

★ A **bean** is a vegetable. ❗ **been**.

☆ To **bear** something is to carry it and a **bear** is an animal. ❗ **bare**.

○ **Beech** means 'a tree'. ❗ **beach**.

✣ You use **been** in e.g. *I've been to the zoo.* ❗ **bean**.

## be

**begrudge** *verb*
  begrudges
  begrudging
  begrudged

**begun** see **begin**

**behalf**

**behave** *verb*
  behaves
  behaving
  behaved

**behaviour**

**behead** *verb*
  beheads
  beheading
  beheaded

**behind** *adverb and preposition*

**behind** *noun*
  behinds

**beige** *noun*

**being** *noun*
  beings

**belch** *verb*
  belches
  belching
  belched

**belch** *noun*
  belches

**belfry** *noun*
  belfries

**belief** *noun*
  beliefs

**believe** *verb*
  believes
  believing
  believed

**believable**

**believer**

**bellow** *verb*
  bellows
  bellowing
  bellowed

**bellows**

**belly** *noun*
  bellies

**belong** *verb*
  belongs
  belonging
  belonged

**belongings**

**beloved**

**below**

**belt** *noun*
  belts

**belt** *verb*
  belts
  belting
  belted

**bench** *noun*
  benches

**bend** *verb*
  bends
  bending
  bent

**bend** *noun*
  bends

**beneath**

**benefaction**

**benefactor** *noun*
  benefactors

**benefit** *noun*
  benefits

**beneficial**
  beneficially

**benevolence**

**benevolent**

**bent** see **bend**

**bequeath** *verb*
  bequeaths
  bequeathing
  bequeathed

**bequest**

**bereaved**★

**bereavement**

**bereft**☆

**beret** *noun*
  berets

**berry** *noun*
  berries

**berserk**

**berth** *noun*
  berths

**beside**

**besides**

**besiege** *verb*
  besieges
  besieging
  besieged

**bestseller** *noun*
  bestsellers

**bet** *noun*
  bets

**bet** *verb*
  bets
  betting
  bet
  betted

**betray** *verb*
  betrays
  betraying
  betrayed

**betrayal**

**better** *adjective and adverb*

. . . . . . . . . . . . . . . . . . . . . . . . . . . . . . . . . . . . . . . . . . . . .

★ You use **bereaved** when you mean a person with a close relative who has died. **!bereft**.

☆ You use **bereft** when you mean 'deprived of something', e.g. *bereft of hope*. **!bereaved**.

**better** *verb*
  betters
  bettering
  bettered

**between**

**beware**★ *verb*

**bewilder** *verb*
  bewilders
  bewildering
  bewildered

**bewilderment**

**bewitch** *verb*
  bewitches
  bewitching
  bewitched

**beyond**

**bi-**
*bi-* at the beginning of a word means 'two', e.g. **bicycle** (= a machine with two wheels), **bilateral** (= having two sides).

**bias** *noun*
  biases

**biased**

**bib** *noun*
  bibs

**Bible** *noun*
  Bibles

**biblical**

**bicycle** *noun*
  bicycles

**bid** *noun*
  bids

**bid** *verb*
  bids
  bidding
  bid

**bide** *verb*
  bides
  biding
  bided

**big** *adjective*
  bigger
  biggest

**bigamist**

**bigamous**

**bigamy**

**bike** *noun*
  bikes

**bikini** *noun*
  bikinis

**bile**

**bilge** *noun*
  bilges

**bilingual**

**billiards**

**billion** *noun*
  billions

**billionth**

**billow** *noun*
  billows

**billow** *verb*
  billows
  billowing
  billowed

**billy goat** *noun*
  billy goats

**binary**

**bind** *verb*
  binds
  binding
  bound

**bingo**

**binoculars**

**bio-**
*bio-* at the beginning of a word means 'life', e.g. **biography** (= a story of a person's life), **biology** (= the study of living things).

**biodegradable**

**biographer**

**biographical**

**biography** *noun*
  biographies

**biological**

**biologist**

**biology**

**bionic**

**biosphere**

**birch** *noun*
  birches

**bird** *noun*
  birds

**birdseed**

**Biro** *noun*
  Biros

**birth** *noun*
  births

**birth control**

**birthday** *noun*
  birthdays

**birthmark** *noun*
  birthmarks

**birthplace** *noun*
  birthplaces

**biscuit** *noun*
  biscuits

**bisect** *verb*
  bisects
  bisecting
  bisected

**bishop** *noun*
  bishops

★ **Beware** has no other forms.

a
**b**
c
d
e
f
g
h
i
j
k
l
m
n
o
p
q
r
s
t
u
v
w
x
y
z

21

a

**b**

c

d

e

f

g

h

i

j

k

l

m

n

o

p

q

r

s

t

u

v

w

x

y

z

**bison** *noun*
bison

**bit** *noun*
bits

**bit** see **bite**

**bitch** *noun*
bitches

**bitchy** *adjective*
bitchier
bitchiest

**bite** *verb*
bites
biting
bit
bitten

**bite**★ *noun*
bites

**bitter**

**black** *adjective*
blacker
blackest

**black** *noun*
blacks

**blackberry** *noun*
blackberries

**blackbird** *noun*
blackbirds

**blackboard** *noun*
blackboards

**blacken** *verb*
blackens
blackening
blackened

**blackmail** *verb*
blackmails
blackmailing
blackmailed

**blackout** *noun*
blackouts

**blacksmith** *noun*
blacksmiths

**bladder** *noun*
bladders

**blade** *noun*
blades

**blame** *verb*
blames
blaming
blamed

**blame** *noun*

**blancmange** *noun*
blancmanges

**blank** *adjective* and
*noun*
blanks

**blanket** *noun*
blankets

**blare** *verb*
blares
blaring
blared

**blaspheme** *verb*
blasphemes
blaspheming
blasphemed

**blasphemous**

**blasphemy**

**blast** *noun*
blasts

**blast** *verb*
blasts
blasting
blasted

**blast-off**

**blaze** *noun*
blazes

**blaze** *verb*
blazes
blazing
blazed

**blazer** *noun*
blazers

**bleach** *noun*
bleaches

**bleach** *verb*
bleaches
bleaching
bleached

**bleak** *adjective*
bleaker
bleakest

**bleary** *adjective*
blearier
bleariest
blearily

**bleat** *noun*
bleats

**bleat** *verb*
bleats
bleating
bleated

**bleed** *verb*
bleeds
bleeding
bled

**bleep** *noun*
bleeps

**blemish** *noun*
blemishes

**blend** *verb*
blends
blending
blended

**blend** *noun*
blends

**bless** *verb*
blesses
blessing
blessed

**blessing** *noun*
blessings

**blew**☆ see **blow**

**blight** *noun*
blights

..........................................................

★ A **bite** is an act of biting. **!** byte.
☆ You use **blew** in e.g. *the wind blew hard*. **!** blue.

**blind** *adjective*
blinder
blindest

**blind** *verb*
blinds
blinding
blinded

**blind** *noun*
blinds

**blindfold** *noun*
blindfolds

**blindfold** *verb*
blindfolds
blindfolding
blindfolded

**blink** *verb*
blinks
blinking
blinked

**bliss**

**blissful**
blissfully

**blister** *noun*
blisters

**blitz** *noun*
blitzes

**blizzard** *noun*
blizzards

**bloated**

**block** *noun*
blocks

**block** *verb*
blocks
blocking
blocked

**blockade** *noun*
blockades

**blockage** *noun*
blockages

**blond** *adjective*
blonder
blondest

**blonde★** *noun*
blondes

**blood**

**bloodhound** *noun*
bloodhounds

**bloodshed**

**bloodshot**

**bloodstream**

**bloodthirsty** *adjective*
bloodthirstier
bloodthirstiest

**bloody** *adjective*
bloodier
bloodiest

**bloom** *verb*
blooms
blooming
bloomed

**bloom** *noun*
blooms

**blossom** *noun*
blossoms

**blossom** *verb*
blossoms
blossoming
blossomed

**blot** *noun*
blots

**blot** *verb*
blots
blotting
blotted

**blotch** *noun*
blotches

**blotchy** *adjective*
blotchier
blotchiest

**blouse** *noun*
blouses

**blow** *noun*
blows

**blow** *verb*
blows
blowing
blew
blown

**blowlamp** *noun*
blowlamps

**blowtorch** *noun*
blowtorches

**blue** *adjective*
bluer
bluest

**blue☆** *noun*
blues

**bluebell** *noun*
bluebells

**bluebottle** *noun*
bluebottles

**blueprint** *noun*
blueprints

**bluff** *verb*
bluffs
bluffing
bluffed

**bluff** *noun*
bluffs

**blunder** *verb*
blunders
blundering
blundered

**blunder** *noun*
blunders

**blunt** *adjective*
blunter
bluntest

**blur** *verb*
blurs
blurring
blurred

· · · · · · · · · · · · · · · · · · · · · · · · · · · · · · · · · · · · · · · · · · · · ·
★ You use **blonde** when you are talking about a girl or woman.
☆ **Blue** is the colour. ! **blew**.

a
**b**
c
d
e
f
g
h
i
j
k
l
m
n
o
p
q
r
s
t
u
v
w
x
y
z

23

## bl - bo

**blur** noun
blurs

**blush** verb
blushes
blushing
blushed

**bluster** verb
blusters
blustering
blustered

**blustery**

**boa constrictor** noun
boa constrictors

**boar**★ noun
boars

**board**☆ noun
boards

**board** verb
boards
boarding
boarded

**boarder** noun
boarders

**board game** noun
board games

**boast** verb
boasts
boasting
boasted

**boastful**
boastfully

**boat** noun
boats

**boating**

**bob** verb
bobs
bobbing
bobbed

**bobble** noun
bobbles

**bobsled** noun
bobsleds

**bobsleigh** noun
bobsleighs

**bodice** noun
bodices

**bodily**

**body** noun
bodies

**bodyguard** noun
bodyguards

**boggy** adjective
boggier
boggiest

**bogus**

**boil** verb
boils
boiling
boiled

**boil** noun
boils

**boiler** noun
boilers

**boisterous**
boisterously

**bold** adjective
bolder
boldest

**bollard** noun
bollards

**bolster** verb
bolsters
bolstering
bolstered

**bolster** noun
bolsters

**bolt** noun
bolts

**bolt** verb
bolts
bolting
bolted

**bomb** noun
bombs

**bomb** verb
bombs
bombing
bombed

**bombard** verb
bombards
bombarding
bombarded

**bombardment**

**bomber** noun
bombers

**bond** noun
bonds

**bondage**

**bone** noun
bones

**bonfire** noun
bonfires

**bonnet** noun
bonnets

**bonus** noun
bonuses

**bony** adjective
bonier
boniest

**boo** verb
boos
booing
booed

**booby** noun
boobies

**book** noun
books

**book** verb
books
booking
booked

**bookcase** noun
bookcases

**booklet** noun
booklets

. . . . . . . . . . . . . . . . . . . . . . . . . . . . . . . . . . . . . . . . . . .

★ A **boar** is a wild pig. ! **bore**.
☆ A **board** is a piece of wood. ! **bored**.

**bookmaker** *noun*
bookmakers

**bookmark** *noun*
bookmarks

**boom** *noun*
booms

**boom** *verb*
booms
booming
boomed

**boomerang** *noun*
boomerangs

**boost** *verb*
boosts
boosting
boosted

**booster** *noun*
boosters

**boot** *noun*
boots

**boot** *verb*
boots
booting
booted

**booth** *noun*
booths

**border** *noun*
borders

**borderline**

**bore** *verb*
bores
boring
bored

**bore★** *noun*
bores

**boredom**

**boring**

**born☆**

**borne✪** see **bear**

**borough** *noun*
boroughs

**borrow** *verb*
borrows
borrowing
borrowed

**bosom** *noun*
bosoms

**boss** *noun*
bosses

**boss** *verb*
bosses
bossing
bossed

**bossy** *adjective*
bossier
bossiest

**botanical**

**botanist**

**botany**

**both**

**bother** *verb*
bothers
bothering
bothered

**bother** *noun*

**bottle** *noun*
bottles

**bottle** *verb*
bottles
bottling
bottled

**bottleneck** *noun*
bottlenecks

**bottom** *noun*
bottoms

**bottomless**

**bough✢** *noun*
boughs

**bought**

**boulder** *noun*
boulders

**bounce** *verb*
bounces
bouncing
bounced

**bounce** *noun*
bounces

**bouncing**

**bouncy** *adjective*
bouncier
bounciest

**bound** *verb*
bounds
bounding
bounded

**bound** *adjective* and *noun*
bounds

**bound** see **bind**

**boundary** *noun*
boundaries

**bounds**

**bouquet** *noun*
bouquets

**bout** *noun*
bouts

**boutique** *noun*
boutiques

**bow✱** *noun*
bows

. . . . . . . . . . . . . . . . . . . . . . . . . . . . . . . . . . . . . . . . . .

★ **Bore** means 'something boring'. !**boar**.

☆ You use **born** in e.g. *He was born in June.* !**borne**.

✪ You use **borne** in e.g. *She has borne three children* and *The cost is borne by the government.* !**born**.

✢ A **bough** is a part of a tree. !**bow**.

✱ A **bow** is a knot with loops and rhymes with 'go'. A **bow** is also the front of a ship or a bending of the body and rhymes with 'cow'.

a
**b**
c
d
e
f
g
h
i
j
k
l
m
n
o
p
q
r
s
t
u
v
w
x
y
z

25

a
**b**
c
d
e
f
g
h
i
j
k
l
m
n
o
p
q
r
s
t
u
v
w
x
y
z

**bow★** *verb*
bows
bowing
bowed

**bowels**

**bowl** *noun*
bowls

**bowl** *verb*
bowls
bowling
bowled

**bow-legged**

**bowler** *noun*
bowlers

**bowling**

**bowls**

**bow tie** *noun*
bow ties

**box** *noun*
boxes

**box** *verb*
boxes
boxing
boxed

**boxer** *noun*
boxers

**Boxing Day** *noun*

**boy** *noun*
boys

**boycott** *verb*
boycotts
boycotting
boycotted

**boyfriend** *noun*
boyfriends

**boyhood**

**boyish**

**bra** *noun*
bras

**brace** *noun*
braces

**bracelet** *noun*
bracelets

**braces**

**bracken**

**bracket** *noun*
brackets

**bracket** *verb*
brackets
bracketing
bracketed

**brag** *verb*
brags
bragging
bragged

**braid** *noun*
braids

**braille**

**brain** *noun*
brains

**brainy** *adjective*
brainier
brainiest

**brake**☆ *noun*
brakes

**bramble** *noun*
brambles

**branch** *noun*
branches

**branch** *verb*
branches
branching
branched

**brand** *noun*
brands

**brand** *verb*
brands
branding
branded

**brandish** *verb*
brandishes
brandishing
brandished

**brand new**

**brandy** *noun*
brandies

**brass**

**brassière** *noun*
brassières

**brassy** *adjective*
brassier
brassiest

**brave** *adjective*
braver
bravest

**brave** *noun*
braves

**bravery**

**brawl** *noun*
brawls

**brawn**

**brawny** *adjective*
brawnier
brawniest

**bray** *verb*
brays
braying
brayed

**brazen**

**brazier** *noun*
braziers

**breach**✪ *noun*
breaches

**bread**

**breadth** *noun*
breadths

**breadwinner** *noun*
breadwinners

. . . . . . . . . . . . . . . . . . . . . . . . . . . . . . . . . . . . . . . . . . . . . . . . . . .

★ To **bow** is to bend the body and rhymes with 'cow'.

☆ A **brake** is what makes a car stop. **!** break.

✪ A **breach** is a gap or a breaking of a rule. **!** breech.

26

**break★** *verb*
 breaks
 breaking
 broke
 broken
**break** *noun*
 breaks
**breakable**
**breakage** *noun*
 breakages
**breakdown** *noun*
 breakdowns
**breaker** *noun*
 breakers
**breakfast** *noun*
 breakfasts
**breakneck**
**breakthrough** *noun*
 breakthroughs
**breakwater** *noun*
 breakwaters
**breast** *noun*
 breasts
**breaststroke**
**breath** *noun*
 breaths
**breathalyse**
 breathalyses
 breathalysing
 breathalysed
**breathalyser** *noun*
 breathalysers
**breathe** *verb*
 breathes
 breathing
 breathed
**breather** *noun*
 breathers

**breathless**
**breathtaking**
**bred** see **breed**
**breech**☆ *noun*
 breeches
**breeches** *plural noun*
**breed** *verb*
 breeds
 breeding
 bred
**breed** *noun*
 breeds
**breeder** *noun*
 breeders
**breeze** *noun*
 breezes
**breezy** *adjective*
 breezier
 breeziest
**brethren**
**brevity**
**brew** *verb*
 brews
 brewing
 brewed
**brewer** *noun*
 brewers
**brewery** *noun*
 breweries
**briar**✪ *noun*
 briars
**bribe** *noun*
 bribes
**bribe** *verb*
 bribes
 bribing
 bribed

**bribery**
**brick** *noun*
 bricks
**bricklayer** *noun*
 bricklayers
**bride** *noun*
 brides
**bridal**✜
**bridegroom** *noun*
 bridegrooms
**bridesmaid** *noun*
 bridesmaids
**bridge** *noun*
 bridges
**bridle**✻ *noun*
 bridles
**brief** *adjective*
 briefer
 briefest
**brief** *noun*
 briefs
**brief** *verb*
 briefs
 briefing
 briefed
**briefcase** *noun*
 briefcases
**brigade** *noun*
 brigades
**brigadier** *noun*
 brigadiers
**brigand** *noun*
 brigands
**bright** *adjective*
 brighter
 brightest

★ To **break** something is to make it go into pieces. **! brake**.
☆ A **breech** is a part of a gun. **! breach**.
✪ **Briar** means 'a prickly bush' and 'a pipe'. You will sometimes see it spelt *brier*.
✜ **Bridal** means 'to do with a bride'. **! bridle**.
✻ A **bridle** is part of a horse's harness. **! bridal**.

**brighten** *verb*
brightens
brightening
brightened

**brilliance**

**brilliant**

**brim** *noun*
brims

**brimming**

**brine**

**bring** *verb*
brings
bringing
brought

**brink**

**brisk** *adjective*
brisker
briskest

**bristle** *noun*
bristles

**bristly**
bristlier
bristliest

**British**

**Briton** *noun*
Britons

**brittle** *adjective*
brittler
brittlest

**broach**★ *verb*
broaches
broaching
broached

**broad** *adjective*
broader
broadest
broadly

**broadcast** *noun*
broadcasts

**broadcast** *verb*
broadcasts
broadcasting
broadcast

**broadcaster**

**broaden** *verb*
broadens
broadening
broadened

**broad-minded**

**broadside** *noun*
broadsides

**brochure** *noun*
brochures

**brogue** *noun*
brogues

**broke** see **break**

**broken** see **break**

**bronchitis**

**bronze**

**brooch**☆ *noun*
brooches

**brood** *noun*
broods

**brood** *verb*
broods
brooding
brooded

**broody** *adjective*
broodier
broodiest

**brook** *noun*
brooks

**broom** *noun*
brooms

**broomstick** *noun*
broomsticks

**broth** *noun*
broths

**brother** *noun*
brothers

**brotherly**

**brother-in-law** *noun*
brothers-in-law

**brought** see **bring**

**brow** *noun*
brows

**brown** *adjective*
browner
brownest

**brownie**⚬ *noun*
brownies

**Brownie**✣ *noun*
Brownies

**browse** *verb*
browses
browsing
browsed

**bruise** *noun*
bruises

**bruise** *verb*
bruises
bruising
bruised

**brunette** *noun*
brunettes

**brush** *noun*
brushes

**brush** *verb*
brushes
brushing
brushed

**Brussels sprout** *noun*
Brussels sprouts

**brutal**
brutally

**brutality**
brutalities

. . . . . . . . . . . . . . . . . . . . . . . . . . . . . . . . . . . . . . . . . . . . . . . . . . .

★ **Broach** means 'to mention something'. **!broch**.
☆ A **brooch** is an ornament you wear. **!broach**.
⚬ A **brownie** is a chocolate cake.
✣ A **Brownie** is a junior Guide.

**brute** *noun*
  brutes
**bubble** *noun*
  bubbles
**bubble** *verb*
  bubbles
  bubbling
  bubbled
**bubble gum**
**bubbly** *adjective*
  bubblier
  bubbliest
**buccaneer** *noun*
  buccaneers
**buck** *noun*
  bucks
**buck** *verb*
  bucks
  bucking
  bucked
**bucket** *noun*
  buckets
**bucketful** *noun*
  bucketfuls
**buckle** *noun*
  buckles
**buckle** *verb*
  buckles
  buckling
  buckled
**bud** *noun*
  buds
**Buddhism**
**Buddhist**
**budding**
**budge** *verb*
  budges
  budging
  budged
**budgerigar** *noun*
  budgerigars
**budget** *noun*
  budgets

**budget** *verb*
  budgets
  budgeting
  budgeted
**budgie** *noun*
  budgies
**buff**
**buffalo** *noun*
  buffalo *or* buffaloes
**buffer** *noun*
  buffers
**buffet** *noun*
  buffets
**bug** *noun*
  bugs
**bug** *verb*
  bugs
  bugging
  bugged
**bugle** *noun*
  bugles
**bugler** *noun*
  buglers
**build** *verb*
  builds
  building
  built
**builder** *noun*
  builders
**building** *noun*
  buildings
**built-in**
**built-up**
**bulb** *noun*
  bulbs
**bulge** *noun*
  bulges
**bulge** *verb*
  bulges
  bulging
  bulged
**bulk**

**bulky** *adjective*
  bulkier
  bulkiest
**bull** *noun*
  bulls
**bulldog** *noun*
  bulldogs
**bulldoze** *verb*
  bulldozes
  bulldozing
  bulldozed
**bulldozer** *noun*
  bulldozers
**bullet** *noun*
  bullets
**bulletin** *noun*
  bulletins
**bulletproof**
**bullfight** *noun*
  bullfights
**bullfighter**
**bullion**
**bullock** *noun*
  bullocks
**bull's-eye** *noun*
  bull's-eyes
**bully** *verb*
  bullies
  bullying
  bullied
**bully** *noun*
  bullies
**bulrush** *noun*
  bulrushes
**bulwark**★ *noun*
  bulwarks
**bulwarks**☆ *plural noun*
**bum** *noun*
  bums

★ A **bulwark** is a strong wall.
☆ **Bulwarks** are the sides of a ship.

a
**b**
c
d
e
f
g
h
i
j
k
l
m
n
o
p
q
r
s
t
u
v
w
x
y
z

30

**bumblebee** *noun*
bumblebees

**bump** *verb*
bumps
bumping
bumped

**bump** *noun*
bumps

**bumper** *adjective* and *noun*
bumpers

**bumpy** *adjective*
bumpier
bumpiest

**bunch** *noun*
bunches

**bundle** *noun*
bundles

**bundle** *verb*
bundles
bundling
bundled

**bung** *verb*
bungs
bunging
bunged

**bung** *noun*
bungs

**bungalow** *noun*
bungalows

**bungle** *verb*
bungles
bungling
bungled

**bungler** *noun*
bunglers

**bunk** *noun*
bunks

**bunk bed** *noun*
bunk beds

**bunker** *noun*
bunkers

**bunny** *noun*
bunnies

**bunsen burner** *noun*
bunsen burners

**buoy** *noun*
buoys

**buoyancy**

**buoyant**

**burden** *noun*
burdens

**burdensome**

**bureau**★ *noun*
bureaux

**burglar** *noun*
burglars

**burglary** *noun*
burglaries

**burgle** *verb*
burgles
burgling
burgled

**burial** *noun*
burials

**burly** *adjective*
burlier
burliest

**burn**☆ *verb*
burns
burning
burnt *or* burned

**burn** *noun*
burns

**burner** *noun*
burners

**burning**

**burp** *noun*
burps

**burp** *verb*
burps
burping
burped

**burr** *noun*
burrs

**burrow** *noun*
burrows

**burrow** *verb*
burrows
burrowing
burrowed

**burst** *verb*
bursts
bursting
burst

**burst** *noun*
bursts

**bury** *verb*
buries
burying
buried

**bus** *noun*
buses

**bus stop** *noun*
bus stops

**bush** *noun*
bushes

**bushy** *adjective*
bushier
bushiest

**busily**

**business** *noun*
businesses

**businesslike**

**busker** *noun*
buskers

........................................................

★ **Bureau** is a French word used in English. It means 'a writing desk' or 'an office'.

☆ You use **burned** in e.g. *I burned the cakes*. You use **burnt** in e.g. *I can smell burnt cakes*. You use **burned** or **burnt** in e.g. *I have burned/burnt the cakes*.

**bust** *verb*
 busts
 busting
 bust

**bust** *noun*
 busts

**bust** *adjective*

**bustle** *verb*
 bustles
 bustling
 bustled

**busy** *adjective*
 busier
 busiest

**busybody** *noun*
 busybodies

**but**★

**butcher** *noun*
 butchers

**butchery**

**butler** *noun*
 butlers

**butt**☆ *noun*
 butts

**butt**○ *verb*
 butts
 butting
 butted

**butter**

**buttercup** *noun*
 buttercups

**butterfingers** *noun*
 butterfingers

**butterfly** *noun*
 butterflies

**butterscotch** *noun*
 butterscotches

**buttocks**

**button** *noun*
 buttons

**button** *verb*
 buttons
 buttoning
 buttoned

**buttonhole** *noun*
 buttonholes

**buttress** *noun*
 buttresses

**buy** *verb*
 buys
 buying
 bought

**buy** *noun*
 buys

**buyer** *noun*
 buyers

**buzz** *noun*
 buzzes

**buzz** *verb*
 buzzes
 buzzing
 buzzed

**buzzard** *noun*
 buzzards

**buzzer** *noun*
 buzzers

**by**✢ *preposition*

**bye**✻ *noun*
 byes

**bye-bye**

**by-election** *noun*
 by-elections

**by-law** *noun*
 by-laws

**bypass** *noun*
 bypasses

**by-product** *noun*
 by-products

**bystander** *noun*
 bystanders

**byte**✳ *noun*

# Cc

**CAB** *abbreviation*

**cab** *noun*
 cabs

**cabaret** *noun*
 cabarets

**cabbage** *noun*
 cabbages

**cabin** *noun*
 cabins

**cabinet** *noun*
 cabinets

**cable** *noun*
 cables

**cackle** *verb*
 cackles
 cackling
 cackled

**cackle** *noun*
 cackles

**cactus** *noun*
 cacti

**caddie**○ *noun*
 caddies

- - - - - - - - - - - - - - - - - - - - - - - - - - - - - - - - - - - - - - - - -

★ You use **but** in e.g. *I like fish but I´m not hungry.* ! **butt**.
☆ A **butt** is a barrel or part of a gun. ! **but**.
○ **Butt** means 'to hit with your head'! ! **but**.
✢ You use **by** in e.g. *a book by J. K. Rowling.* ! **bye**.
✻ You use **bye** in e.g *bye for now.* ! **by**.
✳ A **byte** is a unit in computing. ! **bite**.
○ A **caddie** is a person who helps a golfer. ! **caddy**..

a
**b**
**c**
d
e
f
g
h
i
j
k
l
m
n
o
p
q
r
s
t
u
v
w
x
y
z

caddy★ *noun*
caddies

cadet *noun*
cadets

cadge *verb*
cadges
cadging
cadged

cafe *noun*
cafes

cafeteria *noun*
cafeterias

caffeine

caftan *noun*
caftans use **kaftan**

cage *noun*
cages

cagey *adjective*
cagier
cagiest

cagoule *noun*
cagoules

cake *noun*
cakes

caked

calamine

calamitous

calamity *noun*
calamities

calcium

calculate *verb*
calculates
calculating
calculated

calculation *noun*
calculations

calculator *noun*
calculators

calendar *noun*
calendars

calf☆ *noun*
calves

calico

call *noun*
calls

call *verb*
calls
calling
called

calling *noun*
callings

callipers *plural noun*

callous

calm *adjective*
calmer
calmest
calmly

calmness

calorie *noun*
calories

calves◦ see **calf**

calypso *noun*
calypsos

camcorder *noun*
camcorders

came see **come**

camel *noun*
camels

camera *noun*
cameras

cameraman *noun*
cameramen

camouflage

camp *noun*
camps

camp *verb*
camps
camping
camped

campaign *noun*
campaigns

campaign *verb*
campaigns
campaigning
campaigned

camper *noun*
campers

campsite *noun*
campsites

campus *noun*
campuses

can *verb*
could

can✢ *verb*
cans
canning
canned

can *noun*
cans

canal *noun*
canals

canary *noun*
canaries

cancel *verb*
cancels
cancelling
cancelled

cancellation *noun*
cancellations

cancer *noun*
cancers

candidate *noun*
candidates

. . . . . . . . . . . . . . . . . . . . . . . . . . . . . . . . . . . . . . . . . . . . . . . . . . . . . . . . . . .

★ A caddy is a container for tea. **!caddie**.

☆ Calf means 'a young cow' and 'a part of your leg'.

◦ Calves is the plural of calf. **!carves**.

✢ This verb can means 'to put food in a can', and it has normal forms.

a b **c** d e f g h i j k l m n o p q r s t u v w x y z

32

**candle** *noun*
candles

**candlelight**

**candlestick** *noun*
candlesticks

**candy** *noun*
candies

**candyfloss**

**cane** *noun*
canes

**cane** *verb*
canes
caning
caned

**canine**

**cannabis**

**canned music**

**cannibal** *noun*
cannibals

**cannibalism**

**cannon**★ *noun*
cannon *or* cannons

**cannonball** *noun*
cannonballs

**cannot**

**canoe** *noun*
canoes

**canoe** *verb*
canoes
canoeing
canoed

**canoeist**

**canon**☆ *noun*
canons

**canopy** *noun*
canopies

**can't** *verb*

**canteen** *noun*
canteens

**canter** *verb*
canters
cantering
cantered

**canton** *noun*
cantons

**canvas**✪ *noun*
canvases

**canvass**✤ *verb*
canvasses
canvassing
canvassed

**canyon** *noun*
canyons

**cap** *verb*
caps
capping
capped

**cap** *noun*
caps

**capable**
capably

**capability**

**capacity** *noun*
capacities

**cape** *noun*
capes

**caper** *verb*
capers
capering
capered

**caper** *noun*
capers

**capital** *noun*
capitals

**capitalism**

**capitalist**

**capsize** *verb*
capsizes
capsizing
capsized

**capsule** *noun*
capsules

**captain** *noun*
captains

**caption** *noun*
captions

**captivating**

**captive** *adjective* and *noun*
captives

**captivity**

**captor** *noun*
captors

**capture** *verb*
captures
capturing
captured

**capture** *noun*

**car** *noun*
cars

**caramel** *noun*
caramels

**carat** *noun*
carats

**caravan** *noun*
caravans

**carbohydrate** *noun*
carbohydrates

**carbon**

**car boot sale** *noun*
car boot sales

. . . . . . . . . . . . . . . . . . . . . . . . . . . . . . . . . . . . . . . . . . . . . . . . . . . . . . . . . .

★ A **cannon** is a gun. **!canon**. You use **cannons** in e.g. *There are ten cannons on the walls* and **cannon** in e.g. *They use all their cannon.*

☆ A **canon** is a member of the clergy. **!cannon**.

✪ **Canvas** means 'a strong cloth'. **!canvass**.

✤ **Canvass** means 'to ask people for their support'. **!canvas**.

a b **c** d e f g h i j k l m n o p q r s t u v w x y z

**carburettor** *noun*
carburettors

**carcass** *noun*
carcasses

**card** *noun*
cards

**cardboard**

**cardigan** *noun*
cardigans

**cardinal** *noun*
cardinals

**cardphone** *noun*
cardphones

**care** *noun*
cares

**care** *verb*
cares
caring
cared

**career** *noun*
careers

**career** *verb*
careers
careering
careered

**carefree**

**careful** *adjective*
carefully

**careless** *adjective*
carelessly
carelessness

**caress** *verb*
caresses
caressing
caressed

**caress** *noun*
caresses

**caretaker** *noun*
caretakers

**cargo** *noun*
cargoes

**Caribbean**

**caricature** *noun*
caricatures

**carnation** *noun*
carnations

**carnival** *noun*
carnivals

**carnivore** *noun*
carnivores

**carnivorous**

**carol** *noun*
carols

**caroller** *noun*
carollers

**carolling**

**carp** *noun*
carp

**carpenter** *noun*
carpenters

**carpentry**

**carpet** *noun*
carpets

**carriage** *noun*
carriages

**carriageway** *noun*
carriageways

**carrier** *noun*
carriers

**carrot** *noun*
carrots

**carry** *verb*
carries
carrying
carried

**cart** *noun*
carts

**cart** *verb*
carts
carting
carted

**carthorse** *noun*
carthorses

**cartilage**

**carton** *noun*
cartons

**cartoon** *noun*
cartoons

**cartoonist** *noun*
cartoonists

**cartridge** *noun*
cartridges

**cartwheel** *noun*
cartwheels

**carve**★ *verb*
carves
carving
carved

**cascade** *noun*
cascades

**case** *noun*
cases

**cash** *verb*
cashes
cashing
cashed

**cash** *noun*

**cashier** *noun*
cashiers

**cash register** *noun*
cash registers

**cask** *noun*
casks

**casket** *noun*
caskets

**casserole** *noun*
casseroles

**cassette** *noun*
cassettes

**cast** *verb*
casts
casting
cast

**cast** *noun*
casts

**castanets** *plural noun*

................................................

★ You use **carves** in e.g. *He carves the meat with a knife.* ! **calves**.

**castaway** *noun*
castaways

**castle** *noun*
castles

**castor** *noun*
castors

**castor sugar**

**casual** *adjective*
casually

**casualty** *noun*
casualties

**cat** *noun*
cats

**catalogue** *noun*
catalogues

**catalyst** *noun*
catalysts

**catamaran** *noun*
catamarans

**catapult** *noun*
catapults

**catastrophe** *noun*
catastrophes

**catastrophic**

**catch** *verb*
catches
catching
caught

**catch** *noun*
catches

**catching**

**catchphrase** *noun*
catchphrases

**catchy** *adjective*
catchier
catchiest

**category** *noun*
categories

**cater** *verb*
caters
catering
catered

**caterer** *noun*
caterers

**caterpillar** *noun*
caterpillars

**cathedral** *noun*
cathedrals

**Catherine wheel**
*noun*
Catherine wheels

**cathode** *noun*
cathodes

**Catholic** *adjective* and
*noun*
Catholics

**catkin** *noun*
catkins

**Cat's-eye** *noun*
Cat's-eyes

**cattle**

**caught** see **catch**

**cauldron** *noun*
cauldrons

**cauliflower** *noun*
cauliflowers

**cause** *verb*
causes
causing
caused

**cause** *noun*
causes

**caution** *noun*
cautions

**cautious** *adjective*
cautiously

**cavalier** *noun*
cavaliers

**cavalry** *noun*
cavalries

**cave** *noun*
caves

**cave** *verb*
caves
caving
caved

**caveman** *noun*
cavemen

**cavern** *noun*
caverns

**cavity** *noun*
cavities

**CD**

**CD-ROM** *noun*
CD-ROMs

**cease** *verb*
ceases
ceasing
ceased

**ceasefire** *noun*
ceasefires

**ceaseless** *adjective*
ceaselessly

**cedar** *noun*
cedars

**ceiling** *noun*
ceilings

**celebrate** *verb*
celebrates
celebrating
celebrated

**celebration** *noun*
celebrations

**celebrity** *noun*
celebrities

**celery**

**cell★** *noun*
cells

**cellar** *noun*
cellars

**cello** *noun*
cellos

**cellular**

**celluloid**

**cellulose**

a
b
**c**
d
e
f
g
h
i
j
k
l
m
n
o
p
q
r
s
t
u
v
w
x
y
z

· · · · · · · · · · · · · · · · · · · · · · · · · · · · · · · · · · · · · · · · · · · · · · · · · · · · · · · · · · · ·
★ A **cell** is a small room or a part of an organism. **!** sell.

35

a
b
**c**
d
e
f
g
h
i
j
k
l
m
n
o
p
q
r
s
t
u
v
w
x
y
z

**Celsius**

**Celt** *noun*
Celts

**Celtic**

**cement**

**cemetery** *noun*
cemeteries

**censor** *verb*
censors
censoring
censored

**censor**★ *noun*
censors

**censorship**

**censure** *verb*
censures
censured
censuring

**censure**☆ *noun*

**census** *noun*
censuses

**cent**◐ *noun*
cents

**centenary** *noun*
centenaries

**centigrade**

**centimetre** *noun*
centimetres

**centipede** *noun*
centipedes

**central** *adjective*
centrally

**centre** *noun*
centres

**centrifugal force**

**centurion** *noun*
centurions

**century** *noun*
centuries

**ceramic** *adjective*

**ceramics** *plural noun*

**cereal**✣ *noun*
cereals

**ceremony** *noun*
ceremonies

**ceremonial** *adjective*
ceremonially

**certain**

**certainly**

**certainty** *noun*
certainties

**certificate** *noun*
certificates

**certify** *verb*
certifies
certifying
certified

**chaffinch** *noun*
chaffinches

**chain** *noun*
chains

**chair** *noun*
chairs

**chairlift** *noun*
chairlifts

**chairman** *noun*
chairmen

**chairperson** *noun*
chairpersons

**chalet** *noun*
chalets

**chalk** *noun*
chalks

**chalky** *adjective*
chalkier
chalkiest

**challenge** *verb*
challenges
challenging
challenged

**challenge** *noun*
challenges

**challenger** *noun*
challengers

**chamber** *noun*
chambers

**champagne**

**champion** *noun*
champions

**championship** *noun*
championships

**chance** *noun*
chances

**chancel** *noun*
chancels

**chancellor** *noun*
chancellors

**Chancellor of the Exchequer**

**chandelier** *noun*
chandeliers

**change** *verb*
changes
changing
changed

**change** *noun*
changes

**changeable**

**channel** *noun*
channels

**chant** *noun*
chants

. . . . . . . . . . . . . . . . . . . . . . . . . . . . . . . . . . . . . . . . . . . . . . . . . . . . . .

★ A **censor** is someone who makes sure books and films are suitable for people to see. ❗censure.

☆ **Censure** means 'harsh criticism'. ❗censor.

◐ A **cent** is a coin used in America. ❗scent, sent.

✣ A **cereal** is something you eat. ❗serial.

**chant** *verb*
chants
chanting
chanted

**chaos**

**chaotic** *adjective*
chaotically

**chap** *noun*
chaps

**chapatti** *noun*
chapattis

**chapel** *noun*
chapels

**chapped**

**chapter** *noun*
chapters

**char** *verb*
chars
charring
charred

**character** *noun*
characters

**characteristic**
*adjective*
characteristically

**characteristic** *noun*
characteristics

**characterize** *verb*
characterizes
characterizing
characterized

**charades** *plural noun*

**charcoal**

**charge** *verb*
charges
charging
charged

**charge** *noun*
charges

**chariot** *noun*
chariots

**charioteer** *noun*
charioteers

**charitable** *adjective*
charitably

**charity** *noun*
charities

**charm** *verb*
charms
charming
charmed

**charm** *noun*
charms

**charming**

**chart** *noun*
charts

**charter** *noun*
charters

**charter** *verb*
charters
chartering
chartered

**charwoman** *noun*
charwomen

**chase** *verb*
chases
chasing
chased

**chase** *noun*
chases

**chasm** *noun*
chasms

**chassis** *noun*
chassis

**chat** *verb*
chats
chatting
chatted

**chat** *noun*
chats

**chatty** *adjective*
chattier
chattiest

**chateau★** *noun*
chateaux

**chatter** *verb*
chatters
chattering
chattered

**chauffeur** *noun*
chauffeurs

**chauvinism**

**chauvinist**

**cheap**☆ *adjective*
cheaper
cheapest

**cheat** *verb*
cheats
cheating
cheated

**cheat** *noun*
cheats

**check** *verb*
checks
checking
checked

**check** *noun*
checks

**checkmate** *noun*
checkmates

**checkout** *noun*
checkouts

**check-up** *noun*
check-ups

**cheek** *noun*
cheeks

**cheek** *verb*
cheeks
cheeking
cheeked

. . . . . . . . . . . . . . . . . . . . . . . . . . . . . . . . . . . . . . . . . .

★ **Chateau** is a French word used in English. It means 'a castle or large house'.

☆ **Cheap** means 'not costing much'. **!** cheep.

a
b
**c**
d
e
f
g
h
i
j
k
l
m
n
o
p
q
r
s
t
u
v
w
x
y
z

37

# ch

cheeky *adjective*
cheekier
cheekiest
cheekily

cheep★ *verb*
cheeps
cheeping
cheeped

cheer *verb*
cheers
cheering
cheered

cheer *noun*
cheers

cheerful *adjective*
cheerfully

cheerio

cheese *noun*
cheeses

cheesy *adjective*
cheesier
cheesiest

cheetah *noun*
cheetahs

chef *noun*
chefs

chemical *adjective*
chemically

chemical *noun*
chemicals

chemist *noun*
chemists

chemistry

cheque *noun*
cheques

chequebook *noun*
chequebooks

chequered

cherish *verb*
cherishes
cherishing
cherished

cherry *noun*
cherries

chess

chest *noun*
chests

chestnut *noun*
chestnuts

chest of drawers
*noun*
chests of drawers

chew *verb*
chews
chewing
chewed

chewy *adjective*
chewier
chewiest

chic☆

chick *noun*
chicks

chicken *noun*
chickens

chicken *verb*
chickens
chickening
chickened

chickenpox

chief *adjective*
chiefly

chief *noun*
chiefs

chieftain *noun*
chieftains

chilblain *noun*
chilblains

child *noun*
children

childhood *noun*
childhoods

childish

childminder *noun*
childminders

childproof

chill *noun*
chills

chill *verb*
chills
chilling
chilled

chilli☉ *noun*
chillies

chilly✦ *adjective*
chillier
chilliest

chime *noun*
chimes

chime *verb*
chimes
chiming
chimed

chimney *noun*
chimneys

chimpanzee *noun*
chimpanzees

chin *noun*
chins

china

...........................................................

★ Cheep is the noise a bird makes. **!cheap**.
☆ Chic is a French word and means 'smart or elegant'. There is no word *chicly*.
☉ A chilli is a type of hot pepper, added to meat or vegetable dishes. **!chilly**.
✦ You use chilly to describe cold, bleak weather or atmosphere. **!chilli**.

a b **c** d e f g h i j k l m n o p q r s t u v w x y z

38

**chink** noun
chinks

**chip** noun
chips

**chip** verb
chips
chipping
chipped

**chirp** verb
chirps
chirping
chirped

**chirpy** adjective
chirpier
chirpiest

**chisel** noun
chisels

**chisel** verb
chisels
chiselling
chiselled

**chivalrous** adjective
chivalrously

**chivalry**

**chlorine**

**chlorophyll**

**choc ice** noun
choc ices

**chock-a-block**

**chock-full**

**chocolate** noun
chocolates

**choice** noun
choices

**choir** noun
choirs

**choirboy** noun
choirboys

**choirgirl** noun
choirgirls

**choke** verb
chokes
choking
choked

**choke** noun
chokes

**cholera**

**cholesterol**

**choose** verb
chooses
choosing
chose
chosen

**choosy** adjective
choosier
choosiest

**chop** verb
chops
chopping
chopped

**chop** noun
chops

**chopper** noun
choppers

**choppy** adjective
choppier
choppiest

**chopsticks**

**choral**

**chord**★ noun
chords

**chore** noun
chores

**chorister** noun
choristers

**chorus** noun
choruses

**chose** see **choose**

**chosen** see **choose**

**christen** verb
christens
christening
christened

**christening**

**Christian** adjective
and noun
Christians

**Christianity**

**Christmas** noun
Christmases

**chrome**

**chromium**

**chromosome** noun
chromosomes

**chronic** adjective
chronically

**chronicle** noun
chronicles

**chronological**
adjective
chronologically

**chronology**

**chrysalis** noun
chrysalises

**chrysanthemum**
noun
chrysanthemums

**chubby** adjective
chubbier
chubbiest

**chuck** verb
chucks
chucking
chucked

**chuckle** verb
chuckles
chuckling
chuckled

**chuckle** noun
chuckles

**chug** verb
chugs
chugging
chugged

**chum** noun
chums

a
b
c
d
e
f
g
h
i
j
k
l
m
n
o
p
q
r
s
t
u
v
w
x
y
z

. . . . . . . . . . . . . . . . . . . . . . . . . . . . . . . . . . . . . . . . . . . . . . . . . . . . . . . . . . .
★ A **chord** is a number of musical notes played together. **!** **cord**.

a
b
**c**
d
e
f
g
h
i
j
k
l
m
n
o
p
q
r
s
t
u
v
w
x
y
z

**chummy** *adjective*
chummier
chummiest

**chunk** *noun*
chunks

**chunky** *adjective*
chunkier
chunkiest

**church** *noun*
churches

**churchyard** *noun*
churchyards

**churn** *noun*
churns

**churn** *verb*
churns
churning
churned

**chute★** *noun*
chutes

**chutney** *noun*
chutneys

**cider** *noun*
ciders

**cigar** *noun*
cigars

**cigarette** *noun*
cigarettes

**cinder** *noun*
cinders

**cine camera** *noun*
cine cameras

**cinema** *noun*
cinemas

**cinnamon**

**circle** *noun*
circles

**circle** *verb*
circles
circling
circled

**circuit** *noun*
circuits

**circular** *adjective* and
*noun*
circulars

**circulate** *verb*
circulates
circulating
circulated

**circulation** *noun*
circulations

**circumference** *noun*
circumferences

**circumstance** *noun*
circumstances

**circus** *noun*
circuses

**cistern** *noun*
cisterns

**citizen** *noun*
citizens

**citizenship**

**citric acid**

**citrus**

**city** *noun*
cities

**civic**

**civil**

**civilian** *noun*
civilians

**civilization** *noun*
civilizations

**civilize** *verb*
civilizes
civilizing
civilized

**clad**

**claim** *verb*
claims
claiming
claimed

**claim** *noun*
claims

**claimant** *noun*
claimants

**clam** *noun*
clams

**clamber** *verb*
clambers
clambering
clambered

**clammy** *adjective*
clammier
clammiest

**clamp** *noun*
clamps

**clamp** *verb*
clamps
clamping
clamped

**clan** *noun*
clans

**clang** *verb*
clangs
clanging
clanged

**clanger** *noun*
clangers

**clank** *verb*
clanks
clanking
clanked

**clap** *verb*
claps
clapping
clapped

**clap** *noun*
claps

**clapper** *noun*
clappers

**clarification**

**clarify** *verb*
clarifies
clarifying
clarified

★ A **chute** is a funnel for sending things down. **!shoot**.

40

**clarinet** *noun*
clarinets

**clarinettist**

**clarity**

**clash** *verb*
clashes
clashing
clashed

**clash** *noun*
clashes

**clasp** *verb*
clasps
clasping
clasped

**clasp** *noun*
clasps

**class** *noun*
classes

**class** *verb*
classes
classing
classed

**classic** *noun*
classics

**classic**

**classical** *adjective*
classically

**classification**

**classified**

**classify** *verb*
classifies
classifying
classified

**classmate** *noun*
classmates

**classroom** *noun*
classrooms

**clatter** *noun*

**clatter** *verb*
clatters
clattering
clattered

**clause**★ *noun*
clauses

**claw**☆ *noun*
claws

**claw**✪ *verb*
claws
clawing
clawed

**clay**

**clayey**

**clean** *adjective*
cleaner
cleanest
cleanly

**clean** *verb*
cleans
cleaning
cleaned

**cleaner** *noun*
cleaners

**cleanliness**

**cleanse** *verb*
cleanses
cleansing
cleansed

**cleanser**

**clear** *adjective*
clearer
clearest
clearly

**clear** *verb*
clears
clearing
cleared

**clearance** *noun*
clearances

**clearing** *noun*
clearings

**clef** *noun*
clefs

**clench** *verb*
clenches
clenching
clenched

**clergy**

**clergyman** *noun*
clergymen

**clergywoman** *noun*
clergywomen

**clerical**

**clerk** *noun*
clerks

**clever** *adjective*
cleverer
cleverest

**cliché** *noun*
clichés

**click** *noun*
clicks

**client** *noun*
clients

**cliff** *noun*
cliffs

**cliffhanger** *noun*
cliffhangers

**climate** *noun*
climates

**climatic**

**climax** *noun*
climaxes

**climb** *verb*
climbs
climbing
climbed

★ A **clause** is a part of a sentence or contract. ! **claws**.
☆ **Claws** are the hard sharp nails that some animals have on their feet. ! **clause**.
✪ To **claw** is to scratch, maul, or pull a person or thing.

a
b
**c**
d
e
f
g
h
i
j
k
l
m
n
o
p
q
r
s
t
u
v
w
x
y
z

41

**climb** noun
climbs

**climber** noun
climbers

**cling** verb
clings
clinging
clung

**clingfilm**

**clinic** noun
clinics

**clink** verb
clinks
clinking
clinked

**clip** verb
clips
clipping
clipped

**clip** noun
clips

**clipboard** noun
clipboards

**clipper** noun
clippers

**clippers** plural noun

**clipping** noun
clippings

**cloak** noun
cloaks

**cloakroom** noun
cloakrooms

**clobber** verb
clobbers
clobbering
clobbered

**clock** noun
clocks

**clockwise**

**clockwork**

**clog** verb
clogs
clogging
clogged

**clog** noun
clogs

**cloister** noun
cloisters

**clone** noun
clones

**clone** verb
clones
cloning
cloned

**close** verb
closes
closing
closed

**close** adjective and noun
closer
closest
closely

**close** noun
closes

**close-up** noun
close-ups

**closure** noun
closures

**clot** noun
clots

**clot** verb
clots
clotting
clotted

**cloth** noun
cloths

**clothe** verb
clothes
clothing
clothed

**clothes**

**clothing**

**cloud** noun
clouds

**cloud** verb
clouds
clouding
clouded

**cloudless**

**cloudy** adjective
cloudier
cloudiest

**clout** verb
clouts
clouting
clouted

**clove** noun
cloves

**clover**

**clown** noun
clowns

**clown** verb
clowns
clowning
clowned

**club** noun
clubs

**club** verb
clubs
clubbing
clubbed

**cluck** verb
clucks
clucking
clucked

**clue** noun
clues

**clueless**

**clump** noun
clumps

**clumsiness**

**clumsy** adjective
clumsier
clumsiest
clumsily

**clung** see **cling**

**cluster** noun
clusters

**clutch** verb
clutches
clutching
clutched

**clutch** *noun*
clutches

**clutter** *verb*
clutters
cluttering
cluttered

**clutter** *noun*

**co-**

*co-* makes words meaning 'together', e.g. a **co-pilot** is another pilot who sits together with the chief pilot. You often need a hyphen, e.g. **co-author**, **co-driver**, but some words are spelt joined up, e.g. **cooperate**, **coordinate**.

**coach** *verb*
coaches
coaching
coached

**coach** *noun*
coaches

**coal**

**coarse**★ *adjective*
coarser
coarsest
coarsely

**coast** *noun*
coasts

**coast** *verb*
coasts
coasting
coasted

**coastal**

**coastguard** *noun*
coastguards

**coastline**

**coat** *noun*
coats

**coat** *verb*
coats
coating
coated

**coating** *noun*
coatings

**coax** *verb*
coaxes
coaxing
coaxed

**cobalt**

**cobbled**

**cobbler** *noun*
cobblers

**cobbles** *plural noun*

**cobblestone** *noun*
cobblestones

**cobra** *noun*
cobras

**cobweb** *noun*
cobwebs

**cock** *noun*
cocks

**cock** *verb*
cocks
cocking
cocked

**cockerel** *noun*
cockerels

**cocker spaniel** *noun*
cocker spaniels

**cockle** *noun*
cockles

**cockney** *noun*
cockneys

**cockpit** *noun*
cockpits

**cockroach** *noun*
cockroaches

**cocky** *adjective*
cockier
cockiest

**cocoa** *noun*
cocoas

**coconut** *noun*
coconuts

**cocoon** *noun*
cocoons

**cod**☆ *noun*
cod

**code** *noun*
codes

**code** *verb*
codes
coding
coded

**coeducation**

**coeducational**

**coffee** *noun*
coffees

**coffin** *noun*
coffins

**cog** *noun*
cogs

**cohort** *noun*
cohorts

**coil** *verb*
coils
coiling
coiled

**coil** *noun*
coils

**coin** *noun*
coins

**coin** *verb*
coins
coining
coined

**coinage** *noun*
coinages

. . . . . . . . . . . . . . . . . . . . . . . . . . . . . . . . . . . . . . . . . . . . . . . . . .

★ **Coarse** means 'rough' or 'crude'. ! **course**.

☆ You use **cod** for the plural: *The sea is full of cod.*

a
b
**c**
d
e
f
g
h
i
j
k
l
m
n
o
p
q
r
s
t
u
v
w
x
y
z

43

**coincide** verb
coincides
coinciding
coincided

**coincidence** noun
coincidences

**coincidentally**

**coke**

**cola** noun
colas

**colander** noun
colanders

**cold** adjective
colder
coldest
coldly

**cold** noun
colds

**cold-blooded**

**coldness**

**coleslaw**

**collaborate** verb
collaborates
collaborating
collaborated

**collaboration**

**collaborator**

**collage** noun
collages

**collapse** verb
collapses
collapsing
collapsed

**collapse** noun
collapses

**collapsible**

**collar** noun
collars

**collate** verb
collates
collating
collated

**colleague** noun
colleagues

**collect** verb
collects
collecting
collected

**collection** noun
collections

**collective**

**collector**

**college** noun
colleges

**collide** verb
collides
colliding
collided

**collie** noun
collies

**collision** noun
collisions

**colloquial** adjective
colloquially

**colon** noun
colons

**colonel**★ noun
colonels

**colonial**

**colonist** noun
colonists

**colony** noun
colonies

**colossal** adjective
colossally

**colour** noun
colours

**colour** verb
colours
colouring
coloured

**colour-blind**

**coloured**

**colourful** adjective
colourfully

**colouring**

**colourless**

**colt** noun
colts

**column** noun
columns

**coma** noun
comas

**comb** noun
combs

**comb** verb
combs
combing
combed

**combat** noun
combats

**combat** verb
combats
combating
combated

**combatant** noun
combatants

**combination** noun
combinations

**combine** verb
combines
combining
combined

**combine** noun
combines

**combustion**

**come** verb
comes
coming
came

**comeback** noun
comebacks

**comedian** noun
comedians

**comedy** noun
comedies

. . . . . . . . . . . . . . . . . . . . . . . . . . . . . . . . . . . . . . . . . . . . . . . . . . . . . . . . .

★ A **colonel** is an army officer. **!** **kernel**.

**comet** noun
comets
**comfort** verb
comforts
comforting
comforted
**comfort** noun
comforts
**comfortable** adjective
comfortably
**comic** adjective and noun
comics
**comical** adjective
comically
**comma** noun
commas
**command** verb
commands
commanding
commanded
**command** noun
commands
**commander** noun
commanders
**commandment** noun
commandments
**commando** noun
commandos
**commemorate** verb
commemorates
commemorating
commemorated
**commemoration**
**commence** verb
commences
commencing
commenced
**commencement**
**commend** verb
commends
commending
commended
**commendable**
**commendation**

**comment** verb
comments
commenting
commented
**comment** noun
comments
**commentary** noun
commentaries
**commentate**
**commentator** noun
commentators
**commerce**
**commercial** adjective
commercially
**commercial** noun
commercials
**commercialized**
**commit** verb
commits
committing
committed
**commitment** noun
commitments
**committee** noun
committees
**commodity** noun
commodities
**common** adjective
commoner
commonest
**common** noun
commons
**commonplace**
**commonwealth** noun
commonwealths
**commotion** noun
commotions
**communal** adjective
communally
**commune** noun
communes
**communicate** verb
communicates
communicating
communicated

**communication** noun
communications
**communicative**
**communion** noun
communions
**communism**
**communist** noun
communists
**community** noun
communities
**commute**
**commuter** noun
commuters
**compact** adjective
compactly
**compact** noun
compacts
**compact disc** noun
compact discs
**companion** noun
companions
**companionship**
**company** noun
companies
**comparable** adjective
comparably
**comparative** adjective
comparatively
**comparative** noun
comparatives
**compare** verb
compares
comparing
compared
**comparison** noun
comparisons
**compartment** noun
compartments
**compass** noun
compasses
**compassion**

a
b
**c**
d
e
f
g
h
i
j
k
l
m
n
o
p
q
r
s
t
u
v
w
x
y
z

45

**compassionate** *adjective*
compassionately

**compatible** *adjective*
compatibly

**compel** *verb*
compels
compelling
compelled

**compensate** *verb*
compensates
compensating
compensated

**compensation** *noun*
compensations

**compère** *noun*
compères

**compete** *verb*
competes
competing
competed

**competence**

**competent** *adjective*
competently

**competition** *noun*
competitions

**competitive** *adjective*
competitively

**competitor** *noun*
competitors

**compilation** *noun*
compilations

**compile** *verb*
compiles
compiling
compiled

**compiler** *noun*
compilers

**complacent** *adjective*
complacently

**complain** *verb*
complains
complaining
complained

**complaint** *noun*
complaints

**complement**★ *noun*
complements

**complementary**☆

**complete** *adjective*
completely

**complete** *verb*
completes
completing
completed

**completion**

**complex** *adjective* and *noun*
complexes

**complexion** *noun*
complexions

**complexity** *noun*
complexities

**complicated**

**complication** *noun*
complications

**compliment**○ *noun*
compliments

**complimentary**✧

**component** *noun*
components

**compose** *verb*
composes
composing
composed

**composer** *noun*
composers

**composition** *noun*
compositions

**compost**

**compound** *noun*
compounds

**comprehend** *verb*
comprehends
comprehending
comprehended

**comprehension** *noun*
comprehensions

**comprehensive** *adjective*
comprehensively

**comprehensive** *noun*
comprehensives

**compress** *verb*
compresses
compressing
compressed

**compression**

**comprise** *verb*
comprises
comprising
comprised

**compromise** *noun*
compromises

. . . . . . . . . . . . . . . . . . . . . . . . . . . . . . . . . . . . . . . . . . . . . . . . . . .

★ A **complement** is a thing that completes something. **!** **compliment**.

☆ Something **complementary** completes something.
**!** **complimentary**.

○ A **compliment** is something good you say about someone.
**!** **complement**.

✧ Something **complimentary** praises someone. **!** **complementary**.

**compromise** *verb*
compromises
compromising
compromised

**compulsory**

**computation**

**compute** *verb*
computes
computing
computed

**computer** *noun*
computers

**comrade** *noun*
comrades

**comradeship**

**con** *verb*
cons
conning
conned

**concave**

**conceal** *verb*
conceals
concealing
concealed

**concealment**

**conceit**

**conceited**

**conceive** *verb*
conceives
conceiving
conceived

**concentrate** *verb*
concentrates
concentrating
concentrated

**concentrated**

**concentration** *noun*
concentrations

**concentric**

**concept** *noun*
concepts

**conception** *noun*
conceptions

**concern** *verb*
concerns
concerning
concerned

**concern** *noun*
concerns

**concerning**

**concert** *noun*
concerts

**concertina** *noun*
concertinas

**concerto** *noun*
concertos

**concession** *noun*
concessions

**concise** *adjective*
concisely

**conclude** *verb*
concludes
concluding
concluded

**conclusion** *noun*
conclusions

**concrete** *adjective* and *noun*

**concussion**

**condemn** *verb*
condemns
condemning
condemned

**condemnation**

**condensation**

**condense** *verb*
condenses
condensing
condensed

**condition** *noun*
conditions

**condom** *noun*
condoms

**conduct** *verb*
conducts
conducting
conducted

**conduct** *noun*

**conduction**

**conductor** *noun*
conductors

**cone** *noun*
cones

**confectioner** *noun*
confectioners

**confectionery**

**confer** *verb*
confers
conferring
conferred

**conference** *noun*
conferences

**confess** *verb*
confesses
confessing
confessed

**confession** *noun*
confessions

**confetti**

**confide** *verb*
confides
confiding
confided

**confidence** *noun*
confidences

**confident** *adjective*
confidently

**confidential** *adjective*
confidentially

**confine** *verb*
confines
confining
confined

**confinement**

**confirm** *verb*
confirms
confirming
confirmed

**confirmation**

**confiscate** *verb*
confiscates
confiscating
confiscated

a
b
**c**
d
e
f
g
h
i
j
k
l
m
n
o
p
q
r
s
t
u
v
w
x
y
z

47

For words beginning with a k- sound, try also **ch-**

**confiscation** *noun*
confiscations

**conflict** *verb*
conflicts
conflicting
conflicted

**conflict** *noun*
conflicts

**conform** *verb*
conforms
conforming
conformed

**conformity**

**confront** *verb*
confronts
confronting
confronted

**confrontation** *noun*
confrontations

**confuse** *verb*
confuses
confusing
confused

**confusion** *noun*
confusions

**congested**

**congestion**

**congratulate** *verb*
congratulates
congratulating
congratulated

**congratulations**
*plural noun*

**congregation** *noun*
congregations

**congress** *noun*
congresses

**congruence**

**congruent**

**conical**

**conifer** *noun*
conifers

**coniferous**

**conjunction** *noun*
conjunctions

**conjure** *verb*
conjures
conjuring
conjured

**conjuror** *noun*
conjurors

**conker**★ *noun*
conkers

**connect** *verb*
connects
connecting
connected

**connection** *noun*
connections

**conning tower** *noun*
conning towers

**conquer**☆ *verb*
conquers
conquering
conquered

**conqueror** *noun*
conquerors

**conquest** *noun*
conquests

**conscience**

**conscientious**
*adjective*
conscientiously

**conscious** *adjective*
consciously

**consciousness**

**conscription**

**consecutive** *adjective*
consecutively

**consensus**

**consent** *verb*
consents
consenting
consented

**consent** *noun*

**consequence** *noun*
consequences

**consequently**

**conservation**

**conservationist**

**conservative**

**Conservative**♥ *noun*
Conservatives

**conservatory** *noun*
conservatories

**conserve** *verb*
conserves
conserving
conserved

**consider** *verb*
considers
considering
considered

**considerable**
*adjective*
considerably

**considerate** *adjective*
considerately

**consideration** *noun*
considerations

**consist** *verb*
consists
consisting
consisted

**consistency** *noun*
consistencies

**consistent** *adjective*
consistently

**consolation** *noun*
consolations

. . . . . . . . . . . . . . . . . . . . . . . . . . . . . . . . . . . . . . . . . . . . . . . . . . . . . .

★ A **conker** is the fruit of a horse chestnut tree. **!** conquer.
☆ To **conquer** means 'to invade or take over'. **!** conker.
♥ Use a capital C when you mean a member of the political party.

**console** *verb*
consoles
consoling
consoled

**consonant** *noun*
consonants

**conspicuous**
*adjective*
conspicuously

**conspiracy** *noun*
conspiracies

**conspirator**

**conspire** *verb*
conspires
conspiring
conspired

**constable** *noun*
constables

**constancy**

**constant** *adjective*
constantly

**constant** *noun*
constants

**constellation** *noun*
constellations

**constipated**

**constipation**

**constituency** *noun*
constituencies

**constituent** *noun*
constituents

**constitute** *verb*
constitutes
constituting
constituted

**constitution** *noun*
constitutions

**constitutional**

**construct** *verb*
constructs
constructing
constructed

**construction** *noun*
constructions

**constructive**

**consul** *noun*
consuls

**consult** *verb*
consults
consulting
consulted

**consultant** *noun*
consultants

**consultation** *noun*
consultations

**consume** *verb*
consumes
consuming
consumed

**consumer** *noun*
consumers

**consumption**

**contact** *noun*
contacts

**contact** *verb*
contacts
contacting
contacted

**contagious**

**contain** *verb*
contains
containing
contained

**container** *noun*
containers

**contaminate** *verb*
contaminates
contaminating
contaminated

**contamination**

**contemplate** *verb*
contemplates
contemplating
contemplated

**contemplation**

**contemporary**
*adjective* and *noun*
contemporaries

**contempt**

**contemptible**
*adjective*
contemptibly

**contemptuous**
*adjective*
contemptuously

**contend** *verb*
contends
contending
contended

**contender** *noun*
contenders

**content** *adjective* and
*noun*

**contented** *adjective*
contentedly

**contentment**

**contents** *plural noun*

**contest** *verb*
contests
contesting
contested

**contest** *noun*
contests

**contestant** *noun*
contestants

**context** *noun*
contexts

**continent** *noun*
continents

**continental**

**continual** *adjective*
continually

**continuation**

**continue** *verb*
continues
continuing
continued

**continuous** *adjective*
continuously

**continuity**

**contour** *noun*
contours

**contraception**

a
b
**c**
d
e
f
g
h
i
j
k
l
m
n
o
p
q
r
s
t
u
v
w
x
y
z

a

b

**c**

d

e

f

g

h

i

j

k

l

m

n

o

p

q

r

s

t

u

v

w

x

y

z

**contraceptive** *noun*
contraceptives

**contract** *verb*
contracts
contracting
contracted

**contract** *noun*
contracts

**contraction** *noun*
contractions

**contractor** *noun*
contractors

**contradict** *verb*
contradicts
contradicting
contradicted

**contradiction** *noun*
contradictions

**contradictory**

**contraflow** *noun*
contraflows

**contraption** *noun*
contraptions

**contrary** *adjective* and
*noun*

**contrast** *verb*
contrasts
contrasting
contrasted

**contrast** *noun*
contrasts

**contribute** *verb*
contributes
contributing
contributed

**contribution** *noun*
contributions

**contributor** *noun*
contributors

**contrivance** *noun*
contrivances

**contrive** *verb*
contrives
contriving
contrived

**control** *verb*
controls
controlling
controlled

**control** *noun*
controls

**controller** *noun*
controllers

**controversial**
*adjective*
controversially

**controversy** *noun*
controversies

**conundrum** *noun*
conundrums

**convalescence**

**convalescent**

**convection**

**convector** *noun*
convectors

**convenience** *noun*
conveniences

**convenient** *adjective*
conveniently

**convent** *noun*
convents

**convention** *noun*
conventions

**conventional**
*adjective*
conventionally

**converge** *verb*
converges
converging
converged

**conversation** *noun*
conversations

**conversational**
*adjective*
conversationally

**converse** *verb*
converses
conversing
conversed

**converse** *noun*

**conversion** *noun*
conversions

**convert** *verb*
converts
converting
converted

**convert** *noun*
converts

**convertible**

**convex**

**convey** *verb*
conveys
conveying
conveyed

**conveyor belt** *noun*
conveyor belts

**convict** *verb*
convicts
convicting
convicted

**convict** *noun*
convicts

**conviction** *noun*
convictions

**convince** *verb*
convinces
convincing
convinced

**convoy** *noun*
convoys

**cook** *verb*
cooks
cooking
cooked

**cook** *noun*
cooks

**cooker** *noun*
cookers

**cookery**

**cool** *adjective*
cooler
coolest
coolly

**cool** *verb*
cools
cooling
cooled

**cooler**

**coolness**

**coop** *noun*
coops

**cooperate** *verb*
cooperates
cooperating
cooperated

**cooperation**

**cooperative**

**coordinate** *verb*
coordinates
coordinating
coordinated

**coordinate** *noun*
coordinates

**coordination**

**coordinator** *noun*
coordinators

**coot** *noun*
coots

**cop** *verb*
cops
copping
copped

**cop** *noun*
cops

**cope** *verb*
copes
coping
coped

**copier** *noun*
copiers

**copper** *noun*
coppers

**copper sulphate**

**copy** *verb*
copies
copying
copied

**copy** *noun*
copies

**coral**

**cord★** *noun*
cords

**cordial** *adjective*
cordially

**cordial** *noun*
cordials

**cordiality**

**corduroy**

**core** *noun*
cores

**corgi** *noun*
corgis

**cork** *noun*
corks

**corkscrew** *noun*
corkscrews

**cormorant** *noun*
cormorants

**corn** *noun*
corns

**corned beef**

**corner** *noun*
corners

**corner** *verb*
corners
cornering
cornered

**cornet** *noun*
cornets

**cornfield** *noun*
cornfields

**cornflakes**

**cornflour**

**cornflower** *noun*
cornflowers

**Cornish**

**Cornish pasty** *noun*
Cornish pasties

**corny** *adjective*
cornier
corniest

**coronation** *noun*
coronations

**coroner** *noun*
coroners

**corporal** *noun*
corporals

**corporal** *adjective*

**corporation** *noun*
corporations

**corps☆** *noun*
corps

**corpse♦** *noun*
corpses

**corpuscle** *noun*
corpuscles

**corral** *noun*
corrals

**correct** *adjective*
correctly

**correct** *verb*
corrects
correcting
corrected

**correction** *noun*
corrections

**correctness**

**correspond** *verb*
corresponds
corresponding
corresponded

**correspondence**

. . . . . . . . . . . . . . . . . . . . . . . . . . . . . . . . . . . . . . . . . . . .

★ A **cord** is a piece of thin rope. **!** **chord**.
☆ A **corps** is a unit of soldiers. **!** **corpse**.
♦ A **corpse** is a dead body. **!** **corps**.

a
b
**c**
d
e
f
g
h
i
j
k
l
m
n
o
p
q
r
s
t
u
v
w
x
y
z

51

**correspondent** noun
correspondents

**corridor** noun
corridors

**corrode** verb
corrodes
corroding
corroded

**corrosion**

**corrosive**

**corrugated**

**corrupt**

**corruption**

**corset** noun
corsets

**cosmetics** plural noun

**cosmic**

**cosmonaut** noun
cosmonauts

**cost** verb
costs
costing
cost

**cost** noun
costs

**costly** adjective
costlier
costliest

**costume** noun
costumes

**cosy** adjective
cosier
cosiest

**cosy** noun
cosies

**cot** noun
cots

**cottage** noun
cottages

**cotton**

**couch** noun
couches

**cough** verb
coughs
coughing
coughed

**cough** noun
coughs

**could** see **can**

**couldn't**

**council**★ noun
councils

**councillor**☆ noun
councillors

**counsel**♦ noun
counsels

**counsel** verb
counsels
counselling
counselled

**counsellor**✦ noun
counsellors

**count** verb
counts
counting
counted

**count** noun
counts

**countdown** noun
countdowns

**countenance** noun
countenances

**counter-**
*counter-* makes words
meaning 'opposite',
e.g. a **counter-claim**
is a claim someone
makes in response to
a claim from someone
else. You often need a
hyphen, but some
words are spelt joined
up, e.g. **counteract**,
**counterbalance**.

**counter** noun
counters

**counterfeit**

**countess** noun
countesses

**countless**

**country** noun
countries

**countryman** noun
countrymen

**countryside**

**countrywoman** noun
countrywomen

**county** noun
counties

**couple** noun
couples

**couple** verb
couples
coupling
coupled

**coupling** noun
couplings

**coupon** noun
coupons

. . . . . . . . . . . . . . . . . . . . . . . . . . . . . . . . . . . . . . . . . . . . . . . . . .

★ A **council** is a group of people who run the affairs of a town.
! **counsel**.
☆ A **councillor** is a member of a council. ! **counsellor**.
♦ **Counsel** means 'advice'. ! **council**.
✦ A **counsellor** is someone who gives advice. ! **councillor**.

**courage**

**courageous** *adjective*
courageously

**courgette** *noun*
courgettes

**courier** *noun*
couriers

**course★** *noun*
courses

**court** *noun*
courts

**court** *verb*
courts
courting
courted

**courteous** *adjective*
courteously

**courtesy** *noun*
courtesies

**court martial** *noun*
courts martial

**courtship**

**courtyard** *noun*
courtyards

**cousin** *noun*
cousins

**cove** *noun*
coves

**cover** *verb*
covers
covering
covered

**cover** *noun*
covers

**coverage**

**cover-up** *noun*
cover-ups

**cow** *noun*
cows

**coward** *noun*
cowards

**cowardice**

**cowardly**

**cowboy** *noun*
cowboys

**cowslip** *noun*
cowslips

**cox** *noun*
coxes

**coxswain** *noun*
coxswains

**coy** *adjective*
coyly

**coyness**

**crab** *noun*
crabs

**crack** *verb*
cracks
cracking
cracked

**crack** *noun*
cracks

**cracker** *noun*
crackers

**crackle** *verb*
crackles
crackling
crackled

**crackling**

**cradle** *noun*
cradles

**craft** *noun*
crafts

**craftsman** *noun*
craftsmen

**craftsmanship**

**crafty** *adjective*
craftier
craftiest
craftily

**craftiness**

**crag** *noun*
crags

**craggy** *adjective*
craggier
craggiest

**cram** *verb*
crams
cramming
crammed

**cramp** *verb*
cramps
cramping
cramped

**cramp** *noun*
cramps

**crane** *noun*
cranes

**crane** *verb*
cranes
craning
craned

**crane fly** *noun*
crane flies

**crank** *verb*
cranks
cranking
cranked

**crank** *noun*
cranks

**cranky** *adjective*
crankier
crankiest

**cranny** *noun*
crannies

**crash** *verb*
crashes
crashing
crashed

**crash** *noun*
crashes

**crate** *noun*
crates

**crater** *noun*
craters

a
b
c
d
e
f
g
h
i
j
k
l
m
n
o
p
q
r
s
t
u
v
w
x
y
z

★ You use **course** in e.g. *a French course.* ! **coarse.**

53

a b **c** d e f g h i j k l m n o p q r s t u v w x y z

**crave** verb
craves
craving
craved

**crawl** verb
crawls
crawling
crawled

**crawl** noun
crawls

**crayon** noun
crayons

**craze** noun
crazes

**craziness**

**crazy** adjective
crazier
craziest
crazily

**creak** verb
creaks
creaking
creaked

**creak** noun
creaks

**creaky** adjective
creakier
creakiest

**cream** noun
creams

**creamy** adjective
creamier
creamiest

**crease** verb
creases
creasing
creased

**crease** noun
creases

**create** verb
creates
creating
created

**creation** noun
creations

**creative** adjective
creatively

**creativity**

**creator** noun
creators

**creature** noun
creatures

**crèche** noun
crèches

**credibility**

**credible** adjective
credibly

**credit** verb
credits
crediting
credited

**credit** noun

**creditable** adjective
creditably

**creditor** noun
creditors

**creed** noun
creeds

**creek** noun
creeks

**creep** verb
creeps
creeping
crept

**creep** noun
creeps

**creeper** noun
creepers

**creepy** adjective
creepier
creepiest

**cremate** verb
cremates
cremating
cremated

**cremation** noun
cremations

**crematorium** noun
crematoria

**creosote**

**crêpe** noun
crêpes

**crept** see **creep**

**crescendo** noun
crescendos

**crescent** noun
crescents

**cress**

**crest** noun
crests

**crevice** noun
crevices

**crew** noun
crews

**crib** verb
cribs
cribbing
cribbed

**crib** noun
cribs

**cricket★** noun
crickets

**cricketer** noun
cricketers

**cried** see **cry**

**crime** noun
crimes

**criminal** adjective and noun
criminals

**crimson**

**crinkle** verb
crinkles
crinkling
crinkled

★ **Cricket** means 'a game' and 'an insect like a grasshopper'.

**crinkly** *adjective*
crinklier
crinkliest

**cripple** *verb*
cripples
crippling
crippled

**cripple** *noun*
cripples

**crisis** *noun*
crises

**crisp** *adjective*
crisper
crispest

**crisp** *noun*
crisps

**criss-cross** *adjective*

**critic** *noun*
critics

**critical** *adjective*
critically

**criticism** *noun*
criticisms

**criticize** *verb*
criticizes
criticizing
criticized

**croak** *verb*
croaks
croaking
croaked

**croak** *noun*
croaks

**crochet**★ *noun*

**crock** *noun*
crocks

**crockery**

**crocodile** *noun*
crocodiles

**crocus** *noun*
crocuses

**croft** *noun*
crofts

**crofter**

**croissant** *noun*
croissants

**crook** *noun*
crooks

**crook** *verb*
crooks
crooking
crooked

**crooked**

**croon** *verb*
croons
crooning
crooned

**crop** *noun*
crops

**crop** *verb*
crops
cropping
cropped

**cross-**
*cross-* makes words
meaning 'across', e.g.
a *cross-channel ferry*
is one that goes
across the English
Channel. You usually
need a hyphen, but
some words are spelt
joined up, e.g.
**crossroads** and
**crosswind**.

**cross** *adjective*
crossly

**cross** *verb*
crosses
crossing
crossed

**cross** *noun*
crosses

**crossbar** *noun*
crossbars

**crossbow** *noun*
crossbows

**cross-country**

**cross-examine** *verb*
cross-examines
cross-examining
cross-examined

**cross-examination**
*noun*
cross-examinations

**cross-eyed**

**crossing** *noun*
crossings

**cross-legged**

**crossness**

**crossroads** *noun*
crossroads

**cross-section** *noun*
cross-sections

**crosswise**

**crossword** *noun*
crosswords

**crotchet**☆ *noun*
crotchets

**crouch** *verb*
crouches
crouching
crouched

**crow** *noun*
crows

**crow** *verb*
crows
crowing
crowed

**crowbar** *noun*
crowbars

**crowd** *noun*
crowds

. . . . . . . . . . . . . . . . . . . . . . . . . . . . . . . . . . . . . . . . . . . . .

★ **Crochet** is a kind of needlework. **!** **crotchet**.
☆ A **crotchet** is a note in music. **!** **crochet**.

a

b

**c**

d

e

f

g

h

i

j

k

l

m

n

o

p

q

r

s

t

u

v

w

x

y

z

**crowd** *verb*
crowds
crowding
crowded

**crown** *noun*
crowns

**crown** *verb*
crowns
crowning
crowned

**crow's-nest** *noun*
crow's-nests

**crucial** *adjective*
crucially

**crucifix** *noun*
crucifixes

**crucifixion★** *noun*
crucifixions

**crucify** *verb*
crucifies
crucifying
crucified

**crude** *adjective*
cruder
crudest

**cruel** *adjective*
crueller
cruellest
cruelly

**cruelty** *noun*
cruelties

**cruise** *verb*
cruises
cruising
cruised

**cruise** *noun*
cruises

**cruiser** *noun*
cruisers

**crumb** *noun*
crumbs

**crumble** *verb*
crumbles
crumbling
crumbled

**crumbly** *adjective*
crumblier
crumbliest

**crumpet** *noun*
crumpets

**crumple** *verb*
crumples
crumpling
crumpled

**crunch** *noun*
crunches

**crunch** *verb*
crunches
crunching
crunched

**crunchy** *adjective*
crunchier
crunchiest

**crusade** *noun*
crusades

**crusader** *noun*
crusaders

**crush** *verb*
crushes
crushing
crushed

**crush** *noun*
crushes

**crust** *noun*
crusts

**crustacean** *noun*
crustaceans

**crutch** *noun*
crutches

**cry** *verb*
cries
crying
cried

**cry** *noun*
cries

**crypt** *noun*
crypts

**crystal** *noun*
crystals

**crystalline**

**crystallize** *verb*
crystallizes
crystallizing
crystallized

**cub** *noun*
cubs

**cubbyhole** *noun*
cubbyholes

**cube** *noun*
cubes

**cube** *verb*
cubes
cubing
cubed

**cubic**

**cubicle** *noun*
cubicles

**cuboid** *noun*
cuboids

**cuckoo** *noun*
cuckoos

**cucumber** *noun*
cucumbers

**cud**

**cuddle** *verb*
cuddles
cuddling
cuddled

**cuddly**

**cue**☆ *noun*
cues

**cuff** *verb*
cuffs
cuffing
cuffed

. . . . . . . . . . . . . . . . . . . . . . . . . . . . . . . . . . . . . . . . . . . . . . . . . . . . . . . . . . . . . . . .

★ Use a capital C when you are talking about Christ.
☆ A **cue** is a signal for action or a stick used in snooker. **!queue**.

**cuff** *noun*
cuffs
**cul-de-sac** *noun*
cul-de-sacs *or*
culs-de-sac
**culminate** *verb*
culminates
culminating
culminated
**culmination**
**culprit** *noun*
culprits
**cult** *noun*
cults
**cultivate** *verb*
cultivates
cultivating
cultivated
**cultivation**
**cultivated**
**culture** *noun*
cultures
**cultural** *adjective*
culturally
**cultured**
**cunning**
**cup** *noun*
cups
**cup** *verb*
cups
cupping
cupped
**cupboard** *noun*
cupboards
**cupful** *noun*
cupfuls
**curate** *noun*
curates
**curator** *noun*
curators

**curb**★ *verb*
curbs
curbing
curbed
**curd** *noun*
curds
**curdle** *verb*
curdles
curdling
curdled
**cure** *verb*
cures
curing
cured
**cure** *noun*
cures
**curfew** *noun*
curfews
**curiosity** *noun*
curiosities
**curious** *adjective*
curiously
**curl** *verb*
curls
curling
curled
**curl** *noun*
curls
**curly** *adjective*
curlier
curliest
**currant**☆ *noun*
currants
**currency** *noun*
currencies
**current**○ *noun*
currents
**current** *adjective*
currently

**curriculum** *noun*
curriculums *or*
curricula
**curry** *verb*
curries
currying
curried
**curry** *noun*
curries
**curse** *verb*
curses
cursing
cursed
**curse** *noun*
curses
**cursor** *noun*
cursors
**curtain** *noun*
curtains
**curtsy** *verb*
curtsies
curtsying
curtsied
**curtsy** *noun*
curtsies
**curvature** *noun*
curvatures
**curve** *verb*
curves
curving
curved
**curve** *noun*
curves
**cushion** *noun*
cushions
**cushion** *verb*
cushions
cushioning
cushioned
**custard**

. . . . . . . . . . . . . . . . . . . . . . . . . . . . . . . . . . . . . . . . . . . . . . . .

★ To **curb** a feeling is to restrain it. **!kerb**.
☆ A **currant** is a small dried grape. **!current**.
○ A **current** is a flow of water, air, or electricity. **!currant**.

a

b

**c**

**d**

e

f

g

h

i

j

k

l

m

n

o

p

q

r

s

t

u

v

w

x

y

z

**custom** *noun*
customs

**customary** *adjective*
customarily

**customer** *noun*
customers

**customize** *noun*
customizes
customizing
customized

**cut** *verb*
cuts
cutting
cut

**cut** *noun*
cuts

**cute** *adjective*
cuter
cutest

**cutlass** *noun*
cutlasses

**cutlery**

**cutlet** *noun*
cutlets

**cut-out** *noun*
cut-outs

**cut-price**

**cutter** *noun*
cutters

**cutting** *noun*
cuttings

**cycle** *noun*
cycles

**cycle** *verb*
cycles
cycling
cycled

**cyclist** *noun*
cyclists

**cyclone** *noun*
cyclones

**cyclonic**

**cygnet★** *noun*
cygnets

**cylinder** *noun*
cylinders

**cylindrical**

**cymbal** *noun*
cymbals

**cynic** *noun*
cynics

**cynical** *adjective*
cynically

**cynicism**

**cypress** *noun*
cypresses

# Dd

**dab** *verb*
dabs
dabbing
dabbed

**dab** *noun*
dabs

**dabble** *verb*
dabbles
dabbling
dabbled

**dachshund** *noun*
dachshunds

**dad** *noun*
dads

**daddy** *noun*
daddies

**daddy-long-legs**
*noun*
daddy-long-legs

**daffodil** *noun*
daffodils

**daft** *adjective*
dafter
daftest

**dagger** *noun*
daggers

**dahlia** *noun*
dahlias

**daily** *adjective* and
*adverb*

**daintiness**

**dainty** *adjective*
daintier
daintiest
daintily

**dairy** *noun*
dairies

**daisy** *noun*
daisies

**dale** *noun*
dales

**Dalmatian** *noun*
Dalmatians

**dam** *noun*
dams

**dam**☆ *verb*
dams
damming
dammed

**damage** *verb*
damages
damaging
damaged

**damage** *noun*

**damages** *plural noun*

**Dame**✪ *noun*
Dames

★ A **cygnet** is a young swan. **!** signet.
☆ **Dam** means 'to build a dam across water'. **!** damn.
✪ Use a capital D when it is a title, e.g. *Dame Jane Smith*.

**dame**★ *noun*
dames

**damn**☆ *verb*
damns
damning
damned

**damned**

**damp** *adjective* and *noun*
damper
dampest

**dampen** *verb*
dampens
dampening
dampened

**damson** *noun*
damsons

**dance** *verb*
dances
dancing
danced

**dance** *noun*
dances

**dancer** *noun*
dancers

**dandelion** *noun*
dandelions

**dandruff**

**danger** *noun*
dangers

**dangerous** *adjective*
dangerously

**dangle** *verb*
dangles
dangling
dangled

**dappled**

**dare** *verb*
dares
daring
dared

**dare** *noun*
dares

**daredevil** *noun*
daredevils

**daring**

**dark** *adjective* and *noun*
darker
darkest

**darken** *verb*
darkens
darkening
darkened

**darkness**

**darkroom** *noun*
darkrooms

**darling** *noun*
darlings

**darn** *verb*
darns
darning
darned

**dart** *noun*
darts

**dartboard** *noun*
dartboards

**dash** *verb*
dashes
dashing
dashed

**dash** *noun*
dashes

**dashboard** *noun*
dashboards

**data**○ *plural noun*

**database** *noun*
databases

**date** *noun*
dates

**date** *verb*
dates
dating
dated

**daughter** *noun*
daughters

**dawdle** *verb*
dawdles
dawdling
dawdled

**dawn** *noun*
dawns

**dawn** *verb*
dawns
dawning
dawned

**day** *noun*
days

**daybreak**

**daydream** *verb*
daydreams
daydreaming
daydreamed

**daylight**

**day-to-day**

**daze** *verb*
dazes
dazing
dazed

**daze** *noun*

**dazzle** *verb*
dazzles
dazzling
dazzled

- - - - - - - - - - - - - - - - - - - - - - - - - - - - - - - - - - - - -

★ Use a small d when you mean a pantomime woman played by a man.

☆ **Damn** means 'to say that something is very bad'. **!** dam.

○ **Data** is strictly a plural noun, but is often used as a singular noun: *Here is the data.*

# de

**de-** *de-* makes verbs with an opposite meaning, e.g. **deactivate** means 'to stop something working'. You need a hyphen when the word begins with an *e* or *i*, e.g. **de-escalate, de-ice.**

**dead**

**deaden** *verb*
 deadens
 deadening
 deadened

**dead end** *noun*
 dead ends

**deadline** *noun*
 deadlines

**deadlock**

**deadly** *adjective*
 deadlier
 deadliest

**deaf** *adjective*
 deafer
 deafest

**deafness**

**deafen** *verb*
 deafens
 deafening
 deafened

**deal** *verb*
 deals
 dealing
 dealt

**deal** *noun*
 deals

**dealer** *noun*
 dealers

**dean** *noun*
 deans

**dear★** *adjective*
 dearer
 dearest

**death** *noun*
 deaths

**deathly**

**debatable**

**debate** *noun*
 debates

**debate** *verb*
 debates
 debating
 debated

**debris**

**debt** *noun*
 debts

**debtor** *noun*
 debtors

**debug** *verb*
 debugs
 debugging
 debugged

**début** *noun*
 débuts

**decade** *noun*
 decades

**decay** *verb*
 decays
 decaying
 decayed

**decay** *noun*

**deceased**

**deceit**

**deceitful** *adjective*
 deceitfully

**deceive** *verb*
 deceives
 deceiving
 deceived

**December**

**decency**

**decent** *adjective*
 decently

**deception** *noun*
 deceptions

**deceptive**

**decibel** *noun*
 decibels

**decide** *verb*
 decides
 deciding
 decided

**deciduous**

**decimal** *noun*
 decimals

**decimalization**

**decimalize** *verb*
 decimalizes
 decimalizing
 decimalized

**decipher** *verb*
 deciphers
 deciphering
 deciphered

**decision** *noun*
 decisions

**decisive** *adjective*
 decisively

**deck** *noun*
 decks

**deckchair** *noun*
 deckchairs

**declaration** *noun*
 declarations

**declare** *verb*
 declares
 declaring
 declared

**decline** *verb*
 declines
 declining
 declined

. . . . . . . . . . . . . . . . . . . . . . . . . . . . . . . . . . . . . . . . . . . . . . . .

★ **Dear** means 'loved' or 'expensive'. **!** deer.

**decode** *verb*
decodes
decoding
decoded

**decompose** *verb*
decomposes
decomposing
decomposed

**decorate** *verb*
decorates
decorating
decorated

**decoration** *noun*
decorations

**decorative**

**decorator** *noun*
decorators

**decoy** *noun*
decoys

**decrease** *verb*
decreases
decreasing
decreased

**decrease** *noun*
decreases

**decree** *noun*
decrees

**decree** *verb*
decrees
decreeing
decreed

**decrepit**

**dedicate** *verb*
dedicates
dedicating
dedicated

**dedication**

**deduce** *verb*
deduces
deducing
deduced

**deduct** *verb*
deducts
deducting
deducted

**deductible**

**deduction** *noun*
deductions

**deed** *noun*
deeds

**deep** *adjective*
deeper
deepest
deeply

**deepen** *verb*
deepens
deepening
deepened

**deep-freeze** *noun*
deep-freezes

**deer★** *noun*
deer

**deface** *verb*
defaces
defacing
defaced

**default** *noun*
defaults

**defeat** *verb*
defeats
defeating
defeated

**defeat** *noun*
defeats

**defect** *noun*
defects

**defect** *verb*
defects
defecting
defected

**defective** *adjective*
defectively

**defence** *noun*
defences

**defenceless**

**defend** *verb*
defends
defending
defended

**defendant** *noun*
defendants

**defender** *noun*
defenders

**defensible**

**defensive** *adjective*
defensively

**defer** *verb*
defers
deferring
deferred

**deferment**

**defiance**

**defiant** *adjective*
defiantly

**deficiency** *noun*
deficiencies

**deficient**

**deficit** *noun*
deficits

**defile** *verb*
defiles
defiling
defiled

**define** *verb*
defines
defining
defined

**definite** *adjective*
definitely

**definition** *noun*
definitions

**deflate** *verb*
deflates
deflating
deflated

a
b
c
**d**
e
f
g
h
i
j
k
l
m
n
o
p
q
r
s
t
u
v
w
x
y
z

. . . . . . . . . . . . . . . . . . . . . . . . . . . . . . . . . . . . . . . . . . . . . . . . . . . . . . . . . . .

★ A **deer** is an animal. ! **dear**.

deflect *verb*
deflects
deflecting
deflected

deflection

deforestation

deformed

deformity *noun*
deformities

defrost *verb*
defrosts
defrosting
defrosted

deft *adjective*
defter
deftest
deftly

defuse *verb*
defuses
defusing
defused

defy *verb*
defies
defying
defied

degenerate *verb*
degenerates
degenerating
degenerated

degeneration

degradation

degrade *verb*
degrades
degrading
degraded

degree *noun*
degrees

dehydrated

dehydration

de-ice *verb*
de-ices
de-icing
de-iced

de-icer

deity *noun*
deities

dejected

dejection

delay *verb*
delays
delaying
delayed

delay *noun*
delays

delegate *noun*
delegates

delegate *verb*
delegates
delegating
delegated

delegation

delete *verb*
deletes
deleting
deleted

deletion

deliberate *adjective*
deliberately

deliberate *verb*
deliberates
deliberating
deliberated

deliberation

delicacy *noun*
delicacies

delicate *adjective*
delicately

delicatessen *noun*
delicatessens

delicious *adjective*
deliciously

delight *verb*
delights
delighting
delighted

delight *noun*
delights

delightful *adjective*
delightfully

delinquency

delinquent *noun*
delinquents

delirious *adjective*
deliriously

delirium *noun*

deliver *verb*
delivers
delivering
delivered

delivery *noun*
deliveries

delta *noun*
deltas

delude *verb*
deludes
deluding
deluded

deluge *noun*
deluges

deluge *verb*
deluges
deluging
deluged

delusion *noun*
delusions

de luxe

demand *verb*
demands
demanding
demanded

demand *noun*
demands

demanding

demerara

demist *verb*
demists
demisting
demisted

demo *noun*
demos

democracy *noun*
democracies

democrat *noun*
democrats

**democratic** adjective
democratically

**demolish** verb
demolishes
demolishing
demolished

**demolition**

**demon** noun
demons

**demonstrate** verb
demonstrates
demonstrating
demonstrated

**demonstration** noun
demonstrations

**demonstrator** noun
demonstrators

**demoralize** verb
demoralizes
demoralizing
demoralized

**demote** verb
demotes
demoting
demoted

**den** noun
dens

**denial** noun
denials

**denim**

**denominator** noun
denominators

**denote** verb
denotes
denoting
denoted

**denounce** verb
denounces
denouncing
denounced

**denunciation**

**dense** adjective
denser
densest
densely

**density** noun

**dent** noun
dents

**dental**

**dentist** noun
dentists

**dentistry**

**denture** noun
dentures

**deny** verb
denies
denying
denied

**deodorant** noun
deodorants

**depart** verb
departs
departing
departed

**department** noun
departments

**departure** noun
departures

**depend** verb
depends
depending
depended

**dependable**

**dependant*** noun
dependants

**dependence**

**dependent**☆ adjective

**depict** verb
depicts
depicting
depicted

**deplorable** adjective
deplorably

**deplore** verb
deplores
deploring
deplored

**deport** verb
deports
deporting
deported

**deposit** verb
deposits
depositing
deposited

**deposit** noun
deposits

**depot** noun
depots

**depress** verb
depresses
depressing
depressed

**depression** noun
depressions

**deprivation**

**deprive** verb
deprives
depriving
deprived

**depth** noun
depths

**deputize** verb
deputizes
deputizing
deputized

**deputy** noun
deputies

**derail** verb
derails
derailing
derailed

a
b
c
**d**
e
f
g
h
i
j
k
l
m
n
o
p
q
r
s
t
u
v
w
x
y
z

. . . . . . . . . . . . . . . . . . . . . . . . . . . . . . . . . . . . . . . . . . . . .

★ **Dependant** is a noun: *She has three dependants.* **!** dependent.
☆ **Dependent** is an adjective: *She has three dependent children.*
**!** dependant.

# de

derby *noun*
derbies
derelict
deride *verb*
derides
deriding
derided
derision
derive *verb*
derives
deriving
derived
derrick *noun*
derricks
derv
descant★ *noun*
descants
descend *verb*
descends
descending
descended
descendant *noun*
descendants
descent☆
describe *verb*
describes
describing
described
description *noun*
descriptions
descriptive *adjective*
descriptively
desert○ *noun*
deserts
desert *verb*
deserts
deserting
deserted
deserter *noun*
deserters

desertion
deserve *verb*
deserves
deserving
deserved
design *verb*
designs
designing
designed
design *noun*
designs
designate *verb*
designates
designating
designated
designer *noun*
designers
desirable
desire *verb*
desires
desiring
desired
desire *noun*
desires
desk *noun*
desks
desktop
desolate
desolation
despair *verb*
despairs
despairing
despaired
despair *noun*
despatch *verb* use
dispatch
desperate *adjective*
desperately
desperation

despicable *adjective*
despicably
despise *verb*
despises
despising
despised
despite
dessert✢ *noun*
desserts
dessertspoon *noun*
dessertspoons
destination *noun*
destinations
destined
destiny *noun*
destinies
destroy *verb*
destroys
destroying
destroyed
destroyer *noun*
destroyers
destruction
destructive
detach *verb*
detaches
detaching
detached
detachable
detached
detachment *noun*
detachments
detail *noun*
details
detain *verb*
detains
detaining
detained

. . . . . . . . . . . . . . . . . . . . . . . . . . . . . . . . . . . . . . . . . . . . . . . . . . . . . .

★ Descant is a term in music. ! descent.
☆ Descent is a way down. ! descant.
○ A desert is a very dry area of land. ! dessert.
✢ A dessert is a sweet pudding. ! desert.

**detect** *verb*
  detects
  detecting
  detected
**detection**
**detector**
**detective** *noun*
  detectives
**detention** *noun*
  detentions
**deter** *verb*
  deters
  deterring
  deterred
**detergent** *noun*
  detergents
**deteriorate** *verb*
  deteriorates
  deteriorating
  deteriorated
**deterioration**
**determination**
**determine** *verb*
  determines
  determining
  determined
**determined**
**deterrence**
**deterrent** *noun*
  deterrents
**detest** *verb*
  detests
  detesting
  detested
**detestable**
**detonate** *verb*
  detonates
  detonating
  detonated
**detonation**

**detonator**
**detour** *noun*
  detours
**deuce**★
**devastate** *verb*
  devastates
  devastating
  devastated
**devastation**
**develop** *verb*
  develops
  developing
  developed
**development** *noun*
  developments
**device** *noun*
  devices
**devil** *noun*
  devils
**devilish**
**devilment**
**devious** *adjective*
  deviously
**devise** *verb*
  devises
  devising
  devised
**devolution**
**devote** *verb*
  devotes
  devoting
  devoted
**devotee**
**devotion**
**devour** *verb*
  devours
  devouring
  devoured
**devout**
**dew**☆

**dewy**
**dhoti**✪ *noun*
  dhotis
**diabetes**
**diabetic**
**diabolical** *adjective*
  diabolically
**diagnose** *verb*
  diagnoses
  diagnosing
  diagnosed
**diagnosis** *noun*
  diagnoses
**diagonal** *adjective*
  diagonally
**diagonal** *noun*
  diagonals
**diagram** *noun*
  diagrams
**dial** *noun*
  dials
**dial** *verb*
  dials
  dialling
  dialled
**dialect** *noun*
  dialects
**dialogue** *noun*
  dialogues
**diameter** *noun*
  diameters
**diamond** *noun*
  diamonds
**diaphragm** *noun*
  diaphragms
**diarrhoea**
**diary** *noun*
  diaries
**dice** *noun*
  dice

a b c **d** e f g h i j k l m n o p q r s t u v w x y z

· · · · · · · · · · · · · · · · · · · · · · · · · · · · · · · · · · · ·

★ **Deuce** is a score in tennis. ❗juice.
☆ **Dew** is moisture on grass and plants. ❗due.
✪ A **dhoti** is a piece of clothing worn by Hindus.

65

a

b

c

**d**

e

f

g

h

i

j

k

l

m

n

o

p

q

r

s

t

u

v

w

x

y

z

**dictate** *verb*
dictates
dictating
dictated

**dictation**

**dictator** *noun*
dictators

**dictatorial** *adjective*
dictatorially

**dictionary** *noun*
dictionaries

**did** see **do**

**diddle** *verb*
diddles
diddling
diddled

**didn't** *verb*

**die** *verb*
dies
dying
died

**diesel** *noun*
diesels

**diet** *noun*
diets

**diet** *verb*
diets
dieting
dieted

**differ** *verb*
differs
differing
differed

**difference** *noun*
differences

**different** *adjective*
differently

**difficult**

**difficulty** *noun*
difficulties

**dig** *verb*
digs
digging
dug

**dig** *noun*
digs

**digest** *verb*
digests
digesting
digested

**digestible**

**digestion**

**digestive**

**digger**

**digit** *noun*
digits

**digital** *adjective*
digitally

**dignified**

**dignity**

**dike** *noun* use **dyke**

**dilemma** *noun*
dilemmas

**dilute** *verb*
dilutes
diluting
diluted

**dilution**

**dim** *adjective*
dimmer
dimmest
dimly

**dimension** *noun*
dimensions

**diminish** *verb*
diminishes
diminishing
diminished

**dimple** *noun*
dimples

**din** *noun*
dins

**dine** *verb*
dines
dining
dined

**diner★** *noun*
diners

**dinghy☆** *noun*
dinghies

**dingy✪** *adjective*
dingier
dingiest

**dinner✚** *noun*
dinners

**dinosaur** *noun*
dinosaurs

**dioxide** *noun*
dioxides

**dip** *verb*
dips
dipping
dipped

**dip** *noun*
dips

**diphtheria**

**diploma** *noun*
diplomas

**diplomacy**

**diplomat**

**diplomatic** *adjective*
diplomatically

**dire** *adjective*
direr
direst

**direct** *adjective*
directly

- - - - - - - - - - - - - - - - - - - - - - - - - - - - - - - - - - - - - - - - - -

★ A **diner** is someone who eats dinner. **! dinner**.

☆ A **dinghy** is a small sailing boat. **! dingy**.

✪ **Dingy** means 'dirty-looking, drab, dull-coloured'. **! dinghy**.

✚ **Dinner** is a meal. **! diner**.

66

**direct** *verb*
  directs
  directing
  directed

**direction** *noun*
  directions

**director** *noun*
  directors

**directory** *noun*
  directories

**dirt**

**dirtiness**

**dirty** *adjective*
  dirtier
  dirtiest
  dirtily

**dis-**
dis- makes a word
with an opposite
meaning, e.g.
**disobey** means 'to
refuse to obey' and
**disloyal** means 'not
loyal'. These words
are spelt joined up.

**disability** *noun*
  disabilities

**disabled**

**disadvantage** *noun*
  disadvantages

**disagree** *verb*
  disagrees
  disagreeing
  disagreed

**disagreeable**
  *adjective*
  disagreeably

**disagreement** *noun*
  disagreements

**disappear** *verb*
  disappears
  disappearing
  disappeared

**disappearance** *noun*
  disappearances

**disappoint** *verb*
  disappoints
  disappointing
  disappointed

**disappointing**

**disappointment**
  *noun*
  disappointments

**disapproval**

**disapprove** *verb*
  disapproves
  disapproving
  disapproved

**disarm** *verb*
  disarms
  disarming
  disarmed

**disarmament**

**disaster** *noun*
  disasters

**disastrous** *adjective*
  disastrously

**disc★** *noun*
  discs

**discard** *verb*
  discards
  discarding
  discarded

**discharge** *verb*
  discharges
  discharging
  discharged

**disciple** *noun*
  disciples

**discipline**

**disc jockey** *noun*
  disc jockeys

**disclose** *verb*
  discloses
  disclosing
  disclosed

**disclosure**

**disco** *noun*
  discos

**discomfort**

**disconnect** *verb*
  disconnects
  disconnecting
  disconnected

**disconnection**

**discontent**

**discontented**

**discotheque** *noun*
  discotheques

**discount** *noun*
  discounts

**discourage** *verb*
  discourages
  discouraging
  discouraged

**discouragement**

**discover** *verb*
  discovers
  discovering
  discovered

**discovery** *noun*
  discoveries

**discreet** *adjective*
  discreetly

**discriminate** *verb*
  discriminates
  discriminating
  discriminated

**discrimination**

**discus** *noun*
  discuses

**discuss** *verb*
  discusses
  discussing
  discussed

★ A **disc** is a flat round object. **! disk**.

## di

discussion *noun*
discussions

disease *noun*
diseases

diseased

**disgrace** *verb*
disgraces
disgracing
disgraced

disgrace *noun*

disgraceful *adjective*
disgracefully

disguise *verb*
disguises
disguising
disguised

disguise *noun*
disguises

disgust *verb*
disgusts
disgusting
disgusted

disgust *noun*

disgusting

dish *noun*
dishes

dish *verb*
dishes
dishing
dished

dishcloth *noun*
dishcloths

dishevelled

dishonest *adjective*
dishonestly

dishonesty

dishwasher *noun*
dishwashers

disinfect *verb*
disinfects
disinfecting
disinfected

disinfectant *noun*
disinfectants

disintegrate *verb*
disintegrates
disintegrating
disintegrated

disintegration

disinterested

disk★ *noun*
disks

dislike *verb*
dislikes
disliking
disliked

dislike *noun*
dislikes

dislocate *verb*
dislocates
dislocating
dislocated

dislodge *verb*
dislodges
dislodging
dislodged

disloyal *adjective*
disloyally

disloyalty

dismal *adjective*
dismally

dismantle *verb*
dismantles
dismantling
dismantled

dismay

dismayed

dismiss *verb*
dismisses
dismissing
dismissed

dismissal

dismount *verb*
dismounts
dismounting
dismounted

disobedience

disobedient

disobey *verb*
disobeys
disobeying
disobeyed

disorder *noun*
disorders

disorderly

dispatch *verb*
dispatches
dispatching
dispatched

dispense *verb*
dispenses
dispensing
dispensed

dispenser *noun*
dispensers

dispersal

disperse *verb*
disperses
dispersing
dispersed

display *verb*
displays
displaying
displayed

display *noun*
displays

displease *verb*
displeases
displeasing
displeased

disposable

disposal

★ A **disk** is what you put in a computer. **!disc**.

**dispose** verb
disposes
disposing
disposed

**disprove** verb
disproves
disproving
disproved

**dispute** noun
disputes

**disqualification**

**disqualify** verb
disqualifies
disqualifying
disqualified

**disregard** verb
disregards
disregarding
disregarded

**disrespect**

**disrespectful**
adjective
disrespectfully

**disrupt** verb
disrupts
disrupting
disrupted

**disruption**

**disruptive**

**dissatisfaction**

**dissatisfied**

**dissect** verb
dissects
dissecting
dissected

**dissection**

**dissolve** verb
dissolves
dissolving
dissolved

**dissuade** verb
dissuades
dissuading
dissuaded

**distance** noun
distances

**distant** adjective
distantly

**distil** verb
distils
distilling
distilled

**distillery** noun
distilleries

**distinct** adjective
distinctly

**distinction** noun
distinctions

**distinctive**

**distinguish** verb
distinguishes
distinguishing
distinguished

**distinguished**

**distort** verb
distorts
distorting
distorted

**distortion** noun
distortions

**distract** verb
distracts
distracting
distracted

**distraction** noun
distractions

**distress** verb
distresses
distressing
distressed

**distress** noun

**distribute** verb
distributes
distributing
distributed

**distribution**

**distributor**

**district** noun
districts

**distrust**

**distrustful**

**disturb** verb
disturbs
disturbing
disturbed

**disturbance** noun
disturbances

**disused**

**ditch** noun
ditches

**dither** verb
dithers
dithering
dithered

**divan** noun
divans

**dive** verb
dives
diving
dived

**diver** noun
divers

**diverse**

**diversify** verb
diversifies
diversifying
diversified

**diversion** noun
diversions

**diversity**

**divert** verb
diverts
diverting
diverted

**divide** verb
divides
dividing
divided

**dividend** noun
dividends

**dividers** plural noun

**divine** adjective
divinely

a
b
c
**d**
e
f
g
h
i
j
k
l
m
n
o
p
q
r
s
t
u
v
w
x
y
z

**divine** *verb*
  divines
  divining
  divined

**divinity**

**divisible**

**division** *noun*
  divisions

**divorce** *verb*
  divorces
  divorcing
  divorced

**divorce** *noun*
  divorces

**Diwali**★

**dizziness**

**dizzy** *adjective*
  dizzier
  dizziest
  dizzily

**do** *verb*
  does
  doing
  did
  done

**docile** *adjective*
  docilely

**dock** *noun*
  docks

**dock** *verb*
  docks
  docking
  docked

**dock** *noun*
  docks

**docker** *noun*
  dockers

**dockyard** *noun*
  dockyards

**doctor** *noun*
  doctors

**doctrine** *noun*
  doctrines

**document** *noun*
  documents

**documentary** *noun*
  documentaries

**doddery**

**dodge** *verb*
  dodges
  dodging
  dodged

**dodge** *noun*
  dodges

**dodgem** *noun*
  dodgems

**dodgy** *adjective*
  dodgier
  dodgiest

**doe**☆ *noun*
  does

**doesn't** *abbreviation*

**dog** *noun*
  dogs

**dog-eared**

**dogged** *adjective*
  doggedly

**doldrums** *plural noun*

**dole** *verb*
  doles
  doling
  doled

**dole** *noun*

**doll** *noun*
  dolls

**dollar** *noun*
  dollars

**dolly** *noun*
  dollies

**dolphin** *noun*
  dolphins

**-dom**
*-dom* makes nouns,
e.g. **kingdom**. Other
noun suffixes are
-hood, -ment, -ness,
and -ship.

**domain** *noun*
  domains

**dome** *noun*
  domes

**domestic** *adjective*
  domestically

**domesticated**

**dominance**

**dominant** *adjective*
  dominantly

**dominate** *verb*
  dominates
  dominating
  dominated

**domination**

**dominion** *noun*
  dominions

**domino** *noun*
  dominoes

**donate** *verb*
  donates
  donating
  donated

**donation** *noun*
  donations

**done** see **do**

**donkey** *noun*
  donkeys

**donor** *noun*
  donors

**don't** *abbreviation*

★ **Diwali** is a Hindu festival.
☆ A **doe** is a female deer. ! **dough**.

**doodle** *verb*
doodles
doodling
doodled

**doodle** *noun*
doodles

**doom** *verb*
dooms
dooming
doomed

**doom** *noun*

**door** *noun*
doors

**doorstep** *noun*
doorsteps

**doorway** *noun*
doorways

**dope** *noun*
dopes

**dopey** *adjective*
dopier
dopiest

**dormitory** *noun*
dormitories

**dose** *noun*
doses

**dossier** *noun*
dossiers

**dot** *verb*
dots
dotting
dotted

**dot** *noun*
dots

**dottiness**

**dotty** *adjective*
dottier
dottiest
dottily

**double** *adjective*
doubly

**double** *noun*
doubles

**double** *verb*
doubles
doubling
doubled

**double-cross** *verb*
double-crosses
double-crossing
double-crossed

**double-decker** *noun*
double-deckers

**doubt** *verb*
doubts
doubting
doubted

**doubt** *noun*
doubts

**doubtful** *adjective*
doubtfully

**doubtless**

**dough**★

**doughnut** *noun*
doughnuts

**doughy** *adjective*
doughier
doughiest

**dove** *noun*
doves

**dowel** *noun*
dowels

**down**

**downcast**

**downfall** *noun*
downfalls

**downhill**

**downpour** *noun*
downpours

**downright** *adjective*

**downs** *plural noun*

**downstairs**

**downstream**

**downward** *adjective*
and *adverb*

**downwards** *adverb*

**downy** *adjective*
downier
downiest

**doze** *verb*
dozes
dozing
dozed

**dozen** *noun*
dozens

**dozy** *adjective*
dozier
doziest

**drab** *adjective*
drabber
drabbest

**draft** *verb*
drafts
drafting
drafted

**draft** *noun*
drafts

**drag** *verb*
drags
dragging
dragged

**drag** *noun*

**dragon** *noun*
dragons

**dragonfly** *noun*
dragonflies

**drain** *verb*
drains
draining
drained

**drain** *noun*
drains

**drainage**

**drake** *noun*
drakes

**drama** *noun*
dramas

a
b
c
**d**
e
f
g
h
i
j
k
l
m
n
o
p
q
r
s
t
u
v
w
x
y
z

. . . . . . . . . . . . . . . . . . . . . . . . . . . . . . . . . . . . . . . . . . . . . . . . . . . . . . . . .

★ **Dough** is a mixture of flour and water used for baking. **!** **doe**.

**dramatic** *adjective*
dramatically

**dramatist** *noun*
dramatists

**dramatization**

**dramatize** *verb*
dramatizes
dramatizing
dramatized

**drank** see **drink**

**drape** *verb*
drapes
draping
draped

**drastic** *adjective*
drastically

**draught** *noun*
draughts

**draughty** *adjective*
draughtier
draughtiest

**draughts** *noun*

**draughtsman** *noun*
draughtsmen

**draw★** *verb*
draws
drawing
drew
drawn

**draw** *noun*
draws

**drawback** *noun*
drawbacks

**drawbridge** *noun*
drawbridges

**drawer☆** *noun*
drawers

**drawing** *noun*
drawings

**drawl** *verb*
drawls
drawling
drawled

**dread** *verb*
dreads
dreading
dreaded

**dread** *noun*

**dreadful** *adjective*
dreadfully

**dreadlocks**

**dream** *noun*
dreams

**dream** *verb*
dreams
dreaming
dreamt *or* dreamed

**dreamy** *adjective*
dreamier
dreamiest

**dreariness**

**dreary** *adjective*
drearier
dreariest
drearily

**dredge** *verb*
dredges
dredging
dredged

**dredger**

**drench** *verb*
drenches
drenching
drenched

**dress** *verb*
dresses
dressing
dressed

**dress** *noun*
dresses

**dresser** *noun*
dressers

**dressing** *noun*
dressings

**dressmaker** *noun*
dressmakers

**drew** see **draw**

**dribble** *verb*
dribbles
dribbling
dribbled

**dried** see **dry**

**drier** *noun*
driers

**drift** *verb*
drifts
drifting
drifted

**drift** *noun*
drifts

**driftwood**

**drill** *verb*
drills
drilling
drilled

**drill** *noun*
drills

**drink** *verb*
drinks
drinking
drank
drunk

**drink** *noun*
drinks

**drinker** *noun*
drinkers

**drip** *noun*
drips

......................................................................

★ To **draw** is to make a picture with a pencil, pen, or crayon.
 **!drawer**.
☆ A **drawer** is part of a cupboard. **!draw**.

a
b
c
**d**
e
f
g
h
i
j
k
l
m
n
o
p
q
r
s
t
u
v
w
x
y
z

**drip** *verb*
drips
dripping
dripped

**dripping**

**drive** *verb*
drives
driving
drove
driven

**drive** *noun*
drives

**driver** *noun*
drivers

**drizzle** *verb*
drizzles
drizzling
drizzled

**drizzle** *noun*

**drone** *verb*
drones
droning
droned

**drone** *noun*
drones

**drool** *verb*
drools
drooling
drooled

**droop** *verb*
droops
drooping
drooped

**drop** *verb*
drops
dropping
dropped

**drop** *noun*
drops

**droplet** *noun*
droplets

**drought** *noun*
droughts

**drove** see **drive**

**drown** *verb*
drowns
drowning
drowned

**drowsiness**

**drowsy** *adjective*
drowsier
drowsiest
drowsily

**drug** *noun*
drugs

**drug** *verb*
drugs
drugging
drugged

**Druid** *noun*
Druids

**drum** *noun*
drums

**drum** *verb*
drums
drumming
drummed

**drummer** *noun*
drummers

**drumstick** *noun*
drumsticks

**drunk** see **drink**

**drunk** *adjective* and
*noun*
drunks

**drunkard** *noun*
drunkards

**dry** *adjective*
drier
driest
drily

**dry** *verb*
dries
drying
dried

**dryness**

**dual**★ *adjective*
dually

**dub** *verb*
dubs
dubbing
dubbed

**duchess** *noun*
duchesses

**duck** *noun*
ducks

**duck** *verb*
ducks
ducking
ducked

**duckling** *noun*
ducklings

**duct** *noun*
ducts

**dud** *noun*
duds

**due**☆

**duel**⊙ *noun*
duels

**duet** *noun*
duets

**duff**

**duffel coat** *noun*
duffel coats

**dug** see **dig**

**dugout** *noun*
dugouts

**duke** *noun*
dukes

a
b
c
**d**
e
f
g
h
i
j
k
l
m
n
o
p
q
r
s
t
u
v
w
x
y
z

★ **Dual** means 'having two parts'. **!** **duel**.
☆ **Due** means 'expected'. **!** **dew**.
⊙ A **duel** is a fight between two people. **!** **dual**.

73

a
b
c

**d**
**e**

f
g
h
i
j
k
l
m
n
o
p
q
r
s
t
u
v
w
x
y
z

**dull** *adjective*
  duller
  dullest
  dully
**dullness**
**duly**
**dumb** *adjective*
  dumber
  dumbest
**dumbfounded**
**dummy** *noun*
  dummies
**dump** *verb*
  dumps
  dumping
  dumped
**dump** *noun*
  dumps
**dumpling** *noun*
  dumplings
**dumpy** *adjective*
  dumpier
  dumpiest
**dune** *noun*
  dunes
**dung**
**dungarees**
**dungeon** *noun*
  dungeons
**duo** *noun*
  duos
**duplicate** *noun*
  duplicates
**duplicate** *verb*
  duplicates
  duplicating
  duplicated
**duplication**
**durability**
**durable**
**duration**
**during**

**dusk**
**dust**
**dust** *verb*
  dusts
  dusting
  dusted
**dustbin** *noun*
  dustbins
**duster** *noun*
  dusters
**dustman** *noun*
  dustmen
**dustpan** *noun*
  dustpans
**dusty** *adjective*
  dustier
  dustiest
**dutiful** *adjective*
  dutifully
**duty** *noun*
  duties
**duvet** *noun*
  duvets
**dwarf** *noun*
  dwarfs *or* dwarves
**dwarf** *verb*
  dwarfs
  dwarfing
  dwarfed
**dwell** *verb*
  dwells
  dwelling
  dwelt
**dwelling** *noun*
  dwellings
**dwindle** *verb*
  dwindles
  dwindling
  dwindled
**dye★** *verb*
  dyes
  dyeing
  dyed

**dye** *noun*
  dyes
**dying** see **die**
**dyke** *noun*
  dykes
**dynamic** *adjective*
  dynamically
**dynamite**
**dynamo** *noun*
  dynamos
**dynasty** *noun*
  dynasties
**dyslexia**
**dyslexic**
**dystrophy** *noun*

# Ee

e-
*e-* stands for 'electronic' and makes words about computers and the Internet, e.g. **email** (spelt joined up), **e-commerce** and **e-shopping** (spelt with hyphens).

**each**
**eager** *adjective*
  eagerly
**eagerness**
**eagle** *noun*
  eagles
**ear** *noun*
  ears
**earache**

......................................................................

★ **Dye** means 'to change the colour of something'. **!** **die**.

**eardrum** *noun*
eardrums

**earl** *noun*
earls

**early** *adjective and adverb*
earlier
earliest

**earmark** *verb*
earmarks
earmarking
earmarked

**earn** *verb*
earns
earning
earned

**earnest** *adjective*
earnestly

**earnings** *plural noun*

**earphones**

**earring** *noun*
earrings

**earth** *noun*
earths

**earthenware**

**earthly**

**earthquake** *noun*
earthquakes

**earthworm** *noun*
earthworms

**earthy** *adjective*
earthier
earthiest

**earwig** *noun*
earwigs

**ease** *verb*
eases
easing
eased

**ease** *noun*

**easel** *noun*
easels

**east** *adjective and adverb*

**east★** *noun*

**Easter**

**easterly** *adjective and noun*
easterlies

**eastern**

**eastward** *adjective and adverb*

**eastwards** *adverb*

**easy** *adjective and adverb*
easier
easiest
easily

**eat** *verb*
eats
eating
ate
eaten

**eatable**

**eaves**

**ebb** *verb*
ebbs
ebbing
ebbed

**ebb**

**ebony**

**eccentric**

**eccentricity** *noun*
eccentricities

**echo** *verb*
echoes
echoing
echoed

**echo** *noun*
echoes

**éclair** *noun*
éclairs

**eclipse** *noun*
eclipses

**ecological**

**ecology**

**economic**

**economical** *adjective*
economically

**economics**

**economist** *noun*
economists

**economize** *verb*
economizes
economizing
economized

**economy** *noun*
economies

**ecstasy** *noun*
ecstasies

**ecstatic** *adjective*
ecstatically

**eczema**

---

**-ed and -t**
Some verbs ending in *l*, *m*, *n*, and *p* have past forms and past participles ending in *-ed* and *-t*, e.g. **burned/burnt**, **leaped/leapt**. Both forms are correct, and the *-t* form is especially common when it comes before a noun, e.g. *burnt cakes*.

---

**edge** *noun*
edges

**edge** *verb*
edges
edging
edged

**edgeways**

★ You use a capital E in the **East**, meaning China, Japan, etc.

**edgy** *adjective*
edgier
edgiest

**edible**

**edit** *verb*
edits
editing
edited

**edition** *noun*
editions

**editor** *noun*
editors

**editorial** *noun*
editorials

**educate** *verb*
educates
educating
educated

**education**

**educational**

**educator**

**eel** *noun*
eels

**eerie** *adjective*
eerier
eeriest
eerily

**eeriness**

**effect**★ *noun*
effects

**effective** *adjective*
effectively

**effectiveness**

**effeminate**

**effervescence**

**effervescent**

**efficiency**

**efficient** *adjective*
efficiently

**effort** *noun*
efforts

**effortless** *adjective*
effortlessly

**egg** *noun*
eggs

**egg** *verb*
eggs
egging
egged

-ei- and -ie-
The rule 'i before e except after c' is true when it is pronounced -ee-, e.g. **thief**, **ceiling**. There are a few exceptions, of which the most important are **seize** and **protein**.

**Eid**☆

**eiderdown** *noun*
eiderdowns

**eight**✪

**eighteen**

**eighteenth**

**eighth**✚ *adjective and noun*
eighthly

**eightieth**

**eighty** *noun*
eighties

**either**

**eject** *verb*
ejects
ejecting
ejected

**ejection**

**elaborate** *adjective*
elaborately

**elaborate** *verb*
elaborates
elaborating
elaborated

**elaboration**

**elastic**

**elated**

**elation**

**elbow** *noun*
elbows

**elbow** *verb*
elbows
elbowing
elbowed

**elder** *adjective and noun*
elders

**elderberry** *noun*
elderberries

**elderly**

**eldest**

**elect** *verb*
elects
electing
elected

**election** *noun*
elections

**electorate**

**electric**

**electrical** *adjective*
electrically

**electrician** *noun*
electricians

**electricity**

**electrification**

---

★ An **effect** is something that is caused by something else. ❗affect.
☆ **Eid** is a Muslim festival.
✪ **Eight** is the number. ❗ate.
✚ Note that there are two h's in **eighth**.

**electrify** verb
electrifies
electrifying
electrified

**electrocute** verb
electrocutes
electrocuting
electrocuted

**electrocution**

**electromagnet** noun
electromagnets

**electron** noun
electrons

**electronic** adjective
electronically

**electronics**

**elegance**

**elegant** adjective
elegantly

**element** noun
elements

**elementary**

**elephant** noun
elephants

**elevate** verb
elevates
elevating
elevated

**elevation** noun
elevations

**eleven**

**eleventh**

**elf** noun
elves

**eligibility**

**eligible**

**eliminate** verb
eliminates
eliminating
eliminated

**elimination**

**élite** noun
élites

**elk** noun
elk or elks

**ellipse** noun
ellipses

**elliptical** adjective
elliptically

**elm** noun
elms

**elocution**

**eloquence**

**eloquent**

**else**

**elsewhere**

**elude** verb
eludes
eluding
eluded

**elusive** adjective
elusively

**elves** see elf

**email**★ noun
emails

**email** verb
emails
emailing
emailed

**emancipate** verb
emancipates
emancipating
emancipated

**emancipation**

**embankment** noun
embankments

**embark** verb
embarks
embarking
embarked

**embarkation**

**embarrass**☆ verb
embarrasses
embarrassing
embarrassed

**embarrassment**

**embassy** noun
embassies

**embedded**

**embers** plural noun

**emblem** noun
emblems

**embrace** verb
embraces
embracing
embraced

**embroider** verb
embroiders
embroidering
embroidered

**embroidery** noun
embroideries

**embryo** noun
embryos

**emerald** noun
emeralds

**emerge** verb
emerges
emerging
emerged

**emergence**

**emergency** noun
emergencies

**emery paper**

**emigrant** noun
emigrants

**emigrate** verb
emigrates
emigrating
emigrated

a
b
c
d
e
f
g
h
i
j
k
l
m
n
o
p
q
r
s
t
u
v
w
x
y
z

★ **Email** is short for **electronic mail**.
☆ Note that there are two rs in **embarrass** and **embarrassment**.

77

**emigration**

**eminence**

**eminent**

**emission** ★ *noun*
emissions

**emit** *verb*
emits
emitting
emitted

**emotion** *noun*
emotions

**emotional** *adjective*
emotionally

**emperor** *noun*
emperors

**emphasis** *noun*
emphases

**emphasize** *verb*
emphasizes
emphasizing
emphasized

**emphatic** *adjective*
emphatically

**empire** *noun*
empires

**employ** *verb*
employs
employing
employed

**employee** *noun*
employees

**employer** *noun*
employers

**employment**

**empress** *noun*
empresses

**empties** *plural noun*

**emptiness**

**empty** *adjective*
emptier
emptiest

**empty** *verb*
empties
emptying
emptied

**emu** *noun*
emus

**emulsion** *noun*
emulsions

**enable** *verb*
enables
enabling
enabled

**enamel** *noun*
enamels

**encampment** *noun*
encampments

**-ence**
See the note at -ance.

**enchant** *verb*
enchants
enchanting
enchanted

**enchantment**

**encircle** *verb*
encircles
encircling
encircled

**enclose** *verb*
encloses
enclosing
enclosed

**enclosure**

**encore** *noun*
encores

**encounter** *verb*
encounters
encountering
encountered

**encourage** *verb*
encourages
encouraging
encouraged

**encouragement**

**encyclopedia** *noun*
encyclopedias

**encyclopedic**

**end** *verb*
ends
ending
ended

**end** *noun*
ends

**endanger** *verb*
endangers
endangering
endangered

**endeavour** *verb*
endeavours
endeavouring
endeavoured

**ending** *noun*
endings

**endless** *adjective*
endlessly

**endurance**

**endure** *verb*
endures
enduring
endured

**enemy** *noun*
enemies

**energetic** *adjective*
energetically

**energy** *noun*
energies

**enforce** *verb*
enforces
enforcing
enforced

★ An **emission** is something that escapes, like fumes. **!** omission.

a b c d e f g h i j k l m n o p q r s t u v w x y z

**enforceable**

**enforcement**

**engage** *verb*
engages
engaging
engaged

**engagement** *noun*
engagements

**engine** *noun*
engines

**engineer** *noun*
engineers

**engineering**

**engrave** *verb*
engraves
engraving
engraved

**engraver**

**engrossed**

**engulf** *verb*
engulfs
engulfing
engulfed

**enhance** *verb*
enhances
enhancing
enhanced

**enhancement**

**enjoy** *verb*
enjoys
enjoying
enjoyed

**enjoyable**

**enjoyment**

**enlarge** *verb*
enlarges
enlarging
enlarged

**enlargement** *noun*
enlargements

**enlist** *verb*
enlists
enlisting
enlisted

**enmity** *noun*
enmities

**enormity**★ *noun*
enormities

**enormous** *adjective*
enormously

**enormousness**

**enough**

**enquire** *verb*
enquires
enquiring
enquired

**enquiry**☆ *noun*
enquiries

**enrage** *verb*
enrages
enraging
enraged

**enrich** *verb*
enriches
enriching
enriched

**enrichment**

**enrol** *verb*
enrols
enrolling
enrolled

**enrolment**

**ensemble** *noun*
ensembles

**ensue** *verb*
ensues
ensuing
ensued

**ensure** *verb*
ensures
ensuring
ensured

**-ent**
See the note at **-ant**.

**entangle** *verb*
entangles
entangling
entangled

**entanglement**

**enter** *verb*
enters
entering
entered

**enterprise** *noun*
enterprises

**enterprising**

**entertain** *verb*
entertains
entertaining
entertained

**entertainer** *noun*
entertainers

**entertainment** *noun*
entertainments

**enthusiasm** *noun*
enthusiasms

**enthusiast** *noun*
enthusiasts

**enthusiastic**
*adjective*
enthusiastically

**entire** *adjective*
entirely

**entirety**

**entitle** *verb*
entitles
entitling
entitled

a
b
c
d
e
f
g
h
i
j
k
l
m
n
o
p
q
r
s
t
u
v
w
x
y
z

. . . . . . . . . . . . . . . . . . . . . . . . . . . . . . . . . . . . . . . . . . . . . . . . . . . . . .

★ An **enormity** is a wicked act. If you mean 'large size', use
enormousness.
☆ An **enquiry** is a question. ! inquiry.

a

b

c

d

**e**

f

g

h

i

j

k

l

m

n

o

p

q

r

s

t

u

v

w

x

y

z

**entrance** *noun*
entrances

**entrance** *verb*
entrances
entrancing
entranced

**entrant** *noun*
entrants

**entreat** *verb*
entreats
entreating
entreated

**entreaty** *noun*
entreaties

**entrust** *verb*
entrusts
entrusting
entrusted

**entry** *noun*
entries

**envelop** *verb*
envelops
enveloping
enveloped

**envelope** *noun*
envelopes

**envious** *adjective*
enviously

**environment** *noun*
environments

**environmental**

**environmentalist**
*noun*
environmentalists

**envy** *verb*
envies
envying
envied

**envy** *noun*

**enzyme** *noun*
enzymes

**epic** *noun*
epics

**epidemic** *noun*
epidemics

**epilepsy**

**epileptic** *adjective* and
*noun*
epileptics

**epilogue** *noun*
epilogues

**episode** *noun*
episodes

**epistle** *noun*
epistles

**epitaph** *noun*
epitaphs

**epoch** *noun*
epochs

**equal** *adjective*
equally

**equal** *verb*
equals
equalling
equalled

**equal** *noun*
equals

**equality**

**equalize** *verb*
equalizes
equalizing
equalized

**equalizer** *noun*
equalizers

**equation** *noun*
equations

**equator**

**equatorial**

**equestrian**

**equilateral**

**equilibrium** *noun*
equilibria

**equinox** *noun*
equinoxes

**equip** *verb*
equips
equipping
equipped

**equipment**

**equivalence**

**equivalent**

---

**-er** and **-est**
*-er* and *-est* make
adjectives and
adverbs meaning
'more' or 'most', e.g.
**faster**, **slowest**. You
can do this when the
word has one syllable,
and when a
consonant comes at
the end of the word
after a single vowel
you double it, e.g.
**fatter**, **bigger**. You
can use *-er* and *-est*
with some
two-syllable
adjectives, e.g.
**commoner**,
**pleasantest**, and
words ending in *y*,
which change to *-ier*
and *-iest*, e.g.
**angrier**, **happiest**.

---

**-er** and **-or**
*-er* makes nouns
meaning 'a person or
thing that does
something', e.g. a
**helper** is a person
who helps and an
**opener** is a tool that
opens things. You can
make new words this
way, e.g. **complainer**,
**repairer**. Some words
end in *-or*, e.g. **actor**,
**visitor**, but you can't
use *-or* to make new
words.

---

**era** *noun*
eras

**erase** *verb*
erases
erasing
erased

**eraser**

**erect** *adjective*

**erect** *verb*
erects
erecting
erected

**erection** *noun*
erections

**ermine** *noun*
ermine

**erode** *verb*
erodes
eroding
eroded

**erosion**

**errand** *noun*
errands

**erratic** *adjective*
erratically

**erroneous** *adjective*
erroneously

**error** *noun*
errors

**erupt** *verb*
erupts
erupting
erupted

**eruption**

**escalate** *verb*
escalates
escalating
escalated

**escalation**

**escalator** *noun*
escalators

**escape** *verb*
escapes
escaping
escaped

**escape** *noun*
escapes

**escort** *verb*
escorts
escorting
escorted

**escort** *noun*
escorts

**Eskimo** *noun*
Eskimos *or* Eskimo

**especially**

**espionage**

**esplanade** *noun*
esplanades

**-ess**
-ess makes nouns for female people and animals, e.g. **manageress**, **lioness**.

**essay** *noun*
essays

**essence** *noun*
essences

**essential** *adjective*
essentially

**essential** *noun*
essentials

**establish** *verb*
establishes
establishing
established

**establishment** *noun*
establishments

**estate** *noun*
estates

**esteem** *verb*
esteems
esteeming
esteemed

**estimate** *noun*
estimates

**estimate** *verb*
estimates
estimating
estimated

**estuary** *noun*
estuaries

**etch** *verb*
etches
etching
etched

**etching** *noun*
etchings

**eternal** *adjective*
eternally

**eternity**

**ether**

**ethnic**

**etymology** *noun*
etymologies

**eucalyptus** *noun*
eucalyptuses

**euphemism** *noun*
euphemisms

**euphemistic** *adjective*
euphemistically

**Eurasian**

**euro** *noun*
euro *or* euros

**European** *adjective* and *noun*
Europeans

**euthanasia**

**evacuate** *verb*
evacuates
evacuating
evacuated

**evacuation**

**evacuee**

**evade** *verb*
evades
evading
evaded

**evaluate** *verb*
evaluates
evaluating
evaluated

a
b
c
d
e
f
g
h
i
j
k
l
m
n
o
p
q
r
s
t
u
v
w
x
y
z

81

## ev - ex

a evaluation

b evangelical

evangelism

c evangelist *noun*
evangelists

d evaporate *verb*
evaporates

e evaporating
evaporated

f

evaporation

g evasion *noun*
evasions

h

evasive

i eve *noun*
eves

j

even *adjective*
evenly

k

even *adverb*

l

m even *verb*
evens

n evening
evened

o evening *noun*
evenings

p

evenness

q event *noun*
events

r

eventful *adjective*
eventfully

s

eventual *adjective*
t eventually

u

ever

v evergreen *adjective*
and *noun*

w evergreens

everlasting

x

every

y everybody

everyday

everyone

everything

everywhere

evict *verb*
evicts
evicting
evicted

eviction

evidence

evident *adjective*
evidently

evil *adjective*
evilly

evil *noun*
evils

evolution

evolutionary

evolve *verb*
evolves
evolving
evolved

ewe★ *noun*
ewes

**ex-**
*ex-* makes nouns with
the meaning 'former'
or 'who used to be',
e.g. ex-president,
ex-wife. You use a
hyphen to make these
words.

exact *adjective*
exactly

exactness

exaggerate *verb*
exaggerates
exaggerating
exaggerated

exaggeration

exalt *verb*
exalts
exalting
exalted

exam *noun*
exams

examination *noun*
examinations

examine *verb*
examines
examining
examined

examiner *noun*
examiners

example *noun*
examples

exasperate *verb*
exasperates
exasperating
exasperated

exasperation

excavate *verb*
excavates
excavating
excavated

excavation *noun*
excavations

excavator *noun*
excavators

exceed *verb*
exceeds
exceeding
exceeded

exceedingly

excel *verb*
excels
excelling
excelled

excellence

excellent *adjective*
excellently

★ A ewe is a female sheep. **!**yew, you.

z

except★

exception *noun*
  exceptions

exceptional *adjective*
  exceptionally

excerpt *noun*
  excerpts

excess *noun*
  excesses

excessive *adjective*
  excessively

exchange *verb*
  exchanges
  exchanging
  exchanged

exchange *noun*
  exchanges

excitable *adjective*
  excitably

excite *verb*
  excites
  exciting
  excited

excitedly

excitement *noun*
  excitements

exclaim *verb*
  exclaims
  exclaiming
  exclaimed

exclamation *noun*
  exclamations

exclude *verb*
  excludes
  excluding
  excluded

exclusion

exclusive *adjective*
  exclusively

excrement

excrete *verb*
  excretes
  excreting
  excreted

excretion

excursion *noun*
  excursions

excusable

excuse *verb*
  excuses
  excusing
  excused

excuse *noun*
  excuses

execute *verb*
  executes
  executing
  executed

execution *noun*
  executions

executioner *noun*
  executioners

executive *noun*
  executives

exempt *adjective*

exemption *noun*

exercise *noun*
  exercises

exercise☆ *verb*
  exercises
  exercising
  exercised

exert *verb*
  exerts
  exerting
  exerted

exertion *noun*
  exertions

exhale *verb*
  exhales
  exhaling
  exhaled

exhalation

exhaust *verb*
  exhausts
  exhausting
  exhausted

exhaust *noun*
  exhausts

exhaustion

exhibit *verb*
  exhibits
  exhibiting
  exhibited

exhibit *noun*
  exhibits

exhibition *noun*
  exhibitions

exhibitor *noun*
  exhibitors

exile *verb*
  exiles
  exiling
  exiled

exile *noun*
  exiles

exist *verb*
  exists
  existing
  existed

existence *noun*
  existences

exit *verb*
  exits
  exiting
  exited

exit *noun*
  exits

exorcism

exorcist

a
b
c
d
e
f
g
h
i
j
k
l
m
n
o
p
q
r
s
t
u
v
w
x
y
z

. . . . . . . . . . . . . . . . . . . . . . . . . . . . . . . . . . . . . . . . . . . . . . . . . . . . . . . .

★ You use except in e.g. *everyone except me*. ! accept.
☆ To exercise is to keep your body fit. ! exorcise.

## ex

exorcize★ *verb*
exorcizes
exorcizing
exorcized

exotic *adjective*
exotically

expand *verb*
expands
expanding
expanded

expanse *noun*
expanses

expansion

expect *verb*
expects
expecting
expected

expectant *adjective*
expectantly

expectation *noun*
expectations

expedition *noun*
expeditions

expel *verb*
expels
expelling
expelled

expenditure

expense *noun*
expenses

expensive

experience *verb*
experiences
experiencing
experienced

experience *noun*
experiences

experienced

experiment *verb*
experiments
experimenting
experimented

experiment *noun*
experiments

experimental
*adjective*
experimentally

experimentation

expert *adjective* and
*noun*
experts

expertise

expire *verb*
expires
expiring
expired

expiry

explain *verb*
explains
explaining
explained

explanation *noun*
explanations

explanatory

explode *verb*
explodes
exploding
exploded

exploit *noun*
exploits

exploit *verb*
exploits
exploiting
exploited

exploitation

exploration *noun*
explorations

exploratory

explore *verb*
explores
exploring
explored

explorer *noun*
explorers

explosion *noun*
explosions

explosive *adjective*
and *noun*
explosives

export *verb*
exports
exporting
exported

export *noun*
exports

exporter *noun*
exporters

expose *verb*
exposes
exposing
exposed

exposure *noun*
exposures

express *adjective* and
*noun*
expresses

express *verb*
expresses
expressing
expressed

expression *noun*
expressions

expressive *adjective*
expressively

expulsion *noun*
expulsions

exquisite *adjective*
exquisitely

extend *verb*
extends
extending
extended

extension *noun*
extensions

extensive *adjective*
extensively

extent *noun*
extents

. . . . . . . . . . . . . . . . . . . . . . . . . . . . . . . . . . . . . . . . . . . . . . . . . . . . . . . . .

★ To **exorcise** is to get rid of evil spirits. **!exercise.**

**exterior** *noun*
exteriors

**exterminate** *verb*
exterminates
exterminating
exterminated

**extermination**

**external** *adjective*
externally

**extinct**

**extinction**

**extinguish** *verb*
extinguishes
extinguishing
extinguished

**extinguisher** *noun*
extinguishers

**extra** *adjective* and
*noun*
extras

**extract** *verb*
extracts
extracting
extracted

**extract** *noun*
extracts

**extraction** *noun*
extractions

**extraordinary**
*adjective*
extraordinarily

**extrasensory**

**extraterrestrial**
*adjective* and *noun*
extraterrestrials

**extravagance**

**extravagant** *adjective*
extravagantly

**extreme** *adjective*
extremely

**extreme** *noun*
extremes

**extremity** *noun*
extremities

**exuberance**

**exuberant** *adjective*
exuberantly

**exult** *verb*
exults
exulting
exulted

**exultant**

**exultation**

**eye** *noun*
eyes

**eye** *verb*
eyes
eyeing
eyed

**eyeball** *noun*
eyeballs

**eyebrow** *noun*
eyebrows

**eyelash** *noun*
eyelashes

**eyelid** *noun*
eyelids

**eyepiece** *noun*
eyepieces

**eyesight**

**eyesore** *noun*
eyesores

**eyewitness** *noun*
eyewitnesses

# Ff

**-f**
Most nouns ending in
*-f* have plurals ending
in *-ves*, e.g. **shelf -
shelves**, but some
have plurals ending in
*-fs*, e.g. **chiefs**. Nouns
ending in *-ff* have
plurals ending in *-ffs*,
e.g. **cuffs**.

**fable** *noun*
fables

**fabric** *noun*
fabrics

**fabricate** *verb*
fabricates
fabricating
fabricated

**fabulous** *adjective*
fabulously

**face** *noun*
faces

**face** *verb*
faces
facing
faced

**facet** *noun*
facets

**facetious** *adjective*
facetiously

**facial** *adjective*
facially

**facilitate** *verb*
facilitates
facilitating
facilitated

**facility** *noun*
facilities

**fact** *noun*
facts

**factor** *noun*
factors

**factory** *noun*
factories

**factual** *adjective*
factually

**fad** *noun*
fads

**fade** *verb*
fades
fading
faded

**faeces**

**fag** *noun*
fags

a
b
c
d
e
f
g
h
i
j
k
l
m
n
o
p
q
r
s
t
u
v
w
x
y
z

**fagged**

**faggot** *noun*
faggots

**Fahrenheit**

**fail** *verb*
fails
failing
failed

**fail** *noun*
fails

**failing** *noun*
failings

**failure** *noun*
failures

**faint** *adjective*
fainter
faintest
faintly

**faint** *verb*
faints
fainting
fainted

**faint-hearted**

**faintness**

**fair** *adjective*
fairer
fairest

**fair★** *noun*
fairs

**fairground** *noun*
fairgrounds

**fairly**

**fairness**

**fairy** *noun*
fairies

**fairyland**

**faith** *noun*
faiths

**faithful** *adjective*
faithfully

**faithfulness**

**fake** *noun*
fakes

**fake** *verb*
fakes
faking
faked

**faker**

**falcon** *noun*
falcons

**falconry**

**fall** *verb*
falls
falling
fell
fallen

**fall** *noun*
falls

**fallacious** *adjective*
fallaciously

**fallacy** *noun*
fallacies

**fallen** see **fall**

**fallout**

**fallow**

**falls** *plural noun*

**false** *adjective*
falser
falsest
falsely

**falsehood** *noun*
falsehoods

**falseness**

**falter** *verb*
falters
faltering
faltered

**fame**

**famed**

**familiar** *adjective*
familiarly

**familiarity**

**family** *noun*
families

**famine** *noun*
famines

**famished**

**famous** *adjective*
famously

**fan** *verb*
fans
fanning
fanned

**fan** *noun*
fans

**fanatic** *noun*
fanatics

**fanatical** *adjective*
fanatically

**fanciful** *adjective*
fancifully

**fancy** *adjective*
fancier
fanciest

**fancy** *verb*
fancies
fancying
fancied

**fancy** *noun*
fancies

**fanfare** *noun*
fanfares

**fang** *noun*
fangs

**fantastic** *adjective*
fantastically

**fantasy** *noun*
fantasies

**far** *adjective* and *adverb*
farther
farthest

**far-away**

**farce** *noun*
farces

. . . . . . . . . . . . . . . . . . . . . . . . . . . . . . . . . . . . . . . . . . . . . . . . . . . . . . . . . .

★ A **fair** is a group of outdoor entertainments or an exhibition. ! **fare**.

**farcical** *adjective*
farcically

**fare** *verb*
fares
faring
fared

**fare**★ *noun*
fares

**farewell**

**far-fetched**

**farm** *noun*
farms

**farm** *verb*
farms
farming
farmed

**farmer** *noun*
farmers

**farmhouse** *noun*
farmhouses

**farmyard** *noun*
farmyards

**farther**☆

**farthest**۞

**farthing** *noun*
farthings

**fascinate** *verb*
fascinates
fascinating
fascinated

**fascination**

**fascism**

**fascist** *noun*
fascists

**fashion** *noun*
fashions

**fashion** *verb*
fashions
fashioning
fashioned

**fashionable**

**fast** *adjective* and
*adverb*
faster
fastest

**fast** *verb*
fasts
fasting
fasted

**fasten** *verb*
fastens
fastening
fastened

**fastener**

**fastening**

**fat** *adjective*
fatter
fattest

**fat** *noun*
fats

**fatal** *adjective*
fatally

**fatality** *noun*
fatalities

**fate**✢ *noun*
fates

**father** *noun*
fathers

**father-in-law** *noun*
fathers-in-law

**fathom** *noun*
fathoms

**fathom** *verb*
fathoms
fathoming
fathomed

**fatigue**

**fatigued**

**fatten** *verb*
fattens
fattening
fattened

**fattening**

**fatty** *adjective*
fattier
fattiest

**fault** *noun*
faults

**fault** *verb*
faults
faulting
faulted

**faultless** *adjective*
faultlessly

**faulty** *adjective*
faultier
faultiest

**fauna**

**favour** *noun*
favours

**favour** *verb*
favours
favouring
favoured

**favourable** *adjective*
favourably

**favourite** *adjective*
and *noun*
favourites

**favouritism**

. . . . . . . . . . . . . . . . . . . . . . . . . . . . . . . . . . . . . . . . . . . . . . . . . . . . . . . . . . . . . . . . .

★ A **fare** is money you pay, for example on a bus. **!** **fair**.

☆ You can use **farther** or **further** in e.g. *farther up the road*. See **further**.

۞ You can use **farthest** or **furthest** in e.g. *the place farthest from here*. See **furthest**.

✢ **Fate** is a power that is thought to make things happen. **!** **fête**.

a
b
c
d
e
**f**
g
h
i
j
k
l
m
n
o
p
q
r
s
t
u
v
w
x
y
z

87

a
b
c
d
e

**f**

g
h
i
j
k
l
m
n
o
p
q
r
s
t
u
v
w
x
y
z

**fawn** noun
fawns

**fax** noun
faxes

**fax** verb
faxes
faxing
faxed

**-fe**
Most nouns ending in
-fe have plurals
ending in -ves, e.g.
**life - lives**.

**fear** noun
fears

**fear** verb
fears
fearing
feared

**fearful** adjective
fearfully

**fearless** adjective
fearlessly

**fearsome**

**feasible**

**feast** noun
feasts

**feast** verb
feasts
feasting
feasted

**feat**★ noun
feats

**feather** noun
feathers

**feathery**

**feature** noun
features

**feature** verb
features
featuring
featured

**February**☆ noun
Februaries

**fed** see **feed**

**federal**

**federation**

**fee** noun
fees

**feeble** adjective
feebler
feeblest
feebly

**feed** verb
feeds
feeding
fed

**feed** noun
feeds

**feedback**

**feel** verb
feels
feeling
felt

**feel** noun

**feeler** noun
feelers

**feeling** noun
feelings

**feet**○ see **foot**

**feline**

**fell** see **fall**

**fell** verb
fells
felling
felled

**fell** noun
fells

**fellow** noun
fellows

**fellowship** noun
fellowships

**felt** see **feel**

**felt** noun

**felt-tip pen** or
**felt-tipped pen** noun
felt-tip pens or
felt-tipped pens

**female** adjective and
noun
females

**feminine**

**femininity**

**feminism**

**feminist** noun
feminists

**fen** noun
fens

**fence** noun
fences

**fence** verb
fences
fencing
fenced

**fencer** adjective
fencers

**fencing**

**fend** verb
fends
fending
fended

**fender** noun
fenders

**ferment** verb
ferments
fermenting
fermented

**fermentation**

. . . . . . . . . . . . . . . . . . . . . . . . . . . . . . . . . . . . . . . . . . . . . . . . . . . . . . . . .

★ A **feat** is an achievement. **!feet**.
☆ Note that **February** has two rs.
○ **Feet** is the plural of foot. **!feat**.

**ferment**

**fern** *noun*
  ferns

**ferocious** *adjective*
  ferociously

**ferocity**

**ferret** *noun*
  ferrets

**ferret** *verb*
  ferrets
  ferreting
  ferreted

**ferry** *noun*
  ferries

**ferry** *verb*
  ferries
  ferrying
  ferried

**fertile**

**fertility**

**fertilization**

**fertilize** *verb*
  fertilizes
  fertilizing
  fertilized

**fertilizer** *noun*
  fertilizers

**fervent** *adjective*
  fervently

**fervour**

**festival** *noun*
  festivals

**festive**

**festivity**

**festoon** *verb*
  festoons
  festooning
  festooned

**fetal**

**fetch** *verb*
  fetches
  fetching
  fetched

**fête★** *noun*
  fêtes

**fetlock** *noun*
  fetlocks

**fetters** *plural noun*

**fetus**☆ *noun*
  fetuses

**feud** *noun*
  feuds

**feudal**

**feudalism**

**fever** *noun*
  fevers

**fevered**

**feverish** *adjective*
  feverishly

**few** *adjective*
  fewer
  fewest

**fez** *noun*
  fezzes

**fiancé**✪ *noun*
  fiancés

**fiancée**✤ *noun*
  fiancées

**fiasco** *noun*
  fiascos

**fib** *noun*
  fibs

**fibber** *noun*
  fibbers

**fibre** *noun*
  fibres

**fibreglass**

**fibrous**

**fickle**

**fiction** *noun*
  fictions

**fictional** *adjective*
  fictionally

**fictitious** *adjective*
  fictitiously

**fiddle** *verb*
  fiddles
  fiddling
  fiddled

**fiddle** *noun*
  fiddles

**fiddler** *noun*
  fiddlers

**fiddling**

**fiddly**

**fidelity**

**fidget** *verb*
  fidgets
  fidgeting
  fidgeted

**fidgety**

**field** *noun*
  fields

**field** *verb*
  fields
  fielding
  fielded

**fielder** *noun*
  fielders

**field marshal** *noun*
  field marshals

**fieldwork**

**fiend** *noun*
  fiends

**fiendish** *adjective*
  fiendishly

. . . . . . . . . . . . . . . . . . . . . . . . . . . . . . . . . . . . . . . . . . . . . . . . . . . . . . . .
★ A fête is an outdoor entertainment with stalls. ! fate.
☆ You will also see this word spelt **foetus**.
✪ A woman's fiancé is the man who is going to marry her.
✤ A man's fiancée is the woman who is going to marry him.

a
b
c
d
e
**f**
g
h
i
j
k
l
m
n
o
p
q
r
s
t
u
v
w
x
y
z

**fierce** adjective
fiercer
fiercest
fiercely

**fierceness**

**fiery** adjective
fierier
fieriest

**fife** noun
fifes

**fifteen**

**fifteenth**

**fifth**

**fifthly**

**fiftieth**

**fifty** noun
fifties

**fig** noun
figs

**fight** verb
fights
fighting
fought

**fight** noun
fights

**fighter** noun
fighters

**figurative** adjective
figuratively

**figure** noun
figures

**figure** verb
figures
figuring
figured

**filament** noun
filaments

**file** verb
files
filing
filed

**file** noun
files

**filings** plural noun

**fill** verb
fills
filling
filled

**fill** noun
fills

**filler** noun
fillers

**fillet** noun
fillets

**filling** noun
fillings

**filly** noun
fillies

**film** noun
films

**film** verb
films
filming
filmed

**filter** noun
filters

**filter** verb
filters
filtering
filtered

**filth**

**filthy** adjective
filthier
filthiest

**fin** noun
fins

**final** adjective
finally

**final** noun
finals

**finale** noun
finales

**finalist** noun
finalists

**finality**

**finance**

**finance** verb
finances
financing
financed

**finances** plural noun

**financial** adjective
financially

**financier** noun
financiers

**finch** noun
finches

**find** verb
finds
finding
found

**finder** noun
finders

**findings** plural noun

**fine** adjective
finer
finest
finely

**fine** noun
fines

**fine** verb
fines
fining
fined

**finger** noun
fingers

**finger** verb
fingers
fingering
fingered

**fingernail** noun
fingernails

**fingerprint** noun
fingerprints

**finicky**

**finish** verb
finishes
finishing
finished

**finish** noun
finishes

**fir**★ *noun*
firs

**fire** *noun*
fires

**fire** *verb*
fires
firing
fired

**firearm** *noun*
firearms

**firefighter** *noun*
firefighters

**fireman** *noun*
firemen

**fireplace** *noun*
fireplaces

**fireproof**

**fireside** *noun*
firesides

**firewood**

**firework** *noun*
fireworks

**firm** *adjective*
firmer
firmest
firmly

**firm** *noun*
firms

**firmness**

**first** *adjective* and
*adverb*
firstly

**first class**

**first floor** *noun*
first floors

**first-hand** *adjective*

**first-rate**

**fish** *noun*
fish *or* fishes

**fish** *verb*
fishes
fishing
fished

**fisherman** *noun*
fishermen

**fishmonger** *noun*
fishmongers

**fishy** *adjective*
fishier
fishiest

**fission**

**fist** *noun*
fists

**fit** *adjective*
fitter
fittest

**fit** *verb*
fits
fitting
fitted

**fit** *noun*
fits

**fitness**

**fitter** *noun*
fitters

**fitting** *adjective*

**fitting** *noun*
fittings

**five**

**fiver** *noun*
fivers

**fix** *verb*
fixes
fixing
fixed

**fix** *noun*
fixes

**fixture** *noun*
fixtures

**fizz** *verb*
fizzes
fizzing
fizzed

**fizzy** *adjective*
fizzier
fizziest

**fizzle** *verb*
fizzles
fizzling
fizzled

**fjord** *noun*
fjords

**flabbergasted**

**flabby** *adjective*
flabbier
flabbiest

**flag** *noun*
flags

**flag** *verb*
flags
flagging
flagged

**flagpole** *noun*
flagpoles

**flagship** *noun*
flagships

**flagstaff** *noun*
flagstaffs

**flagstone** *noun*
flagstones

**flair**☆ *noun*

**flake** *noun*
flakes

**flake** *verb*
flakes
flaking
flaked

**flaky** *adjective*
flakier
flakiest

. . . . . . . . . . . . . . . . . . . . . . . . . . . . . . . . . . . . . . . . . . . .

★ A **fir** is a tree. **!** **fur**.

☆ **Flair** is a special talent. **!** **flare**.

a
b
c
d
e
**f**
g
h
i
j
k
l
m
n
o
p
q
r
s
t
u
v
w
x
y
z

**flame** *noun*
flames

**flame** *verb*
flames
flaming
flamed

**flamingo** *noun*
flamingos

**flan** *noun*
flans

**flank** *noun*
flanks

**flannel** *noun*
flannels

**flap** *noun*
flaps

**flap** *verb*
flaps
flapping
flapped

**flapjack** *noun*
flapjacks

**flare★** *noun*
flares

**flare** *verb*
flares
flaring
flared

**flash** *noun*
flashes

**flash** *verb*
flashes
flashing
flashed

**flashback** *noun*
flashbacks

**flashy** *adjective*
flashier
flashiest

**flask** *noun*
flasks

**flat** *adjective*
flatter
flattest
flatly

**flat** *noun*
flats

**flatness**

**flatten** *verb*
flattens
flattening
flattened

**flatter** *verb*
flatters
flattering
flattered

**flatterer** *noun*
flatterers

**flattery**

**flaunt** *verb*
flaunts
flaunting
flaunted

**flavour** *noun*
flavours

**flavour** *verb*
flavours
flavouring
flavoured

**flavouring**

**flaw** *noun*
flaws

**flawed**

**flawless** *adjective*
flawlessly

**flax**

**flea☆** *noun*
fleas

**fleck** *noun*
flecks

**flee○** *verb*
flees
fleeing
fled

**fleece** *noun*
fleeces

**fleece** *verb*
fleeces
fleecing
fleeced

**fleecy** *adjective*
fleecier
fleeciest

**fleet** *noun*
fleets

**fleeting**

**flesh**

**fleshy** *adjective*
fleshier
fleshiest

**flew✧** see **fly**

**flex** *noun*
flexes

**flex** *verb*
flexes
flexing
flexed

**flexibility**

**flexible** *adjective*
flexibly

**flick** *verb*
flicks
flicking
flicked

**flick** *noun*
flicks

- - - - - - - - - - - - - - - - - - - - - - - - - - - - - - - - - - - - - - - -

★ A **flare** is a bright light. **!flair**.
☆ A **flea** is an insect. **!flee**.
○ To **flee** is to run away. **!flea**.
✧ **Flew** is the past of **fly**. **!flu, flue**.

92

**flicker** *verb*
 flickers
 flickering
 flickered

**flight** *noun*
 flights

**flimsy** *adjective*
 flimsier
 flimsiest

**flinch** *verb*
 flinches
 flinching
 flinched

**fling** *verb*
 flings
 flinging
 flung

**flint** *noun*
 flints

**flinty** *adjective*
 flintier
 flintiest

**flip** *verb*
 flips
 flipping
 flipped

**flippancy**

**flippant** *adjective*
 flippantly

**flipper** *noun*
 flippers

**flirt** *verb*
 flirts
 flirting
 flirted

**flirtation**

**flit** *verb*
 flits
 flitting
 flitted

**float** *verb*
 floats
 floating
 floated

**float** *noun*
 floats

**flock** *verb*
 flocks
 flocking
 flocked

**flock** *noun*
 flocks

**flog** *verb*
 flogs
 flogging
 flogged

**flood** *verb*
 floods
 flooding
 flooded

**flood** *noun*
 floods

**floodlight** *noun*
 floodlights

**floodlit**

**floor** *noun*
 floors

**floor** *verb*
 floors
 flooring
 floored

**floorboard** *noun*
 floorboards

**flop** *verb*
 flops
 flopping
 flopped

**flop** *noun*
 flops

**floppy** *adjective*
 floppier
 floppiest

**floppy disk** *noun*
 floppy disks

**flora**

**floral**

**florist** *noun*
 florists

**floss**

**flounder** *verb*
 flounders
 floundering
 floundered

**flour**★

**flourish** *verb*
 flourishes
 flourishing
 flourished

**floury** *adjective*
 flourier
 flouriest

**flow** *verb*
 flows
 flowing
 flowed

**flow** *noun*
 flows

**flower**☆ *noun*
 flowers

**flower** *verb*
 flowers
 flowering
 flowered

**flowerpot** *noun*
 flowerpots

**flowery**

**flown**

**flu**✿

a
b
c
d
e
**f**
g
h
i
j
k
l
m
n
o
p
q
r
s
t
u
v
w
x
y
z

. . . . . . . . . . . . . . . . . . . . . . . . . . . . . . . . . . . . . . . . . . . . . . . . . . . . .

★ **Flour** is powder used in making bread. ❗**flower**.
☆ A **flower** is a part of a plant. ❗**flour**.
✿ **Flu** is an illness. ❗**flew, flue**.

93

a

b

c

d

e

**f**

g

h

i

j

k

l

m

n

o

p

q

r

s

t

u

v

w

x

y

z

**fluctuate** *verb*
fluctuates
fluctuating
fluctuated
**fluctuation**
**flue**★ *noun*
flues
**fluency**
**fluent** *adjective*
fluently
**fluff**
**fluffy** *adjective*
fluffier
fluffiest
**fluid** *noun*
fluids
**fluke** *noun*
flukes
**flung** see **fling**
**fluorescent**
**fluoridation**
**fluoride**
**flurry** *noun*
flurries
**flush** *verb*
flushes
flushing
flushed
**flush** *noun*
flushes
**flush** *adjective*
**flustered**
**flute** *noun*
flutes
**flutter** *verb*
flutters
fluttering
fluttered
**flutter** *noun*
flutters

**fly** *verb*
flies
flying
flew
flown
**fly** *noun*
flies
**flyleaf** *noun*
flyleaves
**flyover** *noun*
flyovers
**flywheel** *noun*
flywheels
**foal** *noun*
foals
**foam** *noun*
**foam** *verb*
foams
foaming
foamed
**foamy** *adjective*
foamier
foamiest
**focal**
**focus** *verb*
focuses
focusing
focused
**focus** *noun*
focuses *or* foci
**fodder**
**foe** *noun*
foes
**foetus** *noun* see **fetus**
**fog** *noun*
fogs
**foggy**☆ *adjective*
foggier
foggiest

**foghorn** *noun*
foghorns
**fogy**❍ *noun*
fogies
**foil** *verb*
foils
foiling
foiled
**foil** *noun*
foils
**fold** *verb*
folds
folding
folded
**fold** *noun*
folds
**folder** *noun*
folders
**foliage**
**folk**
**folklore**
**follow** *verb*
follows
following
followed
**follower** *noun*
followers
**fond** *adjective*
fonder
fondest
fondly
**fondness**
**font** *noun*
fonts
**food** *noun*
foods
**fool** *noun*
fools

. . . . . . . . . . . . . . . . . . . . . . . . . . . . . . . . . . . . . . . . . . . . . . . . . . . . . . . . . . .

★ A **flue** is a pipe for smoke and fumes. ! **flew, flu**.

☆ **Foggy** means 'covered in fog'. ! **fogy**.

❍ A **fogy** is someone with old-fashioned ideas. ! **foggy**.

**fool** *verb*
fools
fooling
fooled

**foolhardiness**

**foolhardy** *adjective*
foolhardier
foolhardiest

**foolish** *adjective*
foolishly

**foolishness**

**foolproof**

**foot★** *noun*
feet

**football** *noun*
footballs

**footballer** *noun*
footballers

**foothill** *noun*
foothills

**foothold** *noun*
footholds

**footing**

**footlights**

**footnote** *noun*
footnotes

**footpath** *noun*
footpaths

**footprint** *noun*
footprints

**footstep** *noun*
footsteps

**for☆** *preposition* and
*conjunction*

**forbid** *verb*
forbids
forbidding
forbade
forbidden

**force** *verb*
forces
forcing
forced

**force** *noun*
forces

**forceful** *adjective*
forcefully

**forceps** *plural noun*

**forcible** *adjective*
forcibly

**ford** *verb*
fords
fording
forded

**ford** *noun*
fords

**fore۞** *adjective* and
*noun*

**forecast** *verb*
forecasts
forecasting
forecast
forecasted

**forecast** *noun*
forecasts

**forecourt** *noun*
forecourts

**forefathers** *plural
noun*

**forefinger** *noun*
forefingers

**foregone✢** *adjective*

**foreground** *noun*
foregrounds

**forehead** *noun*
foreheads

**foreign**

**foreigner** *noun*
foreigners

**foreman** *noun*
foremen

**foremost**

**forename** *noun*
forenames

**foresee** *verb*
foresees
foreseeing
foresaw
foreseen

**foreseeable**

**foresight**

**forest** *noun*
forests

**forester** *noun*
foresters

**forestry**

**foretell** *verb*
foretells
foretelling
foretold

**forever*** *adverb*

**forfeit** *verb*
forfeits
forfeiting
forfeited

**forfeit** *noun*
forfeits

**forgave** see **forgive**

a
b
c
d
e
**f**
g
h
i
j
k
l
m
n
o
p
q
r
s
t
u
v
w
x
y
z

95

. . . . . . . . . . . . . . . . . . . . . . . . . . . . . . . . . . . . . . . . . . . . . . . . . . . . .
★ The plural is **foot** in e.g. *a six-foot pole*.
☆ You use **for** in phrases like *a present for you*. ! **fore**.
۞ You use **fore** in phrases like *come to the fore*. ! **for**.
✢ You can use **foregone** in *a foregone conclusion*.
* You use **forever** in e.g. *They are forever complaining*. You can also
use **for ever** in e.g. *The rain seemed to go on for ever*.

**forge** *verb*
forges
forging
forged

**forge** *noun*
forges

**forgery** *noun*
forgeries

**forget** *verb*
forgets
forgetting
forgot
forgotten

**forgetful**

**forgetfulness**

**forget-me-not** *noun*
forget-me-nots

**forgive** *verb*
forgives
forgiving
forgave
forgiven

**forgiveness**

**fork** *noun*
forks

**fork** *verb*
forks
forking
forked

**fork-lift truck** *noun*
fork-lift trucks

**forlorn**

**form** *verb*
forms
forming
formed

**form** *noun*
forms

**formal** *adjective*
formally

**formality** *noun*
formalities

**format** *noun*
formats

**formation** *noun*
formations

**former** *adjective*
formerly

**formidable** *adjective*
formidably

**formula** *noun*
formulas *or* formulae

**formulate** *verb*
formulates
formulating
formulated

**forsake** *verb*
forsakes
forsaking
forsook
forsaken

**fort** *noun*
forts

**forth★**

**fortieth**

**fortification** *noun*
fortifications

**fortify** *verb*
fortifies
fortifying
fortified

**fortnight** *noun*
fortnights

**fortnightly**

**fortress** *noun*
fortresses

**fortunate** *adjective*
fortunately

**fortune** *noun*
fortunes

**fortune-teller** *noun*
fortune-tellers

**forty** *noun*
forties

**forward** *adjective* and *adverb*

**forward** *noun*
forwards

**forwards** *adverb*

**fossil** *noun*
fossils

**fossilized**

**foster** *verb*
fosters
fostering
fostered

**foster child** *noun*
foster children

**foster parent** *noun*
foster parents

**fought** see **fight**

**foul**☆ *adjective*
fouler
foulest
foully

**foul**❂ *verb*
fouls
fouling
fouled

**foul**✛ *noun*
fouls

**foulness**

. . . . . . . . . . . . . . . . . . . . . . . . . . . . . . . . . . . . . . . . . . . . . . . . . . . . . . . .

★ You use **forth** in e.g. *to go forth.* **! fourth.**
☆ **Foul** means 'dirty' or 'disgusting'. **! fowl.**
❂ To **foul** is to break a rule in a game. **! fowl.**
✛ A **foul** is breaking a rule in a game. **! fowl.**

**found** *verb*
founds
founding
founded

**found** see **find**

**foundation** *noun*
foundations

**founder** *noun*
founders

**founder** *verb*
founders
foundering
foundered

**foundry** *noun*
foundries

**fountain** *noun*
fountains

**four** *noun*
fours

**fourteen** *noun*
fourteens

**fourteenth**

**fourth**★

**fourthly**

**fowl**☆ *noun*
fowl *or* fowls

**fox** *noun*
foxes

**fox** *verb*
foxes
foxing
foxed

**foxglove** *noun*
foxgloves

**foxy** *adjective*
foxier
foxiest

**foyer** *noun*
foyers

**fraction** *noun*
fractions

**fractionally**

**fracture** *verb*
fractures
fracturing
fractured

**fracture** *noun*
fractures

**fragile** *adjective*
fragilely

**fragility**

**fragment** *noun*
fragments

**fragmentary**

**fragmentation**

**fragrance** *noun*
fragrances

**fragrant**

**frail** *adjective*
frailer
frailest
frailly

**frailty** *noun*
frailties

**frame** *verb*
frames
framing
framed

**frame** *noun*
frames

**framework** *noun*
frameworks

**franc**☉ *noun*
francs

**franchise** *noun*
franchises

**frank**✢ *adjective*
franker
frankest
frankly

**frank**✱ *verb*
franks
franking
franked

**frankness**

**frantic** *adjective*
frantically

**fraud** *noun*
frauds

**fraudulent** *adjective*
fraudulently

**fraught**

**frayed**

**freak** *noun*
freaks

**freakish**

**freckle** *noun*
freckles

**freckled**

**free** *adjective*
freer
freest
freely

**free** *verb*
frees
freeing
freed

**freedom** *noun*
freedoms

**freehand** *adjective*

**freewheel** *verb*
freewheels
freewheeling
freewheeled

. . . . . . . . . . . . . . . . . . . . . . . . . . . . . . . . . . . . . . . . . . . . . . . . . . . .

★ You use **fourth** in e.g. *for the fourth time*. !**forth**.

☆ A **fowl** is a kind of bird. !**foul**.

☉ A **franc** is a unit of money in Switzerland. !**frank**.

✢ **Frank** means 'speaking honestly'. !**franc**.

✱ To **frank** is to mark a letter with a postmark. !**franc**.

a

**freeze** ★ *verb*
freezes
freezing
froze
frozen

**freezer** *noun*
freezers

**freight**

**freighter** *noun*
freighters

**frenzied**

**frenzy** *noun*
frenzies

**frequency** *noun*
frequencies

**frequent** *adjective*
frequently

**frequent** *verb*
frequents
frequenting
frequented

**fresh** *adjective*
fresher
freshest
freshly

**freshness**

**freshen** *verb*
freshens
freshening
freshened

**freshwater**

**fret** *verb*
frets
fretting
fretted

**fretful** *adjective*
fretfully

**fretsaw** *noun*
fretsaws

**fretwork**

**friar** *noun*
friars

**friary** *noun*
friaries

**friction**

**Friday** *noun*
Fridays

**fridge** *noun*
fridges

**friend** *noun*
friends

**friendless**

**friendliness**

**friendly** *adjective*
friendlier
friendliest

**friendship** *noun*
friendships

**frieze** ☆ *noun*
friezes

**frigate** *noun*
frigates

**fright** *noun*
frights

**frighten** *verb*
frightens
frightening
frightened

**frightful** *adjective*
frightfully

**frill** *noun*
frills

**frilled**

**frilly** *adjective*
frillier
frilliest

**fringe** *noun*
fringes

**fringed**

**frisk** *verb*
frisks
frisking
frisked

**friskiness**

**frisky** *adjective*
friskier
friskiest
friskily

**fritter** *verb*
fritters
frittering
frittered

**fritter** *noun*
fritters

**frivolous** *adjective*
frivolously

**frivolity** *noun*
frivolities

**frizzy** *adjective*
frizzier
frizziest

**fro** ✪

**frock** *noun*
frocks

**frog** *noun*
frogs

**frogman** *noun*
frogmen

**frolic** *noun*
frolics

**frolicsome**

**frolic** *verb*
frolics
frolicking
frolicked

**front** *noun*
fronts

**frontier** *noun*
frontiers

. . . . . . . . . . . . . . . . . . . . . . . . . . . . . . . . . . . . . . . . . . . . . . . . . . . . . . . .

★ To **freeze** is to be very cold. **! frieze**.
☆ A **frieze** is a strip of designs along a wall. **! freeze**.
✪ You use **fro** in *to and fro*.

98

**frost** *noun*
frosts

**frost** *verb*
frosts
frosting
frosted

**frostbite**

**frostbitten**

**frosty** *adjective*
frostier
frostiest

**froth** *noun*

**froth** *verb*
froths
frothing
frothed

**frothy** *adjective*
frothier
frothiest

**froth** *verb*
froths
frothing
frothed

**frown** *verb*
frowns
frowning
frowned

**frown** *noun*
frowns

**froze** see **freeze**

**frozen** see **freeze**

**frugal** *adjective*
frugally

**frugality**

**fruit** *noun*
fruit *or* fruits

**fruitful** *adjective*
fruitfully

**fruitless** *adjective*
fruitlessly

**fruity** *adjective*
fruitier
fruitiest

**frustrate** *verb*
frustrates
frustrating
frustrated

**frustration** *noun*
frustrations

**fry** *verb*
fries
frying
fried

**fudge**

**fuel** *noun*
fuels

**fuel** *verb*
fuels
fuelling
fuelled

**fug** *noun*
fugs

**fuggy** *adjective*
fuggier
fuggiest

**fugitive** *noun*
fugitives

**-ful**
*-ful* makes nouns for amounts, e.g. **handful**, **spoonful**. The plural of these words ends in *-fuls*, e.g. **handfuls**. *-ful* also makes adjectives, e.g. **graceful**, and when the adjective ends in *-y* following a consonant, you change the *y* to *i*, e.g. **beauty - beautiful**.

**fulcrum** *noun*
fulcra *or* fulcrums

**fulfil** *verb*
fulfils
fulfilling
fulfilled

**fulfilment**

**full** *adjective*
fully

**fullness**

**fumble** *verb*
fumbles
fumbling
fumbled

**fume** *verb*
fumes
fuming
fumed

**fumes** *plural noun*

**fun**

**function** *verb*
functions
functioning
functioned

**function** *noun*
functions

**functional** *adjective*
functionally

**fund** *noun*
funds

**fundamental** *adjective*
fundamentally

**funeral** *noun*
funerals

**fungus** *noun*
fungi

**funk** *verb*
funks
funking
funked

**funnel** *noun*
funnels

**funny** *adjective*
funnier
funniest
funnily

a
b
c
d
e
**f**
g
h
i
j
k
l
m
n
o
p
q
r
s
t
u
v
w
x
y
z

99

**fur**★ *noun*
furs

**furious** *adjective*
furiously

**furl** *verb*
furls
furling
furled

**furlong** *noun*
furlongs

**furnace** *noun*
furnaces

**furnish** *verb*
furnishes
furnishing
furnished

**furniture**

**furrow** *noun*
furrows

**furry** *adjective*
furrier
furriest

**further**☆ *adjective*

**further**○ *verb*
furthers
furthering
furthered

**furthermore**

**furthest**✢

**furtive** *adjective*
furtively

**fury** *noun*
furies

**fuse** *verb*
fuses
fusing
fused

**fuse** *noun*
fuses

**fuselage** *noun*
fuselages

**fusion** *noun*
fusions

**fuss** *verb*
fusses
fussing
fussed

**fuss** *noun*
fusses

**fussiness**

**fussy** *adjective*
fussier
fussiest
fussily

**futile** *adjective*
futilely

**futility**

**futon** *noun*
futons

**future**

**fuzz**

**fuzziness** *noun*

**fuzzy** *adjective*
fuzzier
fuzziest
fuzzily

# Gg

**gabardine** *noun*
gabardines

**gabble** *verb*
gabbles
gabbling
gabbled

**gable** *noun*
gables

**gabled**

**gadget** *noun*
gadgets

**Gaelic**

**gag** *verb*
gags
gagging
gagged

**gag** *noun*
gags

**gaiety**

**gaily**

**gain** *verb*
gains
gaining
gained

**gain** *noun*
gains

**gala** *noun*
galas

**galactic**

**galaxy** *noun*
galaxies

**gale** *noun*
gales

**gallant** *adjective*
gallantly

**gallantry**

**galleon**✳ *noun*
galleons

**gallery** *noun*
galleries

**galley** *noun*
galleys

....................................................

★ **Fur** is the hair of animals. **!** **fir**.

☆ You use **further** in e.g. *We need further information.* See **farther**.

○ To **further** something is to make it progress.

✢ You use **furthest** in e.g. *Who has read the furthest?* See **farthest**.

✳ A **galleon** is a type of ship. **!** **gallon**.

**gallon**★ *noun*
gallons

**gallop** *verb*
gallops
galloping
galloped

**gallop** *noun*
gallops

**gallows**

**galore**

**galvanize** *verb*
galvanizes
galvanizing
galvanized

**gamble** *verb*
gambles
gambling
gambled

**gamble** *noun*
gambles

**gambler** *noun*
gamblers

**game** *noun*
games

**gamekeeper** *noun*
gamekeepers

**gammon**

**gander** *noun*
ganders

**gang** *noun*
gangs

**gang** *verb*
gangs
ganging
ganged

**gangplank** *noun*
gangplanks

**gangster** *noun*
gangsters

**gangway** *noun*
gangways

**gaol** *noun* see **jail**

**gaoler** *noun* see **jailer**

**gap** *noun*
gaps

**gape** *verb*
gapes
gaping
gaped

**garage** *noun*
garages

**garbage**

**garden** *noun*
gardens

**gardener** *noun*
gardeners

**gardening**

**gargle** *verb*
gargles
gargling
gargled

**gargoyle** *noun*
gargoyles

**garland** *noun*
garlands

**garlic**

**garment** *noun*
garments

**garnish** *verb*
garnishes
garnishing
garnished

**garrison** *noun*
garrisons

**garter** *noun*
garters

**gas** *noun*
gases

**gas** *verb*
gasses
gassing
gassed

**gaseous**

**gash** *noun*
gashes

**gasket** *noun*
gaskets

**gasoline**

**gasometer** *noun*
gasometers

**gasp** *verb*
gasps
gasping
gasped

**gasp** *noun*
gasps

**gastric**

**gate** *noun*
gates

**gateau**☆ *noun*
gateaux

**gateway** *noun*
gateways

**gather** *verb*
gathers
gathering
gathered

**gathering** *noun*
gatherings

**gaudy** *adjective*
gaudier
gaudiest

**gauge** *verb*
gauges
gauging
gauged

**gauge** *noun*
gauges

**gaunt**

**gauntlet** *noun*
gauntlets

**gauze**

**gave** see **give**

---

★ A **gallon** is a measurement of liquid. **!galleon**.
☆ **Gateau** is a French word used in English. It means 'a rich cream cake'.

a
b
c
d
e
f
**g**
h
i
j
k
l
m
n
o
p
q
r
s
t
u
v
w
x
y
z

a
b
c
d
e
f
**g**
h
i
j
k
l
m
n
o
p
q
r
s
t
u
v
w
x
y
z

**gay** adjective
gayer
gayest

**gaze** verb
gazes
gazing
gazed

**gaze** noun
gazes

**gazetteer** noun
gazetteers

**gear** noun
gears

**geese** see **goose**

**Geiger counter** noun
Geiger counters

**gel** noun
gels

**gelatine**

**gelding** noun
geldings

**gem** noun
gems

**gender** noun
genders

**gene** noun
genes

**genealogy** noun
genealogies

**general** adjective
generally

**general** noun
generals

**generalization** noun
generalizations

**generalize** verb
generalizes
generalizing
generalized

**generate** verb
generates
generating
generated

**generation** noun
generations

**generator** noun
generators

**generosity**

**generous** adjective
generously

**genetic** adjective
genetically

**genetics** plural noun

**genial** adjective
genially

**genie** noun
genies

**genitals** plural noun

**genius** noun
geniuses

**gent** noun
gents

**gentle** adjective
gentler
gentlest
gently

**gentleman** noun
gentlemen

**gentlemanly**

**gentleness**

**genuine** adjective
genuinely

**genus** noun
genera

**geo-**
geo- means 'earth',
e.g. **geography** ( the
study of the earth).

**geographer**

**geographical**
adjective
geographically

**geography**

**geological** adjective
geologically

**geologist**

**geology**

**geometric** adjective
geometrically

**geometrical** adjective
geometrically

**geometry**

**geranium** noun
geraniums

**gerbil** noun
gerbils

**germ** noun
germs

**germinate** verb
germinates
germinating
germinated

**germination**

**gesticulate** verb
gesticulates
gesticulating
gesticulated

**gesture** noun
gestures

**get** verb
gets
getting
got

**getaway** noun
getaways

**geyser** noun
geysers

**ghastly** adjective
ghastlier
ghastliest

**ghetto** noun
ghettos

**ghost** noun
ghosts

**ghostly** adjective
ghostlier
ghostliest

**ghoulish** adjective
ghoulishly

**giant** noun
giants

**giddiness**

**giddy** *adjective*
giddier
giddiest
giddily

**gift** *noun*
gifts

**gifted**

**gigantic** *adjective*
gigantically

**giggle** *verb*
giggles
giggling
giggled

**giggle** *noun*
giggles

**gild★** *verb*
gilds
gilding
gilded

**gills** *plural noun*

**gimmick** *noun*
gimmicks

**gin**

**ginger**

**gingerbread**

**gingerly**

**gingery**

**gipsy** *noun* see **gypsy**

**giraffe** *noun*
giraffes

**girder** *noun*
girders

**girdle** *noun*
girdles

**girl** *noun*
girls

**girlfriend** *noun*
girlfriends

**girlhood**

**girlish**

**giro☆** *noun*
giros

**girth** *noun*
girths

**gist**

**give** *verb*
gives
giving
gave
given

**given** see **give**

**giver** *noun*
givers

**glacial**

**glacier** *noun*
glaciers

**glad** *adjective*
gladder
gladdest
gladly

**gladden** *verb*
gladdens
gladdening
gladdened

**gladiator** *noun*
gladiators

**gladness**

**glamorize** *verb*
glamorizes
glamorizing
glamorized

**glamorous** *adjective*
glamorously

**glamour**

**glance** *verb*
glances
glancing
glanced

**glance** *noun*
glances

**gland** *noun*
glands

**glandular**

**glare** *verb*
glares
glaring
glared

**glare** *noun*
glares

**glass** *noun*
glasses

**glassful** *noun*
glassfuls

**glassy** *adjective*
glassier
glassiest

**glaze** *verb*
glazes
glazing
glazed

**glaze** *noun*
glazes

**glazier** *noun*
glaziers

**gleam** *noun*
gleams

**gleam** *verb*
gleams
gleaming
gleamed

**glee**

**gleeful** *adjective*
gleefully

**glen** *noun*
glens

**glide** *verb*
glides
gliding
glided

**glider** *noun*
gliders

**glimmer** *verb*
glimmers
glimmering
glimmered

a
b
c
d
e
f
**g**
h
i
j
k
l
m
n
o
p
q
r
s
t
u
v
w
x
y
z

★ To **gild** something is to cover it with gold. **!** **guild**.
☆ A **giro** is a system of paying money. **!** **gyro**.

103

**glimmer** noun
glimmers

**glimpse** verb
glimpses
glimpsing
glimpsed

**glimpse** noun
glimpses

**glint** verb
glints
glinting
glinted

**glint** noun
glints

**glisten** verb
glistens
glistening
glistened

**glitter** verb
glitters
glittering
glittered

**gloat** verb
gloats
gloating
gloated

**global** adjective
globally

**globe** noun
globes

**gloom**

**gloominess**

**gloomy** adjective
gloomier
gloomiest
gloomily

**glorification**

**glorify** verb
glorifies
glorifying
glorified

**glorious** adjective
gloriously

**glory** noun
glories

**gloss** noun
glosses

**glossary** noun
glossaries

**glossy** adjective
glossier
glossiest

**glove** noun
gloves

**glow** verb
glows
glowing
glowed

**glow** noun
glows

**glower** verb
glowers
glowering
glowered

**glow-worm** noun
glow-worms

**glucose**

**glue** noun
glues

**glue** verb
glues
gluing
glued

**gluey** adjective
gluier
gluiest

**glum** adjective
glummer
glummest
glumly

**glutton** noun
gluttons

**gluttonous**

**gluttony**

**gnarled**

**gnash**★ verb
gnashes
gnashing
gnashed

**gnat**★ noun
gnats

**gnaw**★ verb
gnaws
gnawing
gnawed

**gnome**★ noun
gnomes

**go** verb
goes
going
went
gone

**go** noun
goes

**goal** noun
goals

**goalie** noun
goalies

**goalkeeper** noun
goalkeepers

**goalpost** noun
goalposts

**goat** noun
goats

**gobble** verb
gobbles
gobbling
gobbled

**gobbledegook**

**goblet** noun
goblets

**goblin** noun
goblins

**God**☆

. . . . . . . . . . . . . . . . . . . . . . . . . . . . . . . . . . . . . . . . . . . . . . . . . . . . . . . . . . . .

★ In these words beginning with **gn-** the 'g' is silent.
☆ You use a capital G when you mean the Christian, Jewish, and Muslim creator.

**god**★ *noun*
 gods

**godchild** *noun*
 godchildren

**goddess** *noun*
 goddesses

**godparent** *noun*
 godparents

**goggles** *plural noun*

**gold**

**golden**

**goldfinch** *noun*
 goldfinches

**goldfish** *noun*
 goldfish

**golf**

**golfer** *noun*
 golfers

**golfing**

**gondola** *noun*
 gondolas

**gondolier** *noun*
 gondoliers

**gone** see **go**

**gong** *noun*
 gongs

**good** *adjective*
 better
 best

**goodbye** *interjection*

**Good Friday**

**good-looking**

**good-natured**

**goodness**

**goods** *plural noun*

**goodwill**

**gooey** *adjective*
 gooier
 gooiest

**goose** *noun*
 geese

**gooseberry** *noun*
 gooseberries

**gore** *verb*
 gores
 goring
 gored

**gorge** *noun*
 gorges

**gorgeous** *adjective*
 gorgeously

**gorilla**☆ *noun*
 gorillas

**gorse**

**gory** *adjective*
 gorier
 goriest

**gosling** *noun*
 goslings

**gospel** *noun*
 gospels

**gossip** *verb*
 gossips
 gossiping
 gossiped

**gossip** *noun*
 gossips

**got** see **get**

**gouge** *verb*
 gouges
 gouging
 gouged

**gourd** *noun*
 gourds

**govern** *verb*
 governs
 governing
 governed

**government** *noun*
 governments

**governor** *noun*
 governors

**gown** *noun*
 gowns

**grab** *verb*
 grabs
 grabbing
 grabbed

**grace** *noun*
 graces

**graceful** *adjective*
 gracefully

**gracefulness**

**gracious** *adjective*
 graciously

**grade** *noun*
 grades

**grade** *verb*
 grades
 grading
 graded

**gradient** *noun*
 gradients

**gradual** *adjective*
 gradually

**graduate** *noun*
 graduates

**graduate** *verb*
 graduates
 graduating
 graduated

**graduation**

**graffiti** *plural noun*

**grain** *noun*
 grains

**grainy** *adjective*
 grainier
 grainiest

**gram** *noun*
 grams

a
b
c
d
e
f
**g**
h
i
j
k
l
m
n
o
p
q
r
s
t
u
v
w
x
y
z

★ You use a small g when you mean any male divine being.
☆ A **gorilla** is a large ape. **!guerrilla**.

105

a
b
c
d
e
f
**g**
h
i
j
k
l
m
n
o
p
q
r
s
t
u
v
w
x
y
z

**grammar** *noun*
grammars

**grammatical**
*adjective*
grammatically

**gramophone** *noun*
gramophones

**grand** *adjective*
grander
grandest
grandly

**grandad** *noun*
grandads

**grandchild** *noun*
grandchildren

**grandeur**

**grandfather** *noun*
grandfathers

**grandma** *noun*
grandmas

**grandmother** *noun*
grandmothers

**grandpa** *noun*
grandpas

**grandparent** *noun*
grandparents

**grandstand** *noun*
grandstands

**granite**

**granny** *noun*
grannies

**grant** *verb*
grants
granting
granted

**grant** *noun*
grants

**granulated**

**grape** *noun*
grapes

**grapefruit** *noun*
grapefruit

**grapevine** *noun*
grapevines

**graph** *noun*
graphs

**graphic** *adjective*
graphically

**graphics** *plural noun*

**graphite**

**-graphy**
*-graphy* makes words
for subjects of study,
e.g. **geography** ( the
study of the earth). A
**bibliography** is a list
of books on a subject,
and the plural is
**bibliographies**.

**grapple** *verb*
grapples
grappling
grappled

**grasp** *verb*
grasps
grasping
grasped

**grasp** *noun*
grasps

**grass** *noun*
grasses

**grasshopper** *noun*
grasshoppers

**grassy** *adjective*
grassier
grassiest

**grate**★ *verb*
grates
grating
grated

**grate**☆ *noun*
grates

**grateful** *adjective*
gratefully

**grating** *noun*
gratings

**gratitude**

**grave** *noun*
graves

**grave** *adjective*
graver
gravest
gravely

**gravel**

**gravelled**

**gravestone** *noun*
gravestones

**graveyard** *noun*
graveyards

**gravitation**

**gravitational**

**gravity**

**gravy**

**graze** *verb*
grazes
grazing
grazed

**graze** *noun*
grazes

**grease**

**greasy** *adjective*
greasier
greasiest

**great** *adjective*
greater
greatest
greatly

**greatness**

**greed**

**greediness**

. . . . . . . . . . . . . . . . . . . . . . . . . . . . . . . . . . . . . . . . . . . . . . . . . .

★ To **grate** something is to shred it. **!** **great**.
☆ A **grate** is a fireplace. **!** **great**.

**greedy** *adjective*
greedier
greediest
greedily

**green** *adjective* and *noun*
greener
greenest

**greenery**

**greengage** *noun*
greengages

**greengrocer** *noun*
greengrocers

**greengrocery** *noun*
greengroceries

**greenhouse** *noun*
greenhouses

**greens** *plural noun*

**greet** *verb*
greets
greeting
greeted

**greeting** *noun*
greetings

**grenade** *noun*
grenades

**grew** see **grow**

**grey** *adjective* and *noun*
greyer
greyest

**greyhound** *noun*
greyhounds

**grid** *noun*
grids

**grief**

**grievance** *noun*
grievances

**grieve** *verb*
grieves
grieving
grieved

**grievous★** *adjective*
grievously

**grill** *verb*
grills
grilling
grilled

**grill** *noun*
grills

**grim** *adjective*
grimmer
grimmest
grimly

**grimace** *noun*
grimaces

**grime**

**grimness**

**grimy** *adjective*
grimier
grimiest

**grin** *noun*
grins

**grin** *verb*
grins
grinning
grinned

**grind** *verb*
grinds
grinding
ground

**grinder** *noun*
grinders

**grindstone** *noun*
grindstones

**grip** *verb*
grips
gripping
gripped

**grip** *noun*
grips

**grisly**☆ *adjective*
grislier
grisliest

**gristle**

**gristly** *adjective*
gristlier
gristliest

**grit** *verb*
grits
gritting
gritted

**grit** *noun*

**gritty** *adjective*
grittier
grittiest

**grizzly**✪ *adjective*

**groan** *verb*
groans
groaning
groaned

**groan** *noun*
groans

**grocer** *noun*
grocers

**grocery** *noun*
groceries

**groggy** *adjective*
groggier
groggiest

**groin** *noun*
groins

**groom** *verb*
grooms
grooming
groomed

**groom** *noun*
grooms

**groove** *noun*
grooves

. . . . . . . . . . . . . . . . . . . . . . . . . . . . . . . . . . . . . . . . . . . . . . . . .
★ Note that this word does not end *-ious*.
☆ **Grisly** means 'revolting' or 'horrible'. **!grizzly**.
✪ You use **grizzly** in *grizzly bear*. **!grisly**.

a
b
c
d
e
f
**g**
h
i
j
k
l
m
n
o
p
q
r
s
t
u
v
w
x
y
z

107

a
b
c
d
e
f
**g**
h
i
j
k
l
m
n
o
p
q
r
s
t
u
v
w
x
y
z

**grope** verb
  gropes
  groping
  groped

**gross** adjective
  grosser
  grossest
  grossly

**gross** noun
  gross

**grossness**

**grotesque**★ adjective
  grotesquely

**grotty** adjective
  grottier
  grottiest

**ground** noun
  grounds

**ground** see **grind**

**grounded**

**grounds** plural noun

**groundsheet** noun
  groundsheets

**groundsman** noun
  groundsmen

**group** noun
  groups

**group** verb
  groups
  grouping
  grouped

**grouse** verb
  grouses
  grousing
  groused

**grouse** noun
  grouse

**grove** noun
  groves

**grovel** verb
  grovels
  grovelling
  grovelled

**grow** verb
  grows
  growing
  grew
  grown

**grower** noun
  growers

**growl** verb
  growls
  growling
  growled

**growl** noun
  growls

**grown-up** noun
  grown-ups

**growth** noun
  growths

**grub** noun
  grubs

**grubby** adjective
  grubbier
  grubbiest

**grudge** verb
  grudges
  grudging
  grudged

**grudge** noun
  grudges

**grudgingly**

**gruelling**

**gruesome**

**gruff** adjective
  gruffer
  gruffest
  gruffly

**grumble** verb
  grumbles
  grumbling
  grumbled

**grumbler** noun
  grumblers

**grumpiness**

**grumpy** adjective
  grumpier
  grumpiest
  grumpily

**grunt** verb
  grunts
  grunting
  grunted

**grunt** noun
  grunts

**guarantee** noun
  guarantees

**guarantee** verb
  guarantees
  guaranteeing
  guaranteed

**guard** verb
  guards
  guarding
  guarded

**guard** noun
  guards

**guardian** noun
  guardians

**guardianship**

**guerrilla**☆ noun
  guerrillas

**guess** verb
  guesses
  guessing
  guessed

**guess** noun
  guesses

**guesswork**

. . . . . . . . . . . . . . . . . . . . . . . . . . . . . . . . . . . . . . . . . . . . . . . . .

★ **Grotesque** means 'strange' and 'ugly'. It sounds like 'grotesk'.
☆ A **guerrilla** is a member of a small army. **!gorilla**.

108

**guest** noun
  guests

**guidance**

**guide** verb
  guides
  guiding
  guided

**guide** noun
  guides

**guidelines** plural noun

**guild**★ noun
  guilds

**guillotine** noun
  guillotines

**guilt**

**guilty** adjective
  guiltier
  guiltiest

**guinea** noun
  guineas

**guinea pig** noun
  guinea pigs

**guitar** noun
  guitars

**guitarist**

**gulf** noun
  gulfs

**gull** noun
  gulls

**gullet** noun
  gullets

**gullible**

**gully** noun
  gullies

**gulp** verb
  gulps
  gulping
  gulped

**gulp** noun
  gulps

**gum** noun
  gums

**gum** verb
  gums
  gumming
  gummed

**gummy** adjective
  gummier
  gummiest

**gun** noun
  guns

**gun** verb
  guns
  gunning
  gunned

**gunboat** noun
  gunboats

**gunfire**

**gunman** noun
  gunmen

**gunner** noun
  gunners

**gunnery**

**gunpowder**

**gunshot** noun
  gunshots

**gurdwara**☆ noun
  gurdwaras

**gurgle** verb
  gurgles
  gurgling
  gurgled

**guru** noun
  gurus

**Guru Granth Sahib**⊙

**gush** verb
  gushes
  gushing
  gushed

**gust** noun
  gusts

**gusty** adjective
  gustier
  gustiest

**gut** noun
  guts

**gut** verb
  guts
  gutting
  gutted

**gutter** noun
  gutters

**guy** noun
  guys

**guzzle** verb
  guzzles
  guzzling
  guzzled

**gym** noun
  gyms

**gymkhana** noun
  gymkhanas

**gymnasium** noun
  gymnasiums

**gymnast** noun
  gymnasts

**gymnastics** plural noun

**gypsy** noun
  gypsies

**gyro**✣ noun
  gyros

**gyroscope** noun
  gyroscopes

a b c d e f **g** h i j k l m n o p q r s t u v w x y z

★ A **guild** is an organization of people. **!gild**.
☆ A Sikh place of worship.
⊙ The holy book of Sikhs.
✣ A **gyro** is type of compass. **!giro**.

109

a
b
c
d
e
f
g

**h**

i
j
k
l
m
n
o
p
q
r
s
t
u
v

# Hh

**habit** noun
habits

**habitat** noun
habitats

**habitual** adjective
habitually

**hack** verb
hacks
hacking
hacked

**hacker** noun
hackers

**hacksaw** noun
hacksaws

**had** see **has**

**haddock** noun
haddock

**hadn't** verb

**hag** noun
hags

**haggard**

**haggis** noun
haggises

**haggle** verb
haggles
haggling
haggled

**haiku**★ noun
haiku

**hail** verb
hails
hailing
hailed

**hail**

**hailstone** noun
hailstones

**hair**☆ noun
hairs

**hairbrush** noun
hairbrushes

**haircut** noun
haircuts

**hairdresser** noun
hairdressers

**hairpin** noun
hairpins

**hair-raising**

**hairstyle** noun
hairstyles

**hairy** adjective
hairier
hairiest

**hake** noun
hake

**halal**

**half** adjective and noun
halves

**half-baked**

**half-hearted** adjective
half-heartedly

**half-life** noun
half-lives

**half-mast**

**halfpenny**◊ noun
halfpennies or
halfpence

**half-term** noun
half-terms

**half-time** noun
half-times

**halfway**

**halibut** noun
halibut

**hall**✦ noun
halls

**hallo**

**Halloween**✱

**hallucination** noun
hallucinations

**halo** noun
haloes

**halt** verb
halts
halting
halted

**halt** noun
halts

**halter** noun
halters

**halting** adjective
haltingly

**halve** verb
halves
halving
halved

**halves** see **half**

**ham** noun
hams

**hamburger** noun
hamburgers

**hammer** noun
hammers

**hammer** verb
hammers
hammering
hammered

**hammock** noun
hammocks

w
x
y
z

. . . . . . . . . . . . . . . . . . . . . . . . . . . . . . . . . . . . . . . . . . . . . . . . . .

★ A Japanese poem.

☆ **Hair** is the covering on the head. **!** **hare**.

◊ You use **halfpennies** when you mean several coins and **halfpence** for a sum of money.

✦ A **hall** is a large space in a building. **!** **haul**.

✱ You will also see this word spelt *Hallowe´en*.

110

**hamper** *verb*
hampers
hampering
hampered

**hamper** *noun*
hampers

**hamster** *noun*
hamsters

**hand** *noun*
hands

**hand** *verb*
hands
handing
handed

**handbag** *noun*
handbags

**handbook** *noun*
handbooks

**handcuffs** *plural noun*

**handful** *noun*
handfuls

**handicap** *noun*
handicaps

**handicapped**

**handicraft** *noun*
handicrafts

**handiwork**

**handkerchief** *noun*
handkerchiefs

**handle** *noun*
handles

**handle** *verb*
handles
handling
handled

**handlebars** *plural noun*

**handrail** *noun*
handrails

**handsome** *adjective*
handsomer
handsomest
handsomely

**hands-on**

**handstand** *noun*
handstands

**handwriting**

**handwritten**

**handy** *adjective*
handier
handiest

**handyman** *noun*
handymen

**hang** *verb*
hangs
hanging
hung

**hangar**★ *noun*
hangars

**hanger**☆ *noun*
hangers

**hang-glider** *noun*
hang-gliders

**hang-gliding**

**hangman** *noun*
hangmen

**hangover** *noun*
hangovers

**hank** *noun*
hanks

**hanker** *verb*
hankers
hankering
hankered

**hanky** *noun*
hankies

**Hanukkah**◯

**haphazard** *adjective*
haphazardly

**happen** *verb*
happens
happening
happened

**happening** *noun*
happenings

**happiness**

**happy** *adjective*
happier
happiest
happily

**happy-go-lucky**

**harass**✢ *verb*
harasses
harassing
harassed

**harassment**

**harbour** *noun*
harbours

**harbour** *verb*
harbours
harbouring
harboured

**hard** *adjective*
harder
hardest

**hard** *adverb*
harder
hardest

**hardboard**

**hard-boiled**

**hard disk** *noun*
hard disks

**harden** *verb*
hardens
hardening
hardened

**hardly**

a
b
c
d
e
f
g
**h**
i
j
k
l
m
n
o
p
q
r
s
t
u
v
w
x
y
z

. . . . . . . . . . . . . . . . . . . . . . . . . . . . . . . . . . . . . . . . . . . . . . . . . . . .

★ A **hangar** is a shed for aircraft. **!hanger**.
☆ A **hanger** is a thing for hanging clothes on. **!hangar**.
◯ A Jewish festival.
✢ Note that there is only one r in **harass** and **harassment**.

111

a
b
c
d
e
f
g
**h**
i
j
k
l
m
n
o
p
q
r
s
t
u
v
w
x
y
z

**hardness**
**hardship** *noun*
  hardships
**hardware**
**hardwood** *noun*
  hardwoods
**hardy** *adjective*
  hardier
  hardiest
**hare**★ *noun*
  hares
**hark** *verb*
  harks
  harking
  harked
**harm** *verb*
  harms
  harming
  harmed
**harm** *noun*
**harmful** *adjective*
  harmfully
**harmless** *adjective*
  harmlessly
**harmonic**
**harmonica** *noun*
  harmonicas
**harmonious** *adjective*
  harmoniously
**harmonization**
**harmonize** *verb*
  harmonizes
  harmonizing
  harmonized
**harmony** *noun*
  harmonies
**harness** *verb*
  harnesses
  harnessing
  harnessed
**harness** *noun*
  harnesses

**harp** *noun*
  harps
**harp** *verb*
  harps
  harping
  harped
**harpist** *noun*
  harpists
**harpoon** *noun*
  harpoons
**harpsichord** *noun*
  harpsichords
**harrow** *noun*
  harrows
**harsh** *adjective*
  harsher
  harshest
  harshly
**harshness**
**harvest** *noun*
  harvests
**harvest** *verb*
  harvests
  harvesting
  harvested
**hash** *noun*
  hashes
**hasn't** *verb*
**hassle** *noun*
  hassles
**haste**
**hasten** *verb*
  hastens
  hastening
  hastened
**hastiness**
**hasty** *adjective*
  hastier
  hastiest
  hastily

**hatch** *verb*
  hatches
  hatching
  hatched
**hatch** *noun*
  hatches
**hatchback** *noun*
  hatchbacks
**hatchet** *noun*
  hatchets
**hate** *verb*
  hates
  hating
  hated
**hate** *noun*
  hates
**hateful** *adjective*
  hatefully
**hatred**
**hat trick** *noun*
  hat tricks
**haughtiness**
**haughty** *adjective*
  haughtier
  haughtiest
  haughtily
**haul**☆ *verb*
  hauls
  hauling
  hauled
**haul** *noun*
  hauls
**haunt** *verb*
  haunts
  haunting
  haunted
**have** *verb*
  has
  having
  had
**haven** *noun*
  havens

. . . . . . . . . . . . . . . . . . . . . . . . . . . . . . . . . . . . . . . . . . . . . . . . . . . . . . . . . .
★ A **hare** is an animal like a large rabbit. **!** hair.
☆ To **haul** is to pull something heavy. **!** hall.

**haven't** *verb*

**haversack** *noun*
haversacks

**hawk** *noun*
hawks

**hawk** *verb*
hawks
hawking
hawked

**hawker** *noun*
hawkers

**hawthorn** *noun*
hawthorns

**hay fever**

**haymaking**

**haystack** *noun*
haystacks

**hazard** *noun*
hazards

**hazardous**

**haze** *noun*
hazes

**hazel** *noun*
hazels

**haziness**

**hazy** *adjective*
hazier
haziest
hazily

**H-bomb** *noun*
H-bombs

**head** *noun*
heads

**head** *verb*
heads
heading
headed

**headache** *noun*
headaches

**headdress** *noun*
headdresses

**header** *noun*
headers

**heading** *noun*
headings

**headland** *noun*
headlands

**headlight** *noun*
headlights

**headline** *noun*
headlines

**headlong**

**headmaster** *noun*
headmasters

**headmistress** *noun*
headmistresses

**head-on**

**headphones**

**headquarters** *noun*
headquarters

**headteacher** *noun*
headteachers

**headway**

**heal** *verb*
heals
healing
healed

**healer** *noun*
healers

**health**

**healthiness**

**healthy** *adjective*
healthier
healthiest
healthily

**heap** *verb*
heaps
heaping
heaped

**heap** *noun*
heaps

**hear★** *verb*
hears
hearing
heard

**hearing** *noun*
hearings

**hearse** *noun*
hearses

**heart** *noun*
hearts

**hearth** *noun*
hearths

**heartiness**

**heartless**

**hearty** *adjective*
heartier
heartiest
heartily

**heat** *verb*
heats
heating
heated

**heat** *noun*
heats

**heater** *noun*
heaters

**heath** *noun*
heaths

**heathen** *noun*
heathens

**heather**

**heatwave** *noun*
heatwaves

**heave☆** *verb*
heaves
heaving
heaved
hove

**heaven**

**heavenly**

**heaviness**

a
b
c
d
e
f
g
**h**
i
j
k
l
m
n
o
p
q
r
s
t
u
v
w
x
y
z

★ You use **hear** in e.g. *I can't hear you.* **!** **here**.
☆ You use **hove** in e.g. *the ship hove to.*

113

a   **heavy** *adjective*
    heavier
b   heaviest
    heavily
c   **heavyweight** *noun*
    heavyweights
d   **Hebrew**
e   **hectare** *noun*
    hectares
f   **hectic** *adjective*
    hectically
g   **he'd** *verb*
**h**  **hedge** *noun*
    hedges
i   **hedge** *verb*
    hedges
j   hedging
    hedged
k   **hedgehog** *noun*
    hedgehogs
l   **hedgerow** *noun*
    hedgerows
m
    **heed** *verb*
n   heeds
    heeding
o   heeded
    **heed** *noun*
p   **heedless**
q   **heel** *noun*
    heels
r   **heel** *verb*
    heels
s   heeling
    heeled
t   **hefty** *adjective*
    heftier
u   heftiest
    **heifer** *noun*
v   heifers
w   **height** *noun*
    heights
x

**heighten** *verb*
heightens
heightening
heightened

**heir**★ *noun*
heirs

**heiress** *noun*
heiresses

**held** see **hold**

**helicopter** *noun*
helicopters

**helium**

**helix** *noun*
helices

**hell**

**he'll** *verb*

**hellish** *adjective*
hellishly

**hello**

**helm** *noun*
helms

**helmsman** *noun*
helmsmen

**helmet** *noun*
helmets

**helmeted**

**help** *verb*
helps
helping
helped

**help** *noun*
helps

**helper** *noun*
helpers

**helpful** *adjective*
helpfully

**helping** *noun*
helpings

**helpless** *adjective*
helplessly

**helter-skelter** *noun*
helter-skelters

**hem** *noun*
hems

**hem** *verb*
hems
hemming
hemmed

**hemisphere** *noun*
hemispheres

**hemp**

**hence**

**henceforth**

**herald** *noun*
heralds

**herald** *verb*
heralds
heralding
heralded

**heraldic**

**heraldry**

**herb** *noun*
herbs

**herbal**

**herbivore** *noun*
herbivores

**herd** *noun*
herds

**herd**☆ *verb*
herds
herding
herded

**here**○

**hereditary**

**heredity**

**heritage** *noun*
heritages

**hermit** *noun*
hermits

**hermitage**

. . . . . . . . . . . . . . . . . . . . . . . . . . . . . . . . . . . . . . . . . . . . . . . . . . . . . . . . . . . .

y   ★ You do not pronounce the 'h' in **heir** (sounds like *air*).
    ☆ A **herd** is a group of sheep. **!heard**.
z   ○ You use **here** in e.g. *come here*. **!hear**.

**hero** *noun*
heroes
**heroic** *adjective*
heroically
**heroin**★ *noun*
**heroine**☆ *noun*
heroines
**heroism**
**heron** *noun*
herons
**herring** *noun*
herring
herrings
**hers**✪
**herself**
**he`s** *verb*
**hesitant** *adjective*
hesitantly
**hesitate** *verb*
hesitates
hesitating
hesitated
**hesitation**
**hexagon** *noun*
hexagons
**hexagonal**
**hibernate** *verb*
hibernates
hibernating
hibernated
**hibernation**
**hiccup** *noun*
hiccups
**hide** *verb*
hides
hiding
hidden
hid
hidden

**hide-and-seek**
**hideous** *adjective*
hideously
**hideout** *noun*
hideouts
**hiding** *noun*
hidings
**hieroglyphics** *plural noun*
**hi-fi** *noun*
hi-fis
**higgledy-piggledy**
**high** *adjective*
higher
highest
**highland** *adjective*
**highlands** *plural noun*
**highlander** *noun*
highlanders
**highlight** *noun*
highlights
**highlighter** *noun*
highlighters
**highly**
**Highness** *noun*
Highnesses
**high-rise**
**highway** *noun*
highways
**highwayman** *noun*
highwaymen
**hijack** *verb*
hijacks
hijacking
hijacked
**hijacker** *noun*
hijackers

**hike** *verb*
hikes
hiking
hiked
**hike** *noun*
hikes
**hiker** *noun*
hikers
**hilarious** *adjective*
hilariously
**hilarity**
**hill** *noun*
hills
**hillside** *noun*
hillsides
**hilly** *adjective*
hillier
hilliest
**hilt** *noun*
hilts
**himself**
**hind** *adjective*
**hind** *noun*
hinds
**hinder** *verb*
hinders
hindering
hindered
**Hindi**
**hindrance** *noun*
hindrances
**Hindu** *noun*
Hindus
**hinge** *noun*
hinges
**hinge** *verb*
hinges
hinging
hinged

a
b
c
d
e
f
g
**h**
i
j
k
l
m
n
o
p
q
r
s
t
u
v
w
x
y
z

. . . . . . . . . . . . . . . . . . . . . . . . . . . . . . . . . . . . . . . . . . . . . . .

★ **Heroin** is a drug. **!heroine**.
☆ A **heroine** is a woman or girl in a story. **!heroin**.
✪ You use **hers** in e.g. *the book is hers*. Note that there is no apostrophe in this word.

115

a
b
c
d
e
f
g
**h**
i
j
k
l
m
n
o
p
q
r
s
t
u
v
w
x
y
z

**hint** *noun*
　hints

**hint** *verb*
　hints
　hinting
　hinted

**hip** *noun*
　hips

**hippo** *noun*
　hippos

**hippopotamus** *noun*
　hippopotamuses

**hire** *verb*
　hires
　hiring
　hired

**hiss** *verb*
　hisses
　hissing
　hissed

**histogram** *noun*
　histograms

**historian** *noun*
　historians

**historic**

**historical** *adjective*
　historically

**history** *noun*
　histories

**hit** *verb*
　hits
　hitting
　hit

**hit** *noun*
　hits

**hitch** *verb*
　hitches
　hitching
　hitched

**hitch** *noun*
　hitches

**hitch-hike** *verb*
　hitch-hikes
　hitch-hiking
　hitch-hiked

**hitch-hiker** *noun*
　hitch-hikers

**hi-tech**

**hither**

**hitherto**

**hive** *noun*
　hives

**hoard** *verb*
　hoards
　hoarding
　hoarded

**hoard**★ *noun*
　hoards

**hoarder** *noun*
　hoarders

**hoarding** *noun*
　hoardings

**hoar frost**

**hoarse**☆ *adjective*
　hoarser
　hoarsest

**hoax** *verb*
　hoaxes
　hoaxing
　hoaxed

**hoax** *noun*
　hoaxes

**hobble** *verb*
　hobbles
　hobbling
　hobbled

**hobby** *noun*
　hobbies

**hockey**

**hoe** *noun*
　hoes

**hoe** *verb*
　hoes
　hoeing
　hoed

**hog** *noun*
　hogs

**hog** *verb*
　hogs
　hogging
　hogged

**Hogmanay**

**hoist** *verb*
　hoists
　hoisting
　hoisted

**hold** *verb*
　holds
　holding
　held

**hold** *noun*
　holds

**holdall** *noun*
　holdalls

**holder** *noun*
　holders

**hold-up** *noun*
　hold-ups

**hole**✪ *noun*
　holes

**holey**✢ *adjective*

**Holi**✷

**holiday** *noun*
　holidays

**holiness**

**hollow** *adjective* and
　*adverb*

. . . . . . . . . . . . . . . . . . . . . . . . . . . . . . . . . . . . . . . . . . . . . . . . . . . . . .

★ A **hoard** is a secret store. **!** horde.
☆ A **hoarse** voice is rough or croaking. **!** horse.
✪ A **hole** is a gap or opening. **!** whole.
✢ **Holey** means 'full of holes'. **!** holy.
✷ A Hindu festival.

**hollow** *verb*
hollows
hollowing
hollowed

**hollow** *noun*
hollows

**holly**

**holocaust** *noun*
holocausts

**hologram** *noun*
holograms

**holster** *noun*
holsters

**holy**★ *adjective*
holier
holiest

**home** *noun*
homes

**home** *verb*
homes
homing
homed

**homeless**

**homely**

**home-made**

**homesick**

**homesickness**

**homestead** *noun*
homesteads

**homeward** *adjective*

**homewards** *adjective*
and *adverb*

**homework**

**homing**

**homosexual**
*adjective* and *noun*
homosexuals

**honest** *adjective*
honestly

**honesty**

**honey** *noun*
honeys

**honeycomb** *noun*
honeycombs

**honeymoon** *noun*
honeymoons

**honeysuckle**

**honk** *verb*
honks
honking
honked

**honk** *noun*
honks

**honour** *verb*
honours
honouring
honoured

**honour** *noun*
honours

**honourable** *adjective*
honourably

**hood** *noun*
hoods

**-hood**
*-hood* makes nouns,
e.g. **childhood**. Other
noun suffixes are
**-dom**, **-ment**, **-ness**,
and **-ship**.

**hooded**

**hoof** *noun*
hoofs

**hook** *noun*
hooks

**hook** *verb*
hooks
hooking
hooked

**hooligan** *noun*
hooligans

**hoop** *noun*
hoops

**hoopla**

**hooray**

**hoot** *verb*
hoots
hooting
hooted

**hoot** *noun*
hoots

**hooter** *noun*
hooters

**hop** *verb*
hops
hopping
hopped

**hop** *noun*
hops

**hope** *verb*
hopes
hoping
hoped

**hope** *noun*
hopes

**hopeful** *adjective*
hopefully

**hopeless** *adjective*
hopelessly

**hopscotch**

**horde**☆ *noun*
hordes

**horizon** *noun*
horizons

**horizontal** *adjective*
horizontally

**hormone** *noun*
hormones

**horn** *noun*
horns

**hornet** *noun*
hornets

. . . . . . . . . . . . . . . . . . . . . . . . . . . . . . . . . . . . . . . . . . . . . .

★ You use **holy** in e.g. *a holy man.* **!holey**.
☆ A **horde** is a large crowd. **!hoard**.

a
b
c
d
e
f
g
**h**
i
j
k
l
m
n
o
p
q
r
s
t
u
v
w
x
y
z

**horoscope** *noun*
horoscopes
**horrible** *adjective*
horribly
**horrid**
**horrific** *adjective*
horrifically
**horrify** *verb*
horrifies
horrifying
horrified
**horror** *noun*
horrors
**horse** *noun*
horses
**horseback**
**horseman** *noun*
horsemen
**horsemanship**
**horsepower** *noun*
horsepower
**horseshoe** *noun*
horseshoes
**horsewoman** *noun*
horsewomen
**horticulture**
**hose** *noun*
hoses
**hospitable** *adjective*
hospitably
**hospital** *noun*
hospitals
**hospitality**
**host** *noun*
hosts
**hostage** *noun*
hostages
**hostel** *noun*
hostels
**hostess** *noun*
hostesses
**hostile**

**hostility** *noun*
hostilities
**hot** *adjective*
hotter
hottest
hotly
**hot** *verb*
hots
hotting
hotted
**hotel** *noun*
hotels
**hothouse** *noun*
hothouses
**hotpot** *noun*
hotpots
**hound** *noun*
hounds
**hound** *verb*
hounds
hounding
hounded
**hour★** *noun*
hours
**hourglass** *noun*
hourglasses
**hourly** *adjective* and
*adverb*
**house** *noun*
houses
**house** *verb*
houses
housing
housed
**houseboat** *noun*
houseboats
**household** *noun*
households
**householder** *noun*
householders
**housekeeper** *noun*
housekeepers
**housekeeping**

**housewife** *noun*
housewives
**housework**
**housing** *noun*
housings
**hove** see **heave**
**hover** *verb*
hovers
hovering
hovered
**hovercraft** *noun*
hovercraft
**however**
**howl** *verb*
howls
howling
howled
**howl** *noun*
howls
**howler** *noun*
howlers
**hub** *noun*
hubs
**huddle** *verb*
huddles
huddling
huddled
**hue** *noun*
hues
**huff**
**hug** *verb*
hugs
hugging
hugged
**hug** *noun*
hugs
**huge** *adjective*
huger
hugest
hugely
**hugeness**
**hulk** *noun*
hulks

- - - - - - - - - - - - - - - - - - - - - - - - - - - - - - - - - - - - - - - - - - - - - -

★ An **hour** is a measure of time. **!our**.

**hulking**

**hull** *noun*
hulls

**hullabaloo** *noun*
hullabaloos

**hullo**

**hum** *verb*
hums
humming
hummed

**hum** *noun*
hums

**human** *adjective* and *noun*
humans

**humane** *adjective*
humanely

**humanitarian**

**humanity** *noun*
humanities

**humble** *adjective*
humbler
humblest
humbly

**humid**

**humidity**

**humiliate** *verb*
humiliates
humiliating
humiliated

**humiliation**

**humility**

**hummingbird** *noun*
hummingbirds

**humorous** *adjective*
humorously

**humour** *noun*

**humour** *verb*
humours
humouring
humoured

**hump** *noun*
humps

**hump** *verb*
humps
humping
humped

**humpback**

**humus**

**hunch** *verb*
hunches
hunching
hunched

**hunch** *noun*
hunches

**hunchback** *noun*
hunchbacks

**hunchbacked**

**hundred** *noun*
hundreds

**hundredth**

**hundredweight** *noun*
hundredweights

**hung** see **hang**

**hunger**

**hungry** *adjective*
hungrier
hungriest
hungrily

**hunk** *noun*
hunks

**hunt** *verb*
hunts
hunting
hunted

**hunt** *noun*
hunts

**hunter** *noun*
hunters

**hurdle** *noun*
hurdles

**hurdler** *noun*
hurdlers

**hurdling**

**hurl** *verb*
hurls
hurling
hurled

**hurrah** or **hurray**

**hurricane** *noun*
hurricanes

**hurriedly**

**hurry** *verb*
hurries
hurrying
hurried

**hurry** *noun*
hurries

**hurt** *verb*
hurts
hurting
hurt

**hurt** *noun*

**hurtle** *verb*
hurtles
hurtling
hurtled

**husband** *noun*
husbands

**hush** *verb*
hushes
hushing
hushed

**hush** *noun*

**husk** *noun*
husks

**huskiness**

**husky** *adjective*
huskier
huskiest
huskily

**husky** *noun*
huskies

**hustle** *verb*
hustles
hustling
hustled

**hutch** *noun*
hutches

**hyacinth** *noun*
hyacinths

**hybrid** *noun*
hybrids

a
b
c
d
e
f
g
**h**
i
j
k
l
m
n
o
p
q
r
s
t
u
v
w
x
y
z

119

a
b
c
d
e
f
g
**h**
**i**
j
k
l
m
n
o
p
q
r
s
t
u
v
w
x
y
z

**hydrangea** *noun*
hydrangeas

**hydrant** *noun*
hydrants

**hydraulic** *adjective*
hydraulically

**hydroelectric**

**hydrofoil** *noun*
hydrofoils

**hydrogen**

**hydrophobia**

**hyena** *noun*
hyenas

**hygiene**

**hygienic** *adjective*
hygienically

**hymn** *noun*
hymns

**hyperactive**

**hypermarket** *noun*
hypermarkets

**hyphen** *noun*
hyphens

**hyphenated**

**hypnosis**

**hypnotism**

**hypnotist**

**hypnotize** *verb*
hypnotizes
hypnotizing
hypnotized

**hypocrisy**

**hypocrite** *noun*
hypocrites

**hypocritical** *adjective*
hypocritically

**hypodermic**

**hypotenuse** *noun*
hypotenuses

**hypothermia**

**hypothesis** *noun*
hypotheses

**hypothetical**
*adjective*
hypothetically

**hysteria**

**hysterical** *adjective*
hysterically

**hysterics** *plural noun*

# Ii

**-i**
Most nouns ending in
*-i*, e.g. **ski**, **taxi**, have
plurals ending in *-is*,
e.g. **skis**, **taxis**.

**-ible**
See the note at **-able**.

**-ic** and **-ically**
Most adjectives
ending in *-ic* have
adverbs ending in
*-ically*, e.g. **heroic -
heroically**, **scientific
- scientifically**. An
exception is **public**,
which has an adverb -
**publicly**.

**ice** *noun*
ices

**ice** *verb*
ices
icing
iced

**iceberg** *noun*
icebergs

**ice cream** *noun*
ice creams

**icicle** *noun*
icicles

**icing**

**icon** *noun*
icons

**icy** *adjective*
icier
iciest
icily

**I'd** *verb*

**idea** *noun*
ideas

**ideal** *adjective*
ideally

**ideal** *noun*
ideals

**identical** *adjective*
identically

**identification**

**identify** *verb*
identifies
identifying
identified

**identity** *noun*
identities

**idiocy** *noun*
idiocies

**idiom** *noun*
idioms

**idiomatic**

**idiot** *noun*
idiots

**idiotic** *adjective*
idiotically

**idle★** *adjective*
idler
idlest
idly

★ **Idle** means 'lazy'. **❗idol**.

idle *verb*
idles
idling
idled

idol★ *noun*
idols

idolatry

idolize *verb*
idolizes
idolizing
idolized

-ie-
See the note at -ei-.

igloo *noun*
igloos

igneous

ignite *verb*
ignites
igniting
ignited

ignition

ignorance

ignorant

ignore *verb*
ignores
ignoring
ignored

I'll *verb*

ill

illegal *adjective*
illegally

illegible *adjective*
illegibly

illegitimate

illiteracy

illiterate

illness *noun*
illnesses

illogical *adjective*
illogically

illuminate *verb*
illuminates
illuminating
illuminated

illumination *noun*
illuminations

illusion *noun*
illusions

illustrate *verb*
illustrates
illustrating
illustrated

illustration *noun*
illustrations

illustrious

I'm *verb*

image *noun*
images

imagery

imaginable

imaginary

imagination *noun*
imaginations

imaginative *adjective*
imaginatively

imagine *verb*
imagines
imagining
imagined

imam☆ *noun*
imams

imbecile *noun*
imbeciles

imitate *verb*
imitates
imitating
imitated

imitation *noun*
imitations

imitator *noun*
imitators

immature

immaturity

immediate *adjective*
immediately

immense *adjective*
immensely

immensity

immerse *verb*
immerses
immersing
immersed

immersion

immigrant *noun*
immigrants

immigrate *verb*
immigrates
immigrating
immigrated

immigration

immobile

immobility

immobilize *verb*
immobilizes
immobilizing
immobilized

immoral *adjective*
immorally

immorality

immortal

immortality

immune

immunity *noun*
immunities

immunization

immunize *verb*
immunizes
immunizing
immunized

imp *noun*
imps

impish

. . . . . . . . . . . . . . . . . . . . . . . . . . . . . . . . . . . . . . . . . . . . .

★ An **idol** is someone people admire. **!idle**.
☆ A Muslim religious leader.

## im

**impact** *noun*
impacts

**impair** *verb*
impairs
impairing
impaired

**impale** *verb*
impales
impaling
impaled

**impartial** *adjective*
impartially

**impartiality**

**impassable**

**impatience**

**impatient** *adjective*
impatiently

**impede** *verb*
impedes
impeding
impeded

**imperative**

**imperceptible**
*adjective*
imperceptibly

**imperfect** *adjective*
imperfectly

**imperfection** *noun*
imperfections

**imperial**

**impersonal** *adjective*
impersonally

**impersonate** *verb*
impersonates
impersonating
impersonated

**impersonation** *noun*
impersonations

**impersonator** *noun*
impersonators

**impertinence**

**impertinent** *adjective*
impertinently

**implement** *verb*
implements
implementing
implemented

**implement** *noun*
implements

**implication** *noun*
implications

**implore** *verb*
implores
imploring
implored

**imply** *verb*
implies
implying
implied

**impolite** *adjective*
impolitely

**import** *verb*
imports
importing
imported

**import** *noun*
imports

**importance**

**important** *adjective*
importantly

**importer** *noun*
importers

**impose** *verb*
imposes
imposing
imposed

**imposition** *noun*
impositions

**impossibility**

**impossible** *adjective*
impossibly

**impostor** *noun*
impostors

**impracticable**

**impractical**

**impress** *verb*
impresses
impressing
impressed

**impression** *noun*
impressions

**impressive** *adjective*
impressively

**imprison** *verb*
imprisons
imprisoning
imprisoned

**imprisonment**

**improbability**

**improbable** *adjective*
improbably

**impromptu**

**improper** *adjective*
improperly

**impropriety** *noun*
improprieties

**improve** *verb*
improves
improving
improved

**improvement** *noun*
improvements

**improvisation** *noun*
improvisations

**improvise** *verb*
improvises
improvising
improvised

**impudence**

**impudent** *adjective*
impudently

**impulse** *noun*
impulses

**impulsive** *adjective*
impulsively

**impure**
**impurity** *adjective*
 impurities

**in-**
*in-* makes words with
the meaning 'not', e.g.
**inedible**, **infertile**.
There is a fixed
number of these, and
you cannot freely add
*in-* as you can with
*un-*. *in-* changes to *il-*
or *im-* before certain
sounds, e.g. **illogical**,
**impossible**.

**inability**
**inaccessible**
**inaccuracy** *noun*
 inaccuracies
**inaccurate** *adjective*
 inaccurately
**inaction**
**inactive**
**inactivity**
**inadequacy**
**inadequate** *adjective*
 inadequately
**inanimate**
**inappropriate**
 *adjective*
 inappropriately
**inattention**
**inattentive**
**inaudible** *adjective*
 inaudibly
**incapable**
**incapacity**
**incendiary**
**incense** *noun*
**incense** *verb*
 incenses
 incensing
 incensed

**incentive** *noun*
 incentives
**incessant** *adjective*
 incessantly
**inch** *noun*
 inches
**incident** *noun*
 incidents
**incidental** *adjective*
 incidentally
**incinerator** *noun*
 incinerators
**inclination** *noun*
 inclinations
**incline** *verb*
 inclines
 inclining
 inclined
**incline** *noun*
 inclines
**include** *verb*
 includes
 including
 included
**inclusion**
**inclusive**
**income** *noun*
 incomes
**incompatible**
**incompetence**
**incompetent**
 *adjective*
 incompetently
**incomplete** *adjective*
 incompletely
**incomprehensible**
 *adjective*
 incomprehensibly
**incongruity**
**incongruous**
 *adjective*
 incongruously

**inconsiderate**
 *adjective*
 inconsiderately
**inconsistency** *noun*
 inconsistencies
**inconsistent**
 *adjective*
 inconsistently
**inconspicuous**
 *adjective*
 inconspicuously
**inconvenience**
**inconvenient**
 *adjective*
 inconveniently
**incorporate** *verb*
 incorporates
 incorporating
 incorporated
**incorporation**
**incorrect** *adjective*
 incorrectly
**increase** *verb*
 increases
 increasing
 increased
**increase** *noun*
 increases
**increasingly**
**incredible** *adjective*
 incredibly
**incredulity**
**incredulous**
**incubate** *verb*
 incubates
 incubating
 incubated
**incubation**
**incubator** *noun*
 incubators
**indebted**

a
b
c
d
e
f
g
h
i
j
k
l
m
n
o
p
q
r
s
t
u
v
w
x
y
z-

**indecency**

**indecent** *adjective*
indecently

**indeed**

**indefinite** *adjective*
indefinitely

**indelible** *adjective*
indelibly

**indent** *verb*
indents
indenting
indented

**indentation**

**independence**

**independent**
*adjective*
independently

**index** *noun*
indexes

**Indian** *adjective* and
*noun*
Indians

**indicate** *verb*
indicates
indicating
indicated

**indication** *noun*
indications

**indicative**

**indicator** *noun*
indicators

**indifference**

**indifferent** *adjective*
indifferently

**indigestible**

**indigestion**

**indignant** *adjective*
indignantly

**indignation**

**indigo**

**indirect** *adjective*
indirectly

**indispensable**
*adjective*
indispensably

**indistinct** *adjective*
indistinctly

**indistinguishable**

**individual** *adjective*
individually

**individual** *noun*
individuals

**individuality**

**indoctrinate** *verb*
indoctrinates
indoctrinating
indoctrinated

**indoctrination**

**indoor** *adjective*

**indoors** *adverb*

**induce** *verb*
induces
inducing
induced

**inducement** *noun*
inducements

**indulge** *verb*
indulges
indulging
indulged

**indulgence** *noun*
indulgences

**indulgent**

**industrial**

**industrialist** *noun*
industrialists

**industrialization**

**industrialize** *verb*
industrializes
industrializing
industrialized

**industrious** *adjective*
industriously

**industry** *noun*
industries

**ineffective** *adjective*
ineffectively

**ineffectual** *adjective*
ineffectually

**inefficiency** *noun*
inefficiencies

**inefficient** *adjective*
inefficiently

**inequality** *noun*
inequalities

**inert**

**inertia**

**inevitability**

**inevitable** *adjective*
inevitably

**inexhaustible**

**inexpensive** *adjective*
inexpensively

**inexperience**

**inexperienced**

**inexplicable** *adjective*
inexplicably

**infallibility**

**infallible** *adjective*
infallibly

**infamous** *adjective*
infamously

**infamy**

**infancy**

**infant** *noun*
infants

**infantile**

**infantry**

**infect** *verb*
infects
infecting
infected

**infection** *noun*
infections

**infectious** *adjective*
infectiously

**infer** *verb*
infers
inferring
inferred

**inference** *noun*
inferences

**inferior** *adjective* and
*noun*
inferiors

**inferiority**

**infernal** *adjective*
infernally

**inferno** *noun*
infernos

**infested**

**infiltrate** *verb*
infiltrates
infiltrating
infiltrated

**infiltration**

**infinite** *adjective*
infinitely

**infinitive** *noun*
infinitives

**infinity**

**infirm**

**infirmary** *noun*
infirmaries

**infirmity**

**inflame** *verb*
inflames
inflaming
inflamed

**inflammable**

**inflammation** *noun*
inflammations

**inflammatory**

**inflatable**

**inflate** *verb*
inflates
inflating
inflated

**inflation**

**inflect** *verb*
inflects
inflecting
inflected

**inflection** *noun*
inflections

**inflexibility**

**inflexible** *adjective*
inflexibly

**inflict** *verb*
inflicts
inflicting
inflicted

**influence** *verb*
influences
influencing
influenced

**influence** *noun*
influences

**influential** *adjective*
influentially

**influenza**

**inform** *verb*
informs
informing
informed

**informal** *adjective*
informally

**informality**

**informant** *noun*
informants

**information**

**informative**

**informed**

**informer** *noun*
informers

**infrequency**

**infrequent** *adjective*
infrequently

**infuriate** *verb*
infuriates
infuriating
infuriated

**-ing**
*-ing* makes present participles and nouns, e.g. hunt - **hunting**. You normally drop an e at the end, e.g. **change - changing, smoke - smoking**. An exception is **ageing**. Words ending in a consonant following a single vowel double the consonant, e.g. **run - running**.

**ingenious** *adjective*
ingeniously

**ingenuity**

**ingot** *noun*
ingots

**ingrained**

**ingredient** *noun*
ingredients

**inhabit** *verb*
inhabits
inhabiting
inhabited

**inhabitant** *noun*
inhabitants

**inhale** *verb*
inhales
inhaling
inhaled

**inhaler** *noun*
inhalers

**inherent** *adjective*
inherently

**inherit** *verb*
inherits
inheriting
inherited

**inheritance**

**inhibited**

# in

**inhospitable**
*adjective*
inhospitably

**inhuman**

**inhumanity**

**initial** *adjective*
initially

**initial** *noun*
initials

**initiate** *verb*
initiates
initiating
initiated

**initiation**

**initiative** *noun*
initiatives

**inject** *verb*
injects
injecting
injected

**injection** *noun*
injections

**injure** *verb*
injures
injuring
injured

**injurious** *adjective*
injuriously

**injury** *noun*
injuries

**injustice** *noun*
injustices

**ink** *noun*
inks

**inkling** *noun*
inklings

**inky** *adjective*
inkier
inkiest

**inland**

**inlet** *noun*
inlets

**inn** *noun*
inns

**innkeeper** *noun*
innkeepers

**inner**

**innermost**

**innings** *noun*
innings

**innocence**

**innocent** *adjective*
innocently

**innocuous** *adjective*
innocuously

**innovation** *noun*
innovations

**innovative**

**innovator** *noun*
innovators

**innumerable**

**inoculate** *verb*
inoculates
inoculating
inoculated

**inoculation**

**input** *verb*
inputs
inputting
input

**input** *noun*
inputs

**inquest** *noun*
inquests

**inquire** *verb*
inquires
inquiring
inquired

**inquiry**★ *noun*
inquiries

**inquisitive** *adjective*
inquisitively

**insane** *adjective*
insanely

**insanitary**

**insanity**

**inscribe** *verb*
inscribes
inscribing
inscribed

**inscription** *noun*
inscriptions

**insect** *noun*
insects

**insecticide** *noun*
insecticides

**insecure** *adjective*
insecurely

**insecurity**

**insensitive** *adjective*
insensitively

**insensitivity**

**inseparable** *adjective*
inseparably

**insert** *verb*
inserts
inserting
inserted

**insertion** *noun*
insertions

**inshore** *adjective* and *adverb*

**inside** *noun*
insides

**inside** *adverb, adjective,* and *preposition*

**insight** *noun*
insights

**insignificance**

**insignificant**
*adjective*
insignificantly

**insincere** *adjective*
insincerely

**insincerity**

........................................................................

★ An **inquiry** is an official investigation. **!** enquiry.

**insist** verb
insists
insisting
insisted

**insistence**

**insistent** adjective
insistently

**insolence**

**insolent** adjective
insolently

**insolubility**

**insoluble** adjective
insolubly

**insomnia**

**inspect** verb
inspects
inspecting
inspected

**inspection** noun
inspections

**inspector** noun
inspectors

**inspiration**

**inspire** verb
inspires
inspiring
inspired

**install** verb
installs
installing
installed

**installation** noun
installations

**instalment** noun
instalments

**instance** noun
instances

**instant** adjective
instantly

**instant** noun
instants

**instantaneous**
adjective
instantaneously

**instead**

**instep** noun
insteps

**instinct** noun
instincts

**instinctive** adjective
instinctively

**institute** verb
institutes
instituting
instituted

**institute** noun
institutes

**institution** noun
institutions

**instruct** verb
instructs
instructing
instructed

**instruction** noun
instructions

**instrument** noun
instruments

**instrumental**

**insufficient** adjective
insufficiently

**insulate** verb
insulates
insulating
insulated

**insulation**

**insulin**

**insult** verb
insults
insulting
insulted

**insult** noun
insults

**insurance**

**insure** verb
insures
insuring
insured

**intact**

**intake** noun
intakes

**integer** noun
integers

**integral** adjective
integrally

**integrate** verb
integrates
integrating
integrated

**integration**

**integrity**

**intellect** noun
intellects

**intellectual** adjective
intellectually

**intellectual** noun
intellectuals

**intelligence**

**intelligent** adjective
intelligently

**intelligibility**

**intelligible** adjective
intelligibly

**intend** verb
intends
intending
intended

**intense** adjective
intensely

**intensification**

**intensify** verb
intensifies
intensifying
intensified

**intensity** noun
intensities

**intensive** adjective
intensively

**intent** adjective
intently

**intent** noun
intents

**intention** noun
intentions

**intentional** adjective
intentionally

**interact** verb
interacts
interacting
interacted

**interaction**

**interactive**

**intercept** verb
intercepts
intercepting
intercepted

**interception**

**interchange** noun
interchanges

**interchangeable**
adjective
interchangeably

**intercom** noun
intercoms

**intercourse**

**interest** verb
interests
interesting
interested

**interest** noun
interests

**interface** noun
interfaces

**interfere** verb
interferes
interfering
interfered

**interference**

**interior** noun
interiors

**interjection** noun
interjections

**interlock** verb
interlocks
interlocking
interlocked

**interlude** noun
interludes

**intermediate**

**interminable**
adjective
interminably

**intermission** noun
intermissions

**intermittent** adjective
intermittently

**intern** verb
interns
interning
interned

**internal** adjective
internally

**international**
adjective
internationally

**internee**

**internment**

**internet**

**interplanetary**

**interpret** verb
interprets
interpreting
interpreted

**interpretation** noun
interpretations

**interpreter** noun
interpreters

**interrogate** verb
interrogates
interrogating
interrogated

**interrogation**

**interrogative**

**interrogator** noun
interrogators

**interrupt** verb
interrupts
interrupting
interrupted

**interruption** noun
interruptions

**intersect** verb
intersects
intersecting
intersected

**intersection** noun
intersections

**interval** noun
intervals

**intervene** verb
intervenes
intervening
intervened

**intervention** noun
interventions

**interview** noun
interviews

**interview** verb
interviews
interviewing
interviewed

**interviewer** noun
interviewers

**intestinal**

**intestine**

**intimacy**

**intimate** adjective
intimately

**intimate** verb
intimates
intimating
intimated

**intimation** noun
intimations

**intimidate** verb
intimidates
intimidating
intimidated

**intimidation**

**into** preposition

**intolerable** adjective
intolerably

**intolerance**

**intolerant** adjective
intolerantly

a b c d e f g h i j k l m n o p q r s t u v w x y z

intonation *noun*
intonations

intoxicate *verb*
intoxicates
intoxicating
intoxicated

intoxication

intransitive

intrepid *adjective*
intrepidly

intricacy *noun*
intricacies

intricate *adjective*
intricately

intrigue *verb*
intrigues
intriguing
intrigued

introduce *verb*
introduces
introducing
introduced

introduction *noun*
introductions

introductory

intrude *verb*
intrudes
intruding
intruded

intruder *noun*
intruders

intrusion *noun*
intrusions

intrusive *adjective*
intrusively

intuition

intuitive *adjective*
intuitively

Inuit *noun*
Inuit *or* Inuits

inundate *verb*
inundates
inundating
inundated

inundation *noun*
inundations

invade *verb*
invades
invading
invaded

invader *noun*
invaders

invalid *noun*
invalids

invalid *adjective*
invalidly

invaluable

invariable *adjective*
invariably

invasion *noun*
invasions

invent *verb*
invents
inventing
invented

invention *noun*
inventions

inventive *adjective*
inventively

inventor *noun*
inventors

inverse *noun and adjective*
inversely

inversion *noun*
inversions

invert *verb*
inverts
inverting
inverted

invertebrate *noun*
invertebrates

invest *verb*
invests
investing
invested

investigate *verb*
investigates
investigating
investigated

investigation *noun*
investigations

investigator *noun*
investigators

investiture *noun*
investitures

investment *noun*
investments

investor *noun*
investors

invigilate *verb*
invigilates
invigilating
invigilated

invigilation

invigilator *noun*
invigilators

invigorate *verb*
invigorates
invigorating
invigorated

invincible

invisibility

invisible *adjective*
invisibly

invitation *noun*
invitations

invite *verb*
invites
inviting
invited

invoice *noun*
invoices

involuntary

involve *verb*
involves
involving
involved

a
b
c
d
e
f
g
h
i
j
k
l
m
n
o
p
q
r
s
t
u
v
w
x
y
z

a **involvement**

**inward** *adjective*
  inwardly

b

**inwards** *adverb*

c

**iodine**

d **ion** *noun*
  ions

e **iris** *noun*
  irises

f

**iron** *noun*
  irons

g **iron** *verb*
  irons
  ironing

h   ironed

**ironic** *adjective*
  ironically

j

**ironmonger** *noun*
  ironmongers

k

l **ironmongery**

m **irony** *noun*
  ironies

n **irrational** *adjective*
  irrationally

o **irregular** *adjective*
  irregularly

p **irregularity** *noun*
  irregularities

q

**irrelevance**

r **irrelevant** *adjective*
  irrelevantly

s **irresistible** *adjective*
  irresistibly

t **irresponsible**
  *adjective*

u   irresponsibly

**irresponsibility**

v

**irreverence**

w **irreverent** *adjective*
  irreverently

x

**irrigate** *verb*
  irrigates
  irrigating
  irrigated

**irrigation**

**irritability**

**irritable** *adjective*
  irritably

**irritant**

**irritate** *verb*
  irritates
  irritating
  irritated

**irritation** *noun*
  irritations

---

**-ish**
*-ish* makes words
meaning 'rather' or
'fairly', e.g. **soft -
softish**. You normally
drop an *e* at the end,
e.g. **blue - bluish**.
Words ending in a
consonant following a
single vowel double
the consonant, e.g.
**fat - fattish**.

---

**Islam**

**Islamic**

**island** *noun*
  islands

**islander** *noun*
  islanders

**isle★** *noun*
  isles

**isn't** *verb*

**isobar** *noun*
  isobars

**isolate** *verb*
  isolates
  isolating
  isolated

**isolation**

**isosceles** *adjective*

**isotope** *noun*
  isotopes

**issue** *verb*
  issues
  issuing
  issued

**issue** *noun*
  issues

**isthmus** *noun*
  isthmuses

**italics**

**itch** *verb*
  itches
  itching
  itched

**itch** *noun*
  itches

**itchy** *adjective*
  itchier
  itchiest

**item** *noun*
  items

**itinerary** *noun*
  itineraries

**it'll** *verb*

**its**☆

**it's**◑ *verb*

**itself**

**I've** *verb*

**ivory** *adjective* and
  *noun*
  ivories

**ivy**

---

★ An isle is a small island. **!**aisle.

☆ You use its in e.g. *the cat licked its paw.* **!**it's.

◑ You use it's in *it's ( it is) raining* and *it's ( it has) been raining.* **!**its.

**-ize and -ise**
You can use *-ize* or *-ise* at the end of many verbs, e.g. **realize** or **realise**, **privatize** or **privatise**. This book prefers *-ize*, but some words have to be spelt *-ise*, e.g. **advertise**, **exercise**, **supervise**. Check each spelling if you are not sure.

# Jj

**jab** *verb*
  jabs
  jabbing
  jabbed

**jab** *noun*
  jabs

**jabber** *verb*
  jabbers
  jabbering
  jabbered

**jack** *noun*
  jacks

**jack** *verb*
  jacks
  jacking
  jacked

**jackal** *noun*
  jackals

**jackass** *noun*
  jackasses

**jackdaw** *noun*
  jackdaws

**jacket** *noun*
  jackets

**jack-in-the-box** *noun*
  jack-in-the-boxes

**jackknife** *verb*
  jackknifes
  jackknifing
  jackknifed

**jackpot** *noun*
  jackpots

**jacuzzi** *noun*
  jacuzzis

**jade**

**jaded**

**jagged**

**jaguar** *noun*
  jaguars

**jail** *noun*
  jails

**jail** *verb*
  jails
  jailing
  jailed

**jailer** *noun*
  jailers

**Jain**★ *noun*
  Jains

**jam** *noun*
  jams

**jam** *verb*
  jams
  jamming
  jammed

**jamboree** *noun*
  jamborees

**jammy** *adjective*
  jammier
  jammiest

**jangle** *verb*
  jangles
  jangling
  jangled

**January** *noun*
  Januaries

**jar** *noun*
  jars

**jar** *verb*
  jars
  jarring
  jarred

**jaundice**

**jaunt** *noun*
  jaunts

**jauntiness**

**jaunty** *adjective*
  jauntier
  jauntiest
  jauntily

**javelin** *noun*
  javelins

**jaw** *noun*
  jaws

**jay** *noun*
  jays

**jazz**

**jazzy** *adjective*
  jazzier
  jazziest

**jealous** *adjective*
  jealously

**jealousy**

**jeans**

**Jeep** *noun*
  Jeeps

**jeer** *verb*
  jeers
  jeering
  jeered

**jellied**

**jelly** *noun*
  jellies

**jellyfish** *noun*
  jellyfish

a
b
c
d
e
f
g
h
i
j
k
l
m
n
o
p
q
r
s
t
u
v
w
x
y
z

★ A member of an Indian religion.

131

a

**jerk** *verb*
jerks

b

jerking
jerked

c

**jerk** *noun*
jerks

d

**jerky** *adjective*
jerkier

e

jerkiest
jerkily

f

**jersey** *noun*
jerseys

g

**jest** *verb*
jests

h

jesting
jested

i

**jest** *noun*
jests

j

**jester** *noun*
jesters

k

**jet** *noun*
jets

l

**jet** *verb*

m

jets
jetting

n

jetted

o

**jet-propelled**

p

**jetty** *noun*
jetties

q

**Jew** *noun*
Jews

r

**jewel** *noun*
jewels

s

**jewelled**

t

**jeweller** *noun*
jewellers

u

**jewellery**

v

**Jewish**

w

**jib** *noun*
jibs

x

**jiffy** *noun*
jiffies

y

**jig** *noun*
jigs

z

**jig** *verb*
jigs
jigging
jigged

**jigsaw** *noun*
jigsaws

**jingle** *verb*
jingles
jingling
jingled

**jingle** *noun*
jingles

**job** *noun*
jobs

**jobcentre** *noun*
jobcentres

**jockey** *noun*
jockeys

**jodhpurs** *plural noun*

**jog** *verb*
jogs
jogging
jogged

**jogger** *noun*
joggers

**jogtrot** *noun*
jogtrots

**join** *verb*
joins
joining
joined

**join** *noun*
joins

**joiner** *noun*
joiners

**joinery**

**joint** *noun*
joints

**joint** *adjective*
jointly

**joist** *noun*
joists

**jojoba**

**joke** *verb*
jokes
joking
joked

**joke** *noun*
jokes

**joker** *noun*
jokers

**jollity**

**jolly** *adjective*
jollier
jolliest

**jolly** *adverb*

**jolly** *verb*
jollies
jollying
jollied

**jolt** *verb*
jolts
jolting
jolted

**jolt** *noun*
jolts

**jostle** *verb*
jostles
jostling
jostled

**jot** *verb*
jots
jotting
jotted

**jot** *noun*
jots

**jotter** *noun*
jotters

**joule** *noun*
joules

**journal** *noun*
journals

**journalism**

**journalist** *noun*
journalists

**journey** *noun*
journeys

**journey** *verb*
 journeys
 journeying
 journeyed

**joust** *verb*
 jousts
 jousting
 jousted

**jovial** *adjective*
 jovially

**joviality**

**joy** *noun*
 joys

**joyful** *adjective*
 joyfully

**joyous** *adjective*
 joyously

**joyride** *noun*
 joyrides

**joystick** *noun*
 joysticks

**jubilant** *adjective*
 jubilantly

**jubilation**

**jubilee** *noun*
 jubilees

**Judaism**

**judge** *verb*
 judges
 judging
 judged

**judge** *noun*
 judges

**judgement** *noun*
 judgements

**judicial** *adjective*
 judicially

**judicious** *adjective*
 judiciously

**judo**

**jug** *noun*
 jugs

**juggernaut** *noun*
 juggernauts

**juggle** *verb*
 juggles
 juggling
 juggled

**juggler** *noun*
 jugglers

**juice**★ *noun*
 juices

**juicy** *adjective*
 juicier
 juiciest

**jukebox** *noun*
 jukeboxes

**July** *noun*
 Julys

**jumble** *verb*
 jumbles
 jumbling
 jumbled

**jumble** *noun*

**jumbo jet** *noun*
 jumbo jets

**jump** *verb*
 jumps
 jumping
 jumped

**jump** *noun*
 jumps

**jumper** *noun*
 jumpers

**jumpy** *adjective*
 jumpier
 jumpiest

**junction** *noun*
 junctions

**June** *noun*
 Junes

**jungle** *noun*
 jungles

**jungly** *adjective*
 junglier
 jungliest

**junior** *adjective* and
 *noun*
 juniors

**junk** *noun*
 junks

**junket** *noun*
 junkets

**juror** *noun*
 jurors

**jury** *noun*
 juries

**just** *adjective*
 justly

**just** *adverb*

**justice** *noun*
 justices

**justifiable** *adjective*
 justifiably

**justification**

**justify** *verb*
 justifies
 justifying
 justified

**jut** *verb*
 juts
 jutting
 jutted

**juvenile**

# Kk

**kaleidoscope** *noun*
 kaleidoscopes

**kangaroo** *noun*
 kangaroos

**karaoke**

**karate**

★ **Juice** is the liquid from fruit. **!deuce**.

a b c d e f g h i **j** **k** l m n o p q r s t u v w x y z

a

b

c

d

e

f

g

h

i

j

**k**

l

m

n

o

p

q

r

s

t

u

v

w

x

y

z

**kayak** *noun*
kayaks

**kebab** *noun*
kebabs

**keel** *noun*
keels

**keel** *verb*
keels
keeling
keeled

**keen** *adjective*
keener
keenest
keenly

**keenness**

**keep** *verb*
keeps
keeping
kept

**keep** *noun*
keeps

**keeper** *noun*
keepers

**keg** *noun*
kegs

**kennel** *noun*
kennels

**kept** see **keep**

**kerb★** *noun*
kerbs

**kerbstone** *noun*
kerbstones

**kernel☆** *noun*
kernels

**kestrel** *noun*
kestrels

**ketchup**

**kettle** *noun*
kettles

**kettledrum** *noun*
kettledrums

**key◌** *noun*
keys

**keyboard** *noun*
keyboards

**keyhole** *noun*
keyholes

**keynote** *noun*
keynotes

**khaki**

**kibbutz** *noun*
kibbutzim

**kick** *verb*
kicks
kicking
kicked

**kick** *noun*
kicks

**kick-off** *noun*
kick-offs

**kid** *noun*
kids

**kid** *verb*
kids
kidding
kidded

**kidnap** *verb*
kidnaps
kidnapping
kidnapped

**kidnapper** *noun*
kidnappers

**kidney** *noun*
kidneys

**kill** *verb*
kills
killing
killed

**killer** *noun*
killers

**kiln** *noun*
kilns

**kilo** *noun*
kilos

**kilogram** *noun*
kilograms

**kilometre** *noun*
kilometres

**kilowatt** *noun*
kilowatts

**kilt** *noun*
kilts

**kin**

**kind** *adjective*
kinder
kindest
kindly

**kind** *noun*
kinds

**kindergarten** *noun*
kindergartens

**kind-hearted**

**kindle** *verb*
kindles
kindling
kindled

**kindliness**

**kindling**

**kindly** *adjective*
kindlier
kindliest

**kindness**

**kinetic**

**king** *noun*
kings

**kingdom** *noun*
kingdoms

**kingfisher** *noun*
kingfishers

**kingly**

. . . . . . . . . . . . . . . . . . . . . . . . . . . . . . . . . . . . . . . . . . . . . . . . . . . . . . . . . .

★ A **kerb** is the edge of a pavement. **!** curb.

☆ **Kernel** is part of a nut. **!** colonel.

◌ A **key** is a device for opening a lock. **!** quay.

**kink** *noun*
kinks

**kinky** *adjective*
kinkier
kinkiest

**kiosk** *noun*
kiosks

**kipper** *noun*
kippers

**kiss** *verb*
kisses
kissing
kissed

**kiss** *noun*
kisses

**kit** *noun*
kits

**kitchen** *noun*
kitchens

**kite** *noun*
kites

**kitten** *noun*
kittens

**kitty** *noun*
kitties

**kiwi** *noun*
kiwis

**knack**

**knapsack** *noun*
knapsacks

**knave** *noun*
knaves

**knead**★ *verb*
kneads
kneading
kneaded

**knee** *noun*
knees

**kneecap** *noun*
kneecaps

**kneel** *verb*
kneels
kneeling
knelt

**knew**☆ see **know**

**knickers** *plural noun*

**knife** *noun*
knives

**knife** *verb*
knifes
knifing
knifed

**knight**❍ *noun*
knights

**knight** *verb*
knights
knighting
knighted

**knighthood** *noun*
knighthoods

**knit** *verb*
knits
knitting
knitted

**knives** see **knife**

**knob** *noun*
knobs

**knobbly** *adjective*
knobblier
knobbliest

**knock** *verb*
knocks
knocking
knocked

**knock** *noun*
knocks

**knocker** *noun*
knockers

**knockout** *noun*
knockouts

**knot** *noun*
knots

**knot** *verb*
knots
knotting
knotted

**knotty** *adjective*
knottier
knottiest

**know** *verb*
knows
knowing
knew
known

**know-all** *noun*
know-alls

**know-how**

**knowing** *adjective*
knowingly

**knowledge**

**knowledgeable** *adjective*
knowledgeably

**knuckle** *noun*
knuckles

**koala** *noun*
koalas

**kookaburra** *noun*
kookaburras

**Koran**

**kosher**

**kung fu**

# Ll

**label** *noun*
labels

---

★ To **knead** is to work a mixture into a dough. ! **need**.
☆ **Knew** is the past tense of know. ! **new**.
❍ A **knight** is a soldier in old times. ! **night**.

a
b
c
d
e
f
g
h
i
j
**k**
**l**
m
n
o
p
q
r
s
t
u
v
w
x
y
z

135

a
**label** verb
  labels
b
  labelling
  labelled
c
**laboratory** noun
  laboratories
d
**laborious** adjective
  laboriously
e
**labour** noun
  labours
f
**labourer** noun
  labourers
g
**Labrador** noun
  Labradors
h
**laburnum** noun
  laburnums
i
**labyrinth** noun
  labyrinths
j
k
**lace** noun
  laces
l
**lace** verb
  laces
m
  lacing
  laced
n
**lack** verb
o
  lacks
  lacking
p
  lacked
q
**lack** noun
**lacquer**
r
**lacrosse**
s
**lad** noun
  lads
t
**ladder** noun
  ladders
u
**laden**
v
**ladle** noun
  ladles
w
**lady** noun
  ladies
x
**ladybird** noun
y
  ladybirds
z
**ladylike**

**ladyship** noun
  ladyships
**lag** verb
  lags
  lagging
  lagged
**lager** noun
  lagers
**lagoon** noun
  lagoons
**laid** see **lay**
**lain** see **lie**
**lair** noun
  lairs
**lake** noun
  lakes
**lama** noun
  lamas
**lamb** noun
  lambs
**lame** adjective
  lamer
  lamest
  lamely
**lameness**
**lament** verb
  laments
  lamenting
  lamented
**lament** noun
  laments
**lamentation** noun
  lamentations
**laminated**
**lamp** noun
  lamps
**lamp-post** noun
  lamp-posts
**lampshade** noun
  lampshades
**lance** noun
  lances
**lance corporal** noun
  lance corporals

**land** noun
  lands
**land** verb
  lands
  landing
  landed
**landing** noun
  landings
**landlady** noun
  landladies
**landlord** noun
  landlords
**landmark** noun
  landmarks
**landowner** noun
  landowners
**landscape** noun
  landscapes
**landslide** noun
  landslides
**lane** noun
  lanes
**language** noun
  languages
**lankiness**
**lanky** adjective
  lankier
  lankiest
**lantern** noun
  lanterns
**lap** verb
  laps
  lapping
  lapped
**lap** noun
  laps
**lapel** noun
  lapels
**lapse** verb
  lapses
  lapsing
  lapsed
**lapse** noun
  lapses

**laptop** *noun*
laptops

**lapwing** *noun*
lapwings

**larch** *noun*
larches

**lard**

**larder** *noun*
larders

**large** *adjective*
larger
largest
largely

**largeness**

**lark** *noun*
larks

**lark** *verb*
larks
larking
larked

**larva** *noun*
larvae

**lasagne** *noun*
lasagnes

**laser** *noun*
lasers

**lash** *verb*
lashes
lashing
lashed

**lash** *noun*
lashes

**lass** *noun*
lasses

**lasso** *noun*
lassos

**lasso** *verb*
lassoes
lassoing
lassoed

**last** *adjective* and
*adverb*
lastly

**last** *verb*
lasts
lasting
lasted

**last** *noun*

**latch** *noun*
latches

**late** *adjective* and
*adverb*
later
latest

**lately**

**lateness**

**latent**

**lateral** *adjective*
laterally

**lathe** *noun*
lathes

**lather** *noun*
lathers

**Latin**

**latitude** *noun*
latitudes

**latter** *adjective*
latterly

**lattice** *noun*
lattices

**laugh** *verb*
laughs
laughing
laughed

**laugh** *noun*
laughs

**laughable** *adjective*
laughably

**laughter**

**launch** *verb*
launches
launching
launched

**launch** *noun*
launches

**launder** *verb*
launders
laundering
laundered

**launderette** *noun*
launderettes

**laundry** *noun*
laundries

**laurel** *noun*
laurels

**lava**

**lavatory** *noun*
lavatories

**lavender**

**lavish** *adjective*
lavishly

**law** *noun*
laws

**lawcourt** *noun*
lawcourts

**lawful** *adjective*
lawfully

**lawless** *adjective*
lawlessly

**lawn** *noun*
lawns

**lawnmower** *noun*
lawnmowers

**lawsuit** *noun*
lawsuits

**lawyer** *noun*
lawyers

**lax** *adjective*
laxly

**laxative** *noun*
laxatives

**lay** *verb*
lays
laying
laid

**lay** see **lie**

**layabout** *noun*
layabouts

a

**layer** noun
layers

**layman** noun
laymen

**layout** noun
layouts

**laze** verb
lazes
lazing
lazed

**laziness**

**lazy** adjective
lazier
laziest
lazily

**lead** verb
leads
leading
led

**lead**★ noun
leads

**leader** noun
leaders

**leadership**

**leaf** noun
leaves

**leaflet** noun
leaflets

**leafy** adjective
leafier
leafiest

**league** noun
leagues

**leak** verb
leaks
leaking
leaked

**leak**☆ noun
leaks

**leakage** noun
leakages

**leaky** adjective
leakier
leakiest

**lean** verb
leans
leaning
leaned or leant

**lean** adjective
leaner
leanest

**leap** verb
leaps
leaping
leapt
leaped

**leap** noun
leaps

**leapfrog**

**leap year** noun
leap years

**learn** verb
learns
learning
learnt or learned

**learned**⊙ adjective

**learner** noun
learners

**lease** noun
leases

**leash** noun
leashes

**least** adjective and noun

**leather** noun
leathers

**leathery**

**leave** verb
leaves
leaving
left

**leave** noun

**leaves** see **leaf**

**lectern** noun
lecterns

**lecture** verb
lectures
lecturing
lectured

**lecture** noun
lectures

**lecturer** noun
lecturers

**led** see **lead**

**ledge** noun
ledges

**lee**

**leek**✣ noun
leeks

**leer** verb
leers
leering
leered

**leeward**

**left** adjective and noun

**left** see **leave**

**left-handed**

**leftovers** plural noun

**leg** noun
legs

**legacy** noun
legacies

. . . . . . . . . . . . . . . . . . . . . . . . . . . . . . . . . . . . . . . .

★ A **lead** (pronounced *leed*) is a cord for leading a dog. Lead (pronounced *led*) is a metal.

☆ A **leak** is a hole or crack that liquid or gas can get through. ❗ leek.

⊙ Pronounced *ler-nid*.

✣ A **leek** is a vegetable. ❗ leak.

138

**legal** *adjective*
legally

**legality**

**legalize** *verb*
legalizes
legalizing
legalized

**legend** *noun*
legends

**legendary**

**legibility**

**legible** *adjective*
legibly

**legion** *noun*
legions

**legislate** *verb*
legislates
legislating
legislated

**legislation**

**legislator** *noun*
legislators

**legitimacy**

**legitimate** *adjective*
legitimately

**leisure**

**leisurely**

**lemon** *noun*
lemons

**lemonade** *noun*
lemonades

**lend** *verb*
lends
lending
lent

**length** *noun*
lengths

**lengthen** *verb*
lengthens
lengthening
lengthened

**lengthways** *adverb*

**lengthwise** *adverb*

**lengthy** *adjective*
lengthier
lengthiest
lengthily

**lenience**

**lenient** *adjective*
leniently

**lens** *noun*
lenses

**Lent**★

**lent** see **lend**

**lentil** *noun*
lentils

**leopard** *noun*
leopards

**leotard** *noun*
leotards

**leper** *noun*
lepers

**leprosy**

**less**

**lessen**☆ *verb*
lessens
lessening
lessened

**lesser**

**lesson**○ *noun*
lessons

**lest** *conjunction*

**let** *verb*
lets
letting
let

-**let**
-*let* makes nouns meaning 'a small version of', e.g. **booklet**, **piglet**. It also makes words for pieces of jewellery, e.g. **anklet** (worn on the ankle), **bracelet** (from a French word *bras* meaning 'arm')

**lethal** *adjective*
lethally

**let's** *verb*

**letter** *noun*
letters

**letter box** *noun*
letter boxes

**lettering**

**lettuce** *noun*
lettuces

**leukaemia**

**level** *verb*
levels
levelling
levelled

**level** *adjective* and *noun*
levels

**lever** *noun*
levers

**leverage**

**liability** *noun*
liabilities

**liable**

**liar** *noun*
liars

**liberal** *adjective*
liberally

★ **Lent** is the Christian time of fasting. ! **lent**.
☆ To **lessen** something is to make it less. ! **lesson**.
○ A **lesson** is a period of learning. ! **lessen**.

a
b
c
d
e
f
g
h
i
j
k
**l**
m
n
o
p
q
r
s
t
u
v
w
x
y
z

139

## li

**liberate** *verb*
liberates
liberating
liberated

**liberation**

**liberty** *noun*
liberties

**librarian** *noun*
librarians

**librarianship**

**library** *noun*
libraries

**licence** *noun*
licences

**license** *verb*
licenses
licensing
licensed

**lichen** *noun*
lichens

**lick** *verb*
licks
licking
licked

**lick** *noun*
licks

**lid** *noun*
lids

**lie★** *verb*
lies
lying
lay
lain

**lie☆** *verb*
lies
lying
lied

**lie** *noun*
lies

**lieutenant** *noun*
lieutenants

**life** *noun*
lives

**lifebelt** *noun*
lifebelts

**lifeboat** *noun*
lifeboats

**life cycle** *noun*
life cycles

**lifeguard** *noun*
lifeguards

**lifeless** *adjective*
lifelessly

**lifelike**

**lifelong**

**lifestyle** *noun*
lifestyles

**lifetime** *noun*
lifetimes

**lift** *verb*
lifts
lifting
lifted

**lift** *noun*
lifts

**lift-off** *noun*
lift-offs

**light** *adjective*
lighter
lightest
lightly

**light** *verb*
lights
lighting
lit *or* lighted

**light** *noun*
lights

**lighten** *verb*
lightens
lightening
lightened

**lighter** *noun*
lighters

**lighthouse** *noun*
lighthouses

**lighting**

**lightning**

**lightweight**

**like** *verb*
likes
liking
liked

**like** *preposition*

**likeable**

**likely** *adjective*
likelier
likeliest

**liken** *verb*
likens
likening
likened

**likeness** *noun*
likenesses

**likewise**

**liking** *noun*
likings

**lilac** *noun*
lilacs

**lily** *noun*
lilies

**limb** *noun*
limbs

**limber** *verb*
limbers
limbering
limbered

**lime** *noun*
limes

**limelight**

**limerick** *noun*
limericks

**limestone**

. . . . . . . . . . . . . . . . . . . . . . . . . . . . . . . . . . . . . . . . . . . . . . . . . . . . . . . .

★ As in *to lie on the bed.*

☆ Meaning 'to say something untrue'.

**limit** *noun*
limits

**limit** *verb*
limits
limiting
limited

**limitation** *noun*
limitations

**limited**

**limitless**

**limp** *adjective*
limper
limpest
limply

**limp** *verb*
limps
limping
limped

**limp** *noun*
limps

**limpet** *noun*
limpets

**line** *noun*
lines

**line** *verb*
lines
lining
lined

**linen**

**liner** *noun*
liners

**linesman** *noun*
linesmen

**-ling**
*-ling* makes words for
small things, e.g.
**duckling**.

**linger** *verb*
lingers
lingering
lingered

**lingerie**

**linguist** *noun*
linguists

**linguistic**

**linguistics**

**lining** *noun*
linings

**link** *verb*
links
linking
linked

**link** *noun*
links

**lino**

**linoleum**

**lint**

**lion** *noun*
lions

**lioness** *noun*
lionesses

**lip** *noun*
lips

**lip-read** *verb*
lip-reads
lip-reading
lip-read

**lipstick** *noun*
lipsticks

**liquid** *adjective* and
*noun*
liquids

**liquidizer** *noun*
liquidizers

**liquor** *noun*
liquors

**liquorice**

**lisp** *noun*
lisps

**lisp** *verb*
lisps
lisping
lisped

**list** *noun*
lists

**list** *verb*
lists
listing
listed

**listen** *verb*
listens
listening
listened

**listener** *noun*
listeners

**listless** *adjective*
listlessly

**lit** see **light**

**literacy**

**literal** *adjective*
literally

**literary**

**literate**

**literature**

**litmus**

**litre** *noun*
litres

**litter** *noun*
litters

**litter** *verb*
litters
littering
littered

**little★** *adjective* and
*adverb*
less
least

**live** *verb*
lives
living
lived

★ You can also use **littler** and **littlest** when you are talking about
size.

a **live** *adjective*
**livelihood** *noun*
  livelihoods
b **liveliness**
c **lively** *adjective*
  livelier
d   liveliest
e **liver** *noun*
  livers
f **livery** *noun*
  liveries
g **lives** see **life**
h **livestock**
i **livid**
**living** *noun*
j   livings
k **lizard** *noun*
  lizards
l **llama** *noun*
  llamas
m **load** *verb*
  loads
n   loading
  loaded
o **load** *noun*
  loads
p **loaf** *noun*
q   loaves
**loaf** *verb*
r   loafs
  loafing
s   loafed
t **loafer** *noun*
  loafers
u **loam**
**loamy** *adjective*
v   loamier
  loamiest
w

**loan★** *noun*
  loans
**loan** *verb*
  loans
  loaning
  loaned
**loath☆** *adjective*
**loathe◐** *verb*
  loathes
  loathing
  loathed
**loathsome**
**loaves** see **loaf**
**lob** *verb*
  lobs
  lobbing
  lobbed
**lobby** *noun*
  lobbies
**lobby** *verb*
  lobbies
  lobbying
  lobbied
**lobe** *noun*
  lobes
**lobster** *noun*
  lobsters
**local** *adjective*
  locally
**local** *noun*
  locals
**locality** *noun*
  localities
**locate** *verb*
  locates
  locating
  located
**location** *noun*
  locations

**loch✤** *noun*
  lochs
**lock✱** *noun*
  locks
**lock** *verb*
  locks
  locking
  locked
**locker** *noun*
  lockers
**locket** *noun*
  lockets
**locomotive** *noun*
  locomotives
**locust** *noun*
  locusts
**lodge** *noun*
  lodges
**lodge** *verb*
  lodges
  lodging
  lodged
**lodger** *noun*
  lodgers
**lodgings** *plural noun*
**loft** *noun*
  lofts
**lofty** *adjective*
  loftier
  loftiest
  loftily
**log** *noun*
  logs
**log** *verb*
  logs
  logging
  logged
**logarithm** *noun*
  logarithms

. . . . . . . . . . . . . . . . . . . . . . . . . . . . . . . . . . . . . . . . . . . . . . . . . . . . . . . . . . . . . . . .

x ★ A **loan** is a thing that is lent to someone. **!** **lone**.
☆ **Loath** means 'unwilling'. **!** **loathe**.
y ◐ To **loathe** is to dislike very much. **!** **loath**.
✤ A **loch** is a lake in Scotland. **!** **lock**.
z ✱ A **lock** is a mechanism for keeping something closed. **!** **loch**.

**logbook** *noun*
logbooks

**logic**

**logical** *adjective*
logically

**logo** *noun*
logos

> **-logy**
> *-logy* makes words for subjects of study, e.g. **archaeology** ( the study of ancient remains). Most of these words end in *-ology*, but an important exception is **genealogy**. Some words have plurals, e.g. **genealogies**.

**loiter** *verb*
loiters
loitering
loitered

**loiterer** *noun*
loiterers

**loll** *verb*
lolls
lolling
lolled

**lollipop** *noun*
lollipops

**lolly** *noun*
lollies

**lone**★

**loneliness**

**lonely** *adjective*
lonelier
loneliest

**long** *adjective* and *adverb*
longer
longest

**long** *verb*
longs
longing
longed

**longitude** *noun*
longitudes

**longitudinal** *adjective*
longitudinally

**loo** *noun*
loos

**look** *verb*
looks
looking
looked

**look** *noun*
looks

**lookout** *noun*
lookouts

**loom** *noun*
looms

**loom** *verb*
looms
looming
loomed

**loop** *noun*
loops

**loop** *verb*
loops
looping
looped

**loophole** *noun*
loopholes

**loose** *adjective*
looser
loosest
loosely

**loose** *verb*
looses
loosing
loosed

**loosen** *verb*
loosens
loosening
loosened

**looseness**

**loot** *verb*
loots
looting
looted

**loot** *noun*

**looter** *noun*
looters

**lopsided**

**lord** *noun*
lords

**lordly**

**lordship**

**lorry** *noun*
lorries

**lose** *verb*
loses
losing
lost

**loser** *noun*
losers

**loss** *noun*
losses

**lot** *noun*
lots

**lotion** *noun*
lotions

**lottery** *noun*
lotteries

**lotto**

**loud** *adjective*
louder
loudest
loudly

**loudness**

**loudspeaker** *noun*
loudspeakers

**lounge** *noun*
lounges

★ Lone means 'alone'. ! loan.

a
b
c
d
e
f
g
h
i
j
k
**l**
m
n
o
p
q
r
s
t
u
v
w
x
y
z

**lounge** *verb*
lounges
lounging
lounged

**louse** *noun*
lice

**lousy** *adjective*
lousier
lousiest
lousily

**lout** *noun*
louts

**lovable** *adjective*
lovably

**love** *verb*
loves
loving
loved

**love** *noun*
loves

**loveliness**

**lovely** *adjective*
lovelier
loveliest

**lover** *noun*
lovers

**loving** *adjective*
lovingly

**low** *adjective*
lower
lowest

**low** *verb*
lows
lowing
lowed

**lower** *verb*
lowers
lowering
lowered

**lowland** *adjective*

**lowlands** *plural nouns*

**lowlander** *noun*
lowlanders

**lowliness**

**lowly** *adjective*
lowlier
lowliest

**lowness**

**loyal** *adjective*
loyally

**loyalty** *noun*
loyalties

**lozenge** *noun*
lozenges

**lubricant** *noun*
lubricants

**lubricate** *verb*
lubricates
lubricating
lubricated

**lubrication**

**lucid** *adjective*
lucidly

**lucidity**

**luck**

**lucky** *adjective*
luckier
luckiest
luckily

**ludicrous** *adjective*
ludicrously

**ludo**

**lug** *verb*
lugs
lugging
lugged

**luggage**

**lukewarm**

**lull** *verb*
lulls
lulling
lulled

**lull** *noun*
lulls

**lullaby** *noun*
lullabies

**lumber** *verb*
lumbers
lumbering
lumbered

**lumber** *noun*

**lumberjack** *noun*
lumberjacks

**luminosity**

**luminous**

**lump** *noun*
lumps

**lump** *verb*
lumps
lumping
lumped

**lumpy** *adjective*
lumpier
lumpiest

**lunacy** *noun*
lunacies

**lunar**

**lunatic** *noun*
lunatics

**lunch** *noun*
lunches

**lung** *noun*
lungs

**lunge** *verb*
lunges
lunging
lungeing *or* lunged

**lupin** *noun*
lupins

**lurch** *verb*
lurches
lurching
lurched

**lurch** *noun*
lurches

**lure** *verb*
lures
luring
lured

a
b
c
d
e
f
g
h
i
j
k
**l**
m
n
o
p
q
r
s
t
u
v
w
x
y
z

**lurk** *verb*
lurks
lurking
lurked

**luscious** *adjective*
lusciously

**lush** *adjective*
lusher
lushest
lushly

**lushness**

**lust** *noun*
lusts

**lustful** *adjective*
lustfully

**lustre** *noun*
lustres

**lustrous**

**lute** *noun*
lutes

**luxury** *noun*
luxuries

**luxurious** *adjective*
luxuriously

**Lycra**

**-ly**
-ly makes adverbs
from adjectives, e.g.
**slow - slowly**. When
the adjective ends in
-y following a
consonant, you
change the *y* to *i*, e.g.
**happy - happily**. -ly is
also used to make
some adjectives, e.g.
**lovely**, and some
words that are
adjectives and
adverbs, e.g. **kindly**,
**hourly**.

**lying** see **lie**

**lynch** *verb*
lynches
lynching
lynched

**lyre** *noun*
lyres

**lyric** *noun*
lyrics

**lyrical** *adjective*
lyrically

**lyrics** *plural noun*

# Mm

**ma** *noun*
mas

**mac** *noun*
macs

**macabre**

**macaroni**

**machine** *noun*
machines

**machinery**

**mackerel** *noun*
mackerel

**mackintosh** *noun*
mackintoshes

**mad** *adjective*
madder
maddest
madly

**madam**

**madden** *verb*
maddens
maddening
maddened

**made★** see **make**

**madman** *noun*
madmen

**madness**

**magazine** *noun*
magazines

**maggot** *noun*
maggots

**magic** *noun* and
*adjective*

**magical** *adjective*
magically

**magician** *noun*
magicians

**magistrate** *noun*
magistrates

**magma**

**magnesium**

**magnet** *noun*
magnets

**magnetism**

**magnetic** *adjective*
magnetically

**magnetize** *verb*
magnetizes
magnetizing
magnetized

**magnificent** *adjective*
magnificently

**magnificence**

**magnification**

**magnifier**

**magnify** *verb*
magnifies
magnifying
magnified

**magnitude** *noun*
magnitudes

**magnolia** *noun*
magnolias

**magpie** *noun*
magpies

**mahogany**

**maid☆** *noun*
maids

★ You use **made** in e.g. *I made a cake*. **!maid**.
☆ A **maid** is a female servant. **!made**.

a b c d e f g h i j k l m n o p q r s t u v w x y z

# ma

a **maiden** noun
maidens

b **mail**★ noun

c **mail** verb
mails
mailing
d mailed

e **maim** verb
maims
maiming
f maimed

g **main**☆ adjective
mainly
h

i **mainland**

**mainly**

j **mains** plural noun

k **maintain** verb
maintains
maintaining
l maintained

m **maintenance**

**maisonette** noun
maisonettes
n

o **maize**

**majestic** adjective
majestically
p

**majesty** noun
majesties
q

**major** adjective

r **major** noun
majors

s **majority** noun
majorities
t

**make** verb
makes
u making
made
v

**make** noun
w makes

**make-believe**

**maker** noun
makers

**make-up**

**maladjusted**

**malaria**

**male**○ adjective and
noun
males

**malevolence**

**malevolent** adjective
malevolently

**malice**

**malicious** adjective
maliciously

**mallet** noun
mallets

**malnourished**

**malnutrition**

**malt**

**malted**

**mammal** noun
mammals

**mammoth** adjective
and noun
mammoths

**man** noun
men

**man** verb
mans
manning
manned

**manage** verb
manages
managing
managed

**manageable**

**management**

**manager** noun
managers

**manageress** noun
manageresses

**mane**✣ noun
manes

**manger** noun
mangers

**mangle** verb
mangles
mangling
mangled

**mango** noun
mangoes

**manhandle** verb
manhandles
manhandling
manhandled

**manhole** noun
manholes

**mania** noun
manias

**maniac** noun
maniacs

**manic** adjective
manically

**manifesto** noun
manifestos

**manipulate** verb
manipulates
manipulating
manipulated

**manipulation**

**manipulator**

**mankind**

**manliness**

**manly** adjective
manlier
manliest

x
y **★ Mail** is letters and parcels sent by post. ! **male.**
**☆ Main** means 'most important'. ! **mane.**
z **○** A **male** is a man or an animal of the same gender as a man. ! **mail.**
**✣** A **mane** is the long piece of hair on a horse or lion. ! **main.**

**manner**★ *noun*
  manners

**manoeuvrable**

**manoeuvre** *verb*
  manoeuvres
  manoeuvring
  manoeuvred

**manoeuvre** *noun*
  manoeuvres

**man-of-war** *noun*
  men-of-war

**manor**☆ *noun*
  manors

**mansion** *noun*
  mansions

**manslaughter**

**mantelpiece** *noun*
  mantelpieces

**mantle** *noun*
  mantles

**manual** *adjective*
  manually

**manual** *noun*
  manuals

**manufacture** *verb*
  manufactures
  manufacturing
  manufactured

**manufacture** *noun*

**manufacturer** *noun*
  manufacturers

**manure**

**manuscript** *noun*
  manuscripts

**Manx**

**many** *adjective* and
*noun*
  more
  most

**Maori** *noun*
  Maoris

**map** *noun*
  maps

**map** *verb*
  maps
  mapping
  mapped

**maple** *noun*
  maples

**mar** *verb*
  mars
  marring
  marred

**marathon** *noun*
  marathons

**marauder** *noun*
  marauders

**marauding**

**marble** *noun*
  marbles

**March** *noun*
  Marches

**march** *verb*
  marches
  marching
  marched

**march** *noun*
  marches

**marcher** *noun*
  marchers

**mare**✪ *noun*
  mares

**margarine**

**margin** *noun*
  margins

**marginal** *adjective*
  marginally

**marigold** *noun*
  marigolds

**marijuana**

**marina** *noun*
  marinas

**marine** *adjective* and
*noun*
  marines

**mariner** *noun*
  mariners

**marionette** *noun*
  marionettes

**mark** *verb*
  marks
  marking
  marked

**mark** *noun*
  marks

**market** *noun*
  markets

**market** *verb*
  markets
  marketing
  marketed

**marksman** *noun*
  marksmen

**marksmanship**

**marmalade**

**maroon** *verb*
  maroons
  marooning
  marooned

**maroon** *adjective* and
*noun*

**marquee** *noun*
  marquees

**marriage** *noun*
  marriages

. . . . . . . . . . . . . . . . . . . . . . . . . . . . . . . . . . . . . . . . . . . . . . . . .

★ You use **manner** in e.g. *a friendly manner*. **!** **manor**.

☆ A **manor** is a big house in the country. **!** **manner**.

✪ A **mare** is a female horse. **!** **mayor**.

a
b
c
d
e
f
g
h
i
j
k
l
**m**
n
o
p
q
r
s
t
u
v
w
x
y
z

147

**marrow** noun
marrows

**marry** verb
marries
marrying
married

**marsh** noun
marshes

**marshal** noun
marshals

**marshmallow** noun
marshmallows

**marshy** adjective
marshier
marshiest

**marsupial** noun
marsupials

**martial**

**Martian** noun
Martians

**martin** noun
martins

**martyr** noun
martyrs

**martyrdom**

**marvel** verb
marvels
marvelling
marvelled

**marvel** noun
marvels

**marvellous** adjective
marvellously

**Marxism**

**Marxist**

**marzipan**

**mascot** noun
mascots

**masculine**

**masculinity**

**mash** verb
mashes
mashing
mashed

**mash** noun

**mask** noun
masks

**mask** verb
masks
masking
masked

**Mason★** noun
Masons

**mason☆** noun
masons

**masonry**

**Mass♦** noun
Masses

**mass** noun
masses

**mass** verb
masses
massing
massed

**massacre** verb
massacres
massacring
massacred

**massacre** noun
massacres

**massage** verb
massages
massaging
massaged

**massage** noun

**massive** adjective
massively

**mast** noun
masts

**master** noun
masters

**master** verb
masters
mastering
mastered

**masterly**

**mastermind** noun
masterminds

**masterpiece** noun
masterpieces

**mastery**

**mat✛** noun
mats

**matador** noun
matadors

**match** verb
matches
matching
matched

**match** noun
matches

**mate** noun
mates

**mate** verb
mates
mating
mated

**material** noun
materials

**materialistic**

**maternal** adjective
maternally

**maternity**

**mathematical**
adjective
mathematically

- - - - - - - - - - - - - - - - - - - - - - - - - - - - - - - - - - - - - - - - - -

★ You use a capital M when you mean a member of the
Freemasons.
☆ Use a small m when you mean someone who builds with stone.
♦ Use a capital M when you mean the Roman Catholic service.
✛ A mat is a covering for a floor. **!** matt.

**mathematician** *noun*
mathematicians

**mathematics**

**maths**

**matinée** *noun*
matinées

**matrimonial**

**matrimony**

**matrix** *noun*
matrices

**matron** *noun*
matrons

**matt**★

**matted**

**matter** *verb*
matters
mattering
mattered

**matter** *noun*
matters

**matting**

**mattress** *noun*
mattresses

**mature**

**maturity**

**mauve**

**maximum** *adjective*
and *noun*
maxima *or* maximums

**May** *noun*
Mays

**may** *verb*
might

**may**

**maybe**

**May Day**

**mayday**✰ *noun*
maydays

**mayonnaise**

**mayor**✇ *noun*
mayors

**mayoress** *noun*
mayoresses

**maypole** *noun*
maypoles

**maze** *noun*
mazes

**meadow** *noun*
meadows

**meagre**

**meal** *noun*
meals

**mean** *adjective*
meaner
meanest
meanly

**mean** *verb*
means
meaning
meant

**meander** *verb*
meanders
meandering
meandered

**meaning** *noun*
meanings

**meaningful** *adjective*
meaningfully

**meaningless**
*adjective*
meaninglessly

**meanness**

**means** *plural noun*

**meantime**

**meanwhile**

**measles** *plural noun*

**measly** *adjective*
measlier
measliest

**measure** *verb*
measures
measuring
measured

**measure** *noun*
measures

**measurement** *noun*
measurements

**meat**✛ *noun*
meats

**meaty** *adjective*
meatier
meatiest

**mechanic** *noun*
mechanics

**mechanical** *adjective*
mechanically

**mechanics**

**mechanism** *noun*
mechanisms

**medal** *noun*
medals

**medallist** *noun*
medallists

**meddle** *verb*
meddles
meddling
meddled

**meddler** *noun*
meddlers

**meddlesome**

**media** *plural noun*

**median** *noun*
medians

**medical** *adjective*
medically

a
b
c
d
e
f
g
h
i
j
k
l
**m**
n
o
p
q
r
s
t
u
v
w
x
y
z

· · · · · · · · · · · · · · · · · · · · · · · · · · · · · · · · · · · · · · · · · · · · ·

★ **Matt** means 'not shiny'. **!** **mat**.
✰ An international radio signal.
✇ You use **mayor** in e.g. *the Mayor of London*. **!** **mare**.
✛ **Meat** is the flesh of an animal. **!** **meet**.

149

## me

medicine *noun*
medicines
medicinal
medieval
mediocre
mediocrity
meditate *verb*
meditates
meditating
meditated
meditation
Mediterranean
medium *adjective*
medium *noun*
media *or* mediums
meek *adjective*
meeker
meekest
meekly
meekness
meet★ *verb*
meets
meeting
met
meeting *noun*
meetings
megaphone *noun*
megaphones
melancholy
mellow *adjective*
mellower
mellowest
melodious *adjective*
melodiously
melodrama *noun*
melodramas
melodramatic
*adjective*
melodramatically
melody *noun*
melodies
melodic

melon *noun*
melons
melt *verb*
melts
melting
melted
member *noun*
members
membership
Member of
Parliament *noun*
Members of
Parliament
membrane *noun*
membranes
memoirs *plural noun*
memorable *adjective*
memorably
memorial *noun*
memorials
memorize *verb*
memorizes
memorizing
memorized
memory *noun*
memories
men see man
menace *verb*
menaces
menacing
menaced
menace *noun*
menaces
menagerie *noun*
menageries
mend *verb*
mends
mending
mended
mender *noun*
menders
menstrual
menstruation

**-ment**
*-ment* makes nouns
from adjectives e.g.
**contentment**. There
is a fixed number of
these, and you cannot
freely add *-ment* as
you can with *-ness*.
When the adjective
ends in *-y* following a
consonant, you
change the *y* to *i*, e.g.
**merry - merriment**.

mental *adjective*
mentally
mention *verb*
mentions
mentioning
mentioned
mention *noun*
mentions
menu *noun*
menus
mercenary *adjective*
and *noun*
mercenaries
merchandise
merchant *noun*
merchants
merciful *adjective*
mercifully
merciless *adjective*
mercilessly
mercury
mercy *noun*
mercies
mere *adjective*
mere *noun*
meres
merely *adverb*

. . . . . . . . . . . . . . . . . . . . . . . . . . . . . . . . . . . . . . . . . . . . . . . . . . .

★ People meet when they come together. ! meat.

150

**merge** *verb*
merges
merging
merged

**merger** *noun*
mergers

**meridian** *noun*
meridians

**meringue** *noun*
meringues

**merit** *noun*
merits

**merit** *verb*
merits
meriting
merited

**mermaid** *noun*
mermaids

**merriment**

**merry** *adjective*
merrier
merriest
merrily

**merry-go-round**
*noun*
merry-go-rounds

**mesh** *noun*
meshes

**mess** *noun*
messes

**mess** *verb*
messes
messing
messed

**message** *noun*
messages

**messenger** *noun*
messengers

**Messiah**

**messiness**

**messy** *adjective*
messier
messiest
messily

**met** see **meet**

**metal**★ *noun*
metals

**metallic**

**metallurgical**

**metallurgist**

**metallurgy**

**metamorphosis**
*noun*
metamorphoses

**metaphor** *noun*
metaphors

**metaphorical**
*adjective*
metaphorically

**meteor** *noun*
meteors

**meteoric**

**meteorite** *noun*
meteorites

**meteorological**

**meteorologist**

**meteorology**

**meter**☆ *noun*
meters

**methane**

**method** *noun*
methods

**methodical** *adjective*
methodically

**Methodist** *noun*
Methodists

**meths**

**methylated spirit**

**meticulous** *adjective*
meticulously

**metre**○ *noun*
metres

**metric** *adjective*

**metrical** *adjective*
metrically

**metronome** *noun*
metronomes

**mettle**✣

**mew** *verb*
mews
mewing
mewed

**miaow** *verb*
miaows
miaowing
miaowed

**mice** see **mouse**

**micro-**
*micro-* makes words
meaning 'small', e.g.
**microwave**. When
the word begins with a
vowel you add a
hyphen, e.g.
**micro-organism**.

**microbe** *noun*
microbes

**microchip** *noun*
microchips

**microcomputer** *noun*
microcomputers

**microfilm** *noun*
microfilms

a
b
c
d
e
f
g
h
i
j
k
l
**m**
n
o
p
q
r
s
t
u
v
w
x
y
z

★ **Metal** is a hard substance used to make things. **!mettle**.
☆ A **meter** is a device that shows how much of something has been used. **!metre**.
○ A **metre** is a unit of length. **!meter**.
✣ As in *to be on your mettle*. **!metal**.

**microphone** *noun*
microphones

**microprocessor**
*noun*
microprocessors

**microscope** *noun*
microscopes

**microscopic**
*adjective*
microscopically

**microwave** *noun*
microwaves

**microwave** *verb*
microwaves
microwaving
microwaved

**mid**★

**midday**

**middle** *noun*
middles

**Middle Ages**

**Middle East**

**midge** *noun*
midges

**midget** *noun*
midgets

**midland** *adjective*

**midnight**

**midst**

**midsummer**

**midway**

**midwife** *noun*
midwives

**midwifery**

**might**☆ *noun*

**might** see **may**

**mightiness**

**mighty** *adjective*
mightier
mightiest
mightily

**migraine** *noun*
migraines

**migrant** *noun*
migrants

**migrate** *verb*
migrates
migrating
migrated

**migration** *noun*
migrations

**migratory**

**mike** *noun*
mikes

**mild** *adjective*
milder
mildest
mildly

**mildness**

**mile** *noun*
miles

**mileage** *noun*
mileages

**milestone** *noun*
milestones

**militancy**

**militant**

**militarism**

**militaristic**

**military**

**milk** *noun*

**milk** *verb*
milks
milking
milked

**milkman** *noun*
milkmen

**milky** *adjective*
milkier
milkiest

**Milky Way**

**mill** *noun*
mills

**mill** *verb*
mills
milling
milled

**millennium** *noun*
millenniums

**miller** *noun*
millers

**millet**

**milligram** *noun*
milligrams

**millilitre** *noun*
millilitres

**millimetre** *noun*
millimetres

**million** *noun*
millions

**millionth**

**millionaire** *noun*
millionaires

**millstone** *noun*
millstones

**milometer** *noun*
milometers

**mime** *verb*
mimes
miming
mimed

**mime** *noun*
mimes

**mimic** *verb*
mimics
mimicking
mimicked

**mimic** *noun*
mimics

- - - - - - - - - - - - - - - - - - - - - - - - - - - - - - - - - - - - - - - - - - - - -

★ You use a hyphen, e.g. *mid-August*.

☆ **Might** means 'force' or 'strength'. **!** mite.

**mimicry**

**minaret** *noun*
minarets

**mince** *verb*
minces
mincing
minced

**mince** *noun*

**mincemeat**

**mincer** *noun*
mincers

**mind** *noun*
minds

**mind** *verb*
minds
minding
minded

**mindless** *adjective*
mindlessly

**mine** *adjective*

**mine** *verb*
mines
mining
mined

**mine** *noun*
mines

**minefield** *noun*
minefields

**miner** *noun*
miners

**mineral** *noun*
minerals

**mingle** *verb*
mingles
mingling
mingled

**mini-**
*mini-* makes words meaning 'small', e.g. **miniskirt**. You do not normally need a hyphen.

**mingy** *adjective*
mingier
mingiest

**miniature** *adjective*
and *noun*
miniatures

**minibus** *noun*
minibuses

**minim** *noun*
minims

**minimal** *adjective*
minimally

**minimize** *verb*
minimizes
minimizing
minimized

**minimum** *adjective*
and *noun*
minima
minimums

**minister** *noun*
ministers

**ministry** *noun*
ministries

**mink** *noun*
minks

**minnow** *noun*
minnows

**minor** *adjective* and
*noun*
minors

**minority** *noun*
minorities

**minstrel** *noun*
minstrels

**mint** *noun*
mints

**mint** *verb*
mints
minting
minted

**minus** *preposition*

**minute** *adjective*
minutely

**minute** *noun*
minutes

**miracle** *noun*
miracles

**miraculous** *adjective*
miraculously

**mirage** *noun*
mirages

**mirror** *noun*
mirrors

**mirth**

**misbehave** *verb*
misbehaves
misbehaving
misbehaved

**misbehaviour**

**miscarriage** *noun*
miscarriages

**miscellaneous**

**miscellany** *noun*
miscellanies

**mischief**

**mischievous**
*adjective*
mischievously

**miser** *noun*
misers

**miserable** *adjective*
miserably

**miserly**

**misery** *noun*
miseries

**misfire** *verb*
misfires
misfiring
misfired

**misfit** *noun*
misfits

**misfortune** *noun*
misfortunes

**mishap** *noun*
mishaps

**misjudge** *verb*
misjudges
misjudging
misjudged

**mislay** *verb*
mislays
mislaying
mislaid

**mislead** *verb*
misleads
misleading
misled

**misprint** *noun*
misprints

**miss** *verb*
misses
missing
missed

**miss** *noun*
misses

**missile** *noun*
missiles

**missing**

**mission** *noun*
missions

**missionary** *noun*
missionaries

**misspell** *verb*
misspells
misspelling
misspelt *or* misspelled

**mist**★ *noun*
mists

**mistake** *noun*
mistakes

**mistake** *verb*
mistakes
mistaking
mistook
mistaken

**mister**

**mistiness**

**mistletoe**

**mistreat** *verb*
mistreats
mistreating
mistreated

**mistreatment**

**mistress** *noun*
mistresses

**mistrust** *verb*
mistrusts
mistrusting
mistrusted

**misty** *adjective*
mistier
mistiest
mistily

**misunderstand** *verb*
misunderstands
misunderstanding
misunderstood

**misunderstanding** *noun*
misunderstandings

**misuse** *verb*
misuses
misusing
misused

**misuse** *noun*
misuses

**mite**☆ *noun*
mites

**mitre** *noun*
mitres

**mitten** *noun*
mittens

**mix** *verb*
mixes
mixing
mixed

**mixer** *noun*
mixers

**mixture** *noun*
mixtures

**mix-up** *noun*
mix-ups

**moan** *verb*
moans
moaning
moaned

**moan** *noun*
moans

**moat** *noun*
moats

**mob** *noun*
mobs

**mob** *verb*
mobs
mobbing
mobbed

**mobile** *adjective* and *noun*
mobiles

**mobility**

**mobilization**

**mobilize** *verb*
mobilizes
mobilizing
mobilized

**moccasin** *noun*
moccasins

**mock** *adjective*

**mock** *verb*
mocks
mocking
mocked

**mockery** *noun*
mockeries

**mock-up** *noun*
mock-ups

**mode** *noun*
modes

**model** *noun*
models

★ **Mist** is damp air that is difficult to see through. **!missed**.
☆ A **mite** is a tiny insect. **!might**.

**model** *verb*
models
modelling
modelled

**modem** *noun*
modems

**moderate** *adjective*
moderately

**moderate** *verb*
moderates
moderating
moderated

**moderation**

**modern**

**modernity**

**modernization**

**modernize** *verb*
modernizes
modernizing
modernized

**modest** *adjective*
modestly

**modesty**

**modification** *noun*
modifications

**modify** *verb*
modifies
modifying
modified

**module** *noun*
modules

**moist** *adjective*
moister
moistest

**moisture**

**moisten** *verb*
moistens
moistening
moistened

**molar** *noun*
molars

**mole** *noun*
moles

**molecular**

**molecule** *noun*
molecules

**molehill** *noun*
molehills

**molest** *verb*
molests
molesting
molested

**mollusc** *noun*
molluscs

**molten**

**moment** *noun*
moments

**momentary** *adjective*
momentarily

**momentous** *adjective*
momentously

**momentum**

**monarch** *noun*
monarchs

**monarchy** *noun*
monarchies

**monastery** *noun*
monasteries

**monastic**

**Monday** *noun*
Mondays

**money**

**mongoose** *noun*
mongooses

**mongrel** *noun*
mongrels

**monitor** *verb*
monitors
monitoring
monitored

**monitor** *noun*
monitors

**monk** *noun*
monks

**monkey** *noun*
monkeys

**monogram** *noun*
monograms

**monologue** *noun*
monologues

**monopolize** *verb*
monopolizes
monopolizing
monopolized

**monopoly** *noun*
monopolies

**monorail** *noun*
monorails

**monotonous**
*adjective*
monotonously

**monotony**

**monsoon** *noun*
monsoons

**monster** *noun*
monsters

**monstrosity** *noun*
monstrosities

**monstrous** *adjective*
monstrously

**month** *noun*
months

**monthly** *adjective* and
*adverb*

**monument** *noun*
monuments

**monumental**
*adjective*
monumentally

**moo** *verb*
moos
mooing
mooed

**mood** *noun*
moods

**moodiness**

**moody** *adjective*
moodier
moodiest
moodily

**moon** *noun*
moons

**moonlight**

a

**moonlit**
**moor**★ *verb*
moors
mooring
moored
**moor**☆ *noun*
moors
**moorhen** *noun*
moorhens
**mooring** *noun*
moorings
**moose**○ *noun*
moose
**mop** *noun*
mops
**mop** *verb*
mops
mopping
mopped
**mope** *verb*
mopes
moping
moped
**moped** *noun*
mopeds
**moraine** *noun*
moraines
**moral** *adjective*
morally
**moral** *noun*
morals
**morale**
**morality**
**morals** *plural noun*
**morbid** *adjective*
morbidly
**more**✢ *adjective, adverb, and noun*
**moreover**

**Mormon** *noun*
Mormons
**morning** *noun*
mornings
**moron** *noun*
morons
**moronic** *adjective*
moronically
**morose** *adjective*
morosely
**morphine**
**morris dance** *noun*
morris dances
**Morse code**
**morsel** *noun*
morsels
**mortal** *adjective*
mortally
**mortality**
**mortar**
**mortgage** *noun*
mortgages
**mortuary** *noun*
mortuaries
**mosaic** *noun*
mosaics
**mosque** *noun*
mosques
**mosquito** *noun*
mosquitoes
**moss** *noun*
mosses
**mossy** *adjective*
mossier
mossiest
**most** *adjective, adverb, and noun*
**mostly** *adverb*

**motel** *noun*
motels
**moth** *noun*
moths
**mother** *noun*
mothers
**motherhood**
**mother-in-law** *noun*
mothers-in-law
**motherly**
**motion** *noun*
motions
**motionless**
**motivate** *verb*
motivates
motivating
motivated
**motive** *noun*
motives
**motor** *noun*
motors
**motorbike** *noun*
motorbikes
**motor boat** *noun*
motor boats
**motor car** *noun*
motor cars
**motorcycle** *noun*
motorcycles
**motorcyclist** *noun*
motorcyclists
**motorist** *noun*
motorists
**motorway** *noun*
motorways
**mottled**
**motto** *noun*
mottoes

. . . . . . . . . . . . . . . . . . . . . . . . . . . . . . . . . . . . . . . . . . . . . . .

★ To **moor** a boat is to tie it up. **!more**.
☆ A **moor** is an area of rough land. **!more**.
○ A **moose** is an American elk. **!mouse, mousse**.
✢ You use **more** in e.g. *I'd like more to eat.* **!moor**.

**mould** *verb*
moulds
moulding
moulded

**mould** *noun*
moulds

**mouldy** *adjective*
mouldier
mouldiest

**moult** *verb*
moults
moulting
moulted

**mound** *noun*
mounds

**mount** *verb*
mounts
mounting
mounted

**mount** *noun*
mounts

**mountain** *noun*
mountains

**mountaineer** *noun*
mountaineers

**mountaineering**

**mountainous**

**mourn** *verb*
mourns
mourning
mourned

**mourner** *noun*
mourners

**mournful** *adjective*
mournfully

**mouse**★ *noun*
mice

**mousetrap** *noun*
mousetraps

**mousse**☆ *noun*
mousses

**moustache** *noun*
moustaches

**mousy** *adjective*
mousier
mousiest

**mouth** *noun*
mouths

**mouthful** *noun*
mouthfuls

**mouthpiece** *noun*
mouthpieces

**movable**

**move** *verb*
moves
moving
moved

**move** *noun*
moves

**movement** *noun*
movements

**movie** *noun*
movies

**mow** *verb*
mows
mowing
mowed
mown

**mower** *noun*
mowers

**much** *adjective,*
*adverb,* and *noun*

**muck** *noun*

**muck** *verb*
mucks
mucking
mucked

**mucky** *adjective*
muckier
muckiest

**mud**

**muddle** *verb*
muddles
muddling
muddled

**muddle** *noun*
muddles

**muddler** *noun*
muddlers

**muddy** *adjective*
muddier
muddiest

**mudguard** *noun*
mudguards

**muesli**

**muezzin**✪ *noun*
muezzins

**muffle** *verb*
muffles
muffling
muffled

**mug** *noun*
mugs

**mug** *verb*
mugs
mugging
mugged

**mugger** *noun*
muggers

**muggy** *adjective*
muggier
muggiest

**mule** *noun*
mules

**multi-**
*multi-* makes words with the meaning 'many', e.g. **multicultural**. You do not normally need a hyphen.

a b c d e f g h i j k l **m** n o p q r s t u v w x y z

★ A **mouse** is a small animal. **!** moose, mousse.
☆ A **mousse** is a creamy pudding. **!** moose, mouse.
✪ A man who calls Muslims to prayer. Pronounced *moo-ezz-in*.

a · b · c · d · e · f · g · h · i · j · k · l · m · n · o · p · q · r · s · t · u · v · w · x · y · z

**multiple** *adjective* and *noun*
multiples

**multiplication**

**multiply** *verb*
multiplies
multiplying
multiplied

**multiracial**

**multitude** *noun*
multitudes

**mumble** *verb*
mumbles
mumbling
mumbled

**mummify** *verb*
mummifies
mummifying
mummified

**mummy** *noun*
mummies

**mumps**

**munch** *verb*
munches
munching
munched

**mundane**

**municipal**

**mural** *noun*
murals

**murder** *verb*
murders
murdering
murdered

**murder** *noun*
murders

**murderer** *noun*
murderers

**murderous** *adjective*
murderously

**murky** *adjective*
murkier
murkiest

**murmur** *verb*
murmurs
murmuring
murmured

**murmur** *noun*
murmurs

**muscle★** *noun*
muscles

**muscle** *verb*
muscles
muscling
muscled

**muscular**

**museum** *noun*
museums

**mushroom** *noun*
mushrooms

**mushroom** *verb*
mushrooms
mushrooming
mushroomed

**music**

**musical** *adjective*
musically

**musical** *noun*
musicals

**musician** *noun*
musicians

**musket** *noun*
muskets

**musketeer** *noun*
musketeers

**Muslim** *noun*
Muslims

**muslin**

**mussel☆** *noun*
mussels

**must**

**mustard**

**muster** *verb*
musters
mustering
mustered

**mustiness**

**musty** *adjective*
mustier
mustiest

**mutation** *noun*
mutations

**mute** *adjective*
mutely

**mute** *noun*
mutes

**muted**

**mutilate** *verb*
mutilates
mutilating
mutilated

**mutilation**

**mutineer** *noun*
mutineers

**mutiny** *noun*
mutinies

**mutinous** *adjective*
mutinously

**mutiny** *verb*
mutinies
mutinying
mutinied

**mutter** *verb*
mutters
muttering
muttered

**mutton**

**mutual** *adjective*
mutually

**muzzle** *verb*
muzzles
muzzling
muzzled

· · · · · · · · · · · · · · · · · · · · · · · · · · · · · · · · · · · · · · · · · · · · · · · · · · · · · ·

★ A **muscle** is a part of the body. **!mussel**.

☆ A **mussel** is a shellfish. **!muscle**.

**muzzle** *noun*
  muzzles

**myself**

**mysterious** *adjective*
  mysteriously

**mystery** *noun*
  mysteries

**mystification**

**mystify** *verb*
  mystifies
  mystifying
  mystified

**myth** *noun*
  myths

**mythical**

**mythological**
  *adjective*

**mythology**

# Nn

**nab** *verb*
  nabs
  nabbing
  nabbed

**nag** *verb*
  nags
  nagging
  nagged

**nag** *noun*
  nags

**nail** *noun*
  nails

**nail** *verb*
  nails
  nailing
  nailed

**naive** *adjective*
  naively

**naivety**

**naked**

**nakedness**

**name** *noun*
  names

**name** *verb*
  names
  naming
  named

**nameless**

**namely**

**nanny** *noun*
  nannies

**nap** *noun*
  naps

**napkin** *noun*
  napkins

**nappy** *noun*
  nappies

**narcissus** *noun*
  narcissi

**narcotic** *noun*
  narcotics

**narrate** *verb*
  narrates
  narrating
  narrated

**narration** *noun*
  narrations

**narrative** *noun*
  narratives

**narrator** *noun*
  narrators

**narrow** *adjective*
  narrower
  narrowest
  narrowly

**nasal** *adjective*
  nasally

**nastiness**

**nasturtium** *noun*
  nasturtiums

**nasty** *adjective*
  nastier
  nastiest
  nastily

**nation** *noun*
  nations

**national** *adjective*
  nationally

**nationalism**

**nationalist**

**nationality** *noun*
  nationalities

**nationalization**

**nationalize** *verb*
  nationalizes
  nationalizing
  nationalized

**nationwide** *adjective*

**native** *adjective* and
  *noun*
  natives

**Native American**
  *noun*
  Native Americans

**nativity** *noun*
  nativities

**natural** *adjective*
  naturally

**natural** *noun*
  naturals

**naturalist** *noun*
  naturalists

**naturalization**

**naturalize** *verb*
  naturalizes
  naturalizing
  naturalized

**nature** *noun*
  natures

**naughtiness**

**naughty** *adjective*
  naughtier
  naughtiest
  naughtily

**nausea**

**nautical**

a
b
c
d
e
f
g
h
i
j
k
l
**m**
**n**
o
p
q
r
s
t
u
v
w
x
y
z

a
b
c
d
e
f
g
h
i
j
k
l
m

**n**

o
p
q
r
s
t
u
v
w
x
y
z

**naval★** *adjective*

**nave** *noun*
naves

**navel☆** *noun*
navels

**navigable**

**navigate** *verb*
navigates
navigating
navigated

**navigation**

**navigator** *noun*
navigators

**navy** *noun*
navies

**Nazi** *noun*
Nazis

**Nazism**

**near** *adjective* and
*adverb*
nearer
nearest

**near** *preposition*

**near** *verb*
nears
nearing
neared

**nearby**

**nearly**

**neat** *adjective*
neater
neatest
neatly

**neatness**

**necessarily**

**necessary**

**necessity** *noun*
necessities

**neck** *noun*
necks

**neckerchief** *noun*
neckerchiefs

**necklace** *noun*
necklaces

**nectar**

**nectarine** *noun*
nectarines

**need©** *verb*
needs
needing
needed

**need** *noun*
needs

**needle** *noun*
needles

**needless** *adjective*
needlessly

**needlework**

**needy** *adjective*
needier
neediest

**negative** *adjective*
negatively

**negative** *noun*
negatives

**neglect** *verb*
neglects
neglecting
neglected

**neglect** *noun*

**neglectful** *adjective*
neglectfully

**negligence**

**negligent** *adjective*
negligently

**negligible** *adjective*
negligibly

**negotiate** *verb*
negotiates
negotiating
negotiated

**negotiation** *noun*
negotiations

**negotiator** *noun*
negotiators

**neigh** *verb*
neighs
neighing
neighed

**neigh** *noun*
neighs

**neighbour** *noun*
neighbours

**neighbouring**

**neighbourhood** *noun*
neighbourhoods

**neighbourly**

**neither** *adjective* and
*conjunction*

**neon**

**nephew** *noun*
nephews

**nerve** *noun*
nerves

**nerve-racking**

**nervous** *adjective*
nervously

**nervousness**

**-ness**

*-ness* makes nouns
from adjectives, e.g.
**soft - softness**.
When the adjective
ends in *-y* following a
consonant, you
change the *y* to *i*, e.g.
**lively - liveliness**.

**nest** *noun*
nests

★ **Naval** means 'to do with a navy'. **!navel**.
☆ A **navel** is a small hollow in your stomach. **!naval**.
© To **need** is to require something. **!knead**.

**nest** *verb*
nests
nesting
nested

**nestle** *verb*
nestles
nestling
nestled

**nestling** *noun*
nestlings

**net** *noun*
nets

**net** *adjective*

**netball**

**nettle** *noun*
nettles

**network** *noun*
networks

**neuter** *adjective*

**neuter** *verb*
neuters
neutering
neutered

**neutral** *adjective*
neutrally

**neutrality**

**neutralize** *verb*
neutralizes
neutralizing
neutralized

**neutron** *noun*
neutrons

**never**

**nevertheless**
*conjunction*

**new★** *adjective*
newer
newest
newly

**newcomer** *noun*
newcomers

**newness**

**news**

**newsagent** *noun*
newsagents

**newsletter** *noun*
newsletters

**newspaper** *noun*
newspapers

**newt** *noun*
newts

**New Testament**

**newton** *noun*
newtons

**next** *adjective* and
*adverb*

**next door**

**nib** *noun*
nibs

**nibble** *verb*
nibbles
nibbling
nibbled

**nice** *adjective*
nicer
nicest
nicely

**niceness**

**nicety** *noun*
niceties

**nick** *verb*
nicks
nicking
nicked

**nick** *noun*
nicks

**nickel** *noun*
nickels

**nickname** *noun*
nicknames

**nicotine**

**niece** *noun*
nieces

**night☆** *noun*
nights

**nightclub** *noun*
nightclubs

**nightdress** *noun*
nightdresses

**nightfall**

**nightingale** *noun*
nightingales

**nightly**

**nightmare** *noun*
nightmares

**nightmarish**

**nil**

**nimble** *adjective*
nimbler
nimblest
nimbly

**nine** *noun*
nines

**nineteen** *noun*
nineteens

**nineteenth**

**ninetieth**

**ninety** *noun*
nineties

**ninth** *adjective*
ninthly

**nip** *verb*
nips
nipping
nipped

**nip** *noun*
nips

**nipple** *noun*
nipples

**nippy** *adjective*
nippier
nippiest

**nit** *noun*
nits

. . . . . . . . . . . . . . . . . . . . . . . . . . . . . . . . . . . . . . . . . . . . . . . . . . . . . . . . . . . . .

★ You use **new** in e.g *She has a new bike.* ! **knew**.

☆ **Night** is the opposite of day. ! **knight**.

a
b
c
d
e
f
g
h
i
j
k
l
m
**n**
o
p
q
r
s
t
u
v
w
x
y
z

a

**nitrate** *noun*
  nitrates

b

**nitric acid**

c

**nitrogen**

**nitty-gritty**

d

**nitwit** *noun*
  nitwits

e

**nobility**

f

**noble** *adjective*
  nobler
  noblest
  nobly

g

h

**noble** *noun*
  nobles

i

j

**nobleman** *noun*
  noblemen

k

**noblewoman** *noun*
  noblewomen

l

**nobody** *noun*
  nobodies

m

**nocturnal** *adjective*
  nocturnally

**n**

**nod** *verb*
  nods
  nodding
  nodded

o

p

**noise** *noun*
  noises

q

**noiseless** *adjective*
  noiselessly

r

**noisiness**

s

**noisy** *adjective*
  noisier
  noisiest
  noisily

t

u

**nomad** *noun*
  nomads

v

**nomadic**

w

**no man's land**

x


**nominate** *verb*
  nominates
  nominating
  nominated

**nomination** *noun*
  nominations

**-nomy**
-nomy makes words
for subjects of study,
e.g. **astronomy** ( the
study of the stars).
Most of these words
end in -onomy.

**none**★

**non-**
non- makes words
meaning 'not', e.g.
**non-existent**,
**non-smoker**. You
use a hyphen to make
these words. When an
un- word has a special
meaning, e.g.
**unprofessional**, you
can use non- to make
a word without the
special meaning, e.g.
**non-professional**.

**non-existent**
**non-fiction**
**non-flammable**
**nonsense**
**nonsensical** *adjective*
  nonsensically
**non-stop**
**noodle**
**noon**
**no one**


**noose** *noun*
  nooses

**normal** *adjective*
  normally

**normality**

**north** *adjective* and
*adverb*

**north**☆ *noun*

**north-east** *noun* and
*adjective*

**northerly** *adjective*
and *noun*
  northerlies

**northern**

**northerner** *noun*
  northerners

**northward** *adjective*
and *adverb*

**northwards** *adverb*

**north-west**

**nose** *noun*
  noses

**nose** *verb*
  noses
  nosing
  nosed

**nosedive** *verb*
  nosedives
  nosediving
  nosedived

**nosedive** *noun*
  nosedives

**nosiness**

**nostalgia**

**nostalgic** *adjective*
  nostalgically

**nostril** *noun*
  nostrils

y

★ You use **none** in e.g. *none of us went.* **!** nun.

z

☆ You use a capital N in **the North**, when you mean a particular
  region.

**nosy** *adjective*
nosier
nosiest
nosily

**notable** *adjective*
notably

**notch** *noun*
notches

**note** *noun*
notes

**note** *verb*
notes
noting
noted

**notebook** *noun*
notebooks

**notepaper**

**nothing**

**notice** *verb*
notices
noticing
noticed

**notice** *noun*
notices

**noticeable** *adjective*
noticeably

**noticeboard** *noun*
noticeboards

**notion** *noun*
notions

**notoriety**

**notorious** *adjective*
notoriously

**nougat**

**nought** *noun*
noughts

**noun** *noun*
nouns

**nourish** *verb*
nourishes
nourishing
nourished

**nourishment**

**novel** *adjective*

**novel** *noun*
novels

**novelist** *noun*
novelists

**novelty** *noun*
novelties

**November** *noun*
Novembers

**novice** *noun*
novices

**nowadays**

**nowhere**

**nozzle** *noun*
nozzles

**nuclear**

**nucleus** *noun*
nuclei

**nude** *adjective* and
*noun*
nudes

**nudge** *verb*
nudges
nudging
nudged

**nudist** *noun*
nudists

**nudity**

**nugget** *noun*
nuggets

**nuisance** *noun*
nuisances

**numb** *adjective*
numbly

**number** *noun*
numbers

**number** *verb*
numbers
numbering
numbered

**numbness**

**numeracy**

**numeral** *noun*
numerals

**numerate**

**numerator** *noun*
numerators

**numerical** *adjective*
numerically

**numerous**

**nun**★ *noun*
nuns

**nunnery** *noun*
nunneries

**nurse** *noun*
nurses

**nurse** *verb*
nurses
nursing
nursed

**nursery** *noun*
nurseries

**nurture** *verb*
nurtures
nurturing
nurtured

**nut** *noun*
nuts

**nutcrackers** *plural
noun*

**nutmeg** *noun*
nutmegs

**nutrient** *noun*
nutrients

**nutrition**

**nutritional** *adjective*
nutritionally

**nutritious**

**nutshell** *noun*
nutshells

**nutty** *adjective*
nuttier
nuttiest

a
b
c
d
e
f
g
h
i
j
k
l
m
**n**
o
p
q
r
s
t
u
v
w
x
y
z

★ A **nun** is a member of a convent. ! **none**.

163

a

**nuzzle** *verb*
nuzzles
nuzzling
nuzzled

b

c

**nylon** *adjective* and *noun*
nylons

d

e

**nymph** *noun*
nymphs

f

g

# Oo

h

i

**-o**
Most nouns ending in -*o*, e.g. **hero**, **potato**, have plurals ending in -*oes*, e.g. **heroes**, **potatoes**, but a few end in -*os*. The most important are **kilos**, **photos**, **pianos**, **radios**, **ratios**, **solos**, **videos**, **zeros**. Verbs ending in -*o* usually have the forms -*oes* and -*oed*, e.g. **video** - **videoes** - **videoed**.

j

k

l

m

**n**

**o**

p

q

r

**oak** *noun*
oaks

**oar**★ *noun*
oars

s

**oarsman** *noun*
oarsmen

t

u

**oarswoman** *noun*
oarswomen

v

**oasis** *noun*
oases

w

**oath** *noun*
oaths

x

**oatmeal**

y

**oats** *plural noun*

**obedience**

**obedient** *adjective*
obediently

**obey** *verb*
obeys
obeying
obeyed

**obituary** *noun*
obituaries

**object** *noun*
objects

**object** *verb*
objects
objecting
objected

**objection** *noun*
objections

**objectionable**

**objective** *adjective*
objectively

**objective** *noun*
objectives

**objector** *noun*
objectors

**obligation** *noun*
obligations

**obligatory**

**oblige** *verb*
obliges
obliging
obliged

**oblique** *adjective*
obliquely

**oblong** *adjective* and *noun*
oblongs

**oboe** *noun*
oboes

**oboist** *noun*
oboists

**obscene** *adjective*
obscenely

**obscenity** *noun*
obscenities

**obscure** *adjective*
obscurer
obscurest
obscurely

**obscurity**

**observance** *noun*
observances

**observant** *adjective*
observantly

**observation** *noun*
observations

**observatory** *noun*
observatories

**observe** *verb*
observes
observing
observed

**observer** *noun*
observers

**obsessed**

**obsession** *noun*
obsessions

**obsolete**

**obstacle** *noun*
obstacles

**obstinacy**

**obstinate** *adjective*
obstinately

**obstruct** *verb*
obstructs
obstructing
obstructed

**obstruction** *noun*
obstructions

**obstructive** *adjective*
obstructively

z

★ An **oar** is used for rowing a boat. ! or, **ore**.

**obtain** *verb*
obtains
obtaining
obtained

**obtainable**

**obtuse** *adjective*
obtuser
obtusest
obtusely

**obvious** *adjective*
obviously

**occasion** *noun*
occasions

**occasional** *adjective*
occasionally

**occupant** *noun*
occupants

**occupation** *noun*
occupations

**occupy** *verb*
occupies
occupying
occupied

**occur** *verb*
occurs
occurring
occurred

**occurrence** *noun*
occurrences

**ocean** *noun*
oceans

**o'clock**

**octagon** *noun*
octagons

**octagonal** *adjective*
octagonally

**octave** *noun*
octaves

**October** *noun*
Octobers

**octopus** *noun*
octopuses

**odd** *adjective*
odder
oddest
oddly

**oddity** *noun*
oddities

**oddments** *plural noun*

**oddness**

**odds** *plural noun*

**odour** *noun*
odours

**odorous**

**oesophagus** *noun*
oesophagi *or*
oesophaguses

**of**★

**off**☆

**offence** *noun*
offences

**offend** *verb*
offends
offending
offended

**offender** *noun*
offenders

**offensive** *adjective*
offensively

**offer** *verb*
offers
offering
offered

**offer** *noun*
offers

**offhand**

**office** *noun*
offices

**officer** *noun*
officers

**official** *adjective*
officially

**official** *noun*
officials

**officious** *adjective*
officiously

**off-licence** *noun*
off-licences

**offset** *verb*
offsets
offsetting
offset

**offshore** *adjective* and
*adverb*

**offside**

**offspring** *noun*
offspring

**often**

**ogre** *noun*
ogres

**ohm** *noun*
ohms

**oil** *noun*
oils

**oil** *verb*
oils
oiling
oiled

**oilfield** *noun*
oilfields

**oilskin** *noun*
oilskins

**oil well** *noun*
oil wells

**oily** *adjective*
oilier
oiliest

**ointment** *noun*
ointments

**old** *adjective*
older
oldest

**Old Testament**

★ You use of in e.g. *a box of matches.* **!** off.
☆ You use off in e.g. *turn off the light.* **!** of.

a

**olive** *noun*
olives

b

**Olympic Games**
*plural noun*

c

**Olympics** *plural noun*

d

**ombudsman** *noun*
ombudsmen

e

**omelette** *noun*
omelettes

f

**omen** *noun*
omens

g

**ominous** *adjective*
ominously

h

**omission★** *noun*
omissions

i

**omit** *verb*
omits
omitting
omitted

j

k

**omnivorous**

l

**once**

m

**one**☆ *adjective* and
*noun*
ones

n

**oneself**

o

**one-sided**

**one-way**

p

**ongoing**

q

**onion** *noun*
onions

r

**onlooker** *noun*
onlookers

s

**only**

t

**onshore** *adjective* and
*adverb*

u

**onto** *preposition*

**onward** *adjective* and
*adverb*

v

w

**onwards** *adverb*

**ooze** *verb*
oozes
oozing
oozed

**opaque**

**open** *adjective*
openly

**open** *verb*
opens
opening
opened

**opener** *noun*
openers

**opening** *noun*
openings

**opera** *noun*
operas

**operate** *verb*
operates
operating
operated

**operatic**

**operation** *noun*
operations

**operator** *noun*
operators

**opinion** *noun*
opinions

**opium**

**opponent** *noun*
opponents

**opportunity** *noun*
opportunities

**oppose** *verb*
opposes
opposing
opposed

**opposite** *adjective*

**opposite** *noun*
opposites

**opposition**

**oppress** *verb*
oppresses
oppressing
oppressed

**oppression**

**oppressive** *adjective*
oppressively

**oppressor** *noun*
oppressors

**opt** *verb*
opts
opting
opted

**optical** *adjective*
optically

**optician** *noun*
opticians

**optimism**

**optimist** *noun*
optimists

**optimistic** *adjective*
optimistically

**option** *noun*
options

**optional** *adjective*
optionally

**opulence**

**opulent** *adjective*
opulently

**or**✪ *conjunction*

**oral**✦ *adjective*
orally

**orange** *adjective* and
*noun*
oranges

**orangeade** *noun*
orangeades

x

y

z

★ An **omission** is something left out. ❗**emission**.

☆ You use **one** in e.g. *one more time*. ❗**won**.

✪ You use **or** in e.g. *Do you want a cake or a biscuit?* ❗**oar**, **ore**.

✦ **Oral** means spoken aloud. ❗**aural**.

orang-utan *noun*
  orang-utans

oration *noun*
  orations

orator *noun*
  orators

oratorical

oratorio *noun*
  oratorios

oratory

orbit *noun*
  orbits

orbit *verb*
  orbits
  orbiting
  orbited

orbital

orchard *noun*
  orchards

orchestra *noun*
  orchestras

orchestral

orchid *noun*
  orchids

ordeal *noun*
  ordeals

order *noun*
  orders

order *verb*
  orders
  ordering
  ordered

orderliness

orderly

ordinal number *noun*
  ordinal numbers

ordinary *adjective*
  ordinarily

ore★ *noun*
  ores

organ *noun*
  organs

organic *adjective*
  organically

organism *noun*
  organisms

organist *noun*
  organists

organization *noun*
  organizations

organize *verb*
  organizes
  organizing
  organized

organizer *noun*
  organizers

oriental

orienteering

origami

origin *noun*
  origins

original *adjective*
  originally

originality

originate *verb*
  originates
  originating
  originated

origination

originator *noun*
  originators

ornament *noun*
  ornaments

ornamental *adjective*
  ornamentally

ornamentation

ornithological

ornithologist

ornithology

orphan *noun*
  orphans

orphanage *noun*
  orphanages

orthodox

Orthodox Church

orthodoxy

oscillate *verb*
  oscillates
  oscillating
  oscillated

oscillation *noun*
  oscillations

ostrich *noun*
  ostriches

other *adjective* and
  *noun*
  others

otherwise

otter *noun*
  otters

ought

ounce *noun*
  ounces

ours

ourselves

outback

outboard motor *noun*
  outboard motors

outbreak *noun*
  outbreaks

outburst *noun*
  outbursts

outcast *noun*
  outcasts

outcome *noun*
  outcomes

outcry *noun*
  outcries

outdated

outdo *verb*
  outdoes
  outdoing
  outdid
  outdone

outdoor *adjective*

outdoors *adverb*

a
b
c
d
e
f
g
h
i
j
k
l
m
n
**o**
p
q
r
s
t
u
v
w
x
y
z

★ Ore is rock with metal in it. ! oar, or.

167

a

outer

b
outfit *noun*
outfits

c
outgrow *verb*
outgrows
outgrowing
outgrew
outgrown

d

e

f
outhouse *noun*
outhouses

g
outing *noun*
outings

h
outlast *verb*
outlasts
outlasting
outlasted

i

j
outlaw *noun*
outlaws

k
outlaw *verb*
outlaws
outlawing
outlawed

l

m

outlet *noun*
outlets

n

**o**

outline *noun*
outlines

p
outline *verb*
outlines
outlining
outlined

q

r
outlook *noun*
outlooks

s
outlying

t
outnumber *verb*
outnumbers
outnumbering
outnumbered

u

v
outpatient *noun*
outpatients

w
outpost *noun*
outposts

x

output *verb*
outputs
outputting
output

y

z

168

output *noun*
outputs

outrage *noun*
outrages

outrage *verb*
outrages
outraging
outraged

outrageous *adjective*
outrageously

outright

outset

outside *adverb* and
*preposition*

outside *noun*
outsides

outsider *noun*
outsiders

outskirts *plural noun*

outspoken

outstanding *adjective*
outstandingly

outward *adjective*
outwardly

outwards *adverb*

outweigh *verb*
outweighs
outweighing
outweighed

outwit *verb*
outwits
outwitting
outwitted

oval *adjective* and *noun*
ovals

ovary *noun*
ovaries

oven *noun*
ovens

over *adverb* and
*preposition*

over *noun*
overs

**over-**
*over-* makes words
meaning 'too' or 'too
much', e.g.
**overactive** and
**overcook**. You do not
need a hyphen,
except in some words
beginning with *e*, e.g.
**over-eager**.

overall *adjective*

overalls *plural noun*

overarm *adjective*

overboard

overcast

overcoat *noun*
overcoats

overcome *verb*
overcomes
overcoming
overcame
overcome

overdo *verb*
overdoes
overdoing
overdid
overdone

overdose *noun*
overdoses

overdue

overflow *verb*
overflows
overflowing
overflowed

overgrown

overhang *verb*
overhangs
overhanging
overhung

overhaul *verb*
overhauls
overhauling
overhauled

overhead *adjective*

overheads *plural noun*

overhear *verb*
overhears
overhearing
overheard

overland *adjective*

overlap *verb*
overlaps
overlapping
overlapped

overlook *verb*
overlooks
overlooking
overlooked

overnight

overpower *verb*
overpowers
overpowering
overpowered

overrun *verb*
overruns
overrunning
overran
overrun

overseas *adjective* and *adverb*

oversight *noun*
oversights

oversleep *verb*
oversleeps
oversleeping
overslept

overtake *verb*
overtakes
overtaking
overtook
overtaken

overthrow *verb*
overthrows
overthrowing
overthrew
overthrown

overthrow *noun*
overthrows

overtime

overture *noun*
overtures

overturn *verb*
overturns
overturning
overturned

overwhelm *verb*
overwhelms
overwhelming
overwhelmed

overwork *verb*
overworks
overworking
overworked

overwork *noun*

ovum *noun*
ova

owe *verb*
owes
owing
owed

owl *noun*
owls

own *adjective*

own *verb*
owns
owning
owned

owner *noun*
owners

ownership

ox *noun*
oxen

oxidation

oxide *noun*
oxides

oxidize *verb*
oxidizes
oxidizing
oxidized

oxygen

oyster *noun*
oysters

ozone

# Pp

pa *noun*
pas

pace *noun*
paces

pace *verb*
paces
pacing
paced

pacemaker *noun*
pacemakers

pacification

pacifism

pacifist *noun*
pacifists

pacify *verb*
pacifies
pacifying
pacified

pack *verb*
packs
packing
packed

pack *noun*
packs

package *noun*
packages

packet *noun*
packets

pad *noun*
pads

pad *verb*
pads
padding
padded

padding

paddle *verb*
paddles
paddling
paddled

paddle *noun*
paddles

a
b
c
d
e
f
g
h
i
j
k
l
m
n
**o**
**p**
q
r
s
t
u
v
w
x
y
z

# pa

a

**paddock** *noun*
paddocks

b

**paddy** *noun*
paddies

c

**padlock** *noun*
padlocks

d

**pagan** *adjective* and
*noun*
pagans

e

f

**page** *noun*
pages

g

**pageant** *noun*
pageants

h

**pageantry**

i

**pagoda** *noun*
pagodas

j

k

**paid** see **pay**

l

**pail**★ *noun*
pails

m

**pain**☆ *noun*
pains

n

**pain** *verb*
pains
paining
pained

o

p

q

**painful** *adjective*
painfully

r

**painkiller** *noun*
painkillers

s

**painless** *adjective*
painlessly

t

**painstaking**

u

**paint** *noun*
paints

v

**paint** *verb*
paints
painting
painted

**paintbox** *noun*
paintboxes

**paintbrush** *noun*
paintbrushes

**painter** *noun*
painters

**painting** *noun*
paintings

**pair**⊙ *noun*
pairs

**pair** *verb*
pairs
pairing
paired

**pal** *noun*
pals

**palace** *noun*
palaces

**palate** *noun*
palates

**pale**✛ *adjective*
paler
palest

**paleness**

**palette** *noun*
palettes

**paling** *noun*
palings

**palisade** *noun*
palisades

**pall** *verb*
palls
palling
palled

**pallid**

**pallor**

**palm** *noun*
palms

**palm** *verb*
palms
palming
palmed

**palmistry**

**Palm Sunday**

**paltry** *adjective*
paltrier
paltriest

**pampas** *plural noun*

**pamper** *verb*
pampers
pampering
pampered

**pamphlet** *noun*
pamphlets

**pan** *noun*
pans

**pancake** *noun*
pancakes

**panda** *noun*
pandas

**pandemonium**

**pander** *verb*
panders
pandering
pandered

**pane**✱ *noun*
panes

**panel** *noun*
panels

**pang** *noun*
pangs

w

x

y

z

★ A **pail** is a bucket. ❢**pale**.
☆ A **pain** is an unpleasant feeling caused by injury or disease.
❢**pane**.
⊙ A **pair** is a set of two. ❢**pear**.
✛ **Pale** means 'almost white'. ❢**pail**.
✱ A **pane** is a piece of glass in a window. ❢**pain**.

170

panic
panic *verb*
  panics
  panicking
  panicked
panicky
pannier *noun*
  panniers
panorama *noun*
  panoramas
panoramic *adjective*
  panoramically
pansy *noun*
  pansies
pant *verb*
  pants
  panting
  panted
panther *noun*
  panthers
panties *plural noun*
pantomime *noun*
  pantomimes
pantry *noun*
  pantries
pants *plural noun*
paper *noun*
  papers
paper *verb*
  papers
  papering
  papered
paperback *noun*
  paperbacks
papier mâché
papyrus *noun*
  papyri
parable *noun*
  parables
parachute *noun*
  parachutes
parachutist
parade *noun*
  parades

parade *verb*
  parades
  parading
  paraded
paradise
paradox *noun*
  paradoxes
paradoxical *adjective*
  paradoxically
paraffin
paragraph *noun*
  paragraphs
parallel
parallelogram *noun*
  parallelograms
paralyse *verb*
  paralyses
  paralysing
  paralysed
paralysis *noun*
  paralyses
paralytic *adjective*
  paralytically
parapet *noun*
  parapets
paraphernalia
paraphrase *verb*
  paraphrases
  paraphrasing
  paraphrased
parasite *noun*
  parasites
parasitic *adjective*
  parasitically
parasol *noun*
  parasols
paratrooper
paratroops *plural noun*
parcel *noun*
  parcels
parched
parchment

pardon *verb*
  pardons
  pardoning
  pardoned
pardon *noun*
  pardons
pardonable
parent *noun*
  parents
parentage
parental
parenthood
parenthesis *noun*
  parentheses
parish *noun*
  parishes
parishioner *noun*
  parishioners
park *noun*
  parks
park *verb*
  parks
  parking
  parked
parka *noun*
  parkas
parliament *noun*
  parliaments
parliamentary
parody *noun*
  parodies
parole
parrot *noun*
  parrots
parsley
parsnip *noun*
  parsnips
parson *noun*
  parsons
parsonage *noun*
  parsonages
part *noun*
  parts

# pa

part *verb*
parts
parting
parted

partial *adjective*
partially

partiality

participant *noun*
participants

participate *verb*
participates
participating
participated

participation

participle *noun*
participles

particle *noun*
particles

particular *adjective*
particularly

particulars *plural noun*

parting *noun*
partings

partition *noun*
partitions

partly

partner *noun*
partners

partnership

partridge *noun*
partridges

part-time *adjective*

party *noun*
parties

pass *verb*
passes
passing
passed

pass *noun*
passes

passable

passage *noun*
passages

passageway *noun*
passageways

passed★ see pass

passenger *noun*
passengers

passer-by *noun*
passers-by

passion *noun*
passions

passionate *adjective*
passionately

passive *adjective*
passively

Passover

passport *noun*
passports

password *noun*
passwords

past☆ *noun, adjective, and preposition*

pasta *noun*
pastas

paste *noun*
pastes

paste *verb*
pastes
pasting
pasted

pastel *noun*
pastels

pasteurization

pasteurize *verb*
pasteurizes
pasteurizing
pasteurized

pastille *noun*
pastilles

pastime *noun*
pastimes

pastoral

pastry *noun*
pastries

pasture *noun*
pastures

pasty *noun*
pasties

pasty *adjective*
pastier
pastiest

pat *verb*
pats
patting
patted

pat *noun*
pats

patch *noun*
patches

patch *verb*
patches
patching
patched

patchwork

patchy *adjective*
patchier
patchiest

patent *adjective*
patently

patent *verb*
patents
patenting
patented

patent *noun*
patents

paternal *adjective*
paternally

path *noun*
paths

pathetic *adjective*
pathetically

. . . . . . . . . . . . . . . . . . . . . . . . . . . . . . . . . . . . . . . . . . . . . . .

★ You use **passed** in e.g. *We passed the house.* **!** past.

☆ You use **past** in e.g. *We went past the house.* **!** passed.

patience

patient *adjective*
 patiently

patient *noun*
 patients

patio *noun*
 patios

patriot *noun*
 patriots

patriotic *adjective*
 patriotically

patriotism

patrol *verb*
 patrols
 patrolling
 patrolled

patrol *noun*
 patrols

patron *noun*
 patrons

patronage

patronize *verb*
 patronizes
 patronizing
 patronized

patter *verb*
 patters
 pattering
 pattered

patter *noun*
 patters

pattern *noun*
 patterns

pause *verb*
 pauses
 pausing
 paused

pause *noun*
 pauses

pave *verb*
 paves
 paving
 paved

pavement *noun*
 pavements

pavilion *noun*
 pavilions

paw *noun*
 paws

paw *verb*
 paws
 pawing
 pawed

pawn *noun*
 pawns

pawn *verb*
 pawns
 pawning
 pawned

pawnbroker *noun*
 pawnbrokers

pay *verb*
 pays
 paying
 paid

pay *noun*

payment *noun*
 payments

pea *noun*
 peas

peace★

peaceful *adjective*
 peacefully

peach *noun*
 peaches

peacock *noun*
 peacocks

peak☆ *noun*
 peaks

peak❂ *verb*
 peaks
 peaking
 peaked

peaked

peal✜ *verb*
 peals
 pealing
 pealed

peal✻ *noun*
 peals

peanut *noun*
 peanuts

pear✲ *noun*
 pears

pearl *noun*
 pearls

pearly *adjective*
 pearlier
 pearliest

peasant *noun*
 peasants

peasantry

peat

pebble *noun*
 pebbles

pebbly *adjective*
 pebblier
 pebbliest

peck *verb*
 pecks
 pecking
 pecked

................................................................

★ **Peace** is a time when there is no war. ❗**piece**.
☆ A **peak** is the top of something. ❗**peek**.
❂ To **peak** is to reach the highest point. ❗**peek**.
✜ To **peal** is to make a ringing sound of bells. ❗**peel**.
✻ A **peal** is a ringing of bells. ❗**peel**.
✲ A **pear** is a fruit. ❗**pair**.

**peck** *noun*
pecks

**peckish**

**peculiar** *adjective*
peculiarly

**peculiarity** *noun*
peculiarities

**pedal** *noun*
pedals

**pedal** *verb*
pedals
pedalling
pedalled

**peddle★** *verb*
peddles
peddling
peddled

**pedestal** *noun*
pedestals

**pedestrian** *noun*
pedestrians

**pedestrian** *adjective*

**pedigree** *noun*
pedigrees

**pedlar** *noun*
pedlars

**peek☆** *verb*
peeks
peeking
peeked

**peel♦** *noun*
peels

**peel✢** *verb*
peels
peeling
peeled

**peep** *verb*
peeps
peeping
peeped

**peep** *noun*
peeps

**peer⊛** *verb*
peers
peering
peered

**peer** *noun*
peers

**peerless**

**peewit** *noun*
peewits

**peg** *noun*
pegs

**peg** *verb*
pegs
pegging
pegged

**Pekinese** *noun*
Pekinese

**pelican** *noun*
pelicans

**pellet** *noun*
pellets

**pelt** *verb*
pelts
pelting
pelted

**pelt** *noun*
pelts

**pen** *noun*
pens

**penalize** *verb*
penalizes
penalizing
penalized

**penalty** *noun*
penalties

**pence** see **penny**

**pencil** *noun*
pencils

**pencil** *verb*
pencils
pencilling
pencilled

**pendant** *noun*
pendants

**pendulum** *noun*
pendulums

**penetrate** *verb*
penetrates
penetrating
penetrated

**penetration**

**penfriend** *noun*
penfriends

**penguin** *noun*
penguins

**penicillin**

**peninsula** *noun*
peninsulas

**peninsular**

**penis** *noun*
penises

**penitence**

**penitent**

**penknife** *noun*
penknives

**pennant** *noun*
pennants

**penniless**

**penny** *noun*
pennies *or* pence

★ To **peddle** is to sell things on the street. ❢ **pedal**.
☆ To **peek** is to look secretly at something. ❢ **peak**.
♦ **Peel** is the skin of fruit and vegetables. ❢ **peal**.
✢ To **peel** something is to take the skin off it. ❢ **peal**.
⊛ To **peer** is to look closely at something. ❢ **pier**.

**pension** *noun*
pensions

**pensioner** *noun*
pensioners

**pentagon** *noun*
pentagons

**pentathlon** *noun*
pentathlons

**peony** *noun*
peonies

**people** *plural noun*

**people** *noun*
peoples

**pepper** *noun*
peppers

**peppermint** *noun*
peppermints

**peppery**

**perceive** *verb*
perceives
perceiving
perceived

**per cent**

**percentage** *noun*
percentages

**perceptible** *adjective*
perceptibly

**perception** *noun*
perceptions

**perceptive** *adjective*
perceptively

**perch** *verb*
perches
perching
perched

**perch** *noun*
perch

**percolator** *noun*
percolators

**percussion**

**percussive**

**perennial** *adjective*
perennially

**perennial** *noun*
perennials

**perfect** *adjective*
perfectly

**perfect** *verb*
perfects
perfecting
perfected

**perfection**

**perforate** *verb*
perforates
perforating
perforated

**perforation** *noun*
perforations

**perform** *verb*
performs
performing
performed

**performance** *noun*
performances

**performer** *noun*
performers

**perfume** *noun*
perfumes

**perhaps**

**peril** *noun*
perils

**perilous** *adjective*
perilously

**perimeter** *noun*
perimeters

**period** *noun*
periods

**periodic** *adjective*
periodically

**periodical** *noun*
periodicals

**periscope** *noun*
periscopes

**perish** *verb*
perishes
perishing
perished

**perishable**

**perm** *noun*
perms

**perm** *verb*
perms
perming
permed

**permanence**

**permanent** *adjective*
permanently

**permissible**

**permission**

**permissive** *adjective*
permissively

**permissiveness**

**permit** *verb*
permits
permitting
permitted

**permit** *noun*
permits

**perpendicular**

**perpetual** *adjective*
perpetually

**perpetuate** *verb*
perpetuates
perpetuating
perpetuated

**perplex** *verb*
perplexes
perplexing
perplexed

**perplexity**

**persecute** *verb*
persecutes
persecuting
persecuted

**persecution** *noun*
persecutions

**persecutor** *noun*
persecutors

**perseverance**

**persevere** *verb*
perseveres
persevering
persevered

persist *verb*
  persists
  persisting
  persisted
**persistence**
**persistent** *adjective*
  persistently
**person**★ *noun*
  persons *or* people
**personal** *adjective*
  personally
**personality** *noun*
  personalities
**personnel** *plural noun*
**perspective** *noun*
  perspectives
**perspiration**
**perspire** *verb*
  perspires
  perspiring
  perspired
**persuade** *verb*
  persuades
  persuading
  persuaded
**persuasion**
**persuasive** *adjective*
  persuasively
**perverse** *adjective*
  perversely
**perversion** *noun*
  perversions
**perversity**
**pervert** *verb*
  perverts
  perverting
  perverted
**pervert** *noun*
  perverts
**Pesach**☆
**pessimism**

**pessimist** *noun*
  pessimists
**pessimistic** *adjective*
  pessimistically
**pest** *noun*
  pests
**pester** *verb*
  pesters
  pestering
  pestered
**pesticide** *noun*
  pesticides
**pestle** *noun*
  pestles
**pet** *noun*
  pets
**petal** *noun*
  petals
**petition** *noun*
  petitions
**petrify** *verb*
  petrifies
  petrifying
  petrified
**petrochemical** *noun*
  petrochemicals
**petrol**
**petroleum**
**petticoat** *noun*
  petticoats
**pettiness**
**petty** *adjective*
  pettier
  pettiest
  pettily
**pew** *noun*
  pews
**pewter**
**pharmacy** *noun*
  pharmacies

**phase** *noun*
  phases
**phase** *verb*
  phases
  phasing
  phased
**pheasant** *noun*
  pheasants
**phenomenal**
  *adjective*
  phenomenally
**phenomenon** *noun*
  phenomena
**philatelist** *noun*
  philatelists
**philately**
**philosopher** *noun*
  philosophers
**philosophical**
  *adjective*
  philosophically
**philosophy** *noun*
  philosophies
**phobia** *noun*
  phobias

**-phobia**
*-phobia* makes words meaning 'a strong fear or dislike', e.g. **xenophobia** ( a dislike of strangers'). It comes from a Greek word and is only used with other Greek or Latin words.

**phoenix** *noun*
  phoenixes
**phone** *noun*
  phones

----

★ The normal plural is **people**: *three people came*. **Persons** is
  formal, e.g. in official reports.
☆ The Hebrew name for Passover. Pronounced *pay-sahk*.

**phone** *verb*
phones
phoning
phoned

**-phone**
*-phone* makes words to do with sound, e.g. **telephone**, **saxophone**. You can sometimes make adjectives by using *-phonic*, e.g. **telephonic**, and nouns by using *-phony*, e.g. **telephony**.

**phonecard** *noun*
phonecards

**phone-in** *noun*
phone-ins

**phosphorescence**

**phosphorescent**

**phosphoric**

**phosphorus**

**photo** *noun*
photos

**photo-**
*photo-* makes words to do with light, e.g. **photograph**, **photocopy**. It is also used in more technical words such as **photochemistry** (the chemistry of light) and as a separate word in **photo** (photograph) and **photo finish** (close finish to a race).

**photocopier** *noun*
photocopiers

**photocopy** *noun*
photocopies

**photocopy** *verb*
photocopies
photocopying
photocopied

**photoelectric**

**photograph** *noun*
photographs

**photograph** *verb*
photographs
photographing
photographed

**photographer** *noun*
photographers

**photographic** *adjective*
photographically

**photography**

**phrase** *noun*
phrases

**phrase** *verb*
phrases
phrasing
phrased

**physical** *adjective*
physically

**physician** *noun*
physicians

**physicist** *noun*
physicists

**physics**

**physiological** *adjective*
physiologically

**physiologist** *noun*
physiologists

**physiology**

**pi**★

**pianist** *noun*
pianists

**piano** *noun*
pianos

**piccolo** *noun*
piccolos

**pick** *verb*
picks
picking
picked

**pick** *noun*
picks

**pickaxe** *noun*
pickaxes

**picket** *noun*
pickets

**picket** *verb*
pickets
picketing
picketed

**pickle** *noun*
pickles

**pickle** *verb*
pickles
pickling
pickled

**pickpocket** *noun*
pickpockets

**pick-up** *noun*
pick-ups

**picnic** *noun*
picnics

**picnic** *verb*
picnics
picnicking
picnicked

**picnicker** *noun*
picnickers

**pictogram** *noun*
pictograms

**pictorial** *adjective*
pictorially

a
b
c
d
e
f
g
h
i
j
k
l
m
n
o
**p**
q
r
s
t
u
v
w
x
y
z

★ **Pi** is a Greek letter, used in mathematics. **!pie**.

177

**picture** *noun*
pictures

**picture** *verb*
pictures
picturing
pictured

**picturesque**

**pie★** *noun*
pies

**piece☆** *noun*
pieces

**piece** *verb*
pieces
piecing
pieced

**piecemeal**

**pie chart** *noun*
pie charts

**pier❍** *noun*
piers

**pierce** *verb*
pierces
piercing
pierced

**pig** *noun*
pigs

**pigeon** *noun*
pigeons

**pigeon-hole** *noun*
pigeon-holes

**piggy** *noun*
piggies

**piggyback** *noun*
piggybacks

**piglet** *noun*
piglets

**pigment** *noun*
pigments

**pigmy** *noun* use
**pygmy**

**pigsty** *noun*
pigsties

**pigtail** *noun*
pigtails

**pike** *noun*
pikes

**pilchard** *noun*
pilchards

**pile** *noun*
piles

**pile** *verb*
piles
piling
piled

**pilfer** *verb*
pilfers
pilfering
pilfered

**pilgrim** *noun*
pilgrims

**pilgrimage** *noun*
pilgrimages

**pill** *noun*
pills

**pillage** *verb*
pillages
pillaging
pillaged

**pillar** *noun*
pillars

**pillion** *noun*
pillions

**pillow** *noun*
pillows

**pillowcase** *noun*
pillowcases

**pilot** *noun*
pilots

**pilot** *verb*
pilots
piloting
piloted

**pimple** *noun*
pimples

**pimply** *adjective*
pimplier
pimpliest

**pin** *noun*
pins

**pin** *verb*
pins
pinning
pinned

**pinafore** *noun*
pinafores

**pincer** *noun*
pincers

**pinch** *verb*
pinches
pinching
pinched

**pinch** *noun*
pinches

**pincushion** *noun*
pincushions

**pine** *noun*
pines

**pine** *verb*
pines
pining
pined

**pineapple** *noun*
pineapples

**ping-pong**

★ A pie is a food with pastry. ! pi.
☆ You use piece in e.g. *a piece of cake*. ! peace.
❍ A pier is a long building on stilts going into the sea. ! peer.

pink *adjective*
pinker
pinkest

pink *noun*
pinks

pint *noun*
pints

pioneer *noun*
pioneers

pious *adjective*
piously

pip *noun*
pips

pipe *noun*
pipes

pipe *verb*
pipes
piping
piped

pipeline *noun*
pipelines

piper *noun*
pipers

piracy

pirate *noun*
pirates

pistil★ *noun*
pistils

pistol☆ *noun*
pistols

piston *noun*
pistons

pit *noun*
pits

pit *verb*
pits
pitting
pitted

pitch *noun*
pitches

pitch *verb*
pitches
pitching
pitched

pitch-black

pitcher *noun*
pitchers

pitchfork *noun*
pitchforks

pitfall *noun*
pitfalls

pitiful *adjective*
pitifully

pitiless *adjective*
pitilessly

pity *verb*
pities
pitying
pitied

pity *noun*

pivot *noun*
pivots

pivot *verb*
pivots
pivoting
pivoted

pixie *noun*
pixies

pizza *noun*
pizzas

pizzicato

placard *noun*
placards

place✧ *noun*
places

place *verb*
places
placing
placed

placid *adjective*
placidly

plague *noun*
plagues

plague *verb*
plagues
plaguing
plagued

plaice✣ *noun*
plaice

plaid *noun*
plaids

plain✲ *adjective*
plainer
plainest
plainly

plain *noun*
plains

plain clothes

plainness

plaintiff *noun*
plaintiffs

plaintive

plaintively

plait *noun*
plaits

plait *verb*
plaits
plaiting
plaited

plan *noun*
plans

plan *verb*
plans
planning
planned

- - - - - - - - - - - - - - - - - - - - - - - - - - - - - - - - - - - - - - - - - - -

★ A **pistil** is a part of a flower.❗ **pistol**.
☆ A **pistol** is a gun.❗ **pistil**.
✪ You use **place** in e.g. *a place in the country*. ❗ **plaice**.
✧ A **plaice** is a fish. ❗ **place**.
✲ **Plain** means 'not pretty or decorated'. ❗ **plane**.

a
b
c
d
e
f
g
h
i
j
k
l
m
n
o
**p**
q
r
s
t
u
v
w
x
y
z

# pl

**plane★** *noun*
planes

**plane☆** *verb*
planes
planing
planed

**planet** *noun*
planets

**planetary**

**plank** *noun*
planks

**plankton**

**planner** *noun*
planners

**plant** *noun*
plants

**plant** *verb*
plants
planting
planted

**plantation** *noun*
plantations

**planter** *noun*
planters

**plaque** *noun*
plaques

**plasma**

**plaster** *noun*
plasters

**plaster** *verb*
plasters
plastering
plastered

**plasterer** *noun*
plasterers

**plaster of Paris**

**plastic** *adjective* and *noun*
plastics

**Plasticine**

**plate** *noun*
plates

**plate** *verb*
plates
plating
plated

**plateau** *noun*
plateaux

**plateful** *noun*
platefuls

**platform** *noun*
platforms

**platinum**

**platoon** *noun*
platoons

**platypus** *noun*
platypuses

**play** *verb*
plays
playing
played

**play** *noun*
plays

**playback** *noun*
playbacks

**player** *noun*
players

**playful** *adjective*
playfully

**playfulness**

**playground** *noun*
playgrounds

**playgroup** *noun*
playgroups

**playmate** *noun*
playmates

**play-off** *noun*
play-offs

**playtime** *noun*
playtimes

**playwright** *noun*
playwrights

**plea** *noun*
pleas

**plead** *verb*
pleads
pleading
pleaded

**pleasant** *adjective*
pleasanter
pleasantest
pleasantly

**please** *verb*
pleases
pleasing
pleased

**pleasurable** *adjective*
pleasurably

**pleasure** *noun*
pleasures

**pleat** *noun*
pleats

**pleated**

**pledge** *verb*
pledges
pledging
pledged

**pledge** *noun*
pledges

**plentiful** *adjective*
plentifully

**plenty**

**pliable**

**pliers** *plural noun*

**plight** *noun*
plights

**plod** *verb*
plods
plodding
plodded

· · · · · · · · · · · · · · · · · · · · · · · · · · · · · · · · · · · · · · · · · ·

★ A **plane** is an aeroplane, a level surface, a tool, or a tree. **! plain.**

☆ To **plane** wood is to make it smooth with a tool. **! plain.**

**plodder** *noun*
plodders

**plop** *verb*
plops
plopping
plopped

**plop** *noun*
plops

**plot** *noun*
plots

**plot** *verb*
plots
plotting
plotted

**plotter** *noun*
plotters

**plough** *noun*
ploughs

**plough** *verb*
ploughs
ploughing
ploughed

**ploughman** *noun*
ploughmen

**plover** *noun*
plovers

**pluck** *verb*
plucks
plucking
plucked

**pluck** *noun*

**plucky** *adjective*
pluckier
pluckiest
pluckily

**plug** *noun*
plugs

**plug** *verb*
plugs
plugging
plugged

**plum★** *noun*
plums

**plumage**

**plumb☆** *verb*
plumbs
plumbing
plumbed

**plumber** *noun*
plumbers

**plumbing**

**plume** *noun*
plumes

**plumed**

**plump** *adjective*
plumper
plumpest

**plump** *verb*
plumps
plumping
plumped

**plunder** *verb*
plunders
plundering
plundered

**plunder** *noun*

**plunderer** *noun*
plunderers

**plunge** *verb*
plunges
plunging
plunged

**plunge** *noun*
plunges

**plural** *adjective* and *noun*
plurals

**plus** *preposition*

**plus** *noun*
pluses

**plutonium**

**plywood**

**pneumatic**

**pneumonia**

**poach** *verb*
poaches
poaching
poached

**poacher** *noun*
poachers

**pocket** *noun*
pockets

**pocket** *verb*
pockets
pocketing
pocketed

**pocketful** *noun*
pocketfuls

**pod** *noun*
pods

**podgy** *adjective*
podgier
podgiest

**poem** *noun*
poems

**poet** *noun*
poets

**poetic** *adjective*
poetically

**poetry**

**point** *noun*
points

**point** *verb*
points
pointing
pointed

**point-blank** *adjective*

**pointed** *adjective*
pointedly

**pointer** *noun*
pointers

**pointless** *adjective*
pointlessly

★ A **plum** is a fruit. **!plumb**.
☆ To **plumb** water is to see how deep it is. **!plum**.

a b c d e f g h i j k l m n o **p** q r s t u v w x y z

181

a

**poise** *noun*

b

**poise** *verb*
poises
poising
poised

c

d

**poison** *noun*
poisons

e

**poison** *verb*
poisons
poisoning
poisoned

f

g

**poisoner** *noun*
poisoners

h

**poisonous** *adjective*
poisonously

i

j

**poke** *verb*
pokes
poking
poked

k

l

**poke** *noun*
pokes

m

**poker** *noun*
pokers

n

**polar**

o

**Polaroid**

**pole**★ *noun*
poles

p

q

**police** *plural noun*

r

**policeman** *noun*
policemen

s

**police officer** *noun*
police officers

t

u

**policewoman** *noun*
policewomen

v

**policy** *noun*
policies

w

**polio**

x

**poliomyelitis**

y

z

**polish** *verb*
polishes
polishing
polished

**polish** *noun*
polishes

**polished**

**polite** *adjective*
politer
politest
politely

**politeness**

**political** *adjective*
politically

**politician** *noun*
politicians

**politics**

**polka** *noun*
polkas

**poll**☆ *noun*
polls

**pollen**

**pollute** *verb*
pollutes
polluting
polluted

**pollution**

**polo**

**polo neck** *noun*
polo necks

**poltergeist** *noun*
poltergeists

**polygon** *noun*
polygons

**polystyrene**

**polythene**

**pomp**

**pomposity**

**pompous** *adjective*
pompously

**pond** *noun*
ponds

**ponder** *verb*
ponders
pondering
pondered

**ponderous** *adjective*
ponderously

**pony** *noun*
ponies

**ponytail** *noun*
ponytails

**pony-trekking**

**poodle** *noun*
poodles

**pool** *noun*
pools

**pool** *verb*
pools
pooling
pooled

**poor** *adjective*
poorer
poorest
poorly

**poorly** *adjective* and *adverb*

**pop** *verb*
pops
popping
popped

**pop** *noun*
pops

**popcorn**

**Pope** *noun*
Popes

**poplar** *noun*
poplars

**poppadom** *noun*
poppadoms

**poppy** *noun*
poppies

. . . . . . . . . . . . . . . . . . . . . . . . . . . . . . . . . . . . . . . . . . . . . . . . . . . . . . . . .

★ A **pole** is a long thin stick. **!** poll.

☆ A **poll** is a vote in an election. **!** pole.

**popular** *adjective*
popularly

**popularity**

**popularize** *verb*
popularizes
popularizing
popularized

**populated**

**population** *noun*
populations

**populous**

**porcelain**

**porch** *noun*
porches

**porcupine** *noun*
porcupines

**pore** *noun*
pores

**pore★** *verb*
pores
poring
pored

**pork**

**pornographic**

**pornography**

**porosity**

**porous**

**porpoise** *noun*
porpoises

**porridge**

**port** *noun*
ports

**portable**

**portcullis** *noun*
portcullises

**porter** *noun*
porters

**porthole** *noun*
portholes

**portion** *noun*
portions

**portliness**

**portly** *adjective*
portlier
portliest

**portrait** *noun*
portraits

**portray** *verb*
portrays
portraying
portrayed

**portrayal** *noun*
portrayals

**pose** *verb*
poses
posing
posed

**pose** *noun*
poses

**poser** *noun*
posers

**posh** *adjective*
posher
poshest

**position** *noun*
positions

**positive** *adjective*
positively

**positive** *noun*
positives

**posse** *noun*
posses

**possess** *verb*
possesses
possessing
possessed

**possession** *noun*
possessions

**possessive** *adjective*
possessively

**possessor** *noun*
possessors

**possibility** *noun*
possibilities

**possible** *adjective*
possibly

**post** *verb*
posts
posting
posted

**post** *noun*
posts

**postage**

**postal**

**postbox** *noun*
postboxes

**postcard** *noun*
postcards

**postcode** *noun*
postcodes

**poster** *noun*
posters

**postman** *noun*
postmen

**postmark** *noun*
postmarks

**post-mortem** *noun*
post-mortems

**postpone** *verb*
postpones
postponing
postponed

**postponement** *noun*
postponements

**postscript** *noun*
postscripts

**posture** *noun*
postures

**posy** *noun*
posies

**pot** *noun*
pots

**pot** *verb*
pots
potting
potted

. . . . . . . . . . . . . . . . . . . . . . . . . . . . . . . . . . . . . . . . . . . . .

★ To **pore** over something is to study it closely. **!pour**.

a

**potassium**

**potato** *noun*
potatoes

**potency**

**potent** *adjective*
potently

**potential** *adjective*
potentially

**potential** *noun*
potentials

**pothole** *noun*
potholes

**potholer** *noun*
potholer

**potholing**

**potion** *noun*
potions

**potter** *noun*
potters

**potter** *verb*
potters
pottering
pottered

**pottery** *noun*
potteries

**potty** *adjective*
pottier
pottiest
pottily

**potty** *noun*
potties

**pouch** *noun*
pouches

**poultry**

**pounce** *verb*
pounces
pouncing
pounced

**pound** *noun*
pounds

**pound** *verb*
pounds
pounding
pounded

**pour★** *verb*
pours
pouring
poured

**pout** *verb*
pouts
pouting
pouted

**poverty**

**powder** *noun*
powders

**powder** *verb*
powders
powdering
powdered

**powdery**

**power** *noun*
powers

**powered**

**powerful** *adjective*
powerfully

**powerhouse** *noun*
powerhouses

**powerless**

**practicable**

**practical** *adjective*
practically

**practice** *noun*
practices

**practise** *verb*
practises
practising
practised

**prairie** *noun*
prairies

**praise** *verb*
praises
praising
praised

**praise** *noun*
praises

**pram** *noun*
prams

**prance** *verb*
prances
prancing
pranced

**prank** *noun*
pranks

**prawn** *noun*
prawns

**pray☆** *verb*
prays
praying
prayed

**prayer** *noun*
prayers

**pre-**
*pre-* makes words
meaning 'before', e.g.
**pre-date** (to exist
before something
else), **prefabricated**
(made in advance).
Many are spelt joined
up, but not all.

**preach** *verb*
preaches
preaching
preached

**preacher** *noun*
preachers

**precarious** *adjective*
precariously

**precaution** *noun*
precautions

b c d e f g h i j k l m n o **p** q r s t u v w x y z

★ To **pour** a liquid is to tip it from a jug etc. **!** pore.
☆ To **pray** is to say prayers. **!** prey.

184

precede *verb*
precedes
preceding
preceded

precedence

precedent *noun*
precedents

precinct *noun*
precincts

precious *adjective*
preciously

precipice *noun*
precipices

précis *noun*
précis

precise *adjective*
precisely

precision

predator *noun*
predators

predatory

predecessor *noun*
predecessors

predict *verb*
predicts
predicting
predicted

predictable *adjective*
predictably

prediction *noun*
predictions

predominance

predominant *adjective*
predominantly

predominate *verb*
predominates
predominating
predominated

preface *noun*
prefaces

prefect *noun*
prefects

prefer *verb*
prefers
preferring
preferred

preferable *adjective*
preferably

preference *noun*
preferences

prefix *noun*
prefixes

pregnancy *noun*
pregnancies

pregnant

prehistoric

prehistory

prejudice *noun*
prejudices

prejudiced

preliminary *adjective*
and *noun*
preliminaries

prelude *noun*
preludes

premier *noun*
premiers

première *noun*
premières

premises *plural noun*

premium *noun*
premiums

Premium Bond *noun*
Premium Bonds

preoccupation *noun*
preoccupations

preoccupied

prep

preparation *noun*
preparations

preparatory

prepare *verb*
prepares
preparing
prepared

preposition *noun*
prepositions

prescribe *verb*
prescribes
prescribing
prescribed

prescription *noun*
prescriptions

presence

present *adjective*
presently

present *noun*
presents

present *verb*
presents
presenting
presented

presentation *noun*
presentations

presenter *noun*
presenters

preservation

preservative *noun*
preservatives

preserve *verb*
preserves
preserving
preserved

preside *verb*
presides
presiding
presided

presidency *noun*
presidencies

president *noun*
presidents

presidential *adjective*
presidentially

press *verb*
presses
pressing
pressed

press *noun*
presses

a

**press-up** noun
press-ups

b

**pressure** noun
pressures

c

**pressurize** verb
pressurizes
pressurizing
pressurized

d

e

**prestige**

f

**prestigious** adjective
prestigiously

g

**presumably**

h

**presume** verb
presumes
presuming
presumed

i

j

**presumption** noun
presumptions

k

**presumptuous**
adjective
presumptuously

l

m

**pretence** noun
pretences

n

o

**pretend** verb
pretends
pretending
pretended

**p**

q

**pretender** noun
pretenders

r

**prettiness**

s

**pretty** adjective and
adverb
prettier
prettiest
prettily

t

u

**prevail** verb
prevails
prevailing
prevailed

v

w

**prevalent**

x

**prevent** verb
prevents
preventing
prevented

**prevention**

**preventive**

**preview** noun
previews

**previous** adjective
previously

**prey★** verb
preys
preying
preyed

**prey** noun

**price** noun
prices

**price** verb
prices
pricing
priced

**priceless**

**prick** verb
pricks
pricking
pricked

**prick** noun
pricks

**prickle** noun
prickles

**prickly** adjective
pricklier
prickliest

**pride** noun
prides

**priest** noun
priests

**priestess** noun
priestesses

**priesthood**

**prig** noun
prigs

**priggish** adjective
priggishly

**prim** adjective
primmer
primmest
primly

**primness**

**primary** adjective
primarily

**primate** noun
primates

**prime** adjective

**prime** verb
primes
priming
primed

**prime** noun
primes

**prime minister** noun
prime ministers

**primer** noun
primers

**primeval**

**primitive** adjective
primitively

**primrose** noun
primroses

**prince** noun
princes

**princely**

**princess** noun
princesses

**principal**☆ adjective
principally

**principal**⊙ noun
principals

. . . . . . . . . . . . . . . . . . . . . . . . . . . . . . . . . . . . . . . . . . . .

y

★ To **prey** on animals is to hunt and kill them. ❗**pray**.

☆ **Principal** means 'chief' or 'main'. ❗**principle**.

z

⊙ A **principal** is a head of a college. ❗**principle**.

**principle★** *noun*
principles

**print** *verb*
prints
printing
printed

**print** *noun*
prints

**printer** *noun*
printers

**printout** *noun*
printouts

**priority** *noun*
priorities

**prise**☆ *verb*
prises
prising
prised

**prism** *noun*
prisms

**prison** *noun*
prisons

**prisoner** *noun*
prisoners

**privacy**

**private** *adjective*
privately

**private** *noun*
privates

**privatization**

**privatize** *verb*
privatizes
privatizing
privatized

**privet**

**privilege** *noun*
privileges

**privileged**

**prize** *noun*
prizes

**prize**○ *verb*
prizes
prizing
prized

**pro** *noun*
pros

> **pro-**
> *pro-* makes words
> meaning 'in favour of',
> e.g. **pro-choice**. In
> this type of word you
> use a hyphen.

**probability** *noun*
probabilities

**probable** *adjective*
probably

**probation**

**probationary**

**probe** *verb*
probes
probing
probed

**probe** *noun*
probes

**problem** *noun*
problems

**procedure** *noun*
procedures

**proceed** *verb*
proceeds
proceeding
proceeded

**proceedings** *plural noun*

**proceeds** *plural noun*

**process** *noun*
processes

**process** *verb*
processes
processing
processed

**procession** *noun*
processions

**proclaim** *verb*
proclaims
proclaiming
proclaimed

**proclamation** *noun*
proclamations

**prod** *verb*
prods
prodding
prodded

**prodigal** *adjective*
prodigally

**produce** *verb*
produces
producing
produced

**produce** *noun*

**producer** *noun*
producers

**product** *noun*
products

**production** *noun*
productions

**productive** *adjective*
productively

**productivity**

**profession** *noun*
professions

**professional** *adjective*
professionally

**professional** *noun*
professionals

**professor** *noun*
professors

a
b
c
d
e
f
g
h
i
j
k
l
m
n
o
**p**
q
r
s
t
u
v
w
x
y
z

★ A **principle** is a rule or belief. **! principal.**
☆ To **prise** something is to open it. **! prize.**
○ To **prize** something is to value it highly. **! prise.**

a

**proficiency**

b **proficient** *adjective*
  proficiently

c **profile** *noun*
  profiles

d **profit★** *noun*
  profits

e **profit** *verb*
  profits
f   profiting
  profited
g
**profitable** *adjective*
h   profitably

i **profound** *adjective*
  profoundly

j **profundity**

k **profuse** *adjective*
  profusely

l **profusion**

m **program**☆ *noun*
  programs

n **program** *verb*
  programs
o   programming
  programmed

**p** **programme**☆ *noun*
  programmes
q
**progress** *noun*
r **progress** *verb*
  progresses
s   progressing
  progressed
t
**progression**
u **progressive** *adjective*
  progressively
v
**prohibit** *verb*
w   prohibits
  prohibiting
x   prohibited

**prohibition** *noun*
  prohibitions

**project** *noun*
  projects

**project** *verb*
  projects
  projecting
  projected

**projection** *noun*
  projections

**projectionist** *noun*
  projectionists

**projector** *noun*
  projectors

**prologue** *noun*
  prologues

**prolong** *verb*
  prolongs
  prolonging
  prolonged

**promenade** *noun*
  promenades

**prominence**

**prominent** *adjective*
  prominently

**promise** *verb*
  promises
  promising
  promised

**promise** *noun*
  promises

**promontory** *noun*
  promontories

**promote** *verb*
  promotes
  promoting
  promoted

**promoter** *noun*
  promoter

**promotion** *noun*
  promotions

**prompt** *adjective*
  prompter
  promptest
  promptly

**prompt** *verb*
  prompts
  prompting
  prompted

**prompter** *noun*
  prompters

**promptness**

**prone**

**prong** *noun*
  prongs

**pronoun** *noun*
  pronouns

**pronounce** *verb*
  pronounces
  pronouncing
  pronounced

**pronouncement**
*noun*
  pronouncements

**pronunciation** *noun*
  pronunciations

**proof** *adjective* and
*noun*
  proofs

**prop** *verb*
  props
  propping
  propped

**prop** *noun*
  props

**propaganda**

**propel** *verb*
  propels
  propelling
  propelled

**propellant** *noun*
  propellants

y
★ A **profit** is extra money made by selling something. **!** **prophet**.
☆ You use **program** when you are talking about computers. In other
z   meanings you use **programme**.

**propeller** *noun*
propellers

**proper** *adjective*
properly

**property** *noun*
properties

**prophecy** *noun*
prophecies

**prophesy** *verb*
prophesies
prophesying
prophesied

**prophet**★ *noun*
prophets

**prophetic** *adjective*
prophetically

**proportion** *noun*
proportions

**proportional** *adjective*
proportionally

**proportionate** *adjective*
proportionately

**propose** *verb*
proposes
proposing
proposed

**proposal** *noun*
proposals

**proprietor** *noun*
proprietors

**propulsion**

**prose**

**prosecute** *verb*
prosecutes
prosecuting
prosecuted

**prosecution** *noun*
prosecutions

**prosecutor** *noun*
prosecutors

**prospect** *noun*
prospects

**prospect** *verb*
prospects
prospecting
prospected

**prospector** *noun*
prospectors

**prosper** *verb*
prospers
prospering
prospered

**prosperity**

**prosperous** *adjective*
prosperously

**prostitute** *noun*
prostitutes

**protect** *verb*
protects
protecting
protected

**protection**

**protective** *adjective*
protectively

**protector** *noun*
protectors

**protein** *noun*
proteins

**protest** *verb*
protests
protesting
protested

**protest** *noun*
protests

**protester** *noun*
protesters

**Protestant** *noun*
Protestants

**proton** *noun*
protons

**protoplasm**

**prototype** *noun*
prototypes

**protractor** *noun*
protractors

**protrude** *verb*
protrudes
protruding
protruded

**protrusion** *noun*
protrusions

**proud** *adjective*
prouder
proudest
proudly

**prove** *verb*
proves
proving
proved

**proverb** *noun*
proverbs

**proverbial** *adjective*
proverbially

**provide** *verb*
provides
providing
provided

**province** *noun*
provinces

**provincial**

**provision** *noun*
provisions

**provisional** *adjective*
provisionally

**provocative** *adjective*
provocatively

**provoke** *verb*
provokes
provoking
provoked

**provocation** *noun*
provocations

★ A **prophet** is someone who makes predictions about the future.
  ! **profit**.

**prow** noun
prows

**prowl** verb
prowls
prowling
prowled

**prowler** noun
prowlers

**prudence**

**prudent** adjective
prudently

**prune** noun
prunes

**prune** verb
prunes
pruning
pruned

**pry** verb
pries
prying
pried

**psalm** noun
psalms

**pseudonym** noun
pseudonyms

**psychiatric**

**psychiatrist** noun
psychiatrists

**psychiatry**

**psychic**

**psychological**
adjective
psychologically

**psychologist** noun
psychologists

**psychology**

**pub** noun
pubs

**puberty**

**public** adjective and
noun
publicly

**publication** noun
publications

**publicity**

**publicize** verb
publicizes
publicizing
publicized

**publish** verb
publishes
publishing
published

**publisher** noun
publishers

**puck** noun
pucks

**pucker** verb
puckers
puckering
puckered

**pudding** noun
puddings

**puddle** noun
puddles

**puff** verb
puffs
puffing
puffed

**puff** noun
puffs

**puffin** noun
puffins

**pull** verb
pulls
pulling
pulled

**pull** noun
pulls

**pulley** noun
pulleys

**pullover** noun
pullovers

**pulp** noun
pulps

**pulp** verb
pulps
pulping
pulped

**pulpit** noun
pulpits

**pulse** noun
pulses

**pulverize** verb
pulverizes
pulverizing
pulverized

**puma** noun
pumas

**pumice**

**pump** verb
pumps
pumping
pumped

**pump** noun
pumps

**pumpkin** noun
pumpkins

**pun** noun
puns

**pun** verb
puns
punning
punned

**punch** verb
punches
punching
punched

**punch** noun
punches

**punch** noun
punches

**punchline** noun
punchlines

**punch-up** noun
punch-ups

**punctual** adjective
punctually

**punctuality**

**punctuate** verb
punctuates
punctuating
punctuated

**punctuation**

a
b
c
d
e
f
g
h
i
j
k
l
m
n
o
**p**
q
r
s
t
u
v
w
x
y
z

**puncture** *noun*
punctures

**punish** *verb*
punishes
punishing
punished

**punishment** *noun*
punishments

**punk** *noun*
punks

**punt** *noun*
punts

**punt** *verb*
punts
punting
punted

**puny** *adjective*
punier
puniest

**pup** *noun*
pups

**pupa** *noun*
pupae

**pupil** *noun*
pupils

**puppet** *noun*
puppets

**puppy** *noun*
puppies

**purchase** *verb*
purchases
purchasing
purchased

**purchase** *noun*
purchases

**purchaser** *noun*
purchasers

**purdah**

**pure** *adjective*
purer
purest
purely

**purge** *verb*
purges
purging
purged

**purge** *noun*
purges

**purification**

**purifier** *noun*
purifiers

**purify** *verb*
purifies
purifying
purified

**Puritan**★ *noun*
Puritans

**puritan** *noun*
puritans

**puritanical** *adjective*
puritanically

**purity**

**purple** *noun*

**purpose** *noun*
purposes

**purposely**

**purr** *verb*
purrs
purring
purred

**purse** *noun*
purses

**pursue** *verb*
pursues
pursuing
pursued

**pursuer** *noun*
pursuers

**pursuit** *noun*
pursuits

**pus**☆ *noun*

**push** *verb*
pushes
pushing
pushed

**push** *noun*
pushes

**pushchair** *noun*
pushchairs

**puss**○ or **pussy** *noun*
pusses *or* pussies

**put**✚ *verb*
puts
putting
put

**putt**✱ *verb*
putts
putting
putted

**putter** *noun*
putters

**putty**

**puzzle** *verb*
puzzles
puzzling
puzzled

**puzzle** *noun*
puzzles

**pygmy** *noun*
pygmies

**pyjamas**

**pylon** *noun*
pylons

a
b
c
d
e
f
g
h
i
j
k
l
m
n
o
**p**
q
r
s
t
u
v
w
x
y
z

191

- - - - - - - - - - - - - - - - - - - - - - - - - - - - - - - - - - - - - - - - -

★ You use a capital P when you are talking about people in history, and a small p when you mean anyone who is morally strict.

☆ Pus is yellow stuff produced in sore places on the body. **!puss**.

○ Puss is a word for a cat. **!pus**.

✚ To put something somewhere is to place it there. **!putt**.

✱ To putt a ball is to tap it gently. **!put**.

a
b
c
d
e
f
g
h
i
j
k
l
m
n
o
**p**
**q**
r
s
t
u
v
w
x
y
z

**pyramid** *noun*
pyramids

**pyramidal**

**python** *noun*
pythons

# Qq

**quack** *verb*
quacks
quacking
quacked

**quack** *noun*
quacks

**quad** *noun*
quads

**quadrangle** *noun*
quadrangles

**quadrant** *noun*
quadrants

**quadrilateral** *noun*
quadrilaterals

**quadruple** *adjective*
and *noun*

**quadruple** *verb*
quadruples
quadrupling
quadrupled

**quadruplet** *noun*
quadruplets

**quail** *verb*
quails
quailing
quailed

**quail** *noun*
quail *or* quails

**quaint** *adjective*
quainter
quaintest
quaintly

**quaintness** *noun*

**quake** *verb*
quakes
quaking
quaked

**Quaker** *noun*
Quakers

**qualification** *noun*
qualifications

**qualify** *verb*
qualifies
qualifying
qualified

**quality** *noun*
qualities

**quantity** *noun*
quantities

**quarantine**

**quarrel** *noun*
quarrels

**quarrel** *verb*
quarrels
quarrelling
quarrelled

**quarrelsome**

**quarry** *noun*
quarries

**quart** *noun*
quarts

**quarter** *noun*
quarters

**quartet** *noun*
quartets

**quartz**

**quaver** *verb*
quavers
quavering
quavered

**quaver** *noun*
quavers

**quay★** *noun*
quays

**queasy** *adjective*
queasier
queasiest

**queen** *noun*
queens

**queer** *adjective*
queerer
queerest

**quench** *verb*
quenches
quenching
quenched

**query** *verb*
queries
querying
queried

**query** *noun*
queries

**quest** *noun*
quests

**question** *noun*
questions

**question** *verb*
questions
questioning
questioned

**questionable**
*adjective*
questionably

**questioner** *noun*
questioner

**questionnaire** *noun*
questionnaires

**queue☆** *noun*
queues

**queue** *verb*
queues
queueing
queued

. . . . . . . . . . . . . . . . . . . . . . . . . . . . . . . . . . . . . . . . . . . . . . . . .

★ A **quay** is a place where ships tie up. **!** key.

☆ A **queue** is a line of people waiting for something. **!** cue.

**quibble** *verb*
quibbles
quibbling
quibbled

**quibble** *noun*
quibbles

**quiche** *noun*
quiches

**quick** *adjective*
quicker
quickest
quickly

**quicken** *verb*
quickens
quickening
quickened

**quicksand** *noun*
quicksands

**quid** *noun*
quid

**quiet** *adjective*
quieter
quietest
quietly

**quieten** *verb*
quietens
quietening
quietened

**quill** *noun*
quills

**quilt** *noun*
quilts

**quintet** *noun*
quintets

**quit** *verb*
quits
quitting
quitted
quit

**quitter** *noun*
quitters

**quite**

**quiver** *verb*
quivers
quivering
quivered

**quiver** *noun*
quivers

**quiz** *noun*
quizzes

**quiz** *verb*
quizzes
quizzing
quizzed

**quoit** *noun*
quoits

**quota** *noun*
quotas

**quotation** *noun*
quotations

**quote** *verb*
quotes
quoting
quoted

**quotient** *noun*
quotients

# Rr

**rabbi** *noun*
rabbis

**rabbit** *noun*
rabbits

**rabid**

**rabies**

**raccoon** *noun*
raccoons

**race** *noun*
races

**race** *verb*
races
racing
raced

**race** *noun*
races

**racecourse** *noun*
racecourses

**racer** *noun*
racers

**racial** *adjective*
racially

**racism**

**racist** *noun*
racists

**rack** *noun*
racks

**rack** *verb*
racks
racking
racked

**racket** *noun*
rackets

**radar**

**radial** *adjective*
radially

**radiance**

**radiant** *adjective*
radiantly

**radiate** *verb*
radiates
radiating
radiated

**radiation**

**radiator** *noun*
radiators

**radical** *adjective*
radically

**radical** *noun*
radicals

**radii** see **radius**

a
b
c
d
e
f
g
h
i
j
k
l
m
n
o
p
**q**
**r**
s
t
u
v
w
x
y
z

a

**radio** *noun*
radios

b

**radioactive**

c

**radioactivity**

**radish** *noun*
radishes

d

**radium**

e

**radius** *noun*
radii

f

**raffle** *noun*
raffles

g

**raffle** *verb*
raffles
raffling
raffled

h

i

**raft** *noun*
rafts

j

**rafter** *noun*
rafters

k

**rag** *noun*
rags

l

m

**rage** *noun*
rages

n

**rage** *verb*
rages
raging
raged

o

p

**ragged**

q

**ragtime**

**raid** *noun*
raids

r

**raid** *verb*
raids
raiding
raided

s

t

**raider** *noun*
raiders

u

**rail** *noun*
rails

v

w

**railings** *plural noun*

**railway** *noun*
railways

x

y

**rain** *verb*
rains
raining
rained

**rain** *noun*
rains

**rainbow** *noun*
rainbows

**raincoat** *noun*
raincoats

**raindrop** *noun*
raindrops

**rainfall**

**rainforest** *noun*
rainforests

**raise** *verb*
raises
raising
raised

**raisin** *noun*
raisins

**rake** *verb*
rakes
raking
raked

**rake** *noun*
rakes

**rally** *verb*
rallies
rallying
rallied

**rally** *noun*
rallies

**ram** *verb*
rams
ramming
rammed

**ram** *noun*
rams

**Ramadan**

**ramble** *noun*
rambles

**ramble** *verb*
rambles
rambling
rambled

**rambler** *noun*
ramblers

**ramp** *noun*
ramps

**rampage** *verb*
rampages
rampaging
rampaged

**rampage** *noun*

**ran** see **run**

**ranch** *noun*
ranches

**random**

**rang** see **ring**

**range** *noun*
ranges

**range** *verb*
ranges
ranging
ranged

**ranger**★ *noun*
rangers

**rank** *noun*
ranks

**rank** *verb*
ranks
ranking
ranked

**ransack** *verb*
ransacks
ransacking
ransacked

**ransom** *verb*
ransoms
ransoming
ransomed

**ransom** *noun*
ransoms

z

★ You use a capital R when you mean a senior Guide.

**rap★** *verb*
raps
rapping
rapped

**rap** *noun*
raps

**rapid** *adjective*
rapidly

**rapidity**

**rapids** *plural noun*

**rare** *adjective*
rarer
rarest
rarely

**rarity** *noun*
rarities

**rascal** *noun*
rascals

**rash** *adjective*
rasher
rashest
rashly

**rash** *noun*
rashes

**rasher** *noun*
rashers

**raspberry** *noun*
raspberries

**Rastafarian** *noun*
Rastafarians

**rat** *noun*
rats

**rate** *noun*
rates

**rate** *verb*
rates
rating
rated

**rather**

**ratio** *noun*
ratios

**ration** *noun*
rations

**ration** *verb*
rations
rationing
rationed

**rational** *adjective*
rationally

**rationalize** *verb*
rationalizes
rationalizing
rationalized

**rattle** *verb*
rattles
rattling
rattled

**rattle** *noun*
rattles

**rattlesnake** *noun*
rattlesnakes

**rave** *verb*
raves
raving
raved

**rave** *noun*
raves

**raven** *noun*
ravens

**ravenous** *adjective*
ravenously

**ravine** *noun*
ravines

**raw** *adjective*
rawer
rawest

**ray** *noun*
rays

**razor** *noun*
razors

**re-**
*re-* makes words
meaning 'again', e.g.
**reproduce**. These
words are normally
spelt joined up, but a
few need a hyphen so
you don't confuse
them with other
words, e.g. **re-cover** (
to put a new cover
on); **recover** has
another meaning. You
also need a hyphen in
words beginning with
*e*, e.g. **re-enter**.

**reach** *verb*
reaches
reaching
reached

**reach** *noun*
reaches

**react** *verb*
reacts
reacting
reacted

**reaction** *noun*
reactions

**reactor** *noun*
reactors

**read**☆ *verb*
reads
reading
read

**readable**

**reader** *noun*
readers

**readily**

**readiness**

**reading** *noun*
readings

★ To **rap** is to knock loudly. ❗**wrap**.

☆ To **read** is to look at something written or printed. ❗**reed**.

a
**ready** *adjective*
readier
b
readiest
**real**★ *adjective*
c
**realism**
d
**realist** *noun*
realists
e
**realistic** *adjective*
realistically
f
**reality** *noun*
realities
g
**realization**
h
**realize** *verb*
realizes
i
realizing
realized
j
**really**
k
**realm** *noun*
realms
l
**reap** *verb*
reaps
m
reaping
reaped
n
**reaper** *noun*
reapers
o
**reappear** *verb*
reappears
p
reappearing
reappeared
q
**reappearance** *noun*
reappearances
**r**
**rear** *adjective* and *noun*
s
rears
**rear** *verb*
t
rears
rearing
u
reared
**rearrange** *verb*
v
rearranges
rearranging
w
rearranged
**rearrangement** *noun*
x
rearrangements
y

**reason** *noun*
reasons
**reason** *verb*
reasons
reasoning
reasoned
**reasonable** *adjective*
reasonably
**reassurance** *noun*
reassurances
**reassure** *verb*
reassures
reassuring
reassured
**rebel** *verb*
rebels
rebelling
rebelled
**rebel** *noun*
rebels
**rebellion** *noun*
rebellions
**rebellious** *adjective*
rebelliously
**rebound** *verb*
rebounds
rebounding
rebounded
**rebuild** *verb*
rebuilds
rebuilding
rebuilt
**recall** *verb*
recalls
recalling
recalled
**recap** *verb*
recaps
recapping
recapped
**recapture** *verb*
recaptures
recapturing
recaptured

**recede** *verb*
recedes
receding
receded
**receipt** *noun*
receipts
**receive** *verb*
receives
receiving
received
**receiver** *noun*
receivers
**recent** *adjective*
recently
**receptacle** *noun*
receptacles
**reception** *noun*
receptions
**receptionist** *noun*
receptionists
**recess** *noun*
recesses
**recession** *noun*
recessions
**recipe** *noun*
recipes
**reciprocal** *adjective*
reciprocally
**reciprocal** *noun*
reciprocals
**recital** *noun*
recitals
**recitation** *noun*
recitations
**recite** *verb*
recites
reciting
recited
**reckless** *adjective*
recklessly
**recklessness**

z

★ **Real** means 'true' or 'existing'. **!** reel.

**reckon** *verb*
reckons
reckoning
reckoned

**reclaim** *verb*
reclaims
reclaiming
reclaimed

**reclamation** *noun*
reclamations

**recline** *verb*
reclines
reclining
reclined

**recognition**

**recognizable** *adjective*
recognizably

**recognize** *verb*
recognizes
recognizing
recognized

**recoil** *verb*
recoils
recoiling
recoiled

**recollect** *verb*
recollects
recollecting
recollected

**recollection** *noun*
recollections

**recommend** *verb*
recommends
recommending
recommended

**recommendation** *noun*
recommendations

**reconcile** *verb*
reconciles
reconciling
reconciled

**reconciliation** *noun*
reconciliations

**reconstruction** *noun*
reconstructions

**record** *noun*
records

**record** *verb*
records
recording
recorded

**recorder** *noun*
recorders

**recover** *verb*
recovers
recovering
recovered

**recovery** *noun*
recoveries

**recreation** *noun*
recreations

**recreational** *adjective*
recreationally

**recruit** *noun*
recruits

**recruit** *verb*
recruits
recruiting
recruited

**rectangle** *noun*
rectangles

**rectangular**

**recur** *verb*
recurs
recurring
recurred

**recurrence** *noun*
recurrences

**recycle** *verb*
recycles
recycling
recycled

**red** *adjective*
redder
reddest

**red** *noun*
reds

**redden** *verb*
reddens
reddening
reddened

**reddish**

**redeem** *verb*
redeems
redeeming
redeemed

**redeemer** *noun*
redeemers

**redemption** *noun*
redemptions

**redhead** *noun*
redheads

**reduce** *verb*
reduces
reducing
reduced

**reduction** *noun*
reductions

**redundancy** *noun*
redundancies

**redundant** *adjective*
redundantly

**reed**★ *noun*
reeds

**reedy**

**reef** *noun*
reefs

**reef knot** *noun*
reef knots

**reek** *verb*
reeks
reeking
reeked

★ A **reed** is a plant or a thin strip. **!** read.

a

**reel**★ *noun*
reels

b

**reel** *verb*
reels
reeling
reeled

c

d

**refer** *verb*
refers
referring
referred

e

f

**referee** *noun*
referees

g

**referee** *verb*
referees
refereeing
refereed

h

i

**reference** *noun*
references

j

**referendum** *noun*
referendums

k

**refill** *verb*
refills
refilling
refilled

l

m

**refill** *noun*
refills

n

**refine** *verb*
refines
refining
refined

o

p

**refinement** *noun*
refinements

q

**r**

**refinery** *noun*
refineries

s

**reflect** *verb*
reflects
reflecting
reflected

t

u

**reflective** *adjective*
reflectively

v

**reflex** *noun*
reflexes

w

x

**reflexive** *adjective*
reflexively

**reform** *verb*
reforms
reforming
reformed

**reform** *noun*
reforms

**reformation** *noun*
reformations

**Reformation**☆

**reformer** *noun*
reformers

**refract** *verb*
refracts
refracting
refracted

**refraction**

**refrain** *verb*
refrains
refraining
refrained

**refrain** *noun*
refrains

**refresh** *verb*
refreshes
refreshing
refreshed

**refreshment** *noun*
refreshments

**refrigerate** *verb*
refrigerates
refrigerating
refrigerated

**refrigeration**

**refrigerator** *noun*
refrigerators

**refuel** *verb*
refuels
refuelling
refuelled

**refuge** *noun*
refuges

**refugee** *noun*
refugees

**refund** *verb*
refunds
refunding
refunded

**refund** *noun*
refunds

**refusal**

**refuse** *verb*
refuses
refusing
refused

**refuse**

**regain** *verb*
regains
regaining
regained

**regard** *verb*
regards
regarding
regarded

**regard** *noun*
regards

**regarding** *preposition*

**regardless**

**regatta** *noun*
regattas

**reggae**

**regiment** *noun*
regiments

**regimental**

**region** *noun*
regions

**regional** *adjective*
regionally

**register** *noun*
registers

. . . . . . . . . . . . . . . . . . . . . . . . . . . . . . . . . . . . . . . . . . . . . . . . . . . . . . .

y

★ A reel is a cylinder on which something is wound. **!** real.

z

☆ You use a capital R when you mean the historical religious movement.

**register** *verb*
registers
registering
registered

**registration** *noun*
registrations

**regret** *noun*
regrets

**regret** *verb*
regrets
regretting
regretted

**regretful** *adjective*
regretfully

**regrettable** *adjective*
regrettably

**regular** *adjective*
regularly

**regularity**

**regulate** *verb*
regulates
regulating
regulated

**regulation** *noun*
regulations

**regulator** *noun*
regulators

**rehearsal** *noun*
rehearsals

**rehearse** *verb*
rehearses
rehearsing
rehearsed

**reign**★ *verb*
reigns
reigning
reigned

**reign** *noun*
reigns

**rein**☆ *noun*
reins

**reindeer** *noun*
reindeer

**reinforce** *verb*
reinforces
reinforcing
reinforced

**reinforcement** *noun*
reinforcements

**reject** *verb*
rejects
rejecting
rejected

**reject** *noun*
rejects

**rejection** *noun*
rejections

**rejoice** *verb*
rejoices
rejoicing
rejoiced

**relate** *verb*
relates
relating
related

**relation** *noun*
relations

**relationship** *noun*
relationships

**relative** *adjective*
relatively

**relative** *noun*
relatives

**relax** *verb*
relaxes
relaxing
relaxed

**relaxation**

**relay** *verb*
relays
relaying
relayed

**relay** *noun*
relays

**release** *verb*
releases
releasing
released

**release** *noun*
releases

**relegate** *verb*
relegates
relegating
relegated

**relegation**

**relent** *verb*
relents
relenting
relented

**relentless** *adjective*
relentlessly

**relevance**

**relevant** *adjective*
relevantly

**reliability**

**reliable** *adjective*
reliably

**reliance**

**reliant**

**relic** *noun*
relics

**relief** *noun*
reliefs

**relieve** *verb*
relieves
relieving
relieved

**religion** *noun*
religions

**religious** *adjective*
religiously

**reluctance**

a
b
c
d
e
f
g
h
i
j
k
l
m
n
o
p
q
**r**
s
t
u
v
w
x
y
z

★ To **reign** is to rule as a king or queen. **!rein**.
☆ A **rein** is a strap used to guide a horse. **!reign**.

a

b

c

d

e

f

g

h

i

j

k

l

m

n

o

p

q

**r**

s

t

u

v

w

x

y

z

**reluctant** *adjective*
reluctantly

**rely** *verb*
relies
relying
relied

**remain** *verb*
remains
remaining
remained

**remainder** *noun*
remainders

**remains**

**remark** *verb*
remarks
remarking
remarked

**remark** *noun*
remarks

**remarkable** *adjective*
remarkably

**remedial** *adjective*
remedially

**remedy** *noun*
remedies

**remember** *verb*
remembers
remembering
remembered

**remembrance**

**remind** *verb*
reminds
reminding
reminded

**reminder** *noun*
reminders

**reminisce** *verb*
reminisces
reminiscing
reminisced

**reminiscence** *noun*
reminiscences

**reminiscent**

**remnant** *noun*
remnants

**remorse**

**remorseful** *adjective*
remorsefully

**remorseless**
*adjective*
remorselessly

**remote** *adjective*
remoter
remotest
remotely

**remoteness**

**removal** *noun*
removals

**remove** *verb*
removes
removing
removed

**Renaissance**★

**render** *verb*
renders
rendering
rendered

**rendezvous** *noun*
rendezvous

**renew** *verb*
renews
renewing
renewed

**renewable**

**renewal** *noun*
renewals

**renown**

**renowned**

**rent** *noun*
rents

**rent** *verb*
rents
renting
rented

**repair** *verb*
repairs
repairing
repaired

**repair** *noun*
repairs

**repay** *verb*
repays
repaying
repaid

**repayment** *noun*
repayments

**repeat** *verb*
repeats
repeating
repeated

**repeat** *noun*
repeats

**repeatedly**

**repel** *verb*
repels
repelling
repelled

**repellent**

**repent** *verb*
repents
repenting
repented

**repentance**

**repentant**

**repetition** *noun*
repetitions

**repetitive** *adjective*
repetitively

**replace** *verb*
replaces
replacing
replaced

**replacement** *noun*
replacements

**replay** *noun*
replays

★ You use a capital R when you mean the historical period.

200

**replica** *noun*
replicas

**reply** *verb*
replies
replying
replied

**reply** *noun*
replies

**report** *verb*
reports
reporting
reported

**report** *noun*
reports

**reporter** *noun*
reporters

**repossess** *verb*
repossesses
repossessing
repossessed

**represent** *verb*
represents
representing
represented

**representation** *noun*
representations

**representative**
*adjective* and *noun*
representatives

**repress** *verb*
represses
repressing
repressed

**repression** *noun*
repressions

**repressive** *adjective*
repressively

**reprieve** *verb*
reprieves
reprieving
reprieved

**reprieve** *noun*
reprieves

**reprimand** *verb*
reprimands
reprimanding
reprimanded

**reprisal** *noun*
reprisals

**reproach** *verb*
reproaches
reproaching
reproached

**reproduce** *verb*
reproduces
reproducing
reproduced

**reproduction** *noun*
reproduction

**reproductive**
*adjective*
reproductively

**reptile** *noun*
reptiles

**republic** *noun*
republics

**republican** *adjective*
and *noun*
republicans

**Republican**★
*adjective* and *noun*
Republicans

**repulsion**

**repulsive** *adjective*
repulsively

**reputation** *noun*
reputations

**request** *verb*
requests
requesting
requested

**request** *noun*
requests

**require** *verb*
requires
requiring
required

**requirement** *noun*
requirements

**reread** *verb*
rereads
rereading
reread

**rescue** *verb*
rescues
rescuing
rescued

**rescue** *noun*
rescues

**rescuer** *noun*
rescuers

**research** *noun*
researches

**researcher** *noun*
researchers

**resemblance** *noun*
resemblances

**resemble** *verb*
resembles
resembling
resembled

**resent** *verb*
resents
resenting
resented

**resentful** *adjective*
resentfully

**resentment**

**reservation** *noun*
reservations

**reserve** *verb*
reserves
reserving
reserved

**reserve** *noun*
reserves

a
b
c
d
e
f
g
h
i
j
k
l
m
n
o
p
q
**r**
s
t
u
v
w
x
y
z

★ You use a capital R when you mean the political party in the USA.

201

**reservoir** *noun*
reservoirs

**reshuffle** *noun*
reshuffles

**reside** *verb*
resides
residing
resided

**residence** *noun*
residences

**resident** *noun*
residents

**resign** *verb*
resigns
resigning
resigned

**resignation** *noun*
resignations

**resin** *noun*
resins

**resinous**

**resist** *verb*
resists
resisting
resisted

**resistance** *noun*
resistances

**resistant**

**resolute** *adjective*
resolutely

**resolution** *noun*
resolutions

**resolve** *verb*
resolves
resolving
resolved

**resort** *noun*
resorts

**resort** *verb*
resorts
resorting
resorted

**resound** *verb*
resounds
resounding
resounded

**resource** *noun*
resources

**respect** *verb*
respects
respecting
respected

**respect** *noun*
respects

**respectability**

**respectable** *adjective*
respectably

**respectful** *adjective*
respectfully

**respective** *adjective*
respectively

**respiration**

**respirator** *noun*
respirators

**respiratory**

**respond** *verb*
responds
responding
responded

**response** *noun*
responses

**responsibility** *noun*
responsibilities

**responsible** *adjective*
responsibly

**rest** *verb*
rests
resting
rested

**rest** *noun*
rests

**restaurant** *noun*
restaurants

**restful** *adjective*
restfully

**restless** *adjective*
restlessly

**restlessness**

**restoration** *noun*
restorations

**restore** *verb*
restores
restoring
restored

**restrain** *verb*
restrains
restraining
restrained

**restraint** *noun*
restraints

**restrict** *verb*
restricts
restricting
restricted

**restriction** *noun*
restrictions

**restrictive** *adjective*
restrictively

**result** *verb*
results
resulting
resulted

**result** *noun*
results

**resume** *verb*
resumes
resuming
resumed

**resumption** *noun*
resumptions

**resuscitate** *verb*
resuscitates
resuscitating
resuscitated

**retail** *verb*
retails
retailing
retailed

**retail** *noun*

**retain** *verb*
retains
retaining
retained

**retina** *noun*
retinas

**retire** *verb*
retires
retiring
retired

**retirement**

**retort** *verb*
retorts
retorting
retorted

**retort** *noun*
retorts

**retrace** *verb*
retraces
retracing
retraced

**retreat** *verb*
retreats
retreating
retreated

**retrievable** *adjective*
retrievably

**retrieval** *noun*
retrievals

**retrieve** *verb*
retrieves
retrieving
retrieved

**retriever** *noun*
retrievers

**return** *verb*
returns
returning
returned

**return** *noun*
returns

**reunion** *noun*
reunions

**rev** *verb*
revs
revving
revved

**rev** *noun*
revs

**reveal** *verb*
reveals
revealing
revealed

**revelation** *noun*
revelations

**revenge**

**revenue** *noun*
revenues

**revere** *verb*
reveres
revering
revered

**reverence**

**Reverend**★

**reverent**★ *adjective*
reverently

**reversal** *noun*
reversals

**reverse** *verb*
reverses
reversing
reversed

**reverse** *noun*
reverses

**reversible** *adjective*
reversibly

**review** *verb*
reviews
reviewing
reviewed

**review**☆ *noun*
reviews

**reviewer** *noun*
reviewers

**revise** *verb*
revises
revising
revised

**revision** *noun*
revisions

**revival** *noun*
revivals

**revive** *verb*
revives
reviving
revived

**revolt** *verb*
revolts
revolting
revolted

**revolt** *noun*
revolts

**revolution** *noun*
revolutions

**revolutionary**
*adjective* and *noun*
revolutionaries

**revolutionize** *verb*
revolutionizes
revolutionizing
revolutionized

**revolve** *verb*
revolves
revolving
revolved

**revolver** *noun*
revolvers

**revue**○ *noun*
revues

a
b
c
d
e
f
g
h
i
j
k
l
m
n
o
p
q
**r**
s
t
u
v
w
x
y
z

★ You use **Reverend** as a title of a member of the clergy, and
  **reverent** as an ordinary word meaning 'showing respect'.
☆ A **review** is a piece of writing about a film, play, etc. ! **revue**.
○ A **revue** is an entertainment of short sketches. ! **review**.

203

a

**reward** *verb*
 rewards
 rewarding
 rewarded

b

c

**reward** *noun*
 rewards

d

**rewind** *verb*
 rewinds
 rewinding
 rewound

e

f

**rewrite** *verb*
 rewrites
 rewriting
 rewrote
 rewritten

g

h

i

**rheumatic**

j

**rheumatism**

**rhinoceros** *noun*
 rhinoceroses
 rhinoceros

k

l

**rhododendron** *noun*
 rhododendrons

m

**rhombus** *noun*
 rhombuses

n

**rhubarb**

o

**rhyme** *verb*
 rhymes
 rhyming
 rhymed

p

q

**rhyme** *noun*
 rhymes

r

**rhythm** *noun*
 rhythms

s

**rhythmic** or
**rhythmical** *adjective*
 rhythmically

t

u

**rib** *noun*
 ribs

v

**ribbon** *noun*
 ribbons

w

x

y

z

**rice**

**rich** *adjective*
 richer
 richest
 richly

**riches** *plural noun*

**richness**

**rick** *noun*
 ricks

**rickety**

**rickshaw** *noun*
 rickshaws

**ricochet** *verb*
 ricochets
 ricocheting
 ricocheted

**rid** *verb*
 rids
 ridding
 rid

**riddance**

**riddle** *noun*
 riddles

**ride** *verb*
 rides
 riding
 rode
 ridden

**ride** *noun*
 rides

**rider** *noun*
 riders

**ridge** *noun*
 ridges

**ridicule** *verb*
 ridicules
 ridiculing
 ridiculed

**ridiculous** *adjective*
 ridiculously

**rifle** *noun*
 rifles

**rift** *noun*
 rifts

**rig** *verb*
 rigs
 rigging
 rigged

**rigging**

**right** *adjective*
 rightly

**right★** *noun*
 rights

**right☆** *verb*
 rights
 righting
 righted

**righteous** *adjective*
 righteously

**righteousness**

**rightful** *adjective*
 rightfully

**right-handed**

**rightness**

**rigid** *adjective*
 rigidly

**rigidity**

**rim** *noun*
 rims

**rind** *noun*
 rinds

**ring** *noun*
 rings

**ring○** *verb*
 rings
 ringing
 rang
 rung

. . . . . . . . . . . . . . . . . . . . . . . . . . . . . . . . . . . . . . . . . . .

★ A **right** is something you are entitled to. **!rite, write.**

☆ To **right** something is to make it right. **!rite, write.**

○ The past tense is **rang** and the past participle is **rung** when you
  mean 'to make a sound like a bell'. **!wring.**

204

**ring**★ *verb*
rings
ringing
ringed

**ring** *noun*
rings

**ringleader** *noun*
ringleaders

**ringlet** *noun*
ringlets

**ringmaster** *noun*
ringmasters

**rink** *noun*
rinks

**rinse** *verb*
rinses
rinsing
rinsed

**rinse** *noun*
rinses

**riot** *verb*
riots
rioting
rioted

**riot** *noun*
riots

**riotous** *adjective*
riotously

**rip** *verb*
rips
ripping
ripped

**rip** *noun*
rips

**ripe** *adjective*
riper
ripest

**ripen** *verb*
ripens
ripening
ripened

**ripeness**

**rip-off** *noun*
rip-offs

**ripple** *noun*
ripples

**ripple** *verb*
ripples
rippling
rippled

**rise** *verb*
rises
rising
rose
risen

**rise** *noun*
rises

**risk** *verb*
risks
risking
risked

**risk** *noun*
risks

**risky** *adjective*
riskier
riskiest
riskily

**risotto** *noun*
risottos

**rissole** *noun*
rissoles

**rite**☆ *noun*
rites

**ritual** *noun*
rituals

**rival** *noun*
rivals

**rival** *verb*
rivals
rivalling
rivalled

**rivalry** *noun*
rivalries

**river** *noun*
rivers

**rivet** *noun*
rivets

**rivet** *verb*
rivets
riveting
riveted

**road**✿ *noun*
roads

**roadroller** *noun*
roadrollers

**roadside** *noun*
roadsides

**roadway** *noun*
roadways

**roam** *verb*
roams
roaming
roamed

**roar** *verb*
roars
roaring
roared

**roar** *noun*
roars

**roast** *verb*
roasts
roasting
roasted

**rob** *verb*
robs
robbing
robbed

a
b
c
d
e
f
g
h
i
j
k
l
m
n
o
p
q
**r**
s
t
u
v
w
x
y
z

★ The past tense and past participle is **ringed** when you mean 'to put a ring round something'. ! **wring**.
☆ A **rite** is a ceremony or ritual. ! **right**, **write**.
✿ A **road** is a hard surface for traffic to use. ! **rode**.

a

**robber** *noun*
robbers

b

**robbery** *noun*
robberies

c

**robe** *noun*
robes

d

**robin** *noun*
robins

e

**robot** *noun*
robots

f

**robust** *adjective*
robustly

g

**rock** *verb*
rocks
rocking
rocked

h

i

**rock** *noun*
rocks

j

k

**rocker** *noun*
rockers

l

**rockery** *noun*
rockeries

m

**rocket** *noun*
rockets

n

**rocky** *adjective*
rockier
rockiest
rockily

o

p

**rod** *noun*
rods

q

**r**

**rode**★ see **ride**

s

**rodent** *noun*
rodents

t

**rodeo** *noun*
rodeos

u

**rogue** *noun*
rogues

v

**roguish** *adjective*
roguishly

w

**role**☆ *noun*
roles

**roll** *verb*
rolls
rolling
rolled

**roll**○ *noun*
rolls

**roller** *noun*
rollers

**Roman** *adjective* and
*noun*
Romans

**Roman Catholic**
*noun*
Roman Catholics

**romance** *noun*
romances

**Roman numeral**

**romantic** *adjective*
romantically

**Romany**

**romp** *verb*
romps
romping
romped

**romp** *noun*
romps

**rompers** *plural noun*

**roof** *noun*
roofs

**rook** *noun*
rooks

**room** *noun*
rooms

**roomful** *noun*
roomfuls

**roomy** *adjective*
roomier
roomiest
roomily

**roost** *noun*
roosts

**root**✢ *noun*
roots

**root** *verb*
roots
rooting
rooted

**rope** *noun*
ropes

**rose** *noun*
roses

**rose** see **rise**

**rosette** *noun*
rosettes

**rosy** *adjective*
rosier
rosiest
rosily

**rot** *verb*
rots
rotting
rotted

**rot** *noun*

**rota** *noun*
rotas

**rotary**

**rotate** *verb*
rotates
rotating
rotated

**rotation** *noun*
rotations

**rotor** *noun*
rotors

**rotten**

x

y

z

★ **Rode** is the past tense of **ride**. ! **road**.
☆ A **role** is a part in a play or film. ! **roll**.
○ A **roll** is a small loaf of bread or an act of rolling. ! **role**.
✢ A **root** is the part of a plant that grows underground. ! **route**.

**rottenness**

**rottweiler** *noun*
rottweilers

**rough** *adjective*
rougher
roughest
roughly

**roughness**

**roughage**

**roughen** *verb*
roughens
roughening
roughened

**round** *adjective,*
*adverb,* and
*preposition*
rounder
roundest
roundly

**round** *noun*
rounds

**round** *verb*
rounds
rounding
rounded

**roundabout** *adjective*
and *noun*
roundabouts

**rounders** *noun*

**Roundhead** *noun*
Roundheads

**rouse** *verb*
rouses
rousing
roused

**rout** *verb*
routs
routing
routed

**rout** *noun*
routs

**route**★ *noun*
routes

**routine** *noun*
routines

**routine** *adjective*
routinely

**rove** *verb*
roves
roving
roved

**rover** *noun*
rovers

**row**☆ *noun*
rows

**row**◐ *verb*
rows
rowing
rowed

**rowdiness**

**rowdy** *adjective*
rowdier
rowdiest
rowdily

**rower** *noun*
rowers

**rowlock** *noun*
rowlocks

**royal** *adjective*
royally

**royalty**

**rub** *verb*
rubs
rubbing
rubbed

**rub** *noun*
rubs

**rubber** *noun*
rubbers

**rubbery**

**rubbish**

**rubble**

**ruby** *noun*
rubies

**rucksack** *noun*
rucksacks

**rudder** *noun*
rudders

**ruddy** *adjective*
ruddier
ruddiest

**rude** *adjective*
ruder
rudest
rudely

**rudeness**

**ruffian** *noun*
ruffians

**ruffle** *verb*
ruffles
ruffling
ruffled

**rug** *noun*
rugs

**rugby**✢

**rugged** *adjective*
ruggedly

**rugger**

- - - - - - - - - - - - - - - - - - - - - - - - - - - - - - - - - - - - - - - - - - - - -

★ A **route** is the way you go to get to a place. **!** root.
☆ A **row** is a line of people or things and rhymes with 'go'. A **row** is also a noise or argument and rhymes with 'cow'.
◐ To **row** means to use oars to make a boat move and rhymes with 'go'.
✢ You can use a small r when you mean the game.

a
b
c
d
e
f
g
h
i
j
k
l
m
n
o
p
q
**r**
s
t
u
v
w
x
y
z

**ruin** *verb*
ruins
ruining
ruined

**ruin** *noun*
ruins

**ruinous** *adjective*
ruinously

**rule** *noun*
rules

**rule** *verb*
rules
ruling
ruled

**ruler** *noun*
rulers

**ruling** *noun*
rulings

**rum** *noun*
rums

**rumble** *verb*
rumbles
rumbling
rumbled

**rumble** *noun*
rumbles

**rummage** *verb*
rummages
rummaging
rummaged

**rummy**

**rumour** *noun*
rumours

**rump** *noun*
rumps

**run** *verb*
runs
running
ran
run

**run** *noun*
runs

**runaway** *noun*
runaways

**rung** *noun*
rungs

**rung** see **ring**

**runner** *noun*
runners

**runner-up** *noun*
runners-up

**runny** *adjective*
runnier
runniest
runnily

**runway** *noun*
runways

**rural**

**rush** *verb*
rushes
rushing
rushed

**rush** *noun*
rushes

**rusk** *noun*
rusks

**rust** *noun*

**rust** *verb*
rusts
rusting
rusted

**rustic**

**rustle** *verb*
rustles
rustling
rustled

**rustler** *noun*
rustlers

**rusty** *adjective*
rustier
rustiest
rustily

**rut** *noun*
ruts

**ruthless** *adjective*
ruthlessly

**ruthlessness**

**rutted**

**rye**★ *noun*

# Ss

**sabbath** *noun*
sabbaths

**sabotage** *noun*

**sabotage** *verb*
sabotages
sabotaging
sabotaged

**saboteur** *noun*
saboteurs

**sac**☆ *noun*
sacs

**saccharin**

**sachet** *noun*
sachets

**sack**○ *noun*
sacks

**sack** *verb*
sacks
sacking
sacked

**sacred**

**sacrifice** *noun*
sacrifices

**sacrificial** *adjective*
sacrificially

★ **Rye** is a type of cereal or bread. **!wry**.
☆ A **sac** is a bag-like part of an animal or plant. **!sack**.
○ A **sack** is a large bag. **!sac**.

a b c d e f g h i j k l m n o p q **r** **s** t u v w x y z

**sacrifice** *verb*
  sacrifices
  sacrificing
  sacrificed

**sad** *adjective*
  sadder
  saddest
  sadly

**sadness**

**sadden** *verb*
  saddens
  saddening
  saddened

**saddle** *noun*
  saddles

**saddle** *verb*
  saddles
  saddling
  saddled

**sadist** *noun*
  sadists

**sadism**

**sadistic** *adjective*
  sadistically

**safari** *noun*
  safaris

**safe** *adjective*
  safer
  safest
  safely

**safe** *noun*
  safes

**safeguard** *noun*
  safeguards

**safety**

**sag** *verb*
  sags
  sagging
  sagged

**saga** *noun*
  sagas

**sago**

**said** see **say**

**sail** *verb*
  sails
  sailing
  sailed

**sail**★ *noun*
  sails

**sailboard** *noun*
  sailboards

**sailor** *noun*
  sailors

**saint** *noun*
  saints

**saintly** *adjective*
  saintlier
  saintliest

**sake**

**salaam** *interjection*

**salad** *noun*
  salads

**salami** *noun*
  salamis

**salary** *noun*
  salaries

**sale**☆ *noun*
  sales

**salesman** *noun*
  salesmen

**salesperson** *noun*
  salespersons

**saleswoman** *noun*
  saleswomen

**saline**

**saliva**

**sally** *verb*
  sallies
  sallying
  sallied

**salmon** *noun*
  salmon

**salon** *noun*
  salons

**saloon** *noun*
  saloons

**salt** *noun*

**salt** *verb*
  salts
  salting
  salted

**salty** *adjective*
  saltier
  saltiest

**salute** *verb*
  salutes
  saluting
  saluted

**salute** *noun*
  salutes

**salvage** *verb*
  salvages
  salvaging
  salvaged

**salvation**

**same**

**samosa** *noun*
  samosas

**sample** *noun*
  samples

**sample** *verb*
  samples
  sampling
  sampled

**sanctuary** *noun*
  sanctuaries

**sand** *noun*
  sands

**sand** *verb*
  sands
  sanding
  sanded

**sander** *noun*
  sanders

. . . . . . . . . . . . . . . . . . . . . . . . . . . . . . . . . . . . . . . . . . . . . .

★ A **sail** is a sheet that catches the wind to make a boat go. **!** sale.
☆ You use **sale** in e.g. *The house is for sale*. **!** sail.

a
b
c
d
e
f
g
h
i
j
k
l
m
n
o
p
q
r
**s**
t
u
v
w
x
y
z

**sandal** *noun*
sandals
**sandbag** *noun*
sandbags
**sandpaper**
**sands** *plural noun*
**sandstone**
**sandwich** *noun*
sandwiches
**sandy** *adjective*
sandier
sandiest
**sane** *adjective*
saner
sanest
sanely
**sang** see **sing**
**sanitary**
**sanitation**
**sanity**
**sank** see **sink**
**Sanskrit**
**sap** *noun*
**sap** *verb*
saps
sapping
sapped
**sapling** *noun*
saplings
**sapphire** *noun*
sapphires
**sarcasm**
**sarcastic** *adjective*
sarcastically
**sardine** *noun*
sardines
**sari** *noun*
saris
**sash** *noun*
sashes
**sat** see **sit**

**satchel** *noun*
satchels
**satellite** *noun*
satellites
**satin**
**satire** *noun*
satires
**satirical** *adjective*
satirically
**satirist** *noun*
satirists
**satisfaction**
**satisfactory** *adjective*
satisfactorily
**satisfy** *verb*
satisfies
satisfying
satisfied
**saturate** *verb*
saturates
saturating
saturated
**saturation**
**Saturday** *noun*
Saturdays
**sauce**★ *noun*
sauces
**saucepan** *noun*
saucepans
**saucer** *noun*
saucers
**saucy** *adjective*
saucier
sauciest
saucily
**sauna** *noun*
saunas
**saunter** *verb*
saunters
sauntering
sauntered
**sausage** *noun*
sausages

**savage** *adjective*
savagely
**savage** *noun*
savages
**savage** *verb*
savages
savaging
savaged
**savagery**
**savannah** *noun*
savannahs
**save** *verb*
saves
saving
saved
**saver** *noun*
savers
**savings** *plural noun*
**saviour** *noun*
saviours
**savoury**
**saw** *noun*
saws
**saw** *verb*
saws
sawing
sawed
sawn
**saw** see **see**
**sawdust**
**saxophone** *noun*
saxophones
**say** *verb*
says
saying
said
**say** *noun*
**saying** *noun*
sayings
**scab** *noun*
scabs

. . . . . . . . . . . . . . . . . . . . . . . . . . . . . . . . . . . . . . . . . . . . . . . . . . . .

★ A **sauce** is a liquid you put on food. **!source**.

**scabbard** noun
scabbards

**scaffold** noun
scaffolds

**scaffolding**

**scald** verb
scalds
scalding
scalded

**scale** noun
scales

**scale** verb
scales
scaling
scaled

**scales** plural noun

**scaly** adjective
scalier
scaliest

**scalp** noun
scalps

**scalp** verb
scalps
scalping
scalped

**scamper** verb
scampers
scampering
scampered

**scampi** plural noun

**scan** verb
scans
scanning
scanned

**scan** noun
scans

**scandal** noun
scandals

**scandalous** adjective
scandalous

**scanner** noun
scanners

**scanty** adjective
scantier
scantiest
scantily

**scapegoat** noun
scapegoats

**scar** noun
scars

**scar** verb
scars
scarring
scarred

**scarce** adjective
scarcer
scarcest
scarcely

**scarcity** noun
scarcities

**scare** verb
scares
scaring
scared

**scare** noun
scares

**scarecrow** noun
scarecrows

**scarf** noun
scarves

**scarlet**

**scary** adjective
scarier
scariest
scarily

**scatter** verb
scatters
scattering
scattered

**scene**★ noun
scenes

**scenery**

**scent**☆ noun
scents

**scent** verb
scents
scenting
scented

**sceptic** noun
sceptics

**sceptical** adjective
sceptically

**scepticism**

**schedule** noun
schedules

**scheme** noun
schemes

**scheme** verb
schemes
scheming
schemed

**schemer** noun
schemers

**scholar** noun
scholars

**scholarly**

**scholarship** noun
scholarships

**school** noun
schools

**schoolboy** noun
schoolboys

**schoolchild** noun
schoolchildren

**schoolgirl** noun
schoolgirls

**schoolteacher** noun
schoolteachers

**schooner** noun
schooners

**science**

**scientific** adjective
scientifically

**scientist** noun
scientists

. . . . . . . . . . . . . . . . . . . . . . . . . . . . . . . . . . . . . . . . . . . . . . . . . . . . . . . . . . .

★ A **scene** is a place or part of a play. ! **seen**.
☆ A **scent** is a smell or perfume. ! **cent**, **sent**.

scissors *plural noun*

scoff *verb*
scoffs
scoffing
scoffed

scold *verb*
scolds
scolding
scolded

scone *noun*
scones

scoop *noun*
scoops

scoop *verb*
scoops
scooping
scooped

scooter *noun*
scooters

scope

scorch *verb*
scorches
scorching
scorched

score *noun*
scores

score *verb*
scores
scoring
scored

scorer *noun*
scorers

scorn *noun*

scorn *verb*
scorns
scorning
scorned

scorpion *noun*
scorpions

Scot *noun*
Scots

scoundrel *noun*
scoundrels

scour *verb*
scours
scouring
scoured

Scout★ *noun*
Scouts

scout *noun*
scouts

scowl *verb*
scowls
scowling
scowled

scramble *verb*
scrambles
scrambling
scrambled

scramble *noun*
scrambles

scrap *verb*
scraps
scrapping
scrapped

scrap *noun*
scraps

scrape *verb*
scrapes
scraping
scraped

scrape *noun*
scrapes

scraper *noun*
scrapers

scrappy *adjective*
scrappier
scrappiest
scrappily

scratch *verb*
scratches
scratching
scratched

scratch *noun*
scratches

scrawl *verb*
scrawls
scrawling
scrawled

scrawl *noun*
scrawls

scream *verb*
screams
screaming
screamed

scream *noun*
screams

screech *verb*
screeches
screeching
screeched

screech *noun*
screeches

screen *noun*
screens

screen *verb*
screens
screening
screened

screw *noun*
screws

screw *verb*
screws
screwing
screwed

screwdriver *noun*
screwdrivers

scribble *verb*
scribbles
scribbling
scribbled

scribble *noun*
scribbles

scribbler *noun*
scribblers

. . . . . . . . . . . . . . . . . . . . . . . . . . . . . . . . . . . . . . .

★ You use a capital S when you mean a member of the Scout Association.

a b c d e f g h i j k l m n o p q r **s** t u v w x y z

**script** *noun*
scripts

**scripture** *noun*
scriptures

**scroll** *noun*
scrolls

**scrotum** *noun*
scrotums *or* scrota

**scrounge** *verb*
scrounges
scrounging
scrounged

**scrounger** *noun*
scroungers

**scrub** *verb*
scrubs
scrubbing
scrubbed

**scrub** *noun*

**scruffy** *adjective*
scruffier
scruffiest
scruffily

**scrum** *noun*
scrums

**scrummage** *noun*
scrummages

**scrutinize** *verb*
scrutinizes
scrutinizing
scrutinized

**scrutiny** *noun*
scrutinies

**scuba diving**

**scuffle** *noun*
scuffles

**scuffle** *verb*
scuffles
scuffling
scuffled

**scullery** *noun*
sculleries

**sculptor** *noun*
sculptors

**sculpture** *noun*
sculptures

**scum**

**scurry** *verb*
scurries
scurrying
scurried

**scurvy**

**scuttle** *verb*
scuttles
scuttling
scuttled

**scuttle** *noun*
scuttles

**scythe** *noun*
scythes

**sea**★ *noun*
seas

**seabed**

**seafarer** *noun*
seafarers

**seafaring**

**seafood**

**seagull** *noun*
seagulls

**sea horse** *noun*
sea horses

**seal** *verb*
seals
sealing
sealed

**seal** *noun*
seals

**sea lion** *noun*
sea lions

**seam**☆ *noun*
seams

**seaman** *noun*
seamen

**seamanship**

**seaplane** *noun*
seaplanes

**seaport** *noun*
seaports

**search** *verb*
searches
searching
searched

**search** *noun*
searches

**searcher** *noun*
searchers

**searchlight** *noun*
searchlights

**seashore** *noun*
seashores

**seasick**

**seasickness**

**seaside**

**season** *noun*
seasons

**season** *verb*
seasons
seasoning
seasoned

**seasonal** *adjective*
seasonally

**seasoning** *noun*
seasonings

**seat** *noun*
seats

**seat** *verb*
seats
seating
seated

**seat belt** *noun*
seat belts

**seaward** *adjective* and *adverb*

**seawards** *adverb*

. . . . . . . . . . . . . . . . . . . . . . . . . . . . . . . . . . . . . . . . . . . .

★ A **sea** is an area of salt water. **!see**.

☆ A **seam** is a line of stitching in cloth. **!seem**.

seaweed *noun*
seaweeds

secateurs *plural noun*

secluded

seclusion

second *adjective*
secondly

second *noun*
seconds

second *verb*
seconds
seconding
seconded

secondary

second-hand
*adjective*

secrecy

secret *adjective*
secretly

secret *noun*
secrets

secretary *noun*
secretaries

secrete *verb*
secretes
secreting
secreted

secretion *noun*
secretions

secretive *adjective*
secretively

secretiveness

sect *noun*
sects

section *noun*
sections

sectional

sector *noun*
sectors

secure *adjective*
securer
securest
securely

secure *verb*
secures
securing
secured

security

sedate *adjective*
sedately

sedation

sedative *noun*
sedatives

sediment

sedimentary

see★ *verb*
sees
seeing
saw
seen

seed *noun*
seeds

seedling *noun*
seedlings

seek *verb*
seeks
seeking
sought

seem☆ *verb*
seems
seeming
seemed

seemingly

seen✪ see see

seep *verb*
seeps
seeping
seeped

seepage

see-saw *noun*
see-saws

seethe *verb*
seethes
seething
seethed

segment *noun*
segments

segmented

segregate *verb*
segregates
segregating
segregated

segregation

seismograph *noun*
seismographs

seize *verb*
seizes
seizing
seized

seizure *noun*
seizures

seldom

select *verb*
selects
selecting
selected

select *adjective*

self *noun*
selves

self-confidence

self-confident
*adjective*
self-confidently

self-conscious
*adjective*
self-consciously

self-contained

selfish *adjective*
selfishly

- - - - - - - - - - - - - - - - - - - - - - - - - - - - - - - - - - - - - - - - - -

★ You use **see** in e.g. *I can´t see anything.* **!sea**.
☆ You use **seem** in e.g. *they seem tired.* **!seam**.
✪ **Seen** is the past participle of **see**. **!scene**.

**selfishness**

**selfless** *adjective*
selflessly

**self-service**

**sell**★ *verb*
sells
selling
sold

**semaphore**

**semen**

---

**semi-**
*semi-* makes words
meaning 'half', e.g.
**semi-automatic**,
**semi-skimmed**. A
few words are spelt
joined up, e.g.
**semicircle**,
**semicolon**, but most
of them have
hyphens.

---

**semibreve** *noun*
semibreves

**semicircle** *noun*
semicircles

**semicircular**

**semicolon** *noun*
semicolons

**semi-detached**

**semi-final** *noun*
semi-finals

**semi-finalist** *noun*
semi-finalists

**semitone** *noun*
semitones

**semolina**

**senate**

**senator** *noun*
senators

**send** *verb*
sends
sending
sent

**senior** *adjective* and
*noun*
seniors

**seniority**

**sensation** *noun*
sensations

**sensational** *adjective*
sensationally

**sense** *noun*
senses

**sense** *verb*
senses
sensing
sensed

**senseless** *adjective*
senselessly

**sensible** *adjective*
sensibly

**sensitive** *adjective*
sensitively

**sensitivity** *noun*
sensitivities

**sensitize** *verb*
sensitizes
sensitizing
sensitized

**sensor** *noun*
sensors

**sent**☆ see **send**

**sentence** *noun*
sentences

**sentence** *verb*
sentences
sentencing
sentenced

**sentiment** *noun*
sentiments

**sentimental** *adjective*
sentimentally

**sentimentality**

**sentinel** *noun*
sentinels

**sentry** *noun*
sentries

**separable**

**separate** *adjective*
separately

**separate** *verb*
separates
separating
separated

**separation** *noun*
separations

**September** *noun*
Septembers

**septic**

**sequel** *noun*
sequels

**sequence** *noun*
sequences

**sequin** *noun*
sequins

**serene** *adjective*
serenely

**serenity**

**sergeant** *noun*
sergeants

**sergeant major** *noun*
sergeant majors

**serial**○ *noun*
serials

**series** *noun*
series

**serious** *adjective*
seriously

**seriousness**

a
b
c
d
e
f
g
h
i
j
k
l
m
n
o
p
q
r
**s**
t
u
v
w
x
y
z

---

★ To **sell** something means 'to exchange it for money'. **!cell**.
☆ You use **sent** in e.g. *he was sent home*. **!cent**, **scent**.
○ A **serial** is a story or programme in separate parts. **!cereal**.

**sermon** noun
sermons

**serpent** noun
serpents

**servant** noun
servants

**serve** verb
serves
serving
served

**server** noun
servers

**serve** noun
serves

**service** noun
services

**service** verb
services
servicing
serviced

**serviette** noun
serviettes

**session** noun
sessions

**set** verb
sets
setting
set

**set** noun
sets

**set square** noun
set squares

**sett\*** noun
setts

**settee** noun
settees

**setting** noun
settings

**settle** verb
settles
settling
settled

**settlement** noun
settlements

**settler** noun
settlers

**set-up** noun
set-ups

**seven**

**seventeen**

**seventeenth**

**seventh** adjective and noun
seventhly

**seventieth**

**seventy** adjective and noun
seventies

**sever** verb
severs
severing
severed

**several** adjective
severally

**severe** adjective
severer
severest
severely

**severity**

**sew**☆ verb
sews
sewing
sewed
sewn

**sewage**

**sewer** noun
sewers

**sex** noun
sexes

**sexism**

**sexist** adjective and noun
sexists

**sextet** noun
sextets

**sexual** adjective
sexually

**sexuality**

**sexy** adjective
sexier
sexiest
sexily

**shabbiness**

**shabby** adjective
shabbier
shabbiest
shabbily

**shack** noun
shacks

**shade** noun
shades

**shade** verb
shades
shading
shaded

**shadow** noun
shadows

**shadow** verb
shadows
shadowing
shadowed

**shadowy**

**shady** adjective
shadier
shadiest

**shaft** noun
shafts

**shaggy** adjective
shaggier
shaggiest
shaggily

- - - - - - - - - - - - - - - - - - - - - - - - - - - - - - - - - - - - - - - - - - - - -

★ A **sett** is a badger's burrow.
☆ To **sew** is to work with a needle and thread. **!** sow.

216

**shake** *verb*
shakes
shaking
shook
shaken

**shake**★ *noun*
shakes

**shaky** *adjective*
shakier
shakiest
shakily

**shall** *verb*
should

**shallow** *adjective*
shallower
shallowest
shallowly

**sham** *noun*
shams

**shamble** *verb*
shambles
shambling
shambled

**shambles** *noun*

**shame** *verb*
shames
shaming
shamed

**shame** *noun*

**shameful** *adjective*
shamefully

**shameless** *adjective*
shamelessly

**shampoo** *noun*
shampoos

**shampoo** *verb*
shampoos
shampooing
shampooed

**shamrock**

**shandy** *noun*
shandies

**shan't** *verb*

**shanty** *noun*
shanties

**shape** *noun*
shapes

**shape** *verb*
shapes
shaping
shaped

**shapeless** *adjective*
shapelessly

**shapely** *adjective*
shapelier
shapeliest

**share** *noun*
shares

**share** *verb*
shares
sharing
shared

**shark** *noun*
sharks

**sharp** *adjective*
sharper
sharpest
sharply

**sharp** *noun*
sharps

**sharpen** *verb*
sharpens
sharpening
sharpened

**sharpener** *noun*
sharpeners

**sharpness**

**shatter** *verb*
shatters
shattering
shattered

**shave** *verb*
shaves
shaving
shaved

**shave** *noun*
shaves

**shaver** *noun*
shavers

**shavings** *plural noun*

**shawl** *noun*
shawls

**she**

**sheaf** *noun*
sheaves

**shear**☆ *verb*
shears
shearing
sheared
shorn

**shearer** *noun*
shearers

**shears** *plural noun*

**sheath** *noun*
sheaths

**sheathe** *verb*
sheathes
sheathing
sheathed

**shed** *noun*
sheds

**shed** *verb*
sheds
shedding
shed

**she'd** *verb*

**sheen**

**sheep** *noun*
sheep

**sheepdog** *noun*
sheepdogs

**sheepish** *adjective*
sheepishly

- - - - - - - - - - - - - - - - - - - - - - - - - - - - - - - - - - - - - - - - - - - -

★ To **shake** is to tremble or quiver. **!sheikh**.
☆ To **shear** is to cut wool from a sheep. **!sheer**.

a
b
c
d
e
f
g
h
i
j
k
l
m
n
o
p
q
r
**s**
t
u
v
w
x
y
z

# sh

**sheer★** *adjective*
sheerer
sheerest

**sheet** *noun*
sheets

**sheikh** *noun*
sheikhs

**shelf** *noun*
shelves

**shell** *noun*
shells

**shell** *verb*
shells
shelling
shelled

**she'll** *verb*

**shellfish** *noun*
shellfish

**shelter** *noun*
shelters

**shelter** *verb*
shelters
sheltering
sheltered

**shelve** *verb*
shelves
shelving
shelved

**shepherd** *noun*
shepherds

**sherbet** *noun*
sherbets

**sheriff** *noun*
sheriffs

**sherry** *noun*
sherries

**she's** *verb*

**shield** *noun*
shields

**shield** *verb*
shields
shielding
shielded

**shift** *noun*
shifts

**shift** *verb*
shifts
shifting
shifted

**shilling** *noun*
shillings

**shimmer** *verb*
shimmers
shimmering
shimmered

**shin** *noun*
shins

**shine** *verb*
shines
shining
shone
shined

**shine** *noun*

**shingle**

**shiny** *adjective*
shinier
shiniest

---

**-ship**
*-ship* makes nouns,
e.g. **friendship**. Other
noun suffixes are
**-dom**, **-hood**, **-ment**,
and **-ness**.

---

**ship** *noun*
ships

**ship** *verb*
ships
shipping
shipped

**shipping**

**shipwreck** *noun*
shipwrecks

**shipwrecked**

**shipyard** *noun*
shipyards

**shire** *noun*
shires

**shirk** *verb*
shirks
shirking
shirked

**shirt** *noun*
shirts

**shiver** *verb*
shivers
shivering
shivered

**shiver** *noun*
shivers

**shivery**

**shoal** *noun*
shoals

**shock** *verb*
shocks
shocking
shocked

**shock** *noun*
shocks

**shoddy** *adjective*
shoddier
shoddiest
shoddily

**shoe** *noun*
shoes

**shoelace** *noun*
shoelaces

**shoestring** *noun*
shoestrings

**shone** see **shine**

**shook** see **shake**

**shoot** *verb*
shoots
shooting
shot

---

★ You use **sheer** in e.g. *sheer joy*. **!shear**.

**shoot**★ *noun*
shoots

**shop** *noun*
shops

**shop** *verb*
shops
shopping
shopped

**shopkeeper** *noun*
shopkeepers

**shoplifter** *noun*
shoplifters

**shopper** *noun*
shoppers

**shopping**

**shore** *noun*
shores

**shorn** see **shear**

**short** *adjective*
shorter
shortest
shortly

**shortness**

**shortage** *noun*
shortages

**shortbread**

**shortcake** *noun*
shortcakes

**shortcoming** *noun*
shortcomings

**shorten** *verb*
shortens
shortening
shortened

**shorthand**

**short-handed**

**shortly**

**shorts** *plural noun*

**short-sighted**

**shot** *noun*
shots

**shot** see **shoot**

**shotgun** *noun*
shotguns

**should**

**shoulder** *noun*
shoulders

**shoulder** *verb*
shoulders
shouldering
shouldered

**shout** *verb*
shouts
shouting
shouted

**shout** *noun*
shouts

**shove** *verb*
shoves
shoving
shoved

**shovel** *noun*
shovels

**shovel** *verb*
shovels
shovelling
shovelled

**show** *verb*
shows
showing
showed
shown

**show** *noun*
shows

**shower** *noun*
showers

**shower** *verb*
showers
showering
showered

**showery**

**showjumper** *noun*
showjumpers

**showjumping**

**showman** *noun*
showmen

**showmanship**

**showroom** *noun*
showrooms

**showiness**

**showy** *adjective*
showier
showiest
showily

**shrank** see **shrink**

**shrapnel**

**shred** *noun*
shreds

**shred** *verb*
shreds
shredding
shredded

**shrew** *noun*
shrews

**shrewd** *adjective*
shrewder
shrewdest
shrewdly

**shrewdness**

**shriek** *verb*
shrieks
shrieking
shrieked

**shriek** *noun*
shrieks

**shrill** *adjective*
shriller
shrillest
shrilly

**shrillness**

**shrimp** *noun*
shrimps

**shrine** *noun*
shrines

**shrink** *verb*
shrinks
shrinking
shrank
shrunk

a
b
c
d
e
f
g
h
i
j
k
l
m
n
o
p
q
r
**s**
t
u
v
w
x
y
z

. . . . . . . . . . . . . . . . . . . . . . . . . . . . . . . . . . . . . . . . . . . . . . . . . . . . . . . .

★ To **shoot** is to fire at someone with a gun. **!** **chute**.

a

b

c

d

e

f

g

h

i

j

k

l

m

n

o

p

q

r

**s**

t

u

v

w

x

y

z

**shrinkage** noun

**shrivel** verb
shrivels
shrivelling
shrivelled

**shroud** noun
shrouds

**shroud** verb
shrouds
shrouding
shrouded

**Shrove Tuesday**

**shrub** noun
shrubs

**shrubbery** noun
shrubberies

**shrug** verb
shrugs
shrugging
shrugged

**shrug** noun
shrugs

**shrunk** see **shrink**

**shrunken** adjective

**shudder** verb
shudders
shuddering
shuddered

**shudder** noun
shudders

**shuffle** verb
shuffles
shuffling
shuffled

**shuffle** noun
shuffles

**shunt** verb
shunts
shunting
shunted

**shunter** noun
shunters

**shut** verb
shuts
shutting
shut

**shutter** noun
shutters

**shuttle** noun
shuttles

**shuttlecock** noun
shuttlecocks

**shy** adjective
shyer
shyest
shyly

**Siamese**

**sick** adjective
sicker
sickest

**sicken** verb
sickens
sickening
sickened

**sickly** adjective
sicklier
sickliest

**sickness** noun
sicknesses

**side** noun
sides

**side** verb
sides
siding
sided

**sideboard** noun
sideboards

**sidecar** noun
sidecars

**sideline** noun
sidelines

**sideshow** noun
sideshows

**sideways**

**siding** noun
sidings

**siege** noun
sieges

**sieve** noun
sieves

**sift** verb
sifts
sifting
sifted

**sigh** verb
sighs
sighing
sighed

**sigh** noun
sighs

**sight\*** noun
sights

**sight** verb
sights
sighting
sighted

**sightseer** noun
sightseers

**sightseeing**

**sign** verb
signs
signing
signed

**sign** noun
signs

**signal** noun
signals

**signal** verb
signals
signalling
signalled

**signaller** noun
signallers

**signalman** noun
signalmen

**signature** noun
signatures

· · · · · · · · · · · · · · · · · · · · · · · · · · · · · · · · · · · · · · · · · · · · · · · · · · · · ·

★ A **sight** is something you see. ! **site**.

220

**signet**★ *noun*
signets

**significance**

**significant** *adjective*
significantly

**signify** *verb*
signifies
signifying
signified

**signing**

**signpost** *noun*
signposts

**Sikh** *noun*
Sikhs

**silence** *noun*
silences

**silence** *verb*
silences
silencing
silenced

**silencer** *noun*
silencers

**silent** *adjective*
silently

**silhouette** *noun*
silhouettes

**silicon**

**silk**

**silken**

**silkworm** *noun*
silkworms

**silky** *adjective*
silkier
silkiest
silkily

**sill** *noun*
sills

**silliness**

**silly** *adjective*
sillier
silliest
sillily

**silver**

**silvery**

**similar** *adjective*
similarly

**similarity**

**simile** *noun*
similes

**simmer** *verb*
simmers
simmering
simmered

**simple** *adjective*
simpler
simplest

**simplicity**

**simplification**

**simplify** *verb*
simplifies
simplifying
simplified

**simply**

**simulate** *verb*
simulates
simulating
simulated

**simulation** *noun*
simulations

**simulator** *noun*
simulators

**simultaneous**
*adjective*
simultaneously

**sin** *noun*
sins

**sin** *verb*
sins
sinning
sinned

**since** *preposition,
adverb, and
conjunction*

**sincere** *adjective*
sincerer
sincerest
sincerely

**sincerity**

**sinew** *noun*
sinews

**sinful** *adjective*
sinfully

**sinfulness**

**sing** *verb*
sings
singing
sang
sung

**singer** *noun*
singers

**singe** *verb*
singes
singeing
singed

**single** *adjective*
singly

**single** *noun*
singles

**single** *verb*
singles
singling
singled

**single-handed**

**singular** *adjective*
singularly

**singular** *noun*
singulars

**sinister** *adjective*
sinisterly

**sink** *verb*
sinks
sinking
sank *or* sunk
sunk

**sink** *noun*
sinks

a
b
c
d
e
f
g
h
i
j
k
l
m
n
o
p
q
r
**s**
t
u
v
w
x
y
z

. . . . . . . . . . . . . . . . . . . . . . . . . . . . . . . . . . . . . . . . . . . . . . . . . . . . . . . . . .
★ A **signet** is a seal worn in a ring. ! **cygnet**.

221

a
b
c
d
e
f
g
h
i
j
k
l
m
n
o
p
q
r
**s**
t
u
v
w
x
y
z

**sinner** *noun*
sinners

**sinus** *noun*
sinuses

**sip** *verb*
sips
sipping
sipped

**siphon** *noun*
siphons

**siphon** *verb*
siphons
siphoning
siphoned

**sir**

**siren** *noun*
sirens

**sister** *noun*
sisters

**sisterly**

**sister-in-law** *noun*
sisters-in-law

**sit** *verb*
sits
sitting
sat

**sitter** *noun*
sitters

**site★** *noun*
sites

**site** *verb*
sites
siting
sited

**sit-in** *noun*
sit-ins

**situated**

**situation** *noun*
situations

**six** *noun*
sixes

**sixpence** *noun*
sixpences

**sixteen** *noun*
sixteens

**sixteenth**

**sixth**

**sixthly**

**sixtieth**

**sixty** *noun*
sixties

**size** *noun*
sizes

**size** *verb*
sizes
sizing
sized

**sizeable**

**sizzle** *verb*
sizzles
sizzling
sizzled

**skate** *verb*
skates
skating
skated

**skate☆** *noun*
skates *or* skate

**skateboard** *noun*
skateboards

**skater** *noun*
skaters

**skeletal** *adjective*
skeletally

**skeleton** *noun*
skeletons

**sketch** *noun*
sketches

**sketch** *verb*
sketches
sketching
sketched

**sketchy** *adjective*
sketchier
sketchiest
sketchily

**skewer** *noun*
skewers

**ski** *verb*
skis
skiing
skied
ski'd

**ski** *noun*
skis

**skid** *verb*
skids
skidding
skidded

**skid** *noun*
skids

**skier** *noun*
skiers

**skilful** *adjective*
skilfully

**skill** *noun*
skills

**skilled**

**skim** *verb*
skims
skimming
skimmed

**skimp** *verb*
skimps
skimping
skimped

**skimpy** *adjective*
skimpier
skimpiest
skimpily

**skin** *noun*
skins

. . . . . . . . . . . . . . . . . . . . . . . . . . . . . . . . . . . . . . . . . . . . . . . . . .

★ A **site** is a place where something will be built. **!** **sight**.

☆ The plural is **skate** when you mean the fish.

**skin** verb
skins
skinning
skinned

**skinny** adjective
skinnier
skinniest

**skint**

**skip** verb
skips
skipping
skipped

**skip** noun
skips

**skipper** noun
skippers

**skirt** noun
skirts

**skirt** verb
skirts
skirting
skirted

**skirting** noun
skirtings

**skit** noun
skits

**skittish** adjective
skittishly

**skittle** noun
skittles

**skull** noun
skulls

**skunk** noun
skunks

**sky** noun
skies

**skylark** noun
skylarks

**skylight** noun
skylights

**skyscraper** noun
skyscrapers

**slab** noun
slabs

**slack** adjective
slacker
slackest
slackly

**slacken** verb
slackens
slackening
slackened

**slackness**

**slacks** plural noun

**slag heap** noun
slag heaps

**slain** see **slay**

**slam** verb
slams
slamming
slammed

**slang**

**slant** verb
slants
slanting
slanted

**slant** noun
slants

**slap** verb
slaps
slapping
slapped

**slap** noun
slaps

**slapstick**

**slash** verb
slashes
slashing
slashed

**slash** noun
slashes

**slat** noun
slats

**slate** noun
slates

**slaty** adjective
slatier
slatiest

**slaughter** verb
slaughters
slaughtering
slaughtered

**slaughter** noun

**slaughterhouse**
noun
slaughterhouses

**slave** noun
slaves

**slave** verb
slaves
slaving
slaved

**slavery**

**slay**★ verb
slays
slaying
slew
slain

**sled** noun
sleds

**sledge** noun
sledges

**sledgehammer** noun
sledgehammers

**sleek** adjective
sleeker
sleekest
sleekly

**sleep** verb
sleeps
sleeping
slept

**sleep** noun

**sleeper** noun
sleepers

**sleepiness**

**sleepless**

★ To **slay** people is to kill them. **!sleigh**.

# sl

**sleepwalker** *noun*
sleepwalkers

**sleepwalking**

**sleepy** *adjective*
sleepier
sleepiest
sleepily

**sleet**

**sleeve** *noun*
sleeves

**sleeveless**

**sleigh*** *noun*
sleighs

**slender** *adjective*
slenderer
slenderest

**slept** see **sleep**

**slew** see **slay**

**slice** *noun*
slices

**slice** *verb*
slices
slicing
sliced

**slick** *adjective*
slicker
slickest
slickly

**slick** *noun*
slicks

**slide** *verb*
slides
sliding
slid

**slide** *noun*
slides

**slight** *adjective*
slighter
slightest
slightly

**slim** *adjective*
slimmer
slimmest
slimly

**slim** *verb*
slims
slimming
slimmed

**slime**

**slimmer** *noun*
slimmers

**slimy** *adjective*
slimier
slimiest

**sling** *verb*
slings
slinging
slung

**sling** *noun*
slings

**slink** *verb*
slinks
slinking
slunk

**slip** *verb*
slips
slipping
slipped

**slip** *noun*
slips

**slipper** *noun*
slippers

**slippery**

**slipshod**

**slit** *noun*
slits

**slit** *verb*
slits
slitting
slit

**slither** *verb*
slithers
slithering
slithered

**sliver** *noun*
slivers

**slog** *verb*
slogs
slogging
slogged

**slog** *noun*
slogs

**slogan** *noun*
slogans

**slop** *verb*
slops
slopping
slopped

**slope** *verb*
slopes
sloping
sloped

**slope** *noun*
slopes

**sloppiness**

**sloppy** *adjective*
sloppier
sloppiest
sloppily

**slops** *plural noun*

**slosh** *verb*
sloshes
sloshing
sloshed

**slot** *noun*
slots

**sloth** *noun*
sloths

**slouch** *verb*
slouches
slouching
slouched

**slovenly**

★ A **sleigh** is a vehicle for sliding on snow. **!slay**.

224

**slow** *adjective*
slower
slowest
slowly

**slow** *verb*
slows
slowing
slowed

**slowcoach** *noun*
slowcoaches

**slowness**

**sludge**

**slug** *noun*
slugs

**slum** *noun*
slums

**slumber**

**slumber** *verb*
slumbers
slumbering
slumbered

**slump** *verb*
slumps
slumping
slumped

**slump** *noun*
slumps

**slung** see **sling**

**slunk** see **slink**

**slur** *noun*
slurs

**slush**

**slushy** *adjective*
slushier
slushiest
slushily

**sly** *adjective*
slyer
slyest
slyly

**slyness**

**smack** *verb*
smacks
smacking
smacked

**smack** *noun*
smacks

**small** *adjective*
smaller
smallest

**smallpox**

**smart** *adjective*
smarter
smartest
smartly

**smart** *verb*
smarts
smarting
smarted

**smarten** *verb*
smartens
smartening
smartened

**smartness**

**smash** *verb*
smashes
smashing
smashed

**smash** *noun*
smashes

**smashing**

**smear** *verb*
smears
smearing
smeared

**smear** *noun*
smears

**smell** *verb*
smells
smelling
smelt *or* smelled

**smell** *noun*
smells

**smelly** *adjective*
smellier
smelliest

**smelt** *verb*
smelts
smelting
smelted

**smile** *noun*
smiles

**smile** *verb*
smiles
smiling
smiled

**smith** *noun*
smiths

**smithereens** *plural noun*

**smock** *noun*
smocks

**smog**

**smoke** *noun*

**smoke** *verb*
smokes
smoking
smoked

**smokeless**

**smoker** *noun*
smokers

**smoky** *adjective*
smokier
smokiest

**smooth** *adjective*
smoother
smoothest
smoothly

**smooth** *verb*
smooths
smoothing
smoothed

**smoothness**

**smother** *verb*
smothers
smothering
smothered

**smoulder** *verb*
smoulders
smouldering
smouldered

**smudge** *verb*
smudges
smudging
smudged

## sm - sn

smudge *noun*
smudges

smuggle *verb*
smuggles
smuggling
smuggled

smuggler *noun*
smugglers

smut *noun*
smuts

smutty *adjective*
smuttier
smuttiest
smuttily

snack *noun*
snacks

snag *noun*
snags

snail *noun*
snails

snake *noun*
snakes

snaky *adjective*
snakier
snakiest

snap *verb*
snaps
snapping
snapped

snap *noun*
snaps

snappy *adjective*
snappier
snappiest
snappily

snapshot *noun*
snapshots

snare *noun*
snares

snare *verb*
snares
snaring
snared

snarl *verb*
snarls
snarling
snarled

snarl *noun*
snarls

snatch *verb*
snatches
snatching
snatched

snatch *noun*
snatches

sneak *verb*
sneaks
sneaking
sneaked

sneak *noun*
sneaks

sneaky *adjective*
sneakier
sneakiest
sneakily

sneer *verb*
sneers
sneering
sneered

sneeze *verb*
sneezes
sneezing
sneezed

sneeze *noun*
sneezes

sniff *verb*
sniffs
sniffing
sniffed

sniff *noun*
sniffs

snigger *verb*
sniggers
sniggering
sniggered

snigger *noun*
sniggers

snip *verb*
snips
snipping
snipped

snip *noun*
snips

snipe *verb*
snipes
sniping
sniped

sniper *noun*
snipers

snippet *noun*
snippets

snivel *verb*
snivels
snivelling
snivelled

snob *noun*
snobs

snobbery

snobbish *adjective*
snobbishly

snooker

snoop *verb*
snoops
snooping
snooped

snooper *noun*
snoopers

snore *verb*
snores
snoring
snored

snorkel *noun*
snorkels

snort *verb*
snorts
snorting
snorted

snort *noun*
snorts

snout *noun*
snouts

snow *noun*

a b c d e f g h i j k l m n o p q r **s** t u v w x y z

**snow** *verb*
snows
snowing
snowed

**snowball** *noun*
snowballs

**snowdrop** *noun*
snowdrops

**snowflake** *noun*
snowflakes

**snowman** *noun*
snowmen

**snowplough** *noun*
snowploughs

**snowshoe** *noun*
snowshoes

**snowstorm** *noun*
snowstorms

**snowy** *adjective*
snowier
snowiest

**snub** *verb*
snubs
snubbing
snubbed

**snuff**

**snug** *adjective*
snugger
snuggest
snugly

**snuggle** *verb*
snuggles
snuggling
snuggled

**soak** *verb*
soaks
soaking
soaked

**so-and-so** *noun*
so-and-so's

**soap** *noun*
soaps

**soapiness** *noun*

**soapy** *adjective*
soapier
soapiest
soapily

**soar**★ *verb*
soars
soaring
soared

**sob** *verb*
sobs
sobbing
sobbed

**sob** *noun*
sobs

**sober** *adjective*
soberly

**sobriety**

**so-called**

**soccer**

**sociability**

**sociable** *adjective*
sociably

**social** *adjective*
socially

**socialism**

**socialist** *noun*
socialists

**society** *noun*
societies

**sociological** *adjective*
sociologically

**sociologist** *noun*
sociologists

**sociology**

**sock** *noun*
socks

**sock** *verb*
socks
socking
socked

**socket** *noun*
sockets

**soda**

**sodium**

**sofa** *noun*
sofas

**soft** *adjective*
softer
softest
softly

**soften** *verb*
softens
softening
softened

**softness**

**software**

**soggy** *adjective*
soggier
soggiest
soggily

**soil** *noun*

**soil** *verb*
soils
soiling
soiled

**solar**

**sold** see **sell**

**solder** *noun*

**solder** *verb*
solders
soldering
soldered

**soldier** *noun*
soldiers

**sole**☆ *noun*
soles

**sole** *adjective*
solely

**solemn** *adjective*
solemnly

**solemnity**

a
b
c
d
e
f
g
h
i
j
k
l
m
n
o
p
q
r
**s**
t
u
v
w
x
y
z

★ To **soar** is to rise or fly high. ! **sore**.
☆ A **sole** is a fish or a part of a shoe. ! **soul**.

227

a **solicitor** noun
solicitors

**solid** adjective
solidly

**solid** noun
solids

**solidify** verb
solidifies
solidifying
solidified

**solidity**

**soliloquy** noun
soliloquies

**solitary**

**solitude**

**solo** noun
solos

**soloist** noun
soloists

**solstice** noun
solstices

**solubility**

**soluble** adjective
solubly

**solution** noun
solutions

**solve** verb
solves
solving
solved

**solvent** adjective and
noun
solvents

**sombre** adjective
sombrely

**some**★ adjective and
pronoun

**somebody**

**somehow**

**someone**

**somersault** noun
somersaults

**something**

**sometime**

**sometimes**

**somewhat**

**somewhere**

**son**☆ noun
sons

**sonar** noun
sonars

**song** noun
songs

**songbird** noun
songbirds

**sonic** adjective
sonically

**sonnet** noun
sonnets

**soon** adverb
sooner
soonest

**soot**

**soothe** verb
soothes
soothing
soothed

**sooty** adjective
sootier
sootiest

**sophisticated**

**sophistication**

**sopping**

**soppy** adjective
soppier
soppiest
soppily

**soprano** noun
sopranos

**sorcerer** noun
sorcerers

**sorceress** noun
sorceresses

**sorcery**

**sore**✪ adjective
sorer
sorest
sorely

**sore** noun
sores

**soreness**

**sorrow** noun
sorrows

**sorrowful** adjective
sorrowfully

**sorry** adjective
sorrier
sorriest

**sort** noun
sorts

**sort** verb
sorts
sorting
sorted

**sought** see **seek**

**soul**✢ noun
souls

**sound** noun
sounds

**sound** verb
sounds
sounding
sounded

**sound** adjective
sounder
soundest
soundly

........................................................................................

★ You use **some** in e.g. *Have some cake.* !**sum**.
☆ A **son** is a male child. !**sun**.
✪ You use **sore** in e.g. *I've got a sore tooth.* !**soar**.
✢ A **soul** is a person's spirit. !**sole**.

soundness

soundtrack *noun*
soundtracks

soup *noun*
soups

sour *adjective*
sourer
sourest
sourly

source★ *noun*
sources

sourness

south *adjective* and *adverb*

south☆ *noun*

south-east *noun* and *adjective*

southerly *adjective* and *noun*
southerlies

southern *adjective*

southerner *noun*
southerners

southward *adjective* and *adverb*

southwards *adverb*

south-west *noun* and *adjective*

souvenir *noun*
souvenirs

sovereign *noun*
sovereigns

sow○ *verb*
sows
sowing
sowed
sown

sow *noun*
sows

sower *noun*
sowers

soya bean *noun*
soya beans

space *noun*
spaces

space *verb*
spaces
spacing
spaced

spacecraft *noun*
spacecraft

spaceman *noun*
spacemen

spaceship *noun*
spaceships

spacewoman *noun*
spacewomen

spacious *adjective*
spaciously

spaciousness

spade *noun*
spades

spaghetti

span *verb*
spans
spanning
spanned

span *noun*
spans

spaniel *noun*
spaniels

spank *verb*
spanks
spanking
spanked

spanner *noun*
spanners

spar *noun*
spars

spar *verb*
spars
sparring
sparred

spare *verb*
spares
sparing
spared

spare *adjective* and *noun*
spares

sparing *adjective*
sparingly

spark *noun*
sparks

spark *verb*
sparks
sparking
sparked

sparkle *verb*
sparkles
sparkling
sparkled

sparkler *noun*
sparklers

sparrow *noun*
sparrows

sparse *adjective*
sparser
sparsest
sparsely

sparseness

spastic *noun*
spastics

spat see spit

spatter *verb*
spatters
spattering
spattered

spawn *noun*

. . . . . . . . . . . . . . . . . . . . . . . . . . . . . . . . . . . . . . . . . . . . . . . . . . . . . . . .

★ The **source** is where something comes from. !**sauce**.

☆ You use a capital S in the **South**, when you mean a particular region.

○ To **sow** is to put seed in the ground. !**sew**.

**spawn** verb
spawns
spawning
spawned

**speak** verb
speaks
speaking
spoke
spoken

**speaker** noun
speakers

**spear** noun
spears

**spear** verb
spears
spearing
speared

**special** adjective
specially

**specialist** noun
specialists

**speciality** noun
specialities

**specialization**

**specialize** verb
specializes
specializing
specialized

**species** noun
species

**specific** adjective
specifically

**specification** noun
specifications

**specify** verb
specifies
specifying
specified

**specimen** noun
specimens

**speck** noun
specks

**speckled**

**spectacle** noun
spectacles

**spectacular** adjective
spectacularly

**spectator** noun
spectators

**spectre** noun
spectres

**spectrum** noun
spectra

**speech** noun
speeches

**speechless**

**speed** noun
speeds

**speed**★ verb
speeds
speeding
sped or speeded

**speedboat** noun
speedboats

**speedometer** noun
speedometers

**speedway** noun
speedways

**speedy** adjective
speedier
speediest
speedily

**spell** verb
spells
spelling
spelt
spelled

**spell** noun
spells

**spelling** noun
spellings

**spend** verb
spends
spending
spent

**sperm** noun
sperms or sperm

**sphere** noun
spheres

**spherical** adjective
spherically

**spice** noun
spices

**spicy** adjective
spicier
spiciest

**spider** noun
spiders

**spied** see **spy**

**spike** noun
spikes

**spiky** adjective
spikier
spikiest

**spill**☆ verb
spills
spilling
spilt or spilled

**spill** noun
spills

**spin** verb
spins
spinning
spun

. . . . . . . . . . . . . . . . . . . . . . . . . . . . . . . . . . . . . . . . . . . . . . . . . . . . . . . . .

★ You use **sped** in e.g. *Cars sped past* and **speeded** in e.g. *They speeded up the process.*

☆ You use **spilled** in e.g. *I spilled the milk.* You use **spilt** in e.g. *I can see spilt milk.* You use **spilled** or **spilt** in e.g. *I have spilled/spilt the milk.*

spin *noun*
spins
spinach
spindle *noun*
spindles
spin-drier *noun*
spin-driers
spine *noun*
spines
spinal
spin-off *noun*
spin-offs
spinster *noun*
spinsters
spiny *adjective*
spiniest
spiniest
spiral *adjective*
spirally
spire *noun*
spires
spirit *noun*
spirits
spiritual *adjective*
spiritually
spiritual *noun*
spirituals
spiritualism
spiritualist *noun*
spiritualists
spit *verb*
spits
spitting
spat
spit *noun*
spits
spite
spiteful *adjective*
spitefully
spittle

splash *verb*
splashes
splashing
splashed
splash *noun*
splashes
splashdown *noun*
splashdowns
splendid *adjective*
splendidly
splendour
splint *noun*
splints
splinter *noun*
splinters
splinter *verb*
splinters
splintering
splintered
split *verb*
splits
splitting
split
split *noun*
splits
splutter *verb*
splutters
spluttering
spluttered
spoil★ *verb*
spoils
spoiling
spoilt *or* spoiled
spoils *plural noun*
spoilsport *noun*
spoilsports
spoke *noun*
spokes
spoke see speak
spoken see speak

spokesperson *noun*
spokespersons
sponge *noun*
sponges
sponge *verb*
sponges
sponging
sponged
sponger *noun*
spongers
sponginess *noun*
spongy *adjective*
spongier
spongiest
spongily
sponsor *noun*
sponsors
sponsorship *noun*
sponsorships
spontaneity
spontaneous
*adjective*
spontaneously
spooky *adjective*
spookier
spookiest
spookily
spool *noun*
spools
spoon *noun*
spoons
spoon *verb*
spoons
spooning
spooned
spoonful *noun*
spoonfuls
sport *noun*
sports
sporting

★ You use **spoiled** in e.g. *They spoiled the party*. You use **spoilt** in e.g. *a spoilt child*. You use **spoiled** or **spoilt** in e.g. *They have spoiled/spoilt the party*.

a

**sportsman** *noun*
sportsmen

b

**sportsmanship**

c

**sportswoman** *noun*
sportswomen

d

**spot** *noun*
spots

e

**spot** *verb*
spots
spotting
spotted

f

g

**spotless** *adjective*
spotlessly

h

**spotlight** *noun*
spotlights

i

**spotter** *noun*
spotters

j

k

**spotty** *adjective*
spottier
spottiest
spottily

l

m

**spout** *noun*
spouts

n

**spout** *verb*
spouts
spouting
spouted

o

p

**sprain** *verb*
sprains
spraining
sprained

q

r

**sprain** *noun*
sprains

**s**

**sprang** see **spring**

t

**sprawl** *verb*
sprawls
sprawling
sprawled

u

v

**spray** *verb*
sprays
spraying
sprayed

w

x

y

**spray** *noun*
sprays

z

**spread** *verb*
spreads
spreading
spread

**spread** *noun*
spreads

**spreadsheet** *noun*
spreadsheets

**sprightliness**

**sprightly** *adjective*
sprightlier
sprightliest

**spring** *verb*
springs
springing
sprang
sprung

**spring** *noun*
springs

**springboard** *noun*
springboards

**spring-clean** *verb*
spring-cleans
spring-cleaning
spring-cleaned

**springtime**

**springy** *adjective*
springier
springiest

**sprinkle** *verb*
sprinkles
sprinkling
sprinkled

**sprinkler** *noun*
sprinklers

**sprint** *verb*
sprints
sprinting
sprinted

**sprinter** *noun*
sprinters

**sprout** *verb*
sprouts
sprouting
sprouted

**sprout** *noun*
sprouts

**spruce** *noun*
spruces

**spruce** *adjective*
sprucer
sprucest

**sprung** see **spring**

**spud** *noun*
spuds

**spun** see **spin**

**spur** *noun*
spurs

**spur** *verb*
spurs
spurring
spurred

**spurt** *verb*
spurts
spurting
spurted

**spurt** *noun*
spurts

**spy** *noun*
spies

**spy** *verb*
spies
spying
spied

**squabble** *verb*
squabbles
squabbling
squabbled

**squabble** *noun*
squabbles

**squad** *noun*
squads

**squadron** *noun*
squadrons

**squalid** *adjective*
squalidly

**squall** *noun*
squalls

**squally** *adjective*
squallier
squalliest

**squalor**

**squander** *verb*
squanders
squandering
squandered

**square** *adjective*
squarely

**square** *noun*
squares

**square** *verb*
squares
squaring
squared

**squareness**

**squash** *verb*
squashes
squashing
squashed

**squash** *noun*
squashes

**squat** *verb*
squats
squatting
squatted

**squat** *adjective*
squatter
squattest
squatly

**squatter** *noun*
squatters

**squaw** *noun*
squaws

**squawk** *verb*
squawks
squawking
squawked

**squawk** *noun*
squawks

**squeak** *verb*
squeaks
squeaking
squeaked

**squeak** *noun*
squeaks

**squeaky** *adjective*
squeakier
squeakiest
squeakily

**squeal** *verb*
squeals
squealing
squealed

**squeal** *noun*
squeals

**squeeze** *verb*
squeezes
squeezing
squeezed

**squeeze** *noun*
squeezes

**squeezer** *noun*
squeezers

**squelch** *verb*
squelches
squelching
squelched

**squelch** *noun*
squelches

**squid** *noun*
squid
squids

**squint** *verb*
squints
squinting
squinted

**squint** *noun*
squints

**squire** *noun*
squires

**squirm** *verb*
squirms
squirming
squirmed

**squirrel** *noun*
squirrels

**squirt** *verb*
squirts
squirting
squirted

**stab** *verb*
stabs
stabbing
stabbed

**stab** *noun*
stabs

**stability**

**stabilize** *verb*
stabilizes
stabilizing
stabilized

**stabilizer** *noun*
stabilizers

**stable** *adjective*
stabler
stablest
stably

**stable** *noun*
stables

**stack** *verb*
stacks
stacking
stacked

**stack** *noun*
stacks

**stadium** *noun*
stadiums *or* stadia

**staff** *noun*
staffs

**stag** *noun*
stags

**stage** *noun*
stages

**stage** *verb*
stages
staging
staged

**stagecoach** *noun*
stagecoaches

# st

**stagger** *verb*
staggers
staggering
staggered

**stagnant** *adjective*
stagnantly

**stain** *noun*
stains

**stain** *verb*
stains
staining
stained

**stainless**

**stair**★ *noun*
stairs

**staircase** *noun*
staircases

**stake**☆ *noun*
stakes

**stake** *verb*
stakes
staking
staked

**stalactite** *noun*
stalactites

**stalagmite** *noun*
stalagmites

**stale** *adjective*
staler
stalest

**stalk** *noun*
stalks

**stalk** *verb*
stalks
stalking
stalked

**stall** *noun*
stalls

**stall** *verb*
stalls
stalling
stalled

**stallion** *noun*
stallions

**stalls** *plural noun*

**stamen** *noun*
stamens

**stamina**

**stammer** *verb*
stammers
stammering
stammered

**stammer** *noun*
stammers

**stamp** *noun*
stamps

**stamp** *verb*
stamps
stamping
stamped

**stampede** *noun*
stampedes

**stand** *verb*
stands
standing
stood

**stand** *noun*
stands

**standard** *adjective and noun*
standards

**standardize** *verb*
standardizes
standardizing
standardized

**standby** *noun*
standbys

**standstill** *noun*
standstills

**stank** see **stink**

**stanza** *noun*
stanzas

**staple** *noun*
staples

**staple** *adjective*

**stapler** *noun*
staplers

**star** *noun*
stars

**starry** *adjective*
starrier
starriest
starrily

**star** *verb*
stars
starring
starred

**starboard**

**starch** *noun*
starches

**starchy** *adjective*
starchier
starchiest

**stare**❂ *verb*
stares
staring
stared

**starfish** *noun*
starfish *or* starfishes

**starling** *noun*
starlings

**start** *verb*
starts
starting
started

**start** *noun*
starts

**starter** *noun*
starters

. . . . . . . . . . . . . . . . . . . . . . . . . . . . . . . . . . . . . . . . . . . . . . . . . . . . . . . . . . . . . . .

★ A **stair** is one of a set of steps. **!stare**.

☆ A **stake** is a pointed stick or post. **!steak**.

❂ To **stare** is to look at something without moving your eyes. **!stair**.

234

**startle** *verb*
startles
startling
startled

**starvation**

**starve** *verb*
starves
starving
starved

**state** *noun*
states

**state** *verb*
states
stating
stated

**stateliness**

**stately** *adjective*
statelier
stateliest

**statement** *noun*
statements

**statesman** *noun*
statesmen

**statesmanship**

**stateswoman** *noun*
stateswomen

**static** *adjective*
statically

**station** *noun*
stations

**station** *verb*
stations
stationing
stationed

**stationary**★ *adjective*

**stationery**☆ *noun*

**stationmaster** *noun*
stationmasters

**statistic** *noun*
statistics

**statistical** *adjective*
statistically

**statistician** *noun*
statisticians

**statistics**

**statue** *noun*
statues

**status** *noun*
statuses

**staunch** *adjective*
stauncher
staunchest
staunchly

**stave** *noun*
staves

**stave** *verb*
staves
staving
staved
stove

**stay** *verb*
stays
staying
stayed

**stay** *noun*
stays

**steadiness**

**steady** *adjective*
steadier
steadiest
steadily

**steady** *verb*
steadies
steadying
steadied

**steak**⊙ *noun*
steaks

**steal**✦ *verb*
steals
stealing
stole
stolen

**stealth**

**stealthy** *adjective*
stealthier
stealthiest
stealthily

**steam** *noun*

**steam** *verb*
steams
steaming
steamed

**steamy** *adjective*
steamier
steamiest
steamily

**steamer** *noun*
steamers

**steamroller** *noun*
steamrollers

**steamship** *noun*
steamships

**steed** *noun*
steeds

**steel** *noun*

**steel**❋ *verb*
steels
steeling
steeled

**steely** *adjective*
steelier
steeliest

**steep** *adjective*
steeper
steepest
steeply

a
b
c
d
e
f
g
h
i
j
k
l
m
n
o
p
q
r
**s**
t
u
v
w
x
y
z

★ **Stationary** means 'not moving'. ❗**stationery**.
☆ **Stationery** means 'paper and envelopes'. ❗**stationary**.
⊙ A **steak** is a thick slice of meat. ❗**stake**.
✦ To **steal** is to take something that is not yours. ❗**steel**.
❋ To **steel** yourself is to find courage to do something hard. ❗**steal**.

235

# st

**steepness**

**steeple** *noun*
steeples

**steeplechase** *noun*
steeplechases

**steeplejack** *noun*
steeplejacks

**steer** *verb*
steers
steering
steered

**steer** *noun*
steers

**stem** *noun*
stems

**stem** *verb*
stems
stemming
stemmed

**stench** *noun*
stenches

**stencil** *noun*
stencils

**step**★ *noun*
steps

**step** *verb*
steps
stepping
stepped

**stepchild** *noun*
stepchildren

**stepfather** *noun*
stepfathers

**stepladder** *noun*
stepladders

**stepmother** *noun*
stepmothers

**steppe**☆ *noun*
steppes

**stereo** *adjective* and
*noun*
stereos

**stereophonic**
*adjective*
stereophonically

**sterile**

**sterility**

**sterilization**

**sterilize** *verb*
sterilizes
sterilizing
sterilized

**sterling**

**stern** *noun*
sterns

**stern** *adjective*
sterner
sternest
sternly

**sternness**

**stethoscope** *noun*
stethoscopes

**stew** *verb*
stews
stewing
stewed

**stew** *noun*
stews

**steward** *noun*
stewards

**stewardess** *noun*
stewardesses

**stick** *verb*
sticks
sticking
stuck

**stick** *noun*
sticks

**sticker** *noun*
stickers

**stickiness**

**stickleback** *noun*
sticklebacks

**sticky** *adjective*
stickier
stickiest
stickily

**stiff** *adjective*
stiffer
stiffest
stiffly

**stiffen** *verb*
stiffens
stiffening
stiffened

**stiffness**

**stifle** *verb*
stifles
stifling
stifled

**stile** *noun*
stiles

**still** *adjective*
stiller
stillest

**still** *adverb*

**still** *verb*
stills
stilling
stilled

**stillness**

**stilts**

**stimulant** *noun*
stimulants

**stimulate** *verb*
stimulates
stimulating
stimulated

**stimulation**

**stimulus** *noun*
stimuli

**sting** *noun*
stings

. . . . . . . . . . . . . . . . . . . . . . . . . . . . . . . . . . . . . . . . . . . . . . . . . . . . . . . . .

★ A **step** is a movement of the feet or part of a stair. **!** steppe.
☆ A **steppe** is a grassy plain. **!** step.

**sting** *verb*
stings
stinging
stung

**stingy** *adjective*
stingier
stingiest
stingily

**stink** *noun*
stinks

**stink** *verb*
stinks
stinking
stank
stunk

**stir** *verb*
stirs
stirring
stirred

**stir** *noun*
stirs

**stirrup** *noun*
stirrups

**stitch** *noun*
stitches

**stoat** *noun*
stoats

**stock** *noun*
stocks

**stock** *verb*
stocks
stocking
stocked

**stockade** *noun*
stockades

**stockbroker** *noun*
stockbrokers

**stocking** *noun*
stockings

**stockpile** *noun*
stockpiles

**stocks** *plural noun*

**stocky** *adjective*
stockier
stockiest
stockily

**stodgy** *adjective*
stodgier
stodgiest
stodgily

**stoke** *verb*
stokes
stoking
stoked

**stole** *noun*
stoles

**stole** see **steal**

**stolen** see **steal**

**stomach** *noun*
stomachs

**stomach** *verb*
stomachs
stomaching
stomached

**stone** *noun*
stones *or* stone

**stone** *verb*
stones
stoning
stoned

**stony** *adjective*
stonier
stoniest

**stood** see **stand**

**stool** *noun*
stools

**stoop** *verb*
stoops
stooping
stooped

**stop** *verb*
stops
stopping
stopped

**stop** *noun*
stops

**stoppage** *noun*
stoppages

**stopper** *noun*
stoppers

**stopwatch** *noun*
stopwatches

**storage**

**store** *verb*
stores
storing
stored

**store** *noun*
stores

**storey**★ *noun*
storeys

**stork** *noun*
storks

**storm** *noun*
storms

**storm** *verb*
storms
storming
stormed

**stormy** *adjective*
stormier
stormiest
stormily

**story**☆ *noun*
stories

**stout** *adjective*
stouter
stoutest
stoutly

**stoutness**

**stove** *noun*
stoves

- - - - - - - - - - - - - - - - - - - - - - - - - - - - - - - - - - - - - - - - - - - - - - -

★ A **storey** is a floor of a building. **!story**.

☆ You use **story** in e.g. *read me a story*. **!storey**.

# st

**stove** see **stave**

**stow** verb
stows
stowing
stowed

**stowaway** noun
stowaways

**straddle** verb
straddles
straddling
straddled

**straggle** verb
straggles
straggling
straggled

**straggler** noun
stragglers

**straggly** adjective
stragglier
straggliest

**straight★** adjective
straighter
straightest

**straighten** verb
straightens
straightening
straightened

**straightforward**
adjective
straightforwardly

**strain** verb
strains
straining
strained

**strain** noun
strains

**strainer** noun
strainers

**strait☆** noun
straits

**straits✪** plural noun

**strand** noun
strands

**stranded**

**strange** adjective
stranger
strangest
strangely

**strangeness**

**stranger** noun
strangers

**strangle** verb
strangles
strangling
strangled

**strangler** noun
stranglers

**strangulation**

**strap** noun
straps

**strap** verb
straps
strapping
strapped

**strategic** adjective
strategically

**strategist** noun
strategists

**strategy** noun
strategies

**stratum** noun
strata

**straw** noun
straws

**strawberry** noun
strawberries

**stray** verb
strays
straying
strayed

**stray** adjective

**streak** noun
streaks

**streak** verb
streaks
streaking
streaked

**streaky** adjective
streakier
streakiest
streakily

**stream** noun
streams

**stream** verb
streams
streaming
streamed

**streamer** noun
streamers

**streamline** verb
streamlines
streamlining
streamlined

**street** noun
streets

**strength** noun
strengths

**strengthen** verb
strengthens
strengthening
strengthened

**strenuous** adjective
strenuously

**stress** noun
stresses

**stress** verb
stresses
stressing
stressed

**stretch** verb
stretches
stretching
stretched

- - - - - - - - - - - - - - - - - - - - - - - - - - - - - - - - - - - - - - - - - -

★ **Straight** means 'not curving or bending'. **!** strait.
☆ A **strait** is a narrow stretch of water. **!** straight.
✪ You use **straits** in the phrase *in dire straits*.

238

**stretch** *noun*
stretches

**stretcher** *noun*
stretchers

**strew** *verb*
strews
strewing
strewed
strewn

**stricken**

**strict** *adjective*
stricter
strictest
strictly

**strictness**

**stride** *verb*
strides
striding
strode
stridden

**stride** *noun*
strides

**strife**

**strike** *verb*
strikes
striking
struck

**strike** *noun*
strikes

**striker** *noun*
strikers

**striking** *adjective*
strikingly

**string** *noun*
strings

**string** *verb*
strings
stringing
strung

**stringiness**

**stringy** *adjective*
stringier
stringiest
stringily

**strip** *verb*
strips
stripping
stripped

**strip** *noun*
strips

**stripe** *noun*
stripes

**striped**

**stripy** *adjective*
stripier
stripiest

**strive** *verb*
strives
striving
strove
striven

**strobe** *noun*
strobes

**strode** see **stride**

**stroke** *noun*
strokes

**stroke** *verb*
strokes
stroking
stroked

**stroll** *verb*
strolls
strolling
strolled

**stroll** *noun*
strolls

**strong** *adjective*
stronger
strongest
strongly

**stronghold** *noun*
strongholds

**strove** see **strive**

**struck** see **strike**

**structural** *adjective*
structurally

**structure** *noun*
structures

**struggle** *verb*
struggles
struggling
struggled

**struggle** *noun*
struggles

**strum** *verb*
strums
strumming
strummed

**strung** see **string**

**strut** *verb*
struts
strutting
strutted

**strut** *noun*
struts

**stub** *verb*
stubs
stubbing
stubbed

**stub** *noun*
stubs

**stubble**

**stubborn** *adjective*
stubbornly

**stubbornness**

**stuck** see **stick**

**stuck-up**

**stud** *noun*
studs

**student** *noun*
students

**studio** *noun*
studios

**studious** *adjective*
studiously

**study** *verb*
studies
studying
studied

**study** *noun*
studies

**stuff** *noun*

a
b
c
d
e
f
g
h
i
j
k
l
m
n
o
p
q
r
**s**
t
u
v
w
x
y
z

**stuff** *verb*
stuffs
stuffing
stuffed

**stuffiness**

**stuffing** *noun*
stuffings

**stuffy** *adjective*
stuffier
stuffiest
stuffily

**stumble** *verb*
stumbles
stumbling
stumbled

**stump** *noun*
stumps

**stump** *verb*
stumps
stumping
stumped

**stun** *verb*
stuns
stunning
stunned

**stung** see **sting**

**stunk** see **stink**

**stunt** *noun*
stunts

**stupendous** *adjective*
stupendously

**stupid** *adjective*
stupider
stupidest
stupidly

**stupidity**

**sturdiness**

**sturdy** *adjective*
sturdier
sturdiest
sturdily

**stutter** *verb*
stutters
stuttering
stuttered

**stutter** *noun*
stutters

**sty★** *noun*
sties

**style** *noun*
styles

**style** *verb*
styles
styling
styled

**stylish** *adjective*
stylishly

**stylus** *noun*
styluses

**subcontinent** *noun*
subcontinents

**subdivide** *verb*
subdivides
subdividing
subdivided

**subdivision** *noun*
subdivisions

**subdue** *verb*
subdues
subduing
subdued

**subject** *adjective* and
*noun*
subjects

**subject** *verb*
subjects
subjecting
subjected

**subjective** *adjective*
subjectively

**submarine** *noun*
submarines

**submerge** *verb*
submerges
submerging
submerged

**submersion**

**submission** *noun*
submissions

**submissive** *adjective*
submissively

**submit** *verb*
submits
submitting
submitted

**subordinate** *adjective*
and *noun*
subordinates

**subordinate** *verb*
subordinates
subordinating
subordinated

**subordination**

**subscribe** *verb*
subscribes
subscribing
subscribed

**subscriber** *noun*
subscribers

**subscription** *noun*
subscriptions

**subsequent** *adjective*
subsequently

**subside** *verb*
subsides
subsiding
subsided

**subsidence**

**subsidize** *verb*
subsidizes
subsidizing
subsidized

**subsidy** *noun*
subsidies

. . . . . . . . . . . . . . . . . . . . . . . . . . . . . . . . . . . . . . . . . . . . . . . . . . . . . . . . . . . . . . .

★ A **sty** is a place for pigs or a swelling on the eye. In the second
meaning you can also use *stye*, plural *styes*.

**substance** *noun*
substances

**substantial** *adjective*
substantially

**substitute** *verb*
substitutes
substituting
substituted

**substitute** *noun*
substitutes

**substitution** *noun*
substitutions

**subtle** *adjective*
subtler
subtlest
subtly

**subtlety** *noun*
subtleties

**subtract** *verb*
subtracts
subtracting
subtracted

**subtraction** *noun*
subtractions

**suburb** *noun*
suburbs

**suburban**

**suburbia**

**subway** *noun*
subways

**succeed** *verb*
succeeds
succeeding
succeeded

**success** *noun*
successes

**successful** *adjective*
successfully

**succession** *noun*
successions

**successive** *adjective*
successively

**successor** *noun*
successors

**such**

**suck** *verb*
sucks
sucking
sucked

**suck** *noun*
sucks

**suction**

**sudden** *adjective*
suddenly

**suddenness**

**suds** *plural noun*

**sue** *verb*
sues
suing
sued

**suede**

**suet**

**suffer** *verb*
suffers
suffering
suffered

**sufficiency**

**sufficient** *adjective*
sufficiently

**suffix** *noun*
suffixes

**suffocate** *verb*
suffocates
suffocating
suffocated

**suffocation**

**sugar**

**sugary**

**suggest** *verb*
suggests
suggesting
suggested

**suggestion** *noun*
suggestions

**suicidal** *adjective*
suicidally

**suicide** *noun*
suicides

**suit★** *noun*
suits

**suit** *verb*
suits
suiting
suited

**suitability**

**suitable** *adjective*
suitably

**suitcase** *noun*
suitcases

**suite☆** *noun*
suites

**suitor** *noun*
suitors

**sulk** *verb*
sulks
sulking
sulked

**sulkiness**

**sulky** *adjective*
sulkier
sulkiest
sulkily

**sullen** *adjective*
sullenly

**sullenness**

**sulphur**

**sulphuric acid**

**sultan** *noun*
sultans

**sultana** *noun*
sultanas

a b c d e f g h i j k l m n o p q r s t u v w x y z

★ A **suit** is a set of matching clothes. !**suite**.
☆ A **suite** is a set of furniture or a group of rooms. !**suit**.

241

a

**sum★** *noun*
sums

b

**sum** *verb*
sums
summing
summed

c

d

**summarize** *verb*
summarizes
summarizing
summarized

e

f

**summary** *noun*
summaries

g

**summer** *noun*
summers

h

**summertime**

i

**summit** *noun*
summits

j

k

**summon** *verb*
summons
summoning
summoned

l

m

**summons** *noun*
summonses

n

**sun☆** *noun*
suns

o

**sun** *verb*
suns
sunning
sunned

p

q

r

**sunbathe** *verb*
sunbathes
sunbathing
sunbathed

s

t

**sunburn**

u

**sunburned** or
**sunburnt**

**sundae○** *noun*
sundaes

v

w

**Sunday✢** *noun*
Sundays

---

**sundial** *noun*
sundials

**sunflower** *noun*
sunflowers

**sung** see **sing**

**sunglasses**

**sunk** see **sink**

**sunlight**

**sunlit**

**sunny** *adjective*
sunnier
sunniest
sunnily

**sunrise** *noun*
sunrises

**sunset** *noun*
sunsets

**sunshade** *noun*
sunshades

**sunshine**

**sunspot** *noun*
sunspots

**sunstroke**

**suntan** *noun*
suntans

**suntanned**

**super**

> **super-**
> *super-* makes words
> meaning 'very good'
> or 'extra', e.g.
> **supermarket**,
> **supermodel**. They
> are normally spelt
> joined up.

**superb** *adjective*
superbly

---

**superficial** *adjective*
superficially

**superfluous** *adjective*
superfluously

**superintend** *verb*
superintends
superintending
superintended

**superintendent** *noun*
superintendents

**superior** *adjective* and
*noun*
superiors

**superiority**

**superlative** *adjective*
superlatively

**superlative** *noun*
superlatives

**supermarket** *noun*
supermarkets

**supernatural**
*adjective*
supernaturally

**supersonic** *adjective*
supersonically

**superstition** *noun*
superstitions

**superstitious**
*adjective*
superstitiously

**supervise** *verb*
supervises
supervising
supervised

**supervision**

**supervisor**

**supper** *noun*
suppers

x

y

z

---

★ A **sum** is an amount or total. **!some**.
☆ A **sun** is a large star. **!son**.
○ A **sundae** is a cocktail of fruit and ice cream. **!Sunday**.
✢ **Sunday** is a day of the week. **!sundae**.

**supple** *adjective*
suppler
supplest
supplely

**supplement** *noun*
supplements

**supplementary**

**suppleness**

**supply** *verb*
supplies
supplying
supplied

**supplier** *noun*
suppliers

**supply** *noun*
supplies

**support** *verb*
supports
supporting
supported

**support** *noun*
supports

**supporter** *noun*
supporters

**suppose** *verb*
supposes
supposing
supposed

**supposedly**

**supposition** *noun*
suppositions

**suppress** *verb*
suppresses
suppressing
suppressed

**suppression**

**supremacy**

**supreme** *adjective*
supremely

**sure** *adjective*
surer
surest
surely

**surf** *noun*

**surf** *verb*
surfs
surfing
surfed

**surface** *noun*
surfaces

**surface** *verb*
surfaces
surfacing
surfaced

**surfboard** *noun*
surfboards

**surfer** *noun*
surfers

**surge** *verb*
surges
surging
surged

**surge** *noun*
surges

**surgeon** *noun*
surgeons

**surgery** *noun*
surgeries

**surgical** *adjective*
surgically

**surname** *noun*
surnames

**surpass** *verb*
surpasses
surpassing
surpassed

**surplus** *noun*
surpluses

**surprise** *verb*
surprises
surprising
surprised

**surprise** *noun*
surprises

**surrender** *verb*
surrenders
surrendering
surrendered

**surrender** *noun*
surrenders

**surround** *verb*
surrounds
surrounding
surrounded

**surroundings** *plural noun*

**survey** *noun*
surveys

**survey** *verb*
surveys
surveying
surveyed

**surveyor** *noun*
surveyors

**survival**

**survive** *verb*
survives
surviving
survived

**survivor** *noun*
survivors

**suspect** *verb*
suspects
suspecting
suspected

**suspect** *noun*
suspects

**suspend** *verb*
suspends
suspending
suspended

**suspense**

**suspension** *noun*
suspensions

**suspicion** *noun*
suspicions

**suspicious** *adjective*
suspiciously

**sustain** *verb*
sustains
sustaining
sustained

swagger *verb*
swaggers
swaggering
swaggered

swallow *verb*
swallows
swallowing
swallowed

swallow *noun*
swallows

swam see swim

swamp *verb*
swamps
swamping
swamped

swamp *noun*
swamps

swampy *adjective*
swampier
swampiest

swan *noun*
swans

swank *verb*
swanks
swanking
swanked

swap *verb*
swaps
swapping
swapped

swap *noun*
swaps

swarm *noun*
swarms

swarm *verb*
swarms
swarming
swarmed

swastika *noun*
swastikas

swat⋆ *verb*
swats
swatting
swatted

swatter *noun*
swatters

sway *verb*
sways
swaying
swayed

swear *verb*
swears
swearing
swore
sworn

sweat *verb*
sweats
sweating
sweated

sweat *noun*

sweater *noun*
sweaters

sweatshirt *noun*
sweatshirts

sweaty *adjective*
sweatier
sweatiest
sweatily

swede *noun*
swedes

sweep *verb*
sweeps
sweeping
swept

sweep *noun*
sweeps

sweeper *noun*
sweepers

sweet *adjective*
sweeter
sweetest
sweetly

sweet *noun*
sweets

sweetcorn

sweeten *verb*
sweetens
sweetening
sweetened

sweetener *noun*
sweeteners

sweetheart *noun*
sweethearts

sweetness

swell *verb*
swells
swelling
swelled
swollen

swell *noun*
swells

swelling *noun*
swellings

swelter *verb*
swelters
sweltering
sweltered

swept see sweep

swerve *verb*
swerves
swerving
swerved

swerve *noun*
swerves

swift *adjective*
swifter
swiftest
swiftly

swift *noun*
swifts

swiftness

swill *verb*
swills
swilling
swilled

swill *noun*

⋆ To **swat** an insect is to hit it. **!swot**.

**swim** *verb*
swims
swimming
swam
swum

**swim** *noun*
swims

**swimmer** *noun*
swimmers

**swimsuit** *noun*
swimsuits

**swindle** *verb*
swindles
swindling
swindled

**swindler** *noun*
swindlers

**swindle** *noun*
swindles

**swine** *noun*
swine *or* swines

**swing** *verb*
swings
swinging
swung

**swing** *noun*
swings

**swipe** *verb*
swipes
swiping
swiped

**swipe** *noun*
swipes

**swirl** *verb*
swirls
swirling
swirled

**swirl** *noun*
swirls

**swish** *verb*
swishes
swishing
swished

**swish** *noun*
swishes

**Swiss roll** *noun*
Swiss rolls

**switch** *verb*
switches
switching
switched

**switch** *noun*
switches

**switchboard** *noun*
switchboards

**swivel** *verb*
swivels
swivelling
swivelled

**swollen** see **swell**

**swoon** *verb*
swoons
swooning
swooned

**swoop** *verb*
swoops
swooping
swooped

**swoop** *noun*
swoops

**swop** *verb*
swops
swopping
swopped

**sword** *noun*
swords

**swore** see **swear**

**sworn** see **swear**

**swot**★ *verb*
swots
swotting
swotted

**swot** *noun*
swots

**swum** see **swim**

**swung** see **swing**

**sycamore** *noun*
sycamores

**syllabic** *adjective*
syllabically

**syllable** *noun*
syllables

**syllabus** *noun*
syllabuses

**symbol** *noun*
symbols

**symbolic** *adjective*
symbolically

**symbolism**

**symbolize** *verb*
symbolizes
symbolizing
symbolized

**symmetrical**
*adjective*
symmetrically

**symmetry**

**sympathetic** *adjective*
sympathetically

**sympathize** *verb*
sympathizes
sympathizing
sympathized

**sympathy** *noun*
sympathies

**symphonic** *adjective*
symphonically

**symphony** *noun*
symphonies

**symptom** *noun*
symptoms

**symptomatic**
*adjective*
symptomatically

**synagogue** *noun*
synagogues

**synchronization**

a
b
c
d
e
f
g
h
i
j
k
l
m
n
o
p
q
r
**s**
t
u
v
w
x
y
z

★ To **swot** is to study hard. **!** **swat**.

245

a

**synchronize** *verb*
synchronizes

b
synchronizing
synchronized

c
**syncopated**

d
**synonym** *noun*
synonyms

e
**synonymous**

f
*adjective*
synonymously

g
**synthesis** *noun*
syntheses

h
**synthesize** *verb*
synthesizes

i
synthesizing
synthesized

j
**synthesizer** *noun*
synthesizers

k

l
**synthetic** *adjective*
synthetically

m
**syringe** *noun*
syringes

n
**syrup** *noun*
syrups

o
**syrupy**

p
**system** *noun*
systems

q
**systematic** *adjective*
systematically

r

**Tt**

s
t

u
**-t**
See the note at -ed.

v

w
**tab** *noun*
tabs

x
**tabby** *noun*
tabbies

y

z

**table** *noun*
tables

**tablecloth** *noun*
tablecloths

**tablespoon** *noun*
tablespoons

**tablespoonful** *noun*
tablespoonfuls

**tablet** *noun*
tablets

**tack** *noun*
tacks

**tack** *verb*
tacks
tacking
tacked

**tackle** *verb*
tackles
tackling
tackled

**tackle** *noun*
tackles

**tacky** *adjective*
tackier
tackiest
tackily

**tact**

**tactful** *adjective*
tactfully

**tactical** *adjective*
tactically

**tactics** *plural noun*

**tactless** *adjective*
tactlessly

**tadpole** *noun*
tadpoles

**tag** *noun*
tags

**tag** *verb*
tags
tagging
tagged

**tail**★ *noun*
tails

**tail** *verb*
tails
tailing
tailed

**tailback** *noun*
tailbacks

**tailless**

**tailor** *noun*
tailors

**take** *verb*
takes
taking
took
taken

**takeaway** *noun*
takeaways

**takings** *plural noun*

**talc**

**talcum powder**

**tale**☆ *noun*
tales

**talent** *noun*
talents

**talented**

**talk** *verb*
talks
talking
talked

**talk** *noun*
talks

**talkative** *adjective*
talkatively

**talker** *noun*
talkers

**tall** *adjective*
taller
tallest

......................................................

★ A **tail** is a part at the back of an animal. ❗ tale.
☆ A **tale** is a story. ❗ tail.

246

**tally** *verb*
  tallies
  tallying
  tallied

**Talmud**

**talon** *noun*
  talons

**tambourine** *noun*
  tambourines

**tame** *adjective*
  tamer
  tamest
  tamely

**tame** *verb*
  tames
  taming
  tamed

**tameness**

**tamer** *noun*
  tamers

**tamper** *verb*
  tampers
  tampering
  tampered

**tampon** *noun*
  tampons

**tan** *noun*
  tans

**tan** *verb*
  tans
  tanning
  tanned

**tandem** *noun*
  tandems

**tang** *noun*
  tangs

**tangent** *noun*
  tangents

**tangerine** *noun*
  tangerines

**tangle** *verb*
  tangles
  tangling
  tangled

**tangle** *noun*
  tangles

**tank** *noun*
  tanks

**tankard** *noun*
  tankards

**tanker** *noun*
  tankers

**tanner** *noun*
  tanners

**tantalize** *verb*
  tantalizes
  tantalizing
  tantalized

**tantrum** *noun*
  tantrums

**tap** *noun*
  taps

**tap** *verb*
  taps
  tapping
  tapped

**tap dance** *noun*
  tap dances

**tap dancer** *noun*
  tap dancers

**tap dancing**

**tape** *noun*
  tapes

**tape** *verb*
  tapes
  taping
  taped

**tape-measure** *noun*
  tape-measures

**taper** *verb*
  tapers
  tapering
  tapered

**taper** *noun*
  tapers

**tape recorder** *noun*
  tape recorders

**tapestry** *noun*
  tapestries

**tapeworm** *noun*
  tapeworms

**tapioca**

**tar** *noun*

**tar** *verb*
  tars
  tarring
  tarred

**tarantula** *noun*
  tarantulas

**target** *noun*
  targets

**target** *verb*
  targets
  targeting
  targeted

**tarmac**

**tarmacadam**

**tarnish** *verb*
  tarnishes
  tarnishing
  tarnished

**tarpaulin** *noun*
  tarpaulins

**tarry** *adjective*
  tarrier
  tarriest

**tart** *noun*
  tarts

**tart** *adjective*
  tarter
  tartest
  tartly

**tartan** *noun*
  tartans

**task** *noun*
  tasks

**tassel** *noun*
  tassels

**taste** *verb*
  tastes
  tasting
  tasted

**taste** *noun*
  tastes

a
b
c
d
e
f
g
h
i
j
k
l
m
n
o
p
q
r
s
**t**
u
v
w
x
y
z

**tasteful** *adjective*
tastefully

**tasteless** *adjective*
tastelessly

**tasty** *adjective*
tastier
tastiest
tastily

**tattered**

**tatters** *plural noun*

**tattoo** *noun*
tattoos

**tattoo** *verb*
tattoos
tattooing
tattooed

**tatty** *adjective*
tattier
tattiest
tattily

**taught** see **teach**

**taunt** *verb*
taunts
taunting
taunted

**taunt** *noun*
taunts

**taut** *adjective*
tauter
tautest
tautly

**tautness**

**tavern** *noun*
taverns

**tawny** *adjective*
tawnier
tawniest

**tax** *noun*
taxes

**tax** *verb*
taxes
taxing
taxed

**taxable**

**taxation**

**taxi** *noun*
taxis

**taxi** *verb*
taxis
taxiing
taxied

**taxpayer** *noun*
taxpayers

**tea**★ *noun*
teas

**teabag** *noun*
teabags

**teacake** *noun*
teacakes

**teach** *verb*
teaches
teaching
taught

**teacher** *noun*
teachers

**tea cloth** or **tea towel**
*noun*
tea cloths *or* tea
towels

**teacup** *noun*
teacups

**teak**

**team**☆ *noun*
teams

**teapot** *noun*
teapots

**tear** *verb*
tears
tearing
tore
torn

**tear**✪ *noun*
tears

**tearful** *adjective*
tearfully

**tear gas**

**tease** *verb*
teases
teasing
teased

**teaspoon** *noun*
teaspoons

**teaspoonful** *noun*
teaspoonfuls

**teat** *noun*
teats

**tech** *noun*
techs

**technical** *adjective*
technically

**technicality** *noun*
technicalities

**technician** *noun*
technicians

**technique** *noun*
techniques

**technological**
*adjective*
technologically

**technology** *noun*
technologies

**teddy bear** *noun*
teddy bears

**tedious** *adjective*
tediously

**tediousness**

. . . . . . . . . . . . . . . . . . . . . . . . . . . . . . . . . . . . . . . . . . . . . . . . . . . . . . .

★ **Tea** is a hot drink. ! **tee**.

☆ You use **team** in e.g. *a football team*. ! **teem**.

✪ A **tear** is a drop of water from an eye and rhymes with 'here', or a split in something and rhymes with 'hair'.

**tedium**

**tee★** *noun*
tees

**teem☆** *verb*
teems
teeming
teemed

**teenage**

**teenager** *noun*
teenagers

**teens**

**teeth** see **tooth**

**teetotal**

**teetotaller** *noun*
teetotallers

**telecommunications**
*plural noun*

**telegram** *noun*
telegrams

**telegraph** *noun*
telegraphs

**telegraphic** *adjective*
telegraphically

**telegraphy**

**telepathic** *adjective*
telepathically

**telepathy**

**telephone** *noun*
telephones

**telephone** *verb*
telephones
telephoning
telephoned

**telephonist** *noun*
telephonists

**telescope** *noun*
telescopes

**telescopic** *adjective*
telescopically

**teletext**

**televise** *verb*
televises
televising
televised

**television** *noun*
televisions

**tell** *verb*
tells
telling
told

**tell-tale** *adjective* and
*noun*
tell-tales

**telly** *noun*
tellies

**temper** *noun*
tempers

**temperate**

**temperature** *noun*
temperatures

**tempest** *noun*
tempests

**tempestuous**
*adjective*
tempestuously

**temple** *noun*
temples

**tempo** *noun*
tempos

**temporary** *adjective*
temporarily

**tempt** *verb*
tempts
tempting
tempted

**temptation** *noun*
temptations

**tempter** *noun*
tempters

**temptress** *noun*
temptresses

**ten** *noun*
tens

**tenancy** *noun*
tenancies

**tenant** *noun*
tenants

**tend** *verb*
tends
tending
tended

**tendency** *noun*
tendencies

**tender** *adjective*
tenderer
tenderest
tenderly

**tender** *noun*
tenders

**tender** *verb*
tenders
tendering
tendered

**tenderness**

**tendon** *noun*
tendons

**tendril** *noun*
tendrils

**tennis**

**tenor** *noun*
tenors

**tenpin bowling**

**tense** *adjective*
tenser
tensest
tensely

**tense** *noun*
tenses

**tension** *noun*
tensions

**tent** *noun*
tents

a
b
c
d
e
f
g
h
i
j
k
l
m
n
o
p
q
r
s
**t**
u
v
w
x
y
z

. . . . . . . . . . . . . . . . . . . . . . . . . . . . . . . . . . . . . . . . . . . . . . . .

★ A tee is part of a golf course. **!** **tea**.
☆ You use **teem** in e.g. *a place teeming with people*. **!** **team**.

249

a
b
c
d
e
f
g
h
i
j
k
l
m
n
o
p
q
r
s
**t**
u
v
w
x
y
z

**tentacle** *noun*
  tentacles

**tenth**

**tenthly**

**tepid**

**term** *noun*
  terms

**term** *verb*
  terms
  terming
  termed

**terminal** *noun*
  terminals

**terminate** *verb*
  terminates
  terminating
  terminated

**termination** *noun*
  terminations

**terminus** *noun*
  termini

**terrace** *noun*
  terraces

**terrapin** *noun*
  terrapins

**terrible** *adjective*
  terribly

**terrier** *noun*
  terriers

**terrific** *adjective*
  terrifically

**terrify** *verb*
  terrifies
  terrifying
  terrified

**territorial** *adjective*
  territorially

**territory** *noun*
  territories

**terror** *noun*
  terrors

**terrorism**

**terrorist** *adjective* and
  *noun*
  terrorists

**terrorize** *verb*
  terrorizes
  terrorizing
  terrorized

**tessellation** *noun*
  tessellations

**test** *noun*
  tests

**test** *verb*
  tests
  testing
  tested

**testament** *noun*
  testaments

**testicle** *noun*
  testicles

**testify** *verb*
  testifies
  testifying
  testified

**testimonial** *noun*
  testimonials

**testimony** *noun*
  testimonies

**testy** *adjective*
  testier
  testiest

**tether** *verb*
  tethers
  tethering
  tethered

**tether** *noun*
  tethers

**text** *noun*
  texts

**textbook** *noun*
  textbooks

**textile** *noun*
  textiles

**texture** *noun*
  textures

**than**

**thank** *verb*
  thanks
  thanking
  thanked

**thankful** *adjective*
  thankfully

**thankless** *adjective*
  thanklessly

**thanks** *plural noun*

**that** *adjective,*
  *pronoun,* and
  *conjunction*

**thatch** *noun*

**thatch** *verb*
  thatches
  thatching
  thatched

**thatcher** *noun*
  thatchers

**thaw** *verb*
  thaws
  thawing
  thawed

**theatre** *noun*
  theatres

**theatrical** *adjective*
  theatrically

**thee**

**theft** *noun*
  thefts

**their**★

**theirs**☆

**them**

. . . . . . . . . . . . . . . . . . . . . . . . . . . . . . . . . . . . . . . . . . . . . . . . . . . . . . . . . . . . . . . .

★ You use **their** in e.g. *this is their house.* ! there, they´re.
☆ You use **theirs** in e.g. *the house is theirs*. Note that there is no
  apostrophe in this word.

**theme** *noun*
themes

**theme park** *noun*
theme parks

**themselves**

**then**

**theologian** *noun*
theologians

**theological** *adjective*
theologically

**theology**

**theorem** *noun*
theorems

**theoretical** *adjective*
theoretically

**theory** *noun*
theories

**therapist** *noun*
therapists

**therapy** *noun*
therapies

**there**★ *adverb*

**thereabouts**

**therefore**

**thermal** *adjective*
thermally

**thermometer** *noun*
thermometers

**Thermos** *noun*
Thermoses

**thermostat** *noun*
thermostats

**thermostatic**
*adjective*
thermostatically

**thesaurus** *noun*
thesauri *or*
thesauruses

**these**

**they**

**they'd** *verb*

**they'll** *verb*

**they're**☆ *verb*

**they've** *verb*

**thick** *adjective*
thicker
thickest
thickly

**thicken** *verb*
thickens
thickening
thickened

**thicket** *noun*
thickets

**thickness** *noun*
thicknesses

**thief** *noun*
thieves

**thigh** *noun*
thighs

**thimble** *noun*
thimbles

**thin** *adjective*
thinner
thinnest
thinly

**thin** *verb*
thins
thinning
thinned

**thine**

**thing** *noun*
things

**think** *verb*
thinks
thinking
thought

**thinker** *noun*
thinkers

**thinness**

**third**

**thirdly**

**Third World**

**thirst**

**thirsty** *adjective*
thirstier
thirstiest
thirstily

**thirteen**

**thirteenth**

**thirtieth**

**thirty** *noun*
thirties

**this**

**thistle** *noun*
thistles

**thorn** *noun*
thorns

**thorny** *adjective*
thornier
thorniest

**thorough** *adjective*
thoroughly

**thoroughness**

**those**

**thou**

**though**

**thought** *noun*
thoughts

**thought** see **think**

**thoughtful** *adjective*
thoughtfully

**thoughtfulness**

**thoughtless** *adjective*
thoughtlessly

**thoughtlessness**

**thousand** *noun*
thousands

**thousandth**

. . . . . . . . . . . . . . . . . . . . . . . . . . . . . . . . . . . . . . . . . . . . . . . . . . . .

★ You use there in e.g. *Look over there.* ! their, they´re.
☆ They´re is short for *they are.* ! their, there.

**thrash**★ *verb*
thrashes
thrashing
thrashed

**thread** *noun*
threads

**thread** *verb*
threads
threading
threaded

**threadbare**

**threat** *noun*
threats

**threaten** *verb*
threatens
threatening
threatened

**three** *noun*
threes

**three-dimensional**
*adjective*
three-dimensionally

**thresh**☆ *verb*
threshes
threshing
threshed

**threshold** *noun*
thresholds

**threw** see **throw**

**thrift**

**thrifty** *adjective*
thriftier
thriftiest
thriftily

**thrill** *noun*
thrills

**thrill** *verb*
thrills
thrilling
thrilled

**thriller** *noun*
thrillers

**thrive** *verb*
thrives
thriving
thrived *or* throve *or*
thriven

**throat** *noun*
throats

**throb** *verb*
throbs
throbbing
throbbed

**throb** *noun*
throbs

**throne** *noun*
thrones

**throng** *noun*
throngs

**throttle** *verb*
throttles
throttling
throttled

**throttle** *noun*
throttles

**through**

**throughout**

**throve** see **thrive**

**throw** *verb*
throws
throwing
threw
thrown

**throw** *noun*
throws

**thrush** *noun*
thrushes

**thrust** *verb*
thrusts
thrusting
thrust

**thud** *noun*
thuds

**thud** *verb*
thuds
thudding
thudded

**thumb** *noun*
thumbs

**thump** *verb*
thumps
thumping
thumped

**thump** *noun*
thumps

**thunder** *noun*

**thunder** *verb*
thunders
thundering
thundered

**thunderous** *adjective*
thunderously

**thunderstorm** *noun*
thunderstorms

**Thursday** *noun*
Thursdays

**thus**

**thy**

**tick** *verb*
ticks
ticking
ticked

**tick** *noun*
ticks

**ticket** *noun*
tickets

**tickle** *verb*
tickles
tickling
tickled

**ticklish** *adjective*
ticklishly

**tidal**

**tiddler** *noun*
tiddlers

• • • • • • • • • • • • • • • • • • • • • • • • • • • • • • • • • • • • • • • • • • • • • • • • • • • • • • • • • • •

★ To **thrash** someone is to beat them. **!** **thresh**.

☆ To **thresh** corn is to beat it to separate the grain. **!** **thrash**.

a
b
c
d
e
f
g
h
i
j
k
l
m
n
o
p
q
r
s
t
u
v
w
x
y
z

**tiddlywink** noun
tiddlywinks

**tide** noun
tides

**tide** verb
tides
tiding
tided

**tidiness**

**tidy** adjective
tidier
tidiest
tidily

**tie** verb
ties
tying
tied

**tie** noun
ties

**tie-break** noun
tie-breaks

**tiger** noun
tigers

**tight** adjective
tighter
tightest
tightly

**tighten** verb
tightens
tightening
tightened

**tightness**

**tightrope** noun
tightropes

**tights** plural noun

**tigress** noun
tigresses

**tile** noun
tiles

**tiled**

**till** preposition and
conjunction

**till** noun
tills

**till** verb
tills
tilling
tilled

**tiller** noun
tillers

**tilt** verb
tilts
tilting
tilted

**tilt** noun
tilts

**timber** noun
timbers

**time** noun
times

**time** verb
times
timing
timed

**timer** noun
timers

**times**

**timetable** noun
timetables

**timid** adjective
timidly

**timidity**

**timing**

**timpani** plural noun

**tin** noun
tins

**tin** verb
tins
tinning
tinned

**tingle** verb
tingles
tingling
tingled

**tingle** noun
tingles

**tinker** verb
tinkers
tinkering
tinkered

**tinker** noun
tinkers

**tinkle** verb
tinkles
tinkling
tinkled

**tinkle** noun
tinkles

**tinny** adjective
tinnier
tinniest
tinnily

**tinsel**

**tint** noun
tints

**tint** verb
tints
tinting
tinted

**tiny** adjective
tinier
tiniest

**tip** verb
tips
tipping
tipped

**tip** noun
tips

**tiptoe** verb
tiptoes
tiptoeing
tiptoed

**tiptoe** noun

**tire★** verb
tires
tiring
tired

★ To **tire** is to become tired. **!tyre**.

# ti - to

tired

tireless *adjective*
tirelessly

tiresome *adjective*
tiresomely

tissue *noun*
tissues

tit *noun*
tits

titbit *noun*
titbits

title *noun*
titles

titter *verb*
titters
tittering
tittered

to★ *preposition*

toad *noun*
toads

toadstool *noun*
toadstools

toast *verb*
toasts
toasting
toasted

toast *noun*
toasts

toaster *noun*
toasters

tobacco *noun*
tobaccos

tobacconist *noun*
tobacconists

toboggan *noun*
toboggans

tobogganing

today

toddler *noun*
toddlers

toe☆ *noun*
toes

toffee *noun*
toffees

toga *noun*
togas

together

toil *verb*
toils
toiling
toiled

toilet *noun*
toilets

token *noun*
tokens

told see tell

tolerable *adjective*
tolerably

tolerance

tolerant *adjective*
tolerantly

tolerate *verb*
tolerates
tolerating
tolerated

toll *noun*
tolls

toll *verb*
tolls
tolling
tolled

tomahawk *noun*
tomahawks

tomato *noun*
tomatoes

tomb *noun*
tombs

tomboy *noun*
tomboys

tombstone *noun*
tombstones

tomcat *noun*
tomcats

tommy-gun *noun*
tommy-guns

tomorrow

tom-tom *noun*
tom-toms

ton✪ *noun*
tons

tonal *adjective*
tonally

tone *noun*
tones

tone *verb*
tones
toning
toned

tone-deaf

tongs *plural noun*

tongue *noun*
tongues

tonic *noun*
tonics

tonight

tonne✦ *noun*
tonnes

tonsillitis

tonsils *plural noun*

too✽ *adverb*

took see take

tool *noun*
tools

tooth *noun*
teeth

- - - - - - - - - - - - - - - - - - - - - - - - - - - - - - - - - - - - - - - - - - - - - - - - - - -

★ You use to in e.g. *go to bed* or *I want to stay.* ! too, two.
☆ A toe is a part of a foot. ! tow.
✪ A ton is a non-metric unit of weight. ! tonne.
✦ A tonne is a metric unit of weight. ! ton.
✽ You use too in e.g. *it's too late* or *I want to come too.* ! to, two.

254

**toothache**

**toothbrush** *noun*
  toothbrushes

**toothed**

**toothpaste** *noun*
  toothpastes

**top** *noun*
  tops

**top** *verb*
  tops
  topping
  topped

**topic** *noun*
  topics

**topical** *adjective*
  topically

**topicality**

**topless**

**topmost**

**topping** *noun*
  toppings

**topple** *verb*
  topples
  toppling
  toppled

**topsy-turvy**

**torch** *noun*
  torches

**tore** see **tear**

**toreador** *noun*
  toreadors

**torment** *verb*
  torments
  tormenting
  tormented

**torment** *noun*
  torments

**tormentor** *noun*
  tormentors

**torn** see **tear**

**tornado** *noun*
  tornadoes

**torpedo** *noun*
  torpedoes

**torpedo** *verb*
  torpedoes
  torpedoing
  torpedoed

**torrent** *noun*
  torrents

**torrential** *adjective*
  torrentially

**torso** *noun*
  torsos

**tortoise** *noun*
  tortoises

**torture** *verb*
  tortures
  torturing
  tortured

**torture** *noun*
  tortures

**torturer** *noun*
  torturers

**Tory** *noun*
  Tories

**toss** *verb*
  tosses
  tossing
  tossed

**toss** *noun*
  tosses

**total** *noun*
  totals

**total** *adjective*
  totally

**total** *verb*
  totals
  totalling
  totalled

**totalitarian**

**totem pole** *noun*
  totem poles

**totter** *verb*
  totters
  tottering
  tottered

**touch** *verb*
  touches
  touching
  touched

**touch** *noun*
  touches

**touchy** *adjective*
  touchier
  touchiest
  touchily

**tough** *adjective*
  tougher
  toughest
  toughly

**toughen** *verb*
  toughens
  toughening
  toughened

**toughness**

**tour** *noun*
  tours

**tourism**

**tourist** *noun*
  tourists

**tournament** *noun*
  tournaments

**tow★** *verb*
  tows
  towing
  towed

**tow** *noun*

**toward** or **towards**

**towel** *noun*
  towels

**towelling**

**tower** *noun*
  towers

★ To tow something is to pull it along. **!toe**.

**tower** *verb*
towers
towering
towered

**town** *noun*
towns

**towpath** *noun*
towpaths

**toxic** *adjective*
toxically

**toy** *noun*
toys

**toy** *verb*
toys
toying
toyed

**toyshop** *noun*
toyshops

**trace** *noun*
traces

**trace** *verb*
traces
tracing
traced

**traceable**

**track** *noun*
tracks

**track** *verb*
tracks
tracking
tracked

**tracker** *noun*
trackers

**tracksuit** *noun*
tracksuits

**tract** *noun*
tracts

**traction**

**tractor** *noun*
tractors

**trade** *noun*
trades

**trade** *verb*
trades
trading
traded

**trademark** *noun*
trademarks

**trader** *noun*
traders

**tradesman** *noun*
tradesmen

**trade union** *noun*
trade unions

**tradition** *noun*
traditions

**traditional** *adjective*
traditionally

**traffic** *noun*

**traffic** *verb*
traffics
trafficking
trafficked

**tragedy** *noun*
tragedies

**tragic** *adjective*
tragically

**trail** *noun*
trails

**trail** *verb*
trails
trailing
trailed

**trailer** *noun*
trailers

**train** *noun*
trains

**train** *verb*
trains
training
trained

**trainer** *noun*
trainers

**traitor** *noun*
traitors

**tram** *noun*
trams

**tramp** *noun*
tramps

**tramp** *verb*
tramps
tramping
tramped

**trample** *verb*
tramples
trampling
trampled

**trampoline** *noun*
trampolines

**trance** *noun*
trances

**tranquil** *adjective*
tranquilly

**tranquillity**★

**tranquillizer** *noun*
tranquillizers

**transact** *verb*
transacts
transacting
transacted

**transaction** *noun*
transactions

**transatlantic**

**transfer** *verb*
transfers
transferring
transferred

**transfer** *noun*
transfers

**transferable**

**transference**

**transform** *verb*
transforms
transforming
transformed

**transformation** *noun*
transformations

. . . . . . . . . . . . . . . . . . . . . . . . . . . . . . . . . . . . . . . . . . . . . . . . . . . . . . . . . . .

★ Note that there are two ls in this word.

**transformer** *noun*
transformers

**transfusion** *noun*
transfusions

**transistor** *noun*
transistors

**transition** *noun*
transitions

**transitional** *adjective*
transitionally

**transitive** *adjective*
transitively

**translate** *verb*
translates
translating
translated

**translation** *noun*
translations

**translator** *noun*
translators

**translucent**

**transmission** *noun*
transmissions

**transmit** *verb*
transmits
transmitting
transmitted

**transmitter** *noun*
transmitters

**transparency** *noun*
transparencies

**transparent** *adjective*
transparently

**transpire** *verb*
transpires
transpiring
transpired

**transplant** *verb*
transplants
transplanting
transplanted

**transplant** *noun*
transplants

**transplantation** *noun*
transplantations

**transport** *verb*
transports
transporting
transported

**transportation**

**transport** *noun*

**transporter** *noun*
transporters

**trap** *verb*
traps
trapping
trapped

**trap** *noun*
traps

**trapdoor** *noun*
trapdoors

**trapeze** *noun*
trapezes

**trapezium** *noun*
trapeziums

**trapezoid** *noun*
trapezoids

**trapper** *noun*
trappers

**trash**

**trashy** *adjective*
trashier
trashiest
trashily

**travel** *verb*
travels
travelling
travelled

**travel** *noun*

**traveller** *noun*
travellers

**traveller's cheque**
*noun*
traveller's cheques

**trawler** *noun*
trawlers

**tray** *noun*
trays

**treacherous** *adjective*
treacherously

**treachery**

**treacle**

**tread** *verb*
treads
treading
trod
trodden

**tread** *noun*
treads

**treason**

**treasure** *noun*
treasures

**treasure** *verb*
treasures
treasuring
treasured

**treasurer** *noun*
treasurers

**treasury** *noun*
treasuries

**treat** *verb*
treats
treating
treated

**treat** *noun*
treats

**treatment** *noun*
treatments

**treaty** *noun*
treaties

**treble** *adjective* and
*noun*
trebles

**treble** *verb*
trebles
trebling
trebled

**tree** *noun*
trees

**trek** *verb*
treks
trekking
trekked

**trek** *noun*
treks

a
b
c
d
e
f
g
h
i
j
k
l
m
n
o
p
q
r
s
**t**
u
v
w
x
y
z

# tr

**trellis** noun
trellises

**tremble** verb
trembles
trembling
trembled

**tremble** noun
trembles

**tremendous** adjective
tremendously

**tremor** noun
tremors

**trench** noun
trenches

**trend** noun
trends

**trendiness**

**trendy** adjective
trendier
trendiest
trendily

**trespass** verb
trespasses
trespassing
trespassed

**trespasser** noun
trespassers

**trestle** noun
trestles

**trial** noun
trials

**triangle** noun
triangles

**triangular**

**tribal** adjective
tribally

**tribe** noun
tribes

**tribesman** noun
tribesmen

**tributary** noun
tributaries

**tribute** noun
tributes

**trick** noun
tricks

**trick** verb
tricks
tricking
tricked

**trickery**

**trickster** noun
tricksters

**trickle** verb
trickles
trickling
trickled

**trickle** noun
trickles

**tricky** adjective
trickier
trickiest
trickily

**tricycle** noun
tricycles

**tried** see **try**

**trifle** noun
trifles

**trifle** verb
trifles
trifling
trifled

**trifling**

**trigger** noun
triggers

**trigger** verb
triggers
triggering
triggered

**trillion** noun
trillions

**trim** adjective
trimmer
trimmest
trimly

**trim** verb
trims
trimming
trimmed

**trim** noun
trims

**Trinity**★

**trio** noun
trios

**trip** verb
trips
tripping
tripped

**trip** noun
trips

**tripe**

**triple** adjective
triply

**triple** noun
triples

**triple** verb
triples
tripling
tripled

**triplet** noun
triplets

**tripod** noun
tripods

**triumph** noun
triumphs

**triumphant** adjective
triumphantly

**trivial** adjective
trivially

**triviality** noun
trivialities

**trod** see **tread**

**trodden** see **tread**

. . . . . . . . . . . . . . . . . . . . . . . . . . . . . . . . . . . . . . . . . . . . . . . . . . . . . .

★ You use a capital T when you mean the three persons of God in
Christianity.

troll *noun*
trolls

trolley *noun*
trolleys

trombone *noun*
trombones

troop *noun*
troops

troop *verb*
troops
trooping
trooped

troops *plural noun*

trophy *noun*
trophies

tropic *noun*
tropics

tropical *adjective*

trot *verb*
trots
trotting
trotted

trot *noun*
trots

trouble *noun*
troubles

trouble *verb*
troubles
troubling
troubled

troublesome

trough *noun*
troughs

trousers *plural noun*

trout *noun*
trout

trowel *noun*
trowels

truancy *noun*
truancies

truant *noun*
truants

truce *noun*
truces

truck *noun*
trucks

trudge *verb*
trudges
trudging
trudged

true *adjective*
truer
truest
truly

trump *noun*
trumps

trump *verb*
trumps
trumping
trumped

trumpet *noun*
trumpets

trumpet *verb*
trumpets
trumpeting
trumpeted

trumpeter *noun*
trumpeters

truncheon *noun*
truncheons

trundle *verb*
trundles
trundling
trundled

trunk *noun*
trunks

trunks *plural noun*

trust *verb*
trusts
trusting
trusted

trust

trustful *adjective*
trustfully

trustworthy *adjective*
trustworthily

trusty *adjective*
trustier
trustiest
trustily

truth *noun*
truths

truthful *adjective*
truthfully

truthfulness

try *verb*
tries
trying
tried

try *noun*
tries

T-shirt *noun*
T-shirts

tub *noun*
tubs

tuba *noun*
tubas

tube *noun*
tubes

tuber *noun*
tubers

tubing

tubular

tuck *verb*
tucks
tucking
tucked

tuck *noun*
tucks

Tuesday *noun*
Tuesdays

tuft *noun*
tufts

tug *noun*
tugs

tug *verb*
tugs
tugging
tugged

tulip *noun*
tulips

a
b
c
d
e
f
g
h
i
j
k
l
m
n
o
p
q
r
s
**t**
u
v
w
x
y
z

a
b
c
d
e
f
g
h
i
j
k
l
m
n
o
p
q
r
s
**t**
u
v
w
x
y
z

**tumble** *verb*
tumbles
tumbling
tumbled

**tumble** *noun*
tumbles

**tumble-drier** *noun*
tumble-driers

**tumbler** *noun*
tumblers

**tummy** *noun*
tummies

**tumour** *noun*
tumours

**tumult**

**tumultuous** *adjective*
tumultuously

**tuna** *noun*
tuna *or* tunas

**tundra**

**tune** *noun*
tunes

**tune** *verb*
tunes
tuning
tuned

**tuneful** *adjective*
tunefully

**tunic** *noun*
tunics

**tunnel** *noun*
tunnels

**tunnel** *verb*
tunnels
tunnelling
tunnelled

**turban** *noun*
turbans

**turbine** *noun*
turbines

**turbulence**

**turbulent** *adjective*
turbulently

**turf** *noun*
turfs *or* turves

**turkey** *noun*
turkeys

**Turkish bath** *noun*
Turkish baths

**Turkish delight**

**turmoil**

**turn** *verb*
turns
turning
turned

**turn** *noun*
turns

**turncoat** *noun*
turncoats

**turnip** *noun*
turnips

**turnover** *noun*
turnovers

**turnstile** *noun*
turnstiles

**turntable** *noun*
turntables

**turpentine**

**turquoise**

**turret** *noun*
turrets

**turtle** *noun*
turtles

**tusk** *noun*
tusks

**tussle** *verb*
tussles
tussling
tussled

**tussle** *noun*
tussles

**tutor** *noun*
tutors

**tweak** *verb*
tweaks
tweaking
tweaked

**tweak** *noun*
tweaks

**tweed**

**tweezers** *plural noun*

**twelve** *noun*
twelves

**twelfth**

**twentieth**

**twenty** *noun*
twenties

**twice**

**twiddle** *verb*
twiddles
twiddling
twiddled

**twiddle** *noun*
twiddles

**twig** *noun*
twigs

**twig** *verb*
twigs
twigging
twigged

**twilight**

**twin** *noun*
twins

**twin** *verb*
twins
twinning
twinned

**twine**

**twinkle** *verb*
twinkles
twinkling
twinkled

**twinkle** *noun*
twinkles

**twirl** *verb*
twirls
twirling
twirled

**twirl** *noun*
twirls

**twist** *verb*
twists
twisting
twisted

**twist** *noun*
twists

**twister** *noun*
twisters

**twitch** *verb*
twitches
twitching
twitched

**twitch** *noun*
twitches

**twitter** *verb*
twitters
twittering
twittered

**two**★ *adjective* and *noun*
twos

**tying** see **tie**

**type** *noun*
types

**type** *verb*
types
typing
typed

**typewriter** *noun*
typewriters

**typewritten**

**typhoon** *noun*
typhoons

**typical** *adjective*
typically

**typist** *noun*
typists

**tyranny** *noun*
tyrannies

**tyrannical** *adjective*
tyrannically

**tyrant** *noun*
tyrants

**tyre**☆ *noun*
tyres

# Uu

**udder** *noun*
udders

**ugliness**

**ugly** *adjective*
uglier
ugliest

**ulcer** *noun*
ulcers

**ultimate** *adjective*
ultimately

**ultraviolet**

**umbilical cord** *noun*
umbilical cords

**umbrella** *noun*
umbrellas

**umpire** *noun*
umpires

**un-**
*un-* makes words meaning 'not', e.g. **unable**, **unhappiness**. Some of these words have special meanings, e.g. **unprofessional**. See the note at **non-**.

**unable**

**unaided**

**unanimity**

**unanimous** *adjective*
unanimously

**unavoidable** *adjective*
unavoidably

**unaware**

**unawares**

**unbearable** *adjective*
unbearably

**unbelievable** *adjective*
unbelievably

**unblock** *verb*
unblocks
unblocking
unblocked

**unborn**

**uncalled for**

**uncanny** *adjective*
uncannier
uncanniest

**uncertain** *adjective*
uncertainly

**uncertainty**

**uncle** *noun*
uncles

**uncomfortable** *adjective*
uncomfortably

**uncommon** *adjective*
uncommonly

**unconscious** *adjective*
unconsciously

**unconsciousness**

**uncontrollable** *adjective*
uncontrollably

**uncountable**

**uncouth**

a
b
c
d
e
f
g
h
i
j
k
l
m
n
o
p
q
r
s
**t**
**u**
v
w
x
y
z

★ You use **two** in e.g. *two people* or *there are two of them.* **!to, too.**
☆ A **tyre** is a rubber cover for a wheel. **!tire.**

a

**uncover** *verb*
uncovers
uncovering
uncovered

b

**undecided**

c

**undeniable** *adjective*
undeniably

d

**under**

e

**underarm** *adjective*

f

**underclothes** *plural noun*

g

**underdeveloped**

h

**underdone**

**underfoot**

i

**undergo** *verb*
undergoes
undergoing
underwent
undergone

j

k

**undergraduate** *noun*
undergraduates

l

**underground**
*adjective* and *noun*
undergrounds

m

n

**undergrowth**

o

**underhand**

p

**underlie** *verb*
underlies
underlying
underlay
underlain

q

r

**underline** *verb*
underlines
underlining
underlined

s

t

**undermine** *verb*
undermines
undermining
undermined

**u**

v

**underneath**
*preposition*

w

**underpants** *plural noun*

x

y

**underpass** *noun*
underpasses

z

**underprivileged**

**understand** *verb*
understands
understanding
understood

**understandable**
*adjective*
understandably

**understanding**

**undertake** *verb*
undertakes
undertaking
undertook
undertaken

**undertaker** *noun*
undertakers

**undertaking** *noun*
undertakings

**underwater**

**underwear**

**underworld**

**undesirable** *adjective*
undesirably

**undeveloped**

**undo** *verb*
undoes
undoing
undid
undone

**undoubted** *adjective*
undoubtedly

**undress** *verb*
undresses
undressing
undressed

**unearth** *verb*
unearths
unearthing
unearthed

**unearthly**

**unease**

**uneasiness**

**uneasy** *adjective*
uneasier
uneasiest
uneasily

**uneatable**

**unemployed**

**unemployment**

**uneven** *adjective*
unevenly

**unevenness**

**unexpected** *adjective*
unexpectedly

**unfair** *adjective*
unfairly

**unfairness**

**unfaithful** *adjective*
unfaithfully

**unfamiliar**

**unfamiliarity**

**unfasten** *verb*
unfastens
unfastening
unfastened

**unfavourable**
*adjective*
unfavourably

**unfinished**

**unfit**

**unfold** *verb*
unfolds
unfolding
unfolded

**unforgettable**
*adjective*
unforgettably

**unforgivable**
*adjective*
unforgivably

**unfortunate** *adjective*
unfortunately

**unfreeze** *verb*
unfreezes
unfreezing
unfroze
unfrozen

unfriendliness
unfriendly
ungrateful *adjective*
ungratefully
unhappiness
unhappy *adjective*
unhappier
unhappiest
unhappily
unhealthy *adjective*
unhealthier
unhealthiest
unhealthily
unheard-of
unicorn *noun*
unicorns
unification
uniform *noun*
uniforms
uniform *adjective*
uniformly
uniformed
uniformity
unify *verb*
unifies
unifying
unified
unimportance
unimportant
uninhabited
unintentional *adjective*
unintentionally
uninterested
uninteresting
union *noun*
unions
unique *adjective*
uniquely
uniqueness
unisex
unison
unit *noun*
units

unite *verb*
unites
uniting
united
unity *noun*
unities
universal *adjective*
universally
universe
university *noun*
universities
unjust *adjective*
unjustly
unkind *adjective*
unkinder
unkindest
unkindly
unkindness
unknown
unleaded
unless
unlike
unlikely *adjective*
unlikelier
unlikeliest
unload *verb*
unloads
unloading
unloaded
unlock *verb*
unlocks
unlocking
unlocked
unlucky *adjective*
unluckier
unluckiest
unluckily
unmistakable *adjective*
unmistakably
unnatural *adjective*
unnaturally
unnecessary *adjective*
unnecessarily

unoccupied
unpack *verb*
unpacks
unpacking
unpacked
unpleasant *adjective*
unpleasantly
unpleasantness
unplug *verb*
unplugs
unplugging
unplugged
unpopular *adjective*
unpopularly
unpopularity
unravel *verb*
unravels
unravelling
unravelled
unreal
unreasonable *adjective*
unreasonably
unrest
unroll *verb*
unrolls
unrolling
unrolled
unruliness
unruly *adjective*
unrulier
unruliest
unscrew *verb*
unscrews
unscrewing
unscrewed
unseemly
unseen
unselfish *adjective*
unselfishly
unselfishness
unsightly
unskilled

**unsound** *adjective*
unsoundly

**unsteadiness**

**unsteady** *adjective*
unsteadier
unsteadiest
unsteadily

**unsuccessful**
*adjective*
unsuccessfully

**unsuitable** *adjective*
unsuitably

**unthinkable** *adjective*
unthinkably

**untidiness**

**untidy** *adjective*
untidier
untidiest
untidily

**untie** *verb*
unties
untying
untied

**until**

**untimely**

**unto**

**untold**

**untoward**

**untrue** *adjective*
untruly

**untruthful** *adjective*
untruthfully

**unused**

**unusual** *adjective*
unusually

**unwanted**

**unwell**

**unwilling** *adjective*
unwillingly

**unwillingness**

**unwind** *verb*
unwinds
unwinding
unwound

**unwrap** *verb*
unwraps
unwrapping
unwrapped

**unzip** *verb*
unzips
unzipping
unzipped

**update** *verb*
updates
updating
updated

**upgrade** *verb*
upgrades
upgrading
upgraded

**upheaval** *noun*
upheavals

**uphill**

**uphold** *verb*
upholds
upholding
upheld

**upholstery**

**upkeep**

**uplands** *plural noun*

**upon**

**upper**

**upright** *adjective*
uprightly

**upright** *noun*
uprights

**uprising** *noun*
uprisings

**uproar** *noun*
uproars

**upset** *verb*
upsets
upsetting
upset

**upset** *noun*
upsets

**upshot**

**upside down**

**upstairs**

**upstart** *noun*
upstarts

**upstream** *adjective*

**uptake**

**uptight**

**upward** *adjective* and
*adverb*

**upwards** *adverb*

**uranium**

**urban**

**urbanization**

**urbanize** *verb*
urbanizes
urbanizing
urbanized

**urchin** *noun*
urchins

**Urdu**

**urge** *verb*
urges
urging
urged

**urge** *noun*
urges

**urgency**

**urgent** *adjective*
urgently

**urinary**

**urinate** *verb*
urinates
urinating
urinated

**urination**

**urine**

**urn** *noun*
urns

a b c d e f g h i j k l m n o p q r s t **u** v w x y z

**-us**
Most nouns ending in *-us* come from Latin words, e.g. **bonus** and **terminus**. They normally have plurals ending in *-uses*, e.g. **bonuses** and **terminuses**. Some more technical words have plurals ending in *-i*, e.g. **nucleus - nuclei**.

**usable**

**usage** *noun*
usages

**use** *verb*
uses
using
used

**use** *noun*
uses

**useful** *adjective*
usefully

**usefulness**

**useless** *adjective*
uselessly

**uselessness**

**user** *noun*
users

**user-friendly** *adjective*
user-friendlier
user-friendliest

**usher** *noun*
ushers

**usher** *verb*
ushers
ushering
ushered

**usherette** *noun*
usherettes

**usual** *adjective*
usually

**usurp** *verb*
usurps
usurping
usurped

**usurper** *noun*
usurpers

**utensil** *noun*
utensils

**uterus** *noun*
uteri

**utilization**

**utilize** *verb*
utilizes
utilizing
utilized

**utmost**

**utter** *adjective*

**utter** *verb*
utters
uttering
uttered

**utterance** *noun*
utterances

**utterly** *adverb*

**U-turn** *noun*
U-turns

# Vv

**vacancy** *noun*
vacancies

**vacant** *adjective*
vacantly

**vacate** *verb*
vacates
vacating
vacated

**vacation** *noun*
vacations

**vaccinate** *verb*
vaccinates
vaccinating
vaccinated

**vaccination** *noun*
vaccinations

**vaccine** *noun*
vaccines

**vacuum** *noun*
vacuums

**vagina** *noun*
vaginas

**vague** *adjective*
vaguer
vaguest
vaguely

**vagueness**

**vain**★ *adjective*
vainer
vainest
vainly

**vale**☆ *noun*
vales

**valentine** *noun*
valentines

**valiant** *adjective*
valiantly

**valid** *adjective*
validly

**validity**

**valley** *noun*
valleys

**valour**

**valuable** *adjective*
valuably

**valuables** *plural noun*

a
b
c
d
e
f
g
h
i
j
k
l
m
n
o
p
q
r
s
t
**u**
**v**
w
x
y
z

**265**

. . . . . . . . . . . . . . . . . . . . . . . . . . . . . . . . . . . . . . . . . . . . . . . . . . . . .
★ **Vain** means 'conceited' or 'proud'. **!vane, vein.**
☆ A **vale** is a valley. **!veil.**

a

**valuation** *noun*
valuations

**value** *noun*
values

**value** *verb*
values
valuing
valued

**valueless**

**valuer** *noun*
valuers

**valve** *noun*
valves

**vampire** *noun*
vampires

**van** *noun*
vans

**vandal** *noun*
vandals

**vandalism**

**vane**★ *noun*
vanes

**vanilla**

**vanish** *verb*
vanishes
vanishing
vanished

**vanity**

**vanquish** *verb*
vanquishes
vanquishing
vanquished

**vaporize** *verb*
vaporizes
vaporizing
vaporized

**vapour** *noun*
vapours

**variable** *adjective*
variably

**variable** *noun*
variables

**variation** *noun*
variations

**varied**

**variety** *noun*
varieties

**various** *adjective*
variously

**varnish** *noun*
varnishes

**varnish** *verb*
varnishes
varnishing
varnished

**vary** *verb*
varies
varying
varied

**vase** *noun*
vases

**vast** *adjective*
vastly

**vastness**

**vat** *noun*
vats

**vault** *verb*
vaults
vaulting
vaulted

**vault** *noun*
vaults

**veal**

**vector** *noun*
vectors

**Veda**

**veer** *verb*
veers
veering
veered

**vegan** *noun*
vegans

**vegetable** *noun*
vegetables

**vegetarian** *noun*
vegetarians

**vegetate** *verb*
vegetates
vegetating
vegetated

**vegetation**

**vehicle** *noun*
vehicles

**veil**☆ *noun*
veils

**veil** *verb*
veils
veiling
veiled

**vein**✪ *noun*
veins

**velocity** *noun*
velocities

**velvet**

**velvety**

**vendetta** *noun*
vendettas

**vendor** *noun*
vendors

**venerable** *adjective*
venerably

**venereal disease** *noun*
venereal diseases

**venetian blind** *noun*
venetian blinds

**vengeance**

**venison**

b
c
d
e
f
g
h
i
j
k
l
m
n
o
p
q
r
s
t
u
**v**
w
x
y
z

. . . . . . . . . . . . . . . . . . . . . . . . . . . . . . . . . . . . . . . . . . . . . . . . . . . .

★ A **vane** is a pointer that shows which way the wind is blowing.
❗**vain, vein**.

☆ A **veil** is a covering for the face. ❗**vale**.

✪ A **vein** carries blood to the heart. ❗**vain, vane**.

**Venn diagram** *noun*
Venn diagrams

**venom**

**venomous** *adjective*
venomously

**vent** *noun*
vents

**ventilate** *verb*
ventilates
ventilating
ventilated

**ventilation**

**ventilator** *noun*
ventilators

**ventriloquism**

**ventriloquist** *noun*
ventriloquists

**venture** *verb*
ventures
venturing
ventured

**venture** *noun*
ventures

**veranda** *noun*
verandas

**verb** *noun*
verbs

**verdict** *noun*
verdicts

**verge** *verb*
verges
verging
verged

**verge** *noun*
verges

**verification**

**verify** *verb*
verifies
verifying
verified

**vermin**

**verruca** *noun*
verrucas

**versatile**

**versatility**

**verse** *noun*
verses

**version** *noun*
versions

**versus**

**vertebra** *noun*
vertebrae

**vertebrate** *noun*
vertebrates

**vertex** *noun*
vertices

**vertical** *adjective*
vertically

**very**

**Vesak**

**vessel** *noun*
vessels

**vest** *noun*
vests

**vested** *adjective*
vested

**vestment** *noun*
vestments

**vestry** *noun*
vestries

**vet** *noun*
vets

**veteran** *noun*
veterans

**veterinary**

**veto** *verb*
vetoes
vetoing
vetoed

**veto** *noun*
vetoes

**vex** *verb*
vexes
vexing
vexed

**vexation**

**via**

**viaduct** *noun*
viaducts

**vibrate** *verb*
vibrates
vibrating
vibrated

**vibration** *noun*
vibrations

**vicar** *noun*
vicars

**vicarage** *noun*
vicarages

**vice** *noun*
vices

**vice-president** *noun*
vice-presidents

**vice versa**

**vicinity** *noun*
vicinities

**vicious** *adjective*
viciously

**viciousness**

**victim** *noun*
victims

**victimize** *verb*
victimizes
victimizing
victimized

**victor** *noun*
victors

**Victorian** *adjective*
and *noun*
Victorians

**victorious** *adjective*
victoriously

**victory** *noun*
victories

**video** *noun*
videos

**video** *verb*
videoes
videoing
videoed

**videotape** *noun*
videotapes

a
b
c
d
e
f
g
h
i
j
k
l
m
n
o
p
q
r
s
t
u
**v**
w
x
y
z

a

**view** *noun*
views

b

**view** *verb*
views
viewing
viewed

c

d

**viewer** *noun*
viewers

e

**vigilance**

f

**vigilant** *adjective*
vigilantly

g

**vigorous** *adjective*
vigorously

h

**vigour**

i

**Viking** *noun*
Vikings

j

k

**vile** *adjective*
viler
vilest
vilely

l

m

**villa** *noun*
villas

n

**village** *noun*
villages

o

**villager** *noun*
villagers

p

**villain** *noun*
villains

q

r

**villainous** *adjective*
villainously

s

**villainy**

t

**vine** *noun*
vines

u

**vinegar**

**v**

**vineyard** *noun*
vineyards

w

**vintage** *noun*
vintages

x

**vinyl**

y

**viola** *noun*
violas

z

**violate** *verb*
violates
violating
violated

**violation** *noun*
violations

**violator** *noun*
violators

**violence**

**violent** *adjective*
violently

**violet** *noun*
violets

**violin** *noun*
violins

**violinist** *noun*
violinists

**viper** *noun*
vipers

**virgin** *noun*
virgins

**virginity**

**virtual** *adjective*
virtually

**virtue** *noun*
virtues

**virtuous** *adjective*
virtuously

**virus** *noun*
viruses

**visa** *noun*
visas

**visibility**

**visible** *adjective*
visibly

**vision** *noun*
visions

**visit** *verb*
visits
visiting
visited

**visit** *noun*
visits

**visitor** *noun*
visitors

**visor** *noun*
visors

**visual** *adjective*
visually

**visualize** *verb*
visualizes
visualizing
visualized

**vital** *adjective*
vitally

**vitality**

**vitamin** *noun*
vitamins

**vivid** *adjective*
vividly

**vividness**

**vivisection** *noun*
vivisections

**vixen** *noun*
vixens

**vocabulary** *noun*
vocabularies

**vocal** *adjective*
vocally

**vocalist** *noun*
vocalists

**vocation** *noun*
vocations

**vocational** *adjective*
vocationally

**vodka** *noun*
vodkas

**voice** *noun*
voices

**voice** *verb*
voices
voicing
voiced

**volcanic**

**volcano** *noun*
volcanoes

**vole** noun
voles

**volley** noun
volleys

**volleyball**

**volt** noun
volts

**voltage** noun
voltages

**volume** noun
volumes

**voluntary** adjective
voluntarily

**volunteer** verb
volunteers
volunteering
volunteered

**volunteer** noun
volunteers

**vomit** verb
vomits
vomiting
vomited

**vote** verb
votes
voting
voted

**vote** noun
votes

**voter** noun
voters

**vouch** verb
vouches
vouching
vouched

**voucher** noun
vouchers

**vow** noun
vows

**vow** verb
vows
vowing
vowed

**vowel** noun
vowels

**voyage** noun
voyages

**voyager** noun
voyagers

**vulgar** adjective
vulgarly

**vulnerable** adjective
vulnerably

**vulture** noun
vultures

**vulva** noun
vulvas

**Ww**

**wad** noun
wads

**waddle** verb
waddles
waddling
waddled

**waddle** noun
waddles

**wade** verb
wades
wading
waded

**wafer** noun
wafers

**wag** verb
wags
wagging
wagged

**wag** noun
wags

**wage** noun
wages

**wage** verb
wages
waging
waged

**wager** noun
wagers

**wager** verb
wagers
wagering
wagered

**waggle** verb
waggles
waggling
waggled

**wagon** noun
wagons

**wagtail** noun
wagtails

**wail** verb
wails
wailing
wailed

**wail**★ noun
wails

**waist**☆ noun
waists

**waistcoat** noun
waistcoats

**wait**✪ verb
waits
waiting
waited

**wait** noun
waits

**waiter** noun
waiters

. . . . . . . . . . . . . . . . . . . . . . . . . . . . . . . . . . . . . . . . . . . . . .

★ A **wail** is a loud sad cry. **!** whale.

☆ A person's **waist** is the narrow part around their middle. **!** waste.

✪ To **wait** is to delay, pause, or rest. **!** weight.

a
b
c
d
e
f
g
h
i
j
k
l
m
n
o
p
q
r
s
t
u
**v**
**w**
x
y
z

a

**waitress** *noun*
waitresses

**waive★** *verb*
waives
waiving
waived

**wake** *verb*
wakes
waking
woke
woken

**wake** *noun*
wakes

**waken** *verb*
wakens
wakening
wakened

**walk** *verb*
walks
walking
walked

**walk** *noun*
walks

**walkabout** *noun*
walkabouts

**walker** *noun*
walkers

**walkie-talkie** *noun*
walkie-talkies

**Walkman** *noun*
Walkmans

**wall** *noun*
walls

**wall** *verb*
walls
walling
walled

**wallaby** *noun*
wallabies

**wallet** *noun*
wallets

**wallflower** *noun*
wallflowers

**wallop** *verb*
wallops
walloping
walloped

**wallow** *verb*
wallows
wallowing
wallowed

**wallpaper** *noun*
wallpapers

**walnut** *noun*
walnuts

**walrus** *noun*
walruses

**waltz** *noun*
waltzes

**waltz** *verb*
waltzes
waltzing
waltzed

**wand** *noun*
wands

**wander** *verb*
wanders
wandering
wandered

**wanderer** *noun*
wanderers

**wane** *verb*
wanes
waning
waned

**wangle** *verb*
wangles
wangling
wangled

**wallet** *noun*
wallets

**want** *verb*
wants
wanting
wanted

**want** *noun*
wants

**war** *noun*
wars

**warble** *verb*
warbles
warbling
warbled

**warble** *noun*
warbles

**warbler** *noun*
warblers

**ward** *noun*
wards

**ward** *verb*
wards
warding
warded

**warden** *noun*
wardens

**warder** *noun*
warders

**wardrobe** *noun*
wardrobes

**ware☆** *noun*
wares

**warehouse** *noun*
warehouses

**warfare**

**warhead** *noun*
warheads

**wariness**

**warlike**

**warm** *adjective*
warmer
warmest
warmly

· · · · · · · · · · · · · · · · · · · · · · · · · · · · · · · · · · · · · · · · · · · · · · · · ·

★ To **waive** a right is to say you do not need it. **!** wave.
☆ **Wares** are manufactured goods. **!** wear, where.

**warm** *verb*
warms
warming
warmed

**warmth**

**warn** *verb*
warns
warning
warned

**warning** *noun*
warnings

**warp** *verb*
warps
warping
warped

**warp** *noun*
warps

**warrant** *noun*
warrants

**warrant** *verb*
warrants
warranting
warranted

**warren** *noun*
warrens

**warrior** *noun*
warriors

**warship** *noun*
warships

**wart** *noun*
warts

**wary** *adjective*
warier
wariest
warily

**was**

**wash** *verb*
washes
washing
washed

**wash** *noun*
washes

**washable**

**washbasin** *noun*
washbasins

**washer** *noun*
washers

**washing**

**washing-up**

**wash-out** *noun*
wash-outs

**wasn't** *verb*

**wasp** *noun*
wasps

**wastage**

**waste**★ *verb*
wastes
wasting
wasted

**waste** *adjective* and
*noun*
wastes

**wasteful** *adjective*
wastefully

**watch** *verb*
watches
watching
watched

**watch** *noun*
watches

**watchdog** *noun*
watchdogs

**watcher** *noun*
watchers

**watchful** *adjective*
watchfully

**watchfulness**

**watchman** *noun*
watchmen

**water** *noun*
waters

**water** *verb*
waters
watering
watered

**watercolour** *noun*
watercolours

**watercress**

**waterfall** *noun*
waterfalls

**waterlogged**

**watermark** *noun*
watermarks

**waterproof**

**water-skiing**

**watertight**

**waterway** *noun*
waterways

**waterworks** *noun*
waterworks

**watery**

**watt**☆ *noun*
watts

**wave**❂ *verb*
waves
waving
waved

**wave** *noun*
waves

**waveband** *noun*
wavebands

**wavelength** *noun*
wavelengths

**waver** *verb*
wavers
wavering
wavered

a
b
c
d
e
f
g
h
i
j
k
l
m
n
o
p
q
r
s
t
u
v
**w**
x
y
z

· · · · · · · · · · · · · · · · · · · · · · · · · · · · · · · · · · · · · · · · · · · · · · · · · · · · · · · · · · · · · · · · · · · · · · · · · · · · · · · · · · · · · · · · · · · · · · · · · · ·

★ To **waste** something is to use more of it than is needed. **!waist**.

☆ A **watt** is a unit of electricity. **!what**.

❂ To **wave** is to move your arm in greeting. **!waive**.

**wavy** *adjective*
wavier
waviest
wavily

**wax** *noun*
waxes

**wax** *verb*
waxes
waxing
waxed

**waxwork** *noun*
waxworks

**waxy** *adjective*
waxier
waxiest

**way**★ *noun*
ways

**weak**☆ *adjective*
weaker
weakest
weakly

**weakness**

**weaken** *verb*
weakens
weakening
weakened

**weakling** *noun*
weaklings

**wealth**

**wealthy** *adjective*
wealthier
wealthiest
wealthily

**weapon** *noun*
weapons

**wear**☉ *verb*
wears
wearing
wore
worn

**wear** *noun*

**wearer** *noun*
wearers

**weariness**

**weary** *adjective*
wearier
weariest
wearily

**weasel** *noun*
weasels

**weather** *noun*

**weather** *verb*
weathers
weathering
weathered

**weathercock** *noun*
weathercocks

**weave**✛ *verb*
weaves
weaving
weaved *or* wove
woven

**weaver** *noun*
weavers

**web** *noun*
webs

**webbed**

**website** *noun*
websites

**wed** *verb*
weds
wedding
wedded
wed

**we'd** *verb*

**wedding** *noun*
weddings

**wedge** *noun*
wedges

**wedge** *verb*
wedges
wedging
wedged

**Wednesday** *noun*
Wednesdays

**weed** *noun*
weeds

**weed** *verb*
weeds
weeding
weeded

**weedy** *adjective*
weedier
weediest
weedily

**week**✱ *noun*
weeks

**weekday** *noun*
weekdays

**weekend** *noun*
weekends

**weekly** *adjective* and
*adverb*

**weep** *verb*
weeps
weeping
wept

★ You use **way** in e.g. *can you tell me the way?* ! **weigh, whey**.
☆ **Weak** means 'not strong'. ! **week**.
☉ To **wear** clothes is to be dressed in them. ! **ware, where**.
✛ The past tense is **weaved** in e.g. *she weaved her way through the crowd* and **wove** in e.g. *she wove a shawl*.
✱ A **week** is a period of seven days. ! **weak**.

a b c d e f g h i j k l m n o p q r s t u v **w** x y z

weft

weigh★ *verb*
weighs
weighing
weighed

weight☆ *noun*
weights

weightless

weightlifting

weighty *adjective*
weightier
weightiest
weightily

weir *noun*
weirs

weird *adjective*
weirder
weirdest
weirdly

weirdness

welcome *noun*
welcomes

welcome *verb*
welcomes
welcoming
welcomed

weld *verb*
welds
welding
welded

welder *noun*
welders

welfare

well *noun*
wells

well *adjective* and
  *adverb*
better
best

we'll *verb*

well-being

wellington boots
  *plural noun*

well-known

went see **go**

wept see **weep**

were see **are**

we're *verb*

werewolf *noun*
werewolves

west *adjective* and
  *adverb*

west✪ *noun*

westerly *adjective* and
  *noun*
westerlies

western *adjective*

western *noun*
westerns

westward *adjective*
  and *adverb*

westwards *adverb*

wet *adjective*
wetter
wettest

wet *verb*
wets
wetting
wetted

wetness

we've *abbreviation*

whack *verb*
whacks
whacking
whacked

whack *noun*
whacks

whale✢ *noun*
whales

whaler *noun*
whalers

whaling

wharf *noun*
wharves *or* wharfs

what✱

whatever

wheat

wheel *noun*
wheels

wheel *verb*
wheels
wheeling
wheeled

wheelbarrow *noun*
wheelbarrows

wheelchair *noun*
wheelchairs

wheeze *verb*
wheezes
wheezing
wheezed

whelk *noun*
whelks

when

whenever *conjunction*

★ You use **weigh** in e.g. *how much do you weigh?* **!way, whey**.
☆ **Weight** is how heavy something is. **!wait**.
✪ You use a capital W in the **West**, when you mean a particular region.
✢ A **whale** is a large sea mammal. **!wail**.
✱ You use **what** in e.g. *what are they doing?* or *I don't know what you mean.* **!watt**.

a
b
c
d
e
f
g
h
i
j
k
l
m
n
o
p
q
r
s
t
u
v

**w**

x
y
z

## wh

a where★

whereabouts

b whereas

c whereupon

d wherever

whether *conjunction*

e whey☆

f which❍

g whichever

whiff *noun*
whiffs

h while *adjective* and
*noun*

i

j while *verb*
whiles
k whiling
whiled

l whilst *conjunction*

m whimper *verb*
whimpers
n whimpering
whimpered

o whimper *noun*
whimpers

p whine *verb*
whines
q whining
whined

r whine✧ *noun*
whines

s

t whinny *verb*
whinnies
whinnying
u whinnied

v whip *noun*
whips

w

x

y

z

whip *verb*
whips
whipping
whipped

whirl *verb*
whirls
whirling
whirled

whirl *noun*
whirls

whirlpool *noun*
whirlpools

whirlwind *noun*
whirlwinds

whirr *verb*
whirrs
whirring
whirred

whirr *noun*
whirrs

whisk *verb*
whisks
whisking
whisked

whisk *noun*
whisks

whisker *noun*
whiskers

whisky *noun*
whiskies

whisper *verb*
whispers
whispering
whispered

whisper *noun*
whispers

whist

whistle *verb*
whistles
whistling
whistled

whistle *noun*
whistles

whistler *noun*
whistlers

white *adjective*
whiter
whitest

whiteness

whitish

white *noun*
whites

whiten *verb*
whitens
whitening
whitened

whitewash *noun*

whitewash *verb*
whitewashes
whitewashing
whitewashed

Whitsun

Whit Sunday

whiz *verb*
whizzes
whizzing
whizzed

who

whoever

whole❋ *adjective*
wholly

whole *noun*
wholes

wholefood *noun*
wholefoods

★ You use **where** in e.g. *where are you?* ! ware, wear.
☆ **Whey** is a watery liquid from milk. ! way, weigh.
❍ You use **which** in e.g. *which one is that?* ! witch.
✧ A **whine** is a high piercing sound. ! wine.
❋ You use **whole** in e.g. *I saw the whole lm.* ! hole.

wholemeal

wholesale *adjective*

wholesome

wholly

whom

whoop *noun*
whoops

whoopee *interjection*

whooping cough

who's★ *verb*

whose☆ *adjective*

why

wick *noun*
wicks

wicked *adjective*
wickeder
wickedest
wickedly

wickedness

wicker

wickerwork

wicket *noun*
wickets

wicketkeeper *noun*
wicketkeepers

wide *adjective* and
*adverb*
wider
widest
widely

widen *verb*
widens
widening
widened

widespread

widow *noun*
widows

widower *noun*
widowers

width *noun*
widths

wield *verb*
wields
wielding
wielded

wife *noun*
wives

wig *noun*
wigs

wiggle *verb*
wiggles
wiggling
wiggled

wiggle *noun*
wiggles

wigwam *noun*
wigwams

wild *adjective*
wilder
wildest
wildly

wilderness *noun*
wildernesses

wildness

wildlife

wilful *adjective*
wilfully

wilfulness

wiliness

will *verb*
would

will *noun*
wills

willing *adjective*
willingly

willingness

willow *noun*
willows

wilt *verb*
wilts
wilting
wilted

wily *adjective*
wilier
wiliest

wimp *noun*
wimps

win *verb*
wins
winning
won

win *noun*
wins

wince *verb*
winces
wincing
winced

winch *noun*
winches

winch *verb*
winches
winching
winched

wind *noun*
winds

wind *verb*
winds
winding
wound

windfall *noun*
windfalls

windmill *noun*
windmills

window *noun*
windows

windpipe *noun*
windpipes

★ You use **who's** in *who's* ( who is) *that?* and *I don't know who's*
(who has) *done it.* **!whose.**

☆ You use **whose** in *whose is this?* and *I don't know whose it is.*
**!who's.**

a
b
c
d
e
f
g
h
i
j
k
l
m
n
o
p
q
r
s
t
u
v
**w**
x
y
z

a

b

c

d

e

f

g

h

i

j

k

l

m

n

o

p

q

r

s

t

u

v

**w**

x

y

z

276

**windscreen** *noun*
windscreens

**windsurfer**

**windsurfing**

**windward**

**windy** *adjective*
windier
windiest
windily

**wine★** *noun*
wines

**wing** *noun*
wings

**wing** *verb*
wings
winging
winged

**winged**

**wingless**

**wingspan** *noun*
wingspans

**wink** *verb*
winks
winking
winked

**wink** *noun*
winks

**winkle** *noun*
winkles

**winkle** *verb*
winkles
winkling
winkled

**winner** *noun*
winners

**winnings** *plural noun*

**winter** *noun*
winters

**wintertime**

**wintry** *adjective*
wintrier
wintriest

**wipe** *verb*
wipes
wiping
wiped

**wipe** *noun*
wipes

**wiper** *noun*
wipers

**wire** *noun*
wires

**wire** *verb*
wires
wiring
wired

**wireless** *noun*
wirelesses

**wiring**

**wiry** *adjective*
wirier
wiriest
wirily

**wisdom**

**wise** *adjective*
wiser
wisest
wisely

**wish** *verb*
wishes
wishing
wished

**wish** *noun*
wishes

**wishbone** *noun*
wishbones

**wisp** *noun*
wisps

**wispy** *adjective*
wispier
wispiest
wispily

**wistful** *adjective*
wistfully

**wistfulness**

**wit** *noun*
wits

**witch☆** *noun*
witches

**witchcraft**

**with**

**withdraw** *verb*
withdraws
withdrawing
withdrew
withdrawn

**withdrawal** *noun*
withdrawals

**wither** *verb*
withers
withering
withered

**withhold** *verb*
withholds
withholding
withheld

**within**

**without**

**withstand** *verb*
withstands
withstanding
withstood

**witness** *noun*
witnesses

**wittiness**

. . . . . . . . . . . . . . . . . . . . . . . . . . . . . . . . . . . . . . . . . . . . . .

★ **Wine** is a drink. **!** whine.

☆ A **witch** is someone who uses witchcraft. **!** which.

**witty** *adjective*
wittier
wittiest
wittily

**wizard** *noun*
wizards

**wizardry**

**wobble** *verb*
wobbles
wobbling
wobbled

**wobble** *noun*
wobbles

**wobbly** *adjective*
wobblier
wobbliest

**woe** *noun*
woes

**woeful** *adjective*
woefully

**wok** *noun*
woks

**woke** see **wake**

**woken** see **wake**

**wolf** *noun*
wolves

**woman** *noun*
women

**womb** *noun*
wombs

**won★** see **win**

**wonder** *noun*
wonders

**wonder** *verb*
wonders
wondering
wondered

**wonderful** *adjective*
wonderfully

**won't** *verb*

**wood**☆ *noun*
woods

**wooded**

**wooden**

**woodland** *noun*
woodlands

**woodlouse** *noun*
woodlice

**woodpecker** *noun*
woodpeckers

**woodwind**

**woodwork**

**woodworm** *noun*
woodworm *or*
woodworms

**woody** *adjective*
woodier
woodiest

**wool**

**woollen**

**woollens** *plural noun*

**woolliness**

**woolly** *adjective*
woollier
woolliest

**word** *noun*
words

**word** *verb*
words
wording
worded

**wording**

**wordy** *adjective*
wordier
wordiest

**wore** see **wear**

**work** *noun*
works

**work** *verb*
works
working
worked

**workable**

**worker** *noun*
workers

**workforce** *noun*
workforces

**workman** *noun*
workmen

**workmanship**

**workout** *noun*
workouts

**works** *plural noun*

**worksheet** *noun*
worksheets

**workshop** *noun*
workshops

**world** *noun*
worlds

**worldliness**

**worldly** *adjective*
worldlier
worldliest

**worldwide** *adjective*

**worm** *noun*
worms

**worm** *verb*
worms
worming
wormed

**worn** see **wear**

**worry** *verb*
worries
worrying
worried

**worrier** *noun*
worriers

a
b
c
d
e
f
g
h
i
j
k
l
m
n
o
p
q
r
s
t
u
v
**w**
x
y
z

. . . . . . . . . . . . . . . . . . . . . . . . . . . . . . . . . . . . . . . . . . . . . .

★ You use **won** in e.g. *I won a prize.* **!one**.
☆ **Wood** is material from trees or a lot of trees growing together.
   **!would**.

277

a

**worry** noun
worries

b

**worse** adjective and adverb

c

**worsen** verb
worsens
worsening
worsened

d

e

**worship** verb
worships
worshipping
worshipped

f

g

h

**worship** noun

i

**worshipper** noun
worshippers

j

**worst** adjective and adverb

k

**worth**

l

**worthiness**

m

**worthless** adjective
worthlessly

n

**worthwhile**

**worthy** adjective
worthier
worthiest
worthily

o

p

**would**★ see **will**

q

**wouldn't** verb

r

**wound** noun
wounds

s

**wound** verb
wounds
wounding
wounded

t

u

**wound** see **wind**

v

**wove** see **weave**

**woven** see **weave**

w

**wrap**☆ verb
wraps
wrapping
wrapped

**wrap** noun
wraps

**wrapper** noun
wrappers

**wrapping** noun
wrappings

**wrath**

**wrathful** adjective
wrathfully

**wreath** noun
wreaths

**wreathe** verb
wreathes
wreathing
wreathed

**wreck** verb
wrecks
wrecking
wrecked

**wreck** noun
wrecks

**wreckage** noun
wreckages

**wrecker** noun
wreckers

**wren** noun
wrens

**wrench** verb
wrenches
wrenching
wrenched

**wrench** noun
wrenches

**wrestle** verb
wrestles
wrestling
wrestled

**wrestler** noun
wrestlers

**wretch** noun
wretches

**wretched** adjective
wretchedly

**wriggle** verb
wriggles
wriggling
wriggled

**wriggle** noun
wriggles

**wriggly** adjective
wrigglier
wriggliest

**wring**○ verb
wrings
wringing
wrung

**wrinkle** noun
wrinkles

**wrinkle** verb
wrinkles
wrinkling
wrinkled

**wrist** noun
wrists

**wristwatch** noun
wristwatches

**write**✛ verb
writes
writing
wrote
written

**writer** noun
writers

x

y

z

★ You use **would** in e.g. *would you like to come to tea?* ! **wood**.
☆ To **wrap** something is to cover it in paper etc. ! **rap**.
○ To **wring** something is to squeeze it hard. ! **ring**.
✛ You use **write** in e.g. *to write a letter*. ! **right, rite**.

**writhe** *verb*
writhes
writhing
writhed

**writing** *noun*
writings

**written** see **write**

**wrong** *adjective* and *adverb*
wrongly

**wrong** *noun*
wrongs

**wrong** *verb*
wrongs
wronging
wronged

**wrote** see **write**

**wrung** see **wring**

**wry**★ *adjective*
wryer
wryest

# Xx

**xenophobia**

**Xmas** *noun*
Xmases

**X-ray** *noun*
X-rays

**X-ray** *verb*
X-rays
X-raying
X-rayed

**xylophone** *noun*
xylophones

# Yy

**-y** and **-ey**
Nouns ending in *-y* following a consonant, e.g. **story**, make plurals ending in *-ies*, e.g. **stories**, and verbs, e.g. **try**, make forms in *-ies* and *-ied*, e.g. **tries, tried**. Nouns ending in *-ey*, e.g. **journey**, make plurals ending in *-eys*, e.g. **journeys**.

**yacht** *noun*
yachts

**yachtsman** *noun*
yachtsmen

**yachtswoman** *noun*
yachtswomen

**yam** *noun*
yams

**yank** *verb*
yanks
yanking
yanked

**yap** *verb*
yaps
yapping
yapped

**yap** *noun*
yaps

**yard** *noun*
yards

**yard** *noun*
yards

**yarn** *noun*
yarns

**yawn** *verb*
yawns
yawning
yawned

**yawn** *noun*
yawns

**year** *noun*
years

**yearly** *adjective* and *adverb*

**yearn** *verb*
yearns
yearning
yearned

**yeast**

**yell** *noun*
yells

**yell** *verb*
yells
yelling
yelled

**yellow** *adjective* and *noun*
yellower
yellowest

**yelp** *verb*
yelps
yelping
yelped

**yelp** *noun*
yelps

**yen**☆ *noun*
yens or yen

**yeoman** *noun*
yeomen

a
b
c
d
e
f
g
h
i
j
k
l
m
n
o
p
q
r
s
t
u
v

z

. . . . . . . . . . . . . . . . . . . . . . . . . . . . . . . . . . . . . . . . . . . . . . . . . . . . . . . . . . .

★ You use **wry** in e.g. *a wry smile.* ! **rye**.
☆ The plural is **yens** when you mean 'a longing' and **yen** for Japanese money.

**yesterday** *adjective*
and *noun*
yesterdays

**yet**

**yeti** *noun*
yetis

**yew**★ *noun*
yews

**yield** *verb*
yields
yielding
yielded

**yield** *noun*
yields

**yippee**

**yodel** *verb*
yodels
yodelling
yodelled

**yodeller** *noun*
yodellers

**yoga**

**yoghurt** *noun*
yoghurts

**yoke**☆ *noun*
yokes

**yoke** *verb*
yokes
yoking
yoked

**yolk**❍ *noun*
yolks

**Yom Kippur**

**yonder**

**you**✦

**you'd** *verb*

**you'll** *verb*

**young** *adjective*
younger
youngest

**young** *plural noun*

**youngster** *noun*
youngsters

**your**

**you're** *abbreviation*

**yours**

**yourself** *pronoun*
yourselves

**youth** *noun*
youths

**youthful** *adjective*
youthfully

**you've** *abbreviation*

**yo-yo** *noun*
yo-yos

**yuppie** *noun*
yuppies

# Zz

**zany** *adjective*
zanier
zaniest
zanily

**zap** *verb*
zaps
zapping
zapped

**zeal**

**zealous** *adjective*
zealously

**zebra** *noun*
zebras

**zenith** *noun*
zeniths

**zero** *noun*
zeros

**zest**

**zigzag** *noun*
zigzags

**zigzag** *verb*
zigzags
zigzagging
zigzagged

**zinc**

**zip** *noun*
zips

**zip** *verb*
zips
zipping
zipped

**zodiac**

**zombie** *noun*
zombies

**zone** *noun*
zones

**zoo** *noun*
zoos

**zoological** *adjective*
zoologically

**zoologist** *noun*
zoologists

**zoology**

**zoom** *verb*
zooms
zooming
zoomed

- - - - - - - - - - - - - - - - - - - - - - - - - - - - - - - - - - - - - -

★ A **yew** is a tree. **!** ewe, you.
☆ A **yoke** is a piece of wood put across animals pulling a cart. **!** yolk.
❍ A **yolk** is the yellow part of an egg. **!** yoke.
✦ You use **you** in e.g. *I love you*. **!** ewe, yew.

a b c d e f g h i j k l m n o p q r s t u v w x

**y**
**z**